A FRESH MAP OF LIFE

A Fresh Map of Life

The Emergence of the Third Age

Second Edition

Peter Laslett

Trinity College
Cambridge

First published by George Weidenfeld and Nicolson Ltd 1989
This edition published 1996 by
MACMILLAN PRESS LTD
Houndmills, Basingstoke, Hampshire RG21 6XS
and London
Companies and representatives
throughout the world

ISBN 0–333–66676–3 hardcover
ISBN 0–333–59940–3 paperback

A catalogue record for this book is available
from the British Library.

10   9   8   7   6   5   4   3   2   1
05   04   03   02   01   00   99   98   97   96

Printed in Great Britain by
Ipswich Book Co Ltd
Ipswich, Suffolk

Contents

List of Tables

List of Figures

Preface: A Fresh Map of Life, the Emergence of the Third Age

An assumption which we inherit from our predecessors is that the world of age and ageing is placid, unchanging, the same in one year as it was in another and will be in yet a third. This is not true if it assumes that the people who compose the older population are the same now as they were and will be. Since the first printing of this book in 1989 well over a quarter of that population in Britain has disappeared and been replaced by people who were in the younger ages in that earlier year. The newcomers are better-off, better-educated and better set-up than the departed.

This must mean that a book published at the end of the 1980s on this subject must be out of date to some degree in the middle of the 1990s. I am extremely grateful to the firm of Macmillan, to Tim Farmiloe and Giovanna Davitti especially, for giving me the opportunity in the second edition of bringing its content into line with the present situation. Apart from the updating of the contents to take account of the great mass of new research which has been produced since 1989, these modifications unfortunately have had to be confined for the most part to revisions in the cited figures. I say unfortunately because in only one or two respects has it been possible to detect change in the social position of older people in Britain, in their attitudes to themselves and in attitudes to them. Cultural lag as to age and ageing, that state of false consciousness as I have ventured to call it, still seems to rule OK.[1]

In 1993, for example, a United Nations *Year of the Elderly and Solidarity between the Generations* was mounted. Admirable as this was in focusing attention on what everyone persists in calling the acute world-wide 'problem' of ageing and in eliciting enthusiastic responses, this seems not to have done much to eradicate the stereotypes or to recognize the growth towards an independent society of those in later life. The terms in which it was cast, certainly the language used, seem rather to have perpetuated the *status quo*.

More encouraging has been the conspicuous growth of the educational movement in favour of older persons and among older persons. Much is made in this book of the growth of the Universities of the Third Age (U3As) and there has been a plethora of meetings and above all of publications. It has to be remembered however that even in Britain as yet only some five in a thousand of the retired are associated with such developments. This tiny minority however has some interesting and encouraging connections. Such is the movement which has sprung up in Britain among British designers at the Royal College of Art. Having adopted from the text of *A Fresh Map* the slogan 'Live in the presence of all your future selves!' they have set out with designers in other European countries to provide comely objects which are purposefully accommodated to the needs and capacities of every individual over the whole life course, with emphasis on the slight, mostly physical, changes which affect so many of those in the Third Age.

Perhaps even this is no more than a straw on the water because it remains to convert those engaged in mass manufacture and mass marketing, especially their hired image makers and paid persuaders. There is little sign yet that these crucial individuals, or their even more influential companions in the media, have begun to see what they should see and know what they should know. Nor have the British politicians, as outpaced as they now seem to be by their counterparts in Australia,[2] and almost as impervious as they have shown themselves to the one development since 1989 which might have put our country in the van of a movement of liberation of the elders. This development was the Carnegie Enquiry into the Third Age, which proceeded from 1989 to 1992, and published ten research papers and a final report in the latter year.

I have myself described this remarkable development and these outstanding publications in the following terms. For the furthering of the Third Age,

> The first and most important lap has already been run, the gathering and assembling of authoritative knowledge for general enlightenment and as a base for policy. More is now known about the phase of life under consideration than has ever been known before for any population. Here is a body determined to change the attitude to ageing and to older people, to brush aside the title and attitude of 'old age', the 'elderly' and so on and to establish a fresh set of divisions of the life course.[3]

However, and here we reach an important reason why a second edition of the present work is so much in order, the Carnegie Enquiry, mainly for technical and what might be called housekeeping reasons, proceeded by using a definition of the Third Age in chronological and birthday-age terms, the years between 50 and 74, rather than the volitional and variation-respecting terms used in the present book. If you are not between your fiftieth and seventy-fifth year, you cannot be in the Third Age according to the Carnegie doctrine: you must therefore be in your Fourth Age of dependency and decline. The alienation of many of those older than 75 who like myself identify themselves as being in the Third Age seems inevitable, though this was decidedly not the reason why the Report seems to have had so little effect on British political life and practice.

The question of the definition of the Third Age is not a trivial issue, as will be evident to anyone who becomes acquainted with the argument of the present book, and similar considerations have not been the object of the intense and mounting discussion of age and ageing which has gone on in all countries with an 'old' population in the last six years. The subject in question is of course to do with public money. How is retirement to be afforded? And are those now retired getting too much?

These topics were considered in the original text of this book, but they have become so pressing since its publication that I have decided to change the content of the work so as to deal with them more fully. Accordingly, the original Chapter 12, entitled 'Employment and the Frontier between the Second Age and the Third' has been withdrawn and a new chapter substituted, 'The Burden of the Elderly and Paying for your own Third Age'. The occasion of the original chapter,[4] which was a passing fear lest a demographic time-bomb was about to explode because of the prospective insufficiency of younger workers, has now passed. I have however transferred parts of it into other contexts in the text.

Otherwise the work stands in this second edition where it stood in the first. I have not modified its theoretical claims in the face of the very extensive critical reviewing which it has received in several countries, though I have done my best to correct the errors of fact which have been pointed out. The characteristic of the Third Age which has been most widely attacked and rejected, that it can in exceptional cases be lived alongside the First or Second Age, has accordingly been retained unmodified. I confess myself to be fully aware, however, that this position has a very serious disadvantage, that the whole theory may be discredited because this part of it is unacceptable, as contrary to common sense.

This is not so to my mind, of course. This particular attribute of the Third Age as I see it, moreover, carried nothing else with it except the insistent suggestion that the Third Age cannot be thought of as a chronological period. It is simply not to be grasped in a definition such as that adopted by the Carnegie Enquiry.

If I have been unwilling to discard any of the original positions, however, there are a few which have added themselves to the inventory.

The only one which I shall mention here has to do with the sense of the NB collective future held by those whose personal future is inevitably short. It came as a surprise to find that those in late life have a somewhat higher appreciation of what is to come than younger people have.[5] Evident as it is that the tradition of Western political philosophy, as distinct from its religious and metaphysical heritage, has lacked an account of what I have called processional justice, which would include future people along with people in the present and the past, this strikes me as a circumstance of some ethical importance. Since it is an attribute of the Third Age of such significance I have allowed myself to include some discussion of it in the new chapter, crowded with themes as that chapter has become.

It may be thought that some of the features which I have touched upon here scarcely belong in a treatise expounding in somewhat formal terms a historical sociology of ageing, the object being to convince by demonstration as far as that is possible in a virtually unworked field of enquiry. The same might be said of the passages of poetry which have so tried the patience of the Italian and German translators, Pier Paolo Viazzo and Axel Flügel. Such a judgement must apply even more strongly to what I have called in Chapter 1 the strain of advocacy in the work; advocacy for an order of persons, older persons; advocacy of a radical reform of attitudes towards them and of their attitudes towards themselves; advocacy in favour of the sole instrument which they so far possess for becoming aware of themselves, that is the University of the Third Age. One reviewer actually described the book as a tract written for the purpose of furthering the cause of that institution, or, in Britain, that set of institutions.

This last judgement is undoubtedly disturbing, since it is my view expressed in the course of Chapter 11, that the U3A is a first experimental venture, not to be set in its form and probably to be accompanied and perhaps succeeded by numerous other institutional innovations. I have pondered criticisms of this character and accept their relevance, paying particular attention to those passages in the book where advocacy might have led to misinterpretation of the facts or blindness to what could have been discovered. I have not found myself able to make many revisions as a consequence though I recognize this may be due to my being so much *parti pris*. It seems preferable that conviction, even prejudice, certainly recommendations for a particular policy, should be evident on the surface rather than buried under protestations of objectivity. If this means requiring the reader 'by indirections to find directions out', so be it. All critical reading has to be like that.

As for the use of poetic phrases and passages, I see no reason why historical or sociological prose should be divorced from what is called literature. A work of the present kind has to be engaged to a considerable extent in suggesting by analogy and imagery, and poetry is the supreme discourse of that kind. Much more weighty in my estimation are the one or two empirical objections which have been made to the doctrines of *A Fresh Map of Life*. Jean Thompson, for example, Chairman for several years of the central body of the British U3As, and continuing as its representative on international bodies, declares from her extensive personal experience that it is entirely unrealistic to suppose that people in the Third Age will ever volunteer to keep museums and art galleries going, or ensure that historic churches stay open by mounting guard upon them, as is recommended in Chapter 11. This is not the way in which they think of themselves ór wish to use their time. Barbara Jeffers reports a conversation with nine retired persons and comments that 'the description of the Third Age as the apogee of personal life' means 'the setting up of grandiose expectations which seem likely to occasion the majority to experience as failure what could otherwise give great satisfaction. Moreover it is quite unnecessary to attempt to rank differences in periods of life in a hierarchy of worth or achievement. Laslett's definition is unnecessarily inflated.'[6]

Here I submit it is necessary to leave the reader to judge. It may be an error, a foolish error of inattention to human nature, to expect older people to use their time in the recommended way. There are regrettable signs that volunteering gets less as people grow older. But much depends on social expectation and it is evident that the whole essay is directed towards changing such expectations, as is openly confessed in the sub-titles to Chapters 3 and 4. I am not aware of having recommended anything that I would not do myself, and I am in my Third Age.

This last fact bears upon the judgements made by Barbara Jeffers. The disappointment she describes as arising from failure to reach too high a standard would be deplorable, if it occurred, though she does not actually report its occurrence. She is of course entitled to her own view about value judgements between the Ages, though I am not conscious of having made such judgements in the rather *naïf* fashion which she implies. What she is not entitled to do is to tell people in the Third Age how they should regard sincere advice given to them by an age-mate, what they should think of challenges made to the conventional view of the life course and to conventional judgements about the incapacity of old people to respond to an ideal to be striven for, if not often to be realised. In doing so she may be making unwitting use of the language regularly employed by the Second Age talking to the Third, the language of the bossy daughter telling her anxious mother what she should or should not expect, believe, or try to perform.

She may also be disregarding the principle appealed to in Chapter 11 in justifying the idealism, apparently unpractical idealism, of the educational arrangements suggested. This is the principle that in really extreme situations, such as that of the intellectual and cultural life of British older people in the 1980s in relation to the government and the established social ethos, only idealism will do.

Two things only remain for this over-lengthy Preface. One is to extend a little the self-reproaches made in the Preface of 1989, and the other is to bring up to date its list of acknowledgements. As for the first, I should like to repeat what was said in 'The Third Age, the Fourth Age and the future' (Laslett, 1994a).

> Two of the most respected of theorists of ageing have declared that elevating the Third Age in comparison with the Fourth [which is how they interpret the statements of the present text] is treading down even older, more defenceless people. These views attract growing support amongst members of the community of researchers on ageing. Margot Jeffreys makes an affecting plea for a return to a more restful, more contemplative outlook in later and latest life, reflective rather than active, final arrival rather than feverish progress which can only be imperatively ended. There are elements here which go to the roots of our civilization, indeed of other civilizations too. I only wish that conditions in our time, and our place in time, made it possible to take them up again.

As for acknowledgement of help received since the publication of the first edition I have already named the two translators from whom I have learnt a great deal. Then comes Matilda White Riley whose work I have cited, David Kertzer, my co-editor (first named) in the collective volume *Aging in the Past* (University of California Press, 1995) and my fellow members of the Maximum Length of Life Project associated with the Cambridge Group, James Vaupel, Väinö Kannisto and Roger Thatcher, along with its patient patron, the Wellcome Institute for the History of Medicine. Then there are Barry Jones and Jack McDonell in Australia. It remains to name those who advised me in the revisions made here, especially in Chapter 4, and in composing Chapter 12. Chief among them are Nathan Keyfitz, Jim Mirrlees, and (appearing here on a second occasion) Paul Johnson of the LSE. I cannot omit my patient and affectionate friends (they must be so to have endured it) with whom I have had discussions of *A Fresh Map of Life* at such lengths and who commented on passages in it. Amongst these are David Thomson, Tom Sokoll, Jim Fishkin, Jim Smith, Jean Thompson, Marion Bieber, Ros Morpeth and Roger Coleman. Nor must I forget attenders at the thirty-odd conferences, national and international, which I have been at since 1989, with the original printing of the book in my hand to talk out of.

1 A New Division of the Life Course

During the period when it was accepted that the life of man was three score years and ten, and almost ever since, most individuals have actually survived for less than half as long. Those in advanced societies today are the first population of creatures to exist in which almost every individual has a chance of full experience of the world, full in the sense of being in it for virtually as long as that individual is capable of living. At all times before the middle of the twentieth century and all over the globe the greater part of human life potential has been wasted, by people dying before their allotted time was up, mostly in their infancy and childhood, but many at maturer ages.

It is not yet known, as will be shown in the following chapter, how long we could all go on existing if absolutely everything was entirely favourable to survival. That figure, however, is quite certainly considerably higher than 70 years, or even the 80 years which the Bible allows 'for reason of strength'. This makes the challenge even more imperative. How are we going to use this sudden, unprecedented, unanticipated release from mortality? How are we to conduct ourselves now that all of us can expect to live out something like the full natural span, whatever that may be?

In so far as this challenge has been recognized at all, the response has been one of fear and alarm, or so it seems to me. Instead of so rearranging our affairs, and so dividing up our lives, that we can begin to realize the full potential human experience for the first time in human history, we have taken fright. In our own country at the moment all that we seem to be able to see is the ever growing number of failing elderly people who weigh upon the individuals who support them. Ageing is seen as a burden on society at large because resources have to be found to give older people incomes, to provide for their ever failing health, to maintain institutions for those who cannot be supported otherwise.

Meantime our work-force is changing rapidly, losing or rejecting its younger members to unemployment, and being unable or unwilling to retain its superfluity of older ones who have perforce to enrol themselves in the ranks of the retired. Europe and the West are growing old and never will be young again.

1

A really slow and solemn burden, it has to be admitted, to which to try to write a descant. Yet even if the facts and circumstances on which accepted dogmas about age and ageing are based were all objective truth, which many or most of them are not, there would still be another story to be told. Much of the accepted account of age and ageing is simply the persistence into our own time of perceptions belonging to the past.

It was never true that all those in later life were in reality the decrepit dependants of the story which has so far been set out. Two of the later chapters of this book make frequent reference to a woman believed by the eminent philosopher who left us the record to be over 100 years old in 1681, and who was quite likely to have been well over 90. Yet she was as independent and lively a person, both in mind and body, as could be imagined. What is more, ordinary people in the pre-industrial world do not seem to have represented themselves to themselves as decrepit until after they had passed the eightieth birthday. Nevertheless men and women beyond the ages of 65 and 60, retirement birthdays in our country though no one knows quite why, must more often have been impotent and helpless than persons of such age are today. It was more understandable, if never forgivable, that our predecessors should take the maimed minority for the whole body of the elderly.

The numbers of elderly and old were in any case much fewer then than they now are so that this misjudgement, this culpably false classification, mattered less. What is more (and here is a circumstance which will be accentuated again and again), it was only very recently that those in later life ceased to be a very small proportion of the whole population, and ceased to consist to such an extent of the infirm. When we talk in the accepted pessimistic fashion about age and ageing, we are simply repeating traditional language which was a more understandable form of discourse up to the First or even the Second World War, until in fact the childhood of those who are themselves elderly in the 1990s, more understandable but even then, as we shall see, never fully appropriate.

The categorical error of taking the minority of the problematic elderly, the chronically sick, those who cannot look after themselves, those who have to live in institutions, those about to die, for the whole body of the retired, is the most damaging survival from the past. But it is not the only assumption about age relationships which has been falsified during the present century.

All our ageing expressions have become inaccurate, and many of them obsolete. They provide us with misleading images of children, of those in the prime of life – a phrase to be noted because we are going to shift the prime of life a long way towards the later years – as well as of those in middle age and of those already in retirement. For the age constitution of our society has been transformed, quite suddenly and without our realizing what has happened. In addition to this it has to be reckoned that the institutions and instruments which have been created to meet the *problem* of ageing are in no position to provide us with a policy for that great majority of retired people who present no problem at all. We need a new outlook, a new language and we need above all a new set of institutions.

I have insisted that the air of despondency which surrounds the subject of ageing has arisen to a considerable extent because of a misclassification of the whole society of retired persons as if they belonged to a very small part of themselves. But I have had to be careful to admit that this is not the whole explanation. The elderly have not simply been misclassified, they have also been demeaned by attributing to each and every one of them deleterious descriptions properly belonging only to the afflicted and decrepit minority. 'Senile', 'geriatric', 'paralytic', along with many other adjectives originally quite innocent of an insulting meaning, are standard epithets of abuse. These are not simply errors of description, they are part of that stigmatizing process which has the effect, which some claim may be intentional, of removing signs of effectiveness and worth from the elderly, disposing of them as of no account.[1] Nevertheless, mistakes about classification have been real. They make it imperative for us to be absolutely clear about the terms of our discussion, and to select our vocabulary with some care.

In the terminology to be recommended here the damaging misclassification which we have been discussing would be defined as mistaking the Fourth Age for the Third, or taking the Fourth Age as properly descriptive of all those no longer living in the Second Age. The reference to the Third Age is the real novelty in this sentence, and it implies a different arrangement of the stages of life from any that has previously been suggested.

The Third Age is a phrase of French or Spanish origin, and was used in the title of *Les Universités du Troisième Age* when they began to be instituted in those countries in the 1970s. It seems to have entered Anglo-Saxon vocabulary when the first of the British Universities of the Third Age was founded at Cambridge in the summer of 1981. Because of the spread of these societies in the United Kingdom and elsewhere, perhaps also because of the perennial need for a term to describe older people, a term not already tarnished, the expression is now in fairly common use.

Dividing life experience into numbered stages is as old as the study of age and ageing, and the various usages are often to be met with in our literature. William Shakespeare, for example, was following a commonplace, a threadbare literary tradition when he put the speech about the seven ages of man into the mouth of Jacques in *As You Like It*. Large numbers of titles and principles have been used, a few have been very widely used and survive into our own generation.[2] The phrase which has been the most recent to arrive is the *Third Age*. Before the 1990s the term Third Age was not employed anywhere, as far as I know, as part of a series of numbered life-course stages, a series which included a First, a Second and perhaps a Fourth Age to complement the Third. But during the decade now in progress, and partly perhaps as a consequence of the publication of the first edition of the present book in 1989, all four terms have become to some degree current in Britain.

They have often been used as might be expected in ways inconsistent with the definitions initially laid out in this book, and inconsistent with each other. This development is considered in the Preface to the present edition, particularly in connection with the terminology for the segmentation of the life course used by the recent Carnegie Enquiry into the Third Age. There can be no doubt of the great value of this very thorough British investigation of an entirely new phenomenon with its nine separate Subject Studies (1992) and its Final Report (1993), much cited in the text which follows here. But the Carnegie usage of life-course terms and especially the exclusive reliance on birthday anniversaries as dividers between the Ages, blankly contradict the message of *A Fresh Map of Life*, and unfortunate results may ensue for the study of ageing and even for the position of elderly persons in Britain and elsewhere.[3] Let us proceed here, however, to set out the life course and its constituent Ages in their original form.

THE FIRST, SECOND, THIRD AND FOURTH AGES

First comes an era of dependence, socialization, immaturity and education; second an era of independence, maturity and responsibility, of earning and of saving; third an era of personal fulfilment; and fourth an era of final dependence, decrepitude and death. Such a fourfold numbered system has many precedents and many rivals.[4] The present scheme differs from its predecessors in several ways, one of them quite radical.

In this analysis of life experience the divisions between the four ages do not come at birthdays, nor do they necessarily lie within clusters of years surrounding particular birthdays. Moreover the life career which is divided into these four modules has its culmination in the Third Age, the age of personal achievement and fulfilment, not in the Second Age and emphatically not in the Fourth. It follows logically enough that the ages should not be looked upon exclusively as stretches of years, and the possibility has to be contemplated that the Third Age could be lived simultaneously with the Second Age, or even with the First. Since the Third Age is identified here as that during which the apogee of personal life is achieved, anyone who reaches the goal at the same time as money is being earned and accumulated, a family founded and sustained, a successful career brought to a pitch of attainment, could be said to live the Third Age alongside the Second. No passage from one to the other need occur, for an individual with these characteristics is doing his or her own thing from maturity until the final end. Artists, the consummate artists, are the best examples. An athlete, on the other hand, usually has to attain the peak during the First Age, and so live part of the Third Age then.

We shall have to reflect on the suggested scheme several times in order to convince the reader that this way of looking at things is the best for her or for him. No claim could be made that the system is entirely consistent, and it is difficult to see how any such system could be so. Critics have claimed that leaving open the possibility of an individual living out two Ages simultaneously is a serious incoherence. The new allocation does provide, however, clear and definite ideas for individual thinking about their own ages and ageing prospects, along with those of their spouses, their children and their friends.

Anxiety is often present when people reflect on such prospects, anxiety about the prospect of dependence, becoming dependent yourself or finding others becoming dependent upon you. Such worries are so widespread and dependence is so conspicuous among a proportion of the elderly, that most writings on age and ageing seem to be entirely preoccupied with them. Using the vocabulary just discussed, a great deal of this anxiety can be accounted for by the confusion which has already been identified, the confusion made by an individual in his or her own case between the Third Age and the Fourth, assimilating the age of fulfilment with the age of decline. This makes it crucial that the stretch of life which has been nominated as the Third Age should have its own title, and should be seen as separate from all the rest, even if it can be lived simultaneously with the Second or the First.

There must be no mistake about the message being transmitted to the reader. The separation of the two later phases of life, the Third from the Fourth, makes entirely obsolete the venerable appellation of 'Old Age'. Someone on the later stretch of life should henceforth be assumed to be either in the Third Age or the Fourth. Care should be taken to specify which. All those passing through any of the Ages at any one time in any society could be said to make up separate orders or communities within that society. Which brings us on to something like a formal definition of the Ages. They are *bracketed cohorts*, where cohort means everyone born in the same year, and bracketed a collection of persons in a number of neighbouring cohorts all likewise passing through the same age band. This falls short of being a complete definition because it will be maintained that it is not finally year of birth which places a person in any of the Ages but other characteristics conventionally, but not necessarily, associated with time elapsed since year of birth. Let us look at these associations in relation to the Third and Fourth Ages.

There can be no doubt that dependence and decrepitude have always been inseparably associated with becoming old, however active, useful and healthy people have been at the high, higher, and even highest calendar ages. However, such an association can never have been more than partially justified as a general description of a particular calendar age. The effect of failing to make the distinction implied in the phrase the Third Age, therefore, must have fastened upon a proportion of the senior members of all societies, past and present, inappropriate and damaging descriptions of their physical and mental state and we shall have to devote a whole chapter to this subject. This obstinate unwillingness to see the Third Age apart from the Fourth has sanctioned their exclusion from activities, especially earning activities, for which nearly all of them have been perfectly well suited, has debased their status in the eyes of their juniors, and above all has devalued them in their own estimation of themselves. To live as you wish to live after your sixty-fifth, seventieth and especially your eightieth birthday, you still have to have something of the quality ascribed to Shakespeare by Matthew Arnold:

Self-school'd, self-scanned, self-honour'd, self-secure.

Now that a fifth and more of the whole of our population is classed as retired, the results of this seemingly deliberate mass depreciation scarcely bear contemplation. The waste of talent and experience is incalculable. Some attempt to estimate the loss in terms of compulsory indolence will be attempted later on. The fact that those who write off the elderly are also writing off themselves, as they will be in a decade or two's time, defies understanding. The only explanation which can be offered here calls upon the somewhat unsatisfactory terms of cultural lag, even of false-consciousness. But some help towards understanding our purblind attitude may come from the recognition that what has been called the processional view of living your life has never so far established itself. Neither philosopher, nor social scientist, nor individual at large has yet begun to recognise the force of the command which will insistently be repeated: *Live continually in the presence of all your future selves!*

The physical dependence of failing individuals in their final years, and sometimes their mental depreciation too; the dilemma of younger persons obliged to look after them, and frequently to look after other dependents as well; the burdens on the social services; the difficulties of the social workers; the poverty of the working-class elderly and the intensification of social divisions which come with age; the problems presented by residential homes for the great and growing numbers of those in the Fourth Age and the horrendous cost – all these are extremely serious issues and they are pre-eminently issues of our time. So is the question of how British society will be able to meet the expense of supporting the elderly and of providing ever more expensive medical care. It is easy to see why nearly all the writings about ageing are about need and dependence, and it is understandable, if deplorable, that an effect of this preponderance is to intensify the conviction that the older population is a problem.

We shall return to these issues about dependence in the last chapter but one. We shall try to show that the impression of the old imposing a burden of dependency in fact arises because of a failure to live in the presence of all your future selves. But this is not one more book about dependence, though of course dependence in older persons will be frequently discussed. It is not a book about dependence because so few elderly people are in fact entirely dependent, and because that small minority provides so deceptive and so distortive a guide to all the rest. It is written in the confidence that much may be done by setting out these facts and circumstances as they really are, even if so many of them have to be expressed in figures, international, comparative figures as well as those for our own country. Rearranging these facts by redividing the life course and giving its most important component, from the elderly point of view, a somewhat novel name, may not go very far. But something can be done in this way to make it clear that the challenges are interesting as well as difficult, in human as well as intellectual terms. The abandonment of Old Age as a general, descriptive term has created the opportunity for us to take the forward stride. It is indeed, as I believe, an entirely new world which has opened up and beckoned us within.

If it is necessary to be clear and careful about the terms which have to be used for whole divisions of the course of life, it is also necessary to keep watch on the rest of the language which is used in reference to ageing, even down to the similes and metaphors which have worked themselves into the ordinary discourse. For the subject of this essay, growing old, teems with tired metaphors, unthinkingly applied.

These figures of speech are derived by analogy from many of the characteristics of the natural world, and the implied comparison of the time of
day and the season of the year with the stages of life are prominent
amongst them. Such analogies were natural enough in a traditional society,
close to the land and the vicissitudes of the seasons. But they still pervade
the jocularity, the sentimentality, the sententiousness which are so often
found in discussions of later life, devices no doubt try to ensure that the
more menacing themes shall be kept in the wings.

Being old is not in fact at all like evening or like winter, for the good
reason that the day and the year are not at all like human life itself. Older
people are not cold in terms of the thermometer. They do not feel cold to
the touch, do not need greater warming up than younger people, are no
colder in temperament, emotion or expression than the rest of us.
Whiteness, snowy whiteness is simply an analogy from whiteness of hair.
It no more justifies the vaguely comforting description of being old as the
winter of life, than the colour of the light from the declining sun justifies
the excruciating description 'golden oldies'. Thinking by analogy and
relying upon metaphor makes for muddle: a consistent, realistic vocabulary is imperative if we are to get the fact and circumstance of ageing
clear.

Even the word *age* itself has a range of meanings. When we come to
Chapter 3 we shall distinguish five separate senses for the age of a person:
calendar age will be seen to differ from biological age, from social age,
from personal age and from subjective age. You may think yourself to be
young, or old, in any of these sense and others may judge you in a similar
way. But there can be ambiguities. Consider for a moment what may be
meant by the remark, 'she is young for her age'. And reflect on a very
familiar association, being a grandparent with being very old. This association does not hold, in spite of the way journalists harp on it. A third of all
persons nowadays have grandchildren by the age of fifty and two-thirds by
the age of fifty-five.

No apology is made for the strain of advocacy in the prose which
follows. Someone in the Third Age is here addressing not first and foremost his own coevals, though they are clearly caught up in the discussion
at every point. It is addressed to the middle-aged, and especially middle-
aged women themselves soon to join the ranks of those already in the
Third Age. It is natural that he should see things from the senior point of
view and defend what he sees to be the interests of his companions, as
they now are and as they will inevitably be. It has not been often that the
older part of society has spoken in its own voice in such a way:
championship has usually come from younger sympathizers.

In the later chapters reference is made to the suspicion that those in the Third Age at the present period, or about to succeed to that status, have been privileged by time, enriched in comparative terms to an extent never attained by their predecessors and not being accorded to those who will be their successors.[5] If such can be demonstrated, we are faced with the first recognized and defined opportunity for providing against victimization by lottery of the date of birth. Since, as an age group in society, they can be identified as trustees for the future,[6] those in the Third Age must do all they can to respect the principles of inter-generational equity, and make whatever provision is open to them to see that justice will be done, even if this is to some extent at their own expense.

THE LAYOUT OF A FRESH MAP OF LIFE

Having defined and discussed the new concept of the life course and of the Third Age in this chapter we proceed in the second to the span of life. It has to be concluded that there is no known maximum number of years during which a human can expect to live. Before the present century it was exceedingly rare for anyone to attain 100 in spite of the many un-substantiated claims which have been made. The widespread conviction that particular areas like the Caucasus have large numbers of the very old is also to be rejected. Since the 1920s, and especially since the 1960s, however, centenarians have begun to multiply and there are well over 4000 in Britain. Expectation of life at the latest age is rising faster than at earlier ages. The text continues with an assessment of the fears people have about growing old, and these fears are confronted with the known facts. The remarkable persistence of capacities to think and create until the very latest years of life is dwelt upon, and the aphorism is enunciated 'Live in the presence of all your future selves!'.

Chapter 3 takes up social as contrasted with individual ageing, using British society for the purpose. Britain, it is shown, is not to be described as an old country and the tendency to do this is a disadvantage to us. Complaint is made against conventional literary views on age and ageing, especially those of the Greek and Roman classical writers along with such English poets as William Wordsworth.

Chapter 4 provides much of the demographic substance of the book. The present British population is shown to be by far the oldest ever to have lived on these islands with an expectation of life never before attained by humans. All Western populations, along with that of Japan, are now in this position and the British are by no means the extreme case.

Developing countries will soon join the West and their populations are now ageing faster than ever those of Western countries have done. These facts give the arguments of the book a global coverage. A glimpse into the demographic future follows, showing how the ageing effects may become intimidating after the middle of the twenty-first century.

Chapters 5 and 6 continue the demographic discussion but are concerned with the social consequences of the dramatic changes. An encouraging theory going under the title of the Rectangular Survival Curve is analysed. This maintains that in time we shall all come to survive as active and healthy people until our mid- or late eighties, and then depart within a short interval with little illness. These claims have to be pronounced unproven and the soberer possibility is confronted that health in our extending later years may not improve, and may even get worse.

Towards the end of Chapter 5, long-term historical studies in age are introduced for the first time into gerontological discussion. Under the title of 'The Secular Shift in Ageing' it is shown for the English case that proportions of the population and expectation of life were surprisingly constant over many centuries until the 1890s. Both indices then began to rise precipitately to their present extreme levels with far-reaching effects on the social structure and on attitudes. It is claimed that in the West we have not yet adapted to this transformation. A major thesis of the book is that attitudes and assumptions appropriate to the long, long ages, before the Secular Shift, still continue to distort our image of older people and get in the way of realistic understanding.

Chapter 6 is given over to the description, the demography and the dates in various countries of the appearance of the Third Age, which did not exist before the Secular Shift. It becomes possible only when at least half of all males, which necessarily implies even more than half of females, can expect to live from age 25 to age 70, can expect at the beginning of the Second Age in fact to survive well into the Third Age, and when a quarter or more of all adults (all over 25) have passed the age of 60. Northern and Western European countries attained this condition between 1950 and 1960, but for the full status of the Third Age to be present, other criteria such as national wealth, education and culture should be present.

Chapter 7 discusses the origin, intensity and regrettable consequences of the unfavourable stereotyping of the elderly, a major obstacle to the realization of the Third Age. An important source was the 'scientific' medicine of the early twentieth century. The tendency to look upon the retired as a reserve army is also run over, along with the manipulative attitude of the Second Age towards the Third. The first of a number of pleas is made for the independence of the Third Age.

In Chapters 8 and 9 the position of old persons in the family, past and present, is surveyed along with the origin and character of retirement. The family as a residential group and as a network of kinship is shown to be, and always to have been, an insufficient guarantee of the support and care of those in late life. These have always had to be negotiated between the family and collective institutions. Retirement was mostly confined to the elite before the Secular Shift and only spread to the people at large with the enormous growth of wealth in the developed countries by the mid-twentieth century, an evident precondition in the emergence of the Third Age.

Chapter 10 lays out the theory of the Third Age in full and Chapter 11 analyses British education in relation to its coming, concluding that the present educational system is obsolescent from that point of view. It relies far too much on education through socialization, i.e. during the First Age, and is not yet capable of providing that continuous further instruction over the whole life course which is imperative for Third Age living. The Universities of the Third Age (U3As) are described and the English or Cambridge model contrasted with the French and Continental model. In the first of the two models, now represented by over 300 U3As in Britain, members teach each other, a telling example of Third Age independence. In the second they are taught by Second Age professionals.

The crucial issues as to the manner of paying for those in the Third and Fourth Ages in relation to the so-called 'burden of the elderly' are dealt with in Chapter 12. The new subject of justice between age groups and generations is run over and a fairly general theoretical model of their relationships presented, with the contractual principles which require younger persons to support older persons. It is insisted that as far as possible personal savings should henceforth be the source of social and individual transfers from the value-producers to the value-receivers. What are called the economistic assumptions shown forth in most analyses of these issues are criticized.

The last chapter spells out the duties complementary to the privileges of the Third Age as intimated by what has gone before.

2 How Long Can Anyone Go on Living?

It comes as a surprise to be told that it is uncertain how long anyone can go on living. The idea of expectation of life for the individual is quite familiar, and we are well aware that most of us in Britain will reach our seventies unless some unforeseen disaster strikes – a fatal disease or an accident. We also recognize that no one can ever be quite confident on the one hand that the seventies will in fact be attained, or on the other hand that death will come before that decade of life is over. There are, after all, plenty of people in their eighties, some in their nineties, and talk of centenarians. But if we are fairly reconciled to the uncertainties of the probable length of our own lives in this way, it is more difficult to have to recognize how uncertain it is what the possible life-span could be. No one quite knows at the moment how long an individual might continue if nothing unfortunate happened; no heart condition developed, no cancer, no infectious disease, no accident, none of the myriad of natural shocks to which humans are prone. It is indeed highly dubious whether it ever can be known.

There is considerable interest in this conspicuous piece of ignorance and much speculation on the subject. Human life-spans have been quoted of the order of 110, 120 or even 130 years, and strong suggestions made that the figure was on the way up. The authorities cited have been research scientists and doctors, and it has become evident that some of their work is rather speculative. We shall go on to survey these questions more closely in Chapter 5, which has the unfamiliar and paradoxical-sounding title, 'The Rectangular Survival Curve and the Secular Shift in Ageing'. What has to be reckoned with here is that duration of life is not a straightforward matter. There are intractable problems about the possible human span, and these problems are not confined to biology.

We may begin our discussion of a subject which touches all of us, if only very distantly, by defining the important term. Maximum human life-span is the largest number of years from birth which an individual could possibly live, given absolutely ideal conditions for survival. Accordingly it is always considerably higher than the general expectation of life: only the life expectation of the most fortunate individual ever born could possibly equal it. Although it must finally be controlled genetically and so presumably be subject to evolutionary change, it is a function for the most part of the physical environment for all animals, and, for humans particularly, of the social environment. It could accordingly vary in theory from place to place, though some biologists seem to assume that there is a constant for life-span underlying all historical and regional variation. The difficulty here, as with so many attempts at determining what is 'natural' biologically, is that competition is so strong among creatures in the wild that few individuals can be expected to survive to the limit. Although we shall use 'maximum human life-span' for most of the statements made, we shall find that circumstances lead us to phrases like the 'average life-span' from time to time here and in Chapter 5, it being understood to refer to death at late ages.

Humans cannot be said to live in the wild but deciding upon a figure for maximum human life as it has been or is now, and upon whether it is changing, is not a simple matter nevertheless. The obstacles in the way of observation are manifold, even for the present day. The possible cases all have to be scrutinizéd for the complete accuracy of dates of birth, and for those not still alive, of dates of death. The dates of birth in question must all lie 100, 110 or 120 years or more before the present point in time, that is earlier than 1895, 1885 or 1875. But registration of births and deaths of sufficient reliability was only being carried out during those decades or before in the then developed countries, mostly in Europe. Getting anything like a general sample of very long-lived humans for the whole contemporary world looks impossible.

There are further hindrances. One is the disposition of those advanced in years to exaggerate their ages and another is the willingness of people to believe in the existence of particular localities where life is particularly lengthy. It always turns out that the areas where centenarians are supposed to abound are distant, and as yet relatively undeveloped. Registration of births and deaths in these places may not be of a good standard now compared with what generally obtains in the advanced countries, but it is practically certain to have been very much less accurate before 1895. Yet there has been something like a cult of very old people in certain places, places where registration seems not to have been at all reliable, and where exaggerated, seemingly impossible, claims have been commonplace. This happened on quite a large scale in the former USSR.

Under the circumstances, calculating the absolute maximum human life span from present observation can go no further than the number of years lived by the oldest person whose birth date is certainly known, and if not still alive, the date of death certainly known as well. Even these conditions are never absolutely unquestionable, since the definition of certainty is not quite transparent for such judgements. A crucial example is that of a Japanese individual, Shigechiyo Izumi, who died in February 1986 120 years and 231 days old, the greatest age in the published file of reliable recordings, that is to say the one maintained in the *Guinness Book of Records* in its successive annual issues (1994 edn, p. 64). A highly authoritative expert, Mr A. R. Thatcher, former Registrar-General of England and Wales, who is particularly concerned with longevity, described Izumi's age in the year after he died as 'fully authenticated', thus admitting him to have lived longer than anyone else in known history.

But it turns out that on the Japanese island of Okinawa, still being described by the Japanese as the area of their country where their long-lived population survives best, birth registration was not in operation in 1865 when Izumi is said to have been born. The earliest documentary evidence of his age is in the census of the district of Okinawa taken in the year 1871 where he is given as having passed his fifth birthday. Certainty cannot be finally assumed for his attained age, therefore, and in 1993 in an unpublished paper, Mr Thatcher withdrew his opinion.[1] The most authentic claim to be the oldest person now alive, and, as far as is known, the oldest person who has ever lived, accordingly attaches to the second name on the Guinness list, Madame Jeanne Calment. This ancient lady celebrated her 120th birthday on 21 February 1995 to a fanfare of international publicity. She has now (October 1995) exceeded Izumi's supposed record. It has to be recognized then that 120 is at present the maximum observed length of human life and that it gets longer with every day, hour or minute during which Jeanne Calment goes on living. This invalidates any discussion which bases itself on a younger maximum.

Jeanne Calment's life is very well documented, and the French describe her as 'part of our national heritage, the grand old lady of the entire world' (la doyenne de l'humanité).[2] But it is still possible that Izumi's birth date is correct which would do something to substantiate 120 years as the maximum attainable age as of 1995, rather than 115, which is favoured by Leonard Hayflick, perhaps the best-known American authority (Hayflick, 1994). But it is obvious that the known absolute maximum is at present rising as Jeanne Calment goes on living and that the figures relating to her attained age, or that of any other claimant, are subject to being surpassed directly a still older person, equally or better authenticated, comes to notice. It was reported in 1994 from central China that a man had attained 147 years of age. We would do well to disregard this claim, but in such a situation it is not at all easy to be confident of the very longest life even under our own conditions of reliable public, official, confirmable registration. As for the past, which is always to be reckoned with when an absolute maximum of this kind is being sought, things are inevitably much more dubious. Yet if we are to tackle the issue of whether maximal length of life is now greater than ever before, as everything seems to suggest, historical information is quite indispensable, with no limit as to period of time or area of the world. What may seem a set of fairly straightforward questions as to the longest life ever lived threatens to become a tangle of analytic and evidential problems.

PROVING IDENTITY OVER A LIFE COURSE

The issue confronted when a claim is made that an individual is, or was at death, so many years old on the grounds that a baby bearing that individual's name was born or given a reliable age on a particular, earlier date is whether the identical person is in question on both occasions. Even if reliable recordings were made and have survived to be checked, it has always to be borne in mind that two persons can have the identical name or combination of names. Records of further events in the life of individuals, like marriage, or the birth of siblings will help to confirm the claim, as will references in letters or diaries, or in public sources. The more such recordings exist the stronger the case, provided of course that they are accurate and consistent with each other. Proving this is sometimes difficult. However long the series, there can still be a residual doubt as to whether the identical person was at issue and there are three sets of circumstances which may increase the hesitation of the researcher.

The recordings may be few, or unconfirmed or inconclusive, or a combination of these things, which is the Izumi case. The names in question, on the other hand, may be found very frequently, so commonly in fact that it is not easy to be absolutely confident about which, of two or more choices, makes an acceptable match, say of a birth with a marriage date. Finally, there may be, or have been, a degree of temptation to pretend that it is or was the identical person at issue, temptation arising particularly from the enhanced status to be gained from being, or having been, a very old or a very, very old person. The pretence may be made by the individual or by someone else, sometimes for interested reasons. Unfortunately for the pursuit of absolute accuracy, attaining great age seems always and everywhere to have conferred considerable prestige on the individual concerned and on those connected with him or her. In this way the study of very long life seems to vitiate its own evidence by conferring even further importance on the great survivors.

These difficulties and the elusiveness of certainty, certainty of the order of seeing an object in front of your eyes which is what people seem to expect could be forthcoming, can be illustrated from the case of Jeanne Calment herself. The documentation is ample, perhaps too ample, because Calment turns out to have been an exceedingly common name in the region where she was born and has lived her life: Jeanne is a very frequent French Christian name. So numerous were people of her surname in her acquaintanceship that she actually married a man called Calment.[3] It could be said therefore that though she has by far the best claim to have lived the longest life so far known, it is still not 'certain' that this is so, since 'certainty' cannot be in question.

In view of the importance of the topic to the study of human survival, and for other reasons a project on 'Maximal Length of Life' has been established at the ageing unit of the Cambridge Group for the History of Population and Social Structure. Since 1992 this project has been associated with the Archive of Population Data kept by the Aging Research Unit at the Medical School of the University of Odense in Denmark which was instituted in that year and where what is being called the Kannisto/Thatcher Database on the Oldest Old has been set up.[4] Only three of the multifarious issues and outcomes concerning very late life with which we are engaged can be cited here in relation to questions as to how long anyone can go on living.

The first relates to the numbers of very, very old people. We have conclusively demonstrated from the evidence which has been assembled and examined that these numbers have been growing much faster than the numbers in any other age group, and that their expectation of life at these latest ages has been rising. The second is that a very high proportion of the claims made in the past and up until recently as to individuals having become centenarians in our country must have been false. The general reason why we can be so confident of their falsity is that there are too many of them. Until the secular shift, life expectation was too low and the size of the population in question too small for more than a minute number of persons aged 98 and over to have made an appearance. We cannot be concerned here with the grounds for this statement in demographic theory. Let it simply be said that the two conditions for the presence of appreciable numbers of the very, very old in the population of our country have not been satisfied until our own day.[5] The third outcome of the length-of-life project is the judgement that the problems presented by exaggeration of ages in all societies and at all periods in order to make claims for individuals to have reached the magic age of 100 are so serious that the concept and title 'centenarian' has to be abandoned. Attention should henceforth be concentrated on 98 years which is just as useful for all our purposes, other than publicity.

Once these facts are grasped, it becomes obvious that everything should be done to play down the historic and still flourishing cult of centenarians. This cult encourages age inflation and so tends to distort the evidence at a vital point. Such actions as the arranging of sessions on centenarians at international conferences on ageing, especially sessions on the centenarians of one country, have to be deplored because they may reward falsification.[6] Even the sending of congratulatory messages from Buckingham Palace and the hullabaloo the French have made about Jeanne Calment may have an unfortunate effect since they foster national competitiveness about these magic anniversaries. What is clearly wanted is a thorough examination of the whole body of reliable evidence and a determined attempt to get at the most accurate possible estimate of every age at death of the extremely long-lived. Väinö Kannisto carried out such a task in the 1980s and presented his results in an article of 1988, results which must now be regarded as preliminary. It is worth summarizing what he then said, however, since its content, and the extensions and revisions now being made by him and by Roger Thatcher, with the publications still to come from the Cambridge/Odense collaboration, seem to offer the best chance of getting as close as is possible to an entirely convincing answer to the question of how long it is possible to live, at least from the point of view of observed length of life.[7]

Kannisto's study was based on the largest body of data then collected, concerning persons reaching 100 in 13 countries of high expectation of life and good registration; Australia, Austria, England and Wales, West Germany, Finland, France, Iceland, Italy, the Netherlands, New Zealand (excluding Maoris), Norway, Sweden and Switzerland. The total strength of these populations was over 280 million, though Kannisto's figures were collected for various periods in each country leading up to the late 1980s. Only 67 286 persons out of this very large number had reached the age of 100 – 52 947 females and 14 339 males. Somewhat over half of this total, 37 241, had attained 101, a quarter or more (20 102) 102, and 16 per cent 103. By this age the excess of females over males, already so conspicuous at 100, had grown to nearly five times as many. The series continued to age 109 for both sexes; at 108 – 219 females and 22 males survived; at 109, 74 females and six males – thereafter only females: 27 aged 110, three aged 111 and one aged 112.[8]

This list demonstrates from the known facts how extremely rare it is for anyone to become a centenarian even in highly developed countries at the present day. It also establishes the important point already insisted upon, that survival of 98-year-olds and that of all those in latest life is getting better in our day. They have only about half a chance of surviving from one birthday to another, all the same. The claims about the average attainable age are rather less convincing. Kannisto suggests that the commonest age of dying for the very long-lived is as low as 85, and tentatively proposes this as the average (modal) human life-span, with a lower extreme at the age of 70 and an upper extreme at age 110. He also defends the view that the deaths of at least some of the people occurring between these ages were natural deaths, that is to say those occurring without any detectable illness or injury being present.

THE BIOLOGISTS, THE LIFE-SPAN AND NATURAL DEATH

Although the idea of natural death is very widely accepted among those without expert knowledge, and has been so throughout history, the notion of life ending simply because the human organism has got to the end of its resources is widely contested and seems to be unacceptable to numbers of physiologists, biologists and doctors. In our later discussions we shall have to return to these matters, though we may notice here that Kannisto cites only one item of medical research to underwrite the view which he presents. It is evident, moreover, that he has not seen the original study himself.[9] His inferences from his extensive evidence seem scarcely proven and the average, in the sense of the commonest, age at 85 for the end of the life-span is as yet undemonstrated. The inherent length of life of humans remains as elusive as ever from the observational, the demographic, point of view.

But when we turn to the biologist we find identical difficulties arising. The scientists tend to call the biological limits to the length of life the 'maximum human life-span', sometimes adding the word 'potential'. Some of them also distinguish this from 'average life-span', or simply 'life-span'. There is little consistency in their usage, however, and it is seldom quite clear which is meant, the maximum or the average.

In one study, for example, perhaps the best-known, the life-span is defined as 'the age at which the average individual would die if there were no diseases or accidents'.[10] It is not at all evident how this is distinct from the maximum, but the idea seems to be much the same as Kannisto's. Like the rest of us, exceptionally long-lived people die at various ages: in this biological study the life-span is the average of these ages, though the average in its usual sense, and not the commonest age as with Kannisto. But the whole position can be questioned in much the same way. The important reason why maximum life-span is so problematic biologically is that there is no generally accepted account of how and why humans age. Much is known about the processes, agreed to be numerous and complex, but no overall theory of ageing has been worked out which is generally accepted, rather a number of competing, often tentative and partial, theories abound. What seems to be the latest of these, the theory of postponed senescence put forward by evolutionary biologists, propounds the view that organisms are capable of doubling their 'normal, mean or maximum life-spans'. Experiments with flies are cited which demonstrate this and one prominent researcher has ventured the view that 'I cannot think we could not do similar things for humans someday.'[11]

Estimates for maximum human life-span potential are accordingly freely quoted by researchers into the biology of ageing, if with little agreement among themselves. Some of these maximal estimates lie within the range we have cited from observation (say 110–120), but others go up to 130 or even higher. The fact that biologists have to interest themselves in the question of whether the life-span has changed or is changing leads them furthermore to cite for confirmation or comparison some of the historical and currently observed highest ages at death, whose elusiveness we have already discussed. Because they are concerned with genetic change in the life-span, and because at least 10 000 years or so may be in question in genetic matters, they are also apt to consult the estimates of archaeo-demographers, made for mean age at death and calculated from skeletons buried in the distant or very distant past using anatomical and radiological techniques. But commonest age at death, subject of course to a very high degree of error in such results as these, is only an approximate indicator of expectation of life and only distantly related to maximum or average life-span.[12] An extremely gross change in either value might conceivably be hinted at by palaeo-demography, but this is as far as we ought to go.

The discussion of how long anyone can go on living, then, ends in a considerable degree of uncertainty, for the past, for the present and for the future. Life-span may well be rising along with average life expectation, and along with numbers of centenarians, but we cannot say what the limit is, or what may happen if medical advances, particularly genetic engineering, succeeded in altering the ageing process. It is understandable that some scientists should declare that it is impossible to estimate, or that it does not exist for humans in the same way as it does for animals because the limits on human life are now almost exclusively a matter of the social environment rather than the physical. As for statisticians and demographers, we have seen what Väinö Kannisto has to say, and Roger Thatcher contents himself with the remark that we cannot 'rule out the logical

possibility of an upper limit to life'. But he adds that 'there may alternatively be no precise boundary of this kind, only a highest age so far
known, with the probability of observing a still higher figure becoming
exceedingly small, and eventually negligible'.

To be denied knowledge of the upper bound of human life is something
of a disadvantage to the biologists and medical experts, as we shall see in
Chapter 5. Their object has always been to raise expectation of life at all
ages, for individuals and for populations as a whole, so as to ensure that as
many people as possible come close to the final frontier – the end of the
life-span, that is – in a healthy and active condition. The missing information alike affects economists, sociologists and even those who concern
themselves with questions of justice between age groups.[13] This arises
because uncertainty on the point underlines the fact that the elderly and
old constitute a completely open-ended population, of no determinate size
and with no obvious limit to the length of time any one person might
spend within it.

The obscurity which surrounds the number of years humans might conceivably live is of little practical importance to the rest of us, however,
since it is established well enough that among people like ourselves only
about 19 per cent of women and 8 per cent of men are still alive at the age
of 90, and that by the age of 95 these proportions fall to 6 per cent and
2 per cent. It would need a substantial change in the estimates to make
much difference, although even the slight but real possibility of a prolonged Fourth Age is intimidating, of having to continue in a condition of
half-life, '*sans* teeth, *sans* eyes, *sans* taste, *sans* everything'. And the
needling uncertainty remains. We can be confident that the topic of living
on and on and on will continue to be discussed, and that the very, very old
will perpetually intrigue us. But we cannot be confident of much else
about the extreme limit to existence.

AGEING, ITS PROBLEMS AND FEARS FOR THOSE INDIVIDUALS
IN LATER LIFE

This uncertainty about probable length of individual lives, if not of the
maximum life-span, is nevertheless of considerable significance for
elderly people, who live in a state of perpetual doubt. They never know
how much time they have: whether to begin this, or to promise that;
whether to plan for several years hence, or at most for a month or two.
They cannot tell if they should cling on to what capital they have, and
persist in habits of saving 'just in case', or if they should spend while the

opportunity lasts: they have great difficulty in deciding how much they should give away in their lifetimes, possessions as well as money, should money be at their disposal. As will be seen in Chapter 12 pensions are becoming somewhat problematic in Britain along with such things as maintenance in old people's homes and payment for medical expenses, intensifying this dilemma for those in the Third Age as they grow older. Their strong desire not to burden their children and the precariousness of their personal situations make the position even more unsettled. They can never be confident that a particular relative or associate near them in age will be present at all at any point in the future. In such directions as these the lives of all older persons go forward in a state of hesitation and in-certitude, however active and satisfying those lives may be while the Third Age itself continues.

Maximum human life-span is sufficiently remote from everyday experience nevertheless for its uncertainties to be freely discussed without much fear of touching on the underlying anxieties associated with the prospect of ageing. Death is a different matter. Here elderly people are much more likely to be affected by calculations of expectation of life than those to do with life-span. It is average years to come at their age, for their gender, for their conditions of living which is crucial to them and it is this average which expectation of life expresses. These statistics will be spelt out at length in later chapters.

However, as in almost all the expositions of ageing as a social condition, the individual is easily lost sight of, and may not be at all happy to identify with a figure appearing in a cell in a table. Because this essay is written for particular individuals as well as for the society they live in, it is important that the attitudes of a person to his or to her ageing process be spelt out word for word. For this reason an attempt is made below to list as explicitly as possible all distinguishable sources of anxiety about growing old. These anxieties are not so much those of people already in the Third Age, but rather more of those in the Second Age, who have begun to recognize for the first time how much of their life still to come will be spent as an older person.

FACING THE PENALTIES OF GETTING OLD

First, is the fear of death; it is now almost exclusively the elderly who die.

Second, is the fear of that final enemy of the old, senile decay, the best-known form of which is Alzheimer's Disease.

Third, is the fear of life-destroying, bed-enforcing disease of decline, cancer above all, but heart disease and so on. Heart disease, let it be noted, is clearly the commonest cause of death in our country, and not cancer.

Fourth, is the fear of the less life-threatening but grave afflictions which come mainly to the old: blindness; deafness; lameness; incontinence, severe or mild.

Fifth, is the general fear of physical debility, mental decline and illness, for themselves and for the dependence they bring with them.

Sixth, is the fear of loss of beauty, attractiveness, fertility, potency, in themselves and in their spouses.

Seventh, is the fear of inability to recall names, events, people, experiences.

Eighth, is the fear of loss of keenness of hearing, eyesight and smell; added to those so far listed and especially the sixth- and seventh-named fears this makes up a general apprehension of losing the capacity for enjoyment.

Ninth, is the fear of loss of mobility, over small distances and large, of being confined indoors, and of the consequent loss of choice of places to go, things to do.

Tenth, is the fear of loss of earning-power, being retired or unemployed because of age.

Eleventh, is the fear of falling status, public status and private status within the family, coming from the decline of earnings and from exit from office – political and social as well as economic – incurred without any necessary reference to falling capacity, but solely because of chronological age.

Twelfth, is the fear of the loss of spouse, siblings, kin, friends, family and consequent desolation.

Thirteenth, is the fear of loss of home, having to live with other people, or in an institution.

Fourteenth, is the fear of the contraction of the future, frustration in fulfilling the chosen plan of life.

These fourteen nameable fears are all connected, although supposed here to be relatively independent. Consciousness of any one of them tends to imply consciousness of all the others. The list is evidently open-ended and there is still a further cluster of anxieties, also associated with ageing if not clearly as cause and effect. Like the specific circumstances set out above, each has its part to play in the uniformly unfavourable appreciation of elderly people and of the elderly condition. There is the fear of being passed over, put on the shelf, regarded as of no account. There is the fear of diminution by being less involved with the hopes and plans of society in general, and especially of the younger generation. More specific are such fears as that of the obsolescence of skills – manual, mental or artistic – woeful losses in themselves and economic losses too.

Then there are familial fears. Parents may be afraid of a time when they will have to devote themselves to the task, often unpleasing and sometime intolerable, of tending their own parents or other ageing relatives throughout a prolonged Fourth Age. Simultaneously they may have to maintain, or to resume, responsibility for the casualties among their adult children, the handicapped, the unemployed, the deserted and divorced. This is a particularly feminine fear, for it is women of whom such things are usually demanded. But those of either gender may come to dread getting into the power of a particular child or relative, acquaintance or even a stranger.

They are afraid, therefore, of the causes of this thing happening, of not being able to cope, to manage the lives they wish to lead. Some of these frustrations could be described as barriers against escaping from the Second Age into the Third. Worst of all perhaps of the anxieties about ageing among working people in Britain, is one scarcely itself familial, though it may arise from a lack of funds to support a family, or from familial neglect. This is fear of the 'welfare', of the social worker and the social welfare institution. Still rumbling on the historical horizon for the British poor is the fear of the workhouse, for Americans of the almshouse.

A further and more recent source of disquiet about the prospect of getting old, a worry which arises from the study of the process itself in our present situation, is only now starting to affect the elderly, though it is part of the litany of woe with which we began. This is the widespread and growing concern as to whether our countries can afford to support the elderly in the numbers and condition which can already be forecast. Will the young and productive – as they are always described as being – be prepared to go on finding the means to support their unproductive elders? The notion of what a body of individuals living their lives in the presence of all their future selves can be said to afford will have to come under close scrutiny before this essay reaches its conclusion.[14]

Large, rich and expansive societies like the USA are beginning to show this anxiety, as well as the not so prosperous, not so expansive societies such as Britain. But for the analyst of ageing the most significant thing in the inventory of fears of growing old arises from the fear of simply being

classed as such. For it is at this point that the issue of being stereotyped
arises, of becoming the victim of a set of inseparably interrelated pre-
judices – as outdated, undesirable, unproductive individuals, incapable of
change, making up so large a proportion of the population as the unfortunate and unwanted outcome of an activity which has gone on for other purposes. This purpose, as we shall come to recognize, has been the deliberate
limitation of the numbers of children to a family proceeding since Victorian
times, together with the decision we seem to have made to add as little as
possible to our collective numbers, to risk their diminution in fact. The
success there has been in prolonging life, has intensified the change; it continues and will continue to do so. It has increased the numbers of the old
and of those who will soon grow old, but until recently it has done little to
unsettle the balance between the old and the young in the population. This
has been upset because of the drastic fall in our fertility.

We should not allow this sombre catalogue of fears of becoming old to
stand without mentioning that there are facets of this process which are
attractive rather than intimidating to those who contemplate the condition,
even from their middle age, and to those who actually experience the situation of elderliness. Such is the very love of freedom to be at ease and no
longer subjugated to the boss, the office and routine, routine in the home
as well as at work. Among the really poor and insecure elderliness is
sometimes welcome for a different reason. Because of pensions and other
privileges, age brings an unwonted security. For everyone, however, there
is the sense of having done your bit, of having earned a right to release
from responsibility, and a right to the leisure which alone permits a person
to devote time and energy to what he or she has always wanted to do but
has always been prevented from doing.

We shall fasten on this last sentiment as our point of departure for the
theory of the Third Age, an integral part of which, however, is the
acceptance of the increasing risk of death as the years go by. But this is in
no way a refusal of life in its later and its latest stages. Only at the end of
the story, at the very last moment which we designate here as the Fourth
of the Human Ages, does the notion of release make an appearance. Only
then are we prepared to say of ourselves what was said of the suffering
Lear:

> Vex not his ghost: Oh let him pass; he hates him
> That would upon the rack of this tough world
> Stretch him out longer.

Having looked at the enemy as closely as we can, or as we dare – right up
to the pores of the face – it is right that we should ask ourselves direct

questions about how realistic it is to be as much afraid of these things as so many of us seem to be. How far are these unpleasing circumstances necessarily associated with growing old, as consequences of that and of nothing else? Do they all indeed belong together as a whole, as a crown, a crown of thorns it might be said, resolutely thrust upon those in later life by the facts of physiological and demographic change, and by current social attitudes? Some of the most important of these features of growing old in our time are fresh arrivals historically considered, especially those to do with lengthened life and the multiplication of numbers of elderly people. Unexpected novelties, they may be called, whose sudden irruption on to the temporal stage may have much to do with that condition of false consciousness and cultural lag which has to be attributed to developed nations in respect of ageing in the last decade of this century.

ALLAYING ANXIETIES ABOUT THE CONSEQUENCES OF AGEING

Many of the questions about how realistic our attitudes are towards getting old can easily be answered from the stock of knowledge now at our disposal. It is true that in general it is the old who die, so that it is perfectly correct in our day to associate this immemorial fear with the later years of life. From the point of view of this essay, of course, it is this which interconnects the Third Age with the Fourth Age: death is indeed a conspicuous characteristic of that final episode. A person in the Third Age, especially in its later phases, is liable to fall into the Fourth Age at any time. But it must not be overlooked that a lapse into the Fourth Age can likewise occur at other points in the life course although it is now extremely rare that it supervenes in youth, a circumstance which marks us off from all our predecessors.

Indeed the facts about how many deaths are still to come after particular ages have been reached are now so impressive that it is worth setting them out as in Table 2.1. The differences between men and women indicated in Table 2.1 are truly astonishing, and so also is the change in favour of greater survival for both genders which has occurred since the early 1980s. At age 75, for example, the preceding English Life Table, for 1980–83, gave 46 per cent of male deaths still to come rather than 53 per cent. Who would have supposed that nowadays at 60, their present age of compulsory retirement, 92 per cent of women have still to die, and nearly 80 per cent of men at age 65, when they have to leave work? A decade ago the figures were 90 per cent and 75 per cent respectively. How telling is the claim

Table 2.1   Deaths after certain ages

Age	50	55	60	65	66	67	68	69	70	71	72	73	74	75	76	77	78	79	80	81	82	83	84	85	86	87	88	89	90
Percentages																													
Males	94	91	87	79	77	75	72	70	68	65	62	59	56	53	49	46	43	39	35	32	28	25	22	19	16	14	12	10	8
Females	96	94	92	87	86	82	83	81	80	78	76	74	71	69	67	64	61	58	55	51	48	44	41	37	33	29	26	22	19

Source: Government Actuary, Interim Life Tables, 1989–1991.

which has been made for those in the Third and Fourth Ages that they do virtually all the dying for the whole of the society.

But the truly formidable effect of these newly established circumstances for all those in later life, is that their friends, their acquaintances, all of their coevals and especially their seniors, are liable to disappear in spite of, and in a sense because of, the rise in the life expectation at earlier ages. Each year, each month, the tempo quickens as time and birthdays pass, and brings news of someone lost, or is marked by a sad scene at the bedside, at the graveyard or the crematorium, for those late-life members of the population.

Before the Third Age and even in the earlier years of that phase of life, people are now much freer of mortality than their ancestors were at that stage of life. It can be reckoned that, up to the final years of the nineteenth century, people in the past lost their age-mates in their thirties and forties at about the same rate as people now lose their age-mates in their early seventies. What is more, death at the earlier ages was, and still is on the rare occasion when it happens, much more of a tragedy both for the persons dying and for family and friends than death at the late, later and latest ages which is so characteristic of our own era, and which is absolutely new from the point of view of the incidence of mortality over the life course. The tragedy of the extinction of a young man in his prime, of a Lycidas, of an Adonais, was what brought our ancestors to write their inconsolable laments.

Worse still was the removal of a beautiful girl, the supreme object of love and desire, or the disappearance of a young mother having children, of a young father in the prime of life. These were the things which made bereavement so oppressive to those who lived in the earlier world, and the celebration of death so much more elaborate and poignant than most funerals today. The slipping away of a man or a woman in her eighties or nineties in the contemporary hospital or hospice is something very different from the departure in the cottage, the field, the disease-ridden city-street of a younger person at the prime of life in traditional society.

The significance of death then has changed fundamentally over time. Inescapably, however, being elderly forces us to confront the universal necessity of being prepared to die, and everyone must make of this what can or should be made. In older Europe which formed our own expectations about the length and end of life, the Latin phrase *memento mori*, remember to die, was perhaps the commonest of family mottos in various formulations in various languages.[15] What was meant then was for those at all ages, death at any time. For those in the Third Age at the present day such a sentiment is still entirely appropriate.

But being elderly at this present time decidedly does not of itself mean the expectation of dying so soon that there is little point in caring. Nor does it mean illness, incapacity, restricted vision, hearing or taste, for any but a small minority, and the anticipation of serious decline in mental capacity is largely unnecessary, at least until the later eighties. A third or more of us will probably stay resolutely 'normal' to the end of their lives, though about the same proportion may show 'benign forgetfulness' in their nineties.[16] It is not very realistic either for people to fear being in an institution in the final years. Though a fair number may spend a period in them, say an eighth or a tenth of those at risk to do so, the last census of Great Britain recorded under 3 per cent of those over 60 in institutions, two-thirds of them being in their eighties or nineties. Of these some two-fifths seem to have been in old peoples homes maintained by local authorities, less than a fifth in hospital wards – one in a thousand of the elderly population at large. You are quite likely to die in a hospital, but very unlikely to be there for any length of time before your final illness.[17]

CONTINUING CAPACITIES IN THE THIRD AGE

Age is not illness and it is one of the worst features of an outmoded medical attitude to ageing that it should ever have been seen in this light. The sentence – 'You must expect this [unpleasant symptom] at your age' – should never, never, never be heard in the consulting room again. As for personal appearance, since being elderly is by definition to lose those attributes which society presently associates with beauty, that is to say the attributes of youth, the loss of comeliness will have to be accepted.

Moreover, it is gratuitous to suppose that the values of the cosmetic advertisements are human universals. Over three hundred years ago the best of our English lyric poets could say:

No *Spring*, nor *Summer Beauty* hath such grace,
As I have seen in one *Autumnal* face.

Sexual activity can continue for both men and women almost indefinitely into the Third Age and does so in spite of the still persistent stereotype which would disallow it. Indeed in an American enquiry reported upon in 1981 two-thirds of the men and no less than four-fifths of the women declared that their sexual experience was the same or better after the age of 60 than it had been when they were younger. No one should pay any further attention to the belief that conventional youthful appeal is of conspicuous importance to sexual companionship. Every

woman, indeed every man, should be aware that release from the possibility of conception and being together as a couple after the departure of children are a great reward and an encouragement.[18] It is nevertheless one of
the least fortunate circumstances which we have to consider that there is
and apparently must be a great want of male partners for women in their
later years.

As for intellectual grasp, capacity to learn afresh, to write, paint, fashion
objects, concern about their gradual elimination with age is easily
exaggerated, since experience and maturity may compensate, or more than
compensate. Elderly learners, as we shall see, especially elderly learners
from each other, are usually keener and fresher than their juniors. These
are a self-selected group of course, but we should be delighted to hear that
creativity is surprisingly independent of period of life. Even memory, for
that which is of importance to their purposes, continues to be adequate to
the ends of elderly people, much as they tend to reproach themselves
about its fading.[19] It is highly dubious whether any but a very, very few of
those compelled to give up their jobs at the established retiring age are
objectively unfit to continue should they wish so to do. Nor is it at all clear
how far it is true that those nearing the end of what we call working life
are in fact appreciably slower on the uptake or less efficient at the required
tasks than those junior to them.

The position, outlook and relationship with the rest of us of the really
powerful – the highly successful politicians (males and females), business
people, intellectuals and artists – will concern us as a subject in itself. For
there is a sense in which they never grow old at all, since the passage of
time adds to their influence, and may reinforce their despotism, especially
in the closed worlds of undemocratic politics and of capitalist hegemony.
They may be deposed, outdated, upstaged by their rivals of any age, but as
long as they occupy the positions they have been helped to by inheritance
and or secured by personal merit, achievement and aggressiveness, they
are exempt from many or most of the penalties which have been recited,
even from some of the biological ones. They do not grow old, as we that
are left grow old, that is to say we the great mass of those they have left
behind them in the race for power.

They do not grow old because society at large does not expect them to
do so. The whole body of facts which have been brought forward here
about the remarkably good general health of those in the Third Age goes
to demonstrate that the condition of old age is not so much a bodily state
as a social construction. This is a judgment which could of course be made
on the notion of the Third Age itself, and will have to be considered again.
Before we leave the objective physical and psychological condition of

those in the Third Age we may quote the conclusions of the medical authorities themselves when they were called upon to assess the health of British persons in the Third Age and the tendency of their own profession as well as others to make out that it is markedly worse than is really the case.

> Mental function is crucial to a successful Third Age and other data indicate the prevalent pessimistic view that function declines inexorably with age is largely an artefact. [In spite of decline in some individuals, often because of poor physical health, recent studies] generally show good preservation of abilities through the Third Age. Indeed such functional declines as do occur are often more than adequately counterbalanced by the advantages of increased experience.... Far more positive attitudes to ageing are appropriate and could be put forward more vigorously.

> Older people are still the victims of negative stereotypes. Our data shows that more positive views could be adopted towards the older workers or drivers, for example.

> Older people are able to benefit from training, if the training is of appropriate design. Exercise can delay or reverse physical declines whilst psychological deterioration is not inevitable and is often more than adequately compensated for by knowledge and experience. These positive views could be actively propagated.[20]

We may conclude our recital of misapprehensions about the undesirable and threatening things which happen in later life by being firmly but cautiously optimistic. We must do so with the recognition that what the researchers call successful ageing for any individual depends on her character or his; previous life history, attitude, background, education, success or failure at work and in the family, as a lover and a spouse, as friend, as parent or as manager of public and of private purposes.

The passage of time itself should not be looked upon as the enemy of hope, for life is what you make of it. This is so in spite of the exponential rise in mortality which becomes so marked after the sixth decade of life and the slower but apparently ineluctable increase in the disposition to fall ill, or when ill to recover less quickly. Nevertheless, the extremely gradual ebbing of some, but by no means all, of our socially and economically significant attributes which begins in our twenties and continues at an almost infinitely gradual pace until our seventies or eighties, has no interlude of sudden or catastrophic decline early or late in its progress, at least before the truly final episode. Monotonic is the technical way to describe it, that is always descending, never ascending, at each distinguishable interval, and thus precisely adapted to the most conspicuous feature of the human personality, strategic adaptability over time. Age is a misfortune, no more and no less inevitable than the other misfortunes of life which Machiavelli had in mind in his famous chapter in *The Prince* entitled 'How Far Human Affairs are Governed by Fortune and how Fortune can be Opposed'. 'Fortune is a woman', he declares in his characteristic, phallocratic way, 'and if she is to be submissive it is necessary to beat and to coerce her.'

It is a given fact of the earning careers of nearly all persons at the present time that age-related retirement or redundancy reduces previous regular incomes. This is especially so for men. Women may thus be exiled from earning as well, but for them the great and growing danger is of loss of the earning power of their partners through desertion or divorce. These ineluctables have become, in the way I have just described, the proper subjects of individual strategies. That success in these strategies is surprisingly widespread seems to be amply confirmed by the repeated expressions of satisfaction which are regularly recorded by Western populations of the retired. Above the level of working class few of the careers in the Third Age of generations yet to come seem likely to be careers of poverty, solitude or even lack of opportunities for earning.[21] Alternations between work and leisure may well become a possibility over the whole of the age-range, and not simply late in life.

Loss of spouse, siblings and other relatives is equally a matter of inevitable misfortune and would seem to be more grievous in that so few relatives are available to a generation whose parents had such tiny families. Being left spouseless by desertion, divorce, separation or widowhood bears very much more heavily on women than on men. A fifth are spouseless by 65, over a third by 75 and two-thirds after that, whereas widowers do not comprise a third of all surviving men even after 75. Much as many of them would grieve the loss of a husband, however, it is said that women do not tend to dread or to lament the condition of widowhood to the degree that men expect them to, and as men seem to do themselves. Moreover, the evidence shows that the survival of all persons in our society is now so good that provided divorce is left out of account we can count on the presence of our spouse, our brothers and sisters, in numbers noticeably greater than was the case with our ancestors even though they had such large bevies of siblings in their childhood and their youth.

An unwelcome corollary of this ability to survive is the set of familial dilemmas to which reference has been made. Parents now sometimes go on living even in a Fourth Age condition for long enough to imprison their middle-aged or elderly daughters in the Second Age. Greater numbers of handicapped offspring get past their early years into continuing dependency, and (though this is not itself primarily a function of survival) divorce and desertion multiply among the younger generation and inevitably involve the parents of the parties in the consequent emergencies. Remarriage grows more and more frequent among the elderly, though it is very much the remarriage of men because it is they who are in short supply. Living together without marriage is also being practised. In Canada they call it sharing. Not widowhood, but divorce once again is the great source of abandonment and loneliness for those in later life in the contemporary world as well as for their younger contemporaries. Divorce in its turn is a question of individual strategies, as well as being subject to change in the general outlook. And the outlook is not entirely unfavourable. It is possible that the multiplication of divorces may add to numbers of kin-related individuals to whom older people may turn for companionship and support.

Less amenable, it has to be confessed, is the contracted time space in which the elderly by necessity have to live, and which is such a contrast, such a vividly remembered contrast, with the sense of illimitable future which attaches to the young. From the subjective point of view, however, the failure of a future to proceed into is unimaginable, as much unimaginable as death itself. For the passage of time, as has already been hinted, is irrelevant to subjective life, even though the subjectivity is perfectly aware that certain objects may be unobtainable. The feeling of being at large in an unfamiliar world where less and less is what it was when you were young and at the beginning, and still getting to know the comfortable certainties of life which must surely last until the very end, seems nevertheless to be inescapable for older people. In some moods even the hardiest among them begins to wonder how much more of life is worthwhile.

That this should be a source of melancholy, a persisting note in the still, sad music of humanity, is both understandable and no more than appropriate. It is much less appropriate as a source of dread. Moreover, when it comes to a feeling for the future, the collective, the social future, there is unmistakable evidence of the presence of a sense of what has to be done for posterity on the part of those in the later and their final years.[22] They can, and do, live in the lives of their successors and especially of their children, their grandchildren and increasingly their great-grandchildren. I shall maintain that unless those in later life today create traditions and institutions for such purposes we shall as a whole society fail our juniors and our posterity in general. Those now in the Third Age and their sense of what is to come make up the one and only available resource for meeting the challenge of growing old, growing old individually and collectively, growing old on a universal scale.

There is a principle which I believe we should adopt as we contemplate the facts of growing old. We have perpetually to conduct our lives as far as is possible not simply in remembrance of our former but in the continuous presence of our future selves, all our future selves. The one thing which is certain in a world whose uncertainties we have dwelt upon is that we shall nearly all have a future to cope with, endure, if that is what we have to do, and enjoy if we possibly can. Wherever we now are on the descending monotonic scale we shall all have to count on going through the Third Age (or continue in that condition), and so face what our predecessors faced, build on what they achieved. We all should be aware that we shall become old almost as certainly as that we shall finally die. Much will be made of this when we come to consider justice between the generations, between what we think of as the retired on the one hand and on the other those in work, part of whose earnings go to support them. But who are the retired but those in work transposed in time by a few decades, by four decades at most, and on average not much more than two?

We have to live now, in our present selves, in the company of these threats and limitations. Their futureness, our ability to refer them to the future which we need not face until we have to do so, these are also sources of our lack of realism about our growing old. It is time to direct ourselves to the actual circumstances of how old our society has become and how we are to respond to the changing patterns of life in a social world, suddenly, universally, remorselessly changed towards the late and latest years.

3 The Age of Britain as a Country: Britain Be Your Age! – First Adjuration

We are quite accustomed to Britain being described as old, or very old. It may be an affectionate evocation of the old country, or a reproach against an age-encumbered, backward-looking society which had difficulty in adapting to the twentieth century and is decidedly unprepared for the twenty-first. Approval or disapproval, outside assessment or self-appraisal, we are challenged to be as clear as we can on how old our country can be said to be, and in what senses. Like our ageing as individuals, the ageing of Britain as a nation has to be faced head-on.

The senses in which an individual or a society grows old, however, can be a little complicated. In order to be confident about what is meant by the various notions and expressions which are in use, and which will be used here, it is proper to suggest some definitions and to draw some distinctions.

The age of an individual is one thing and the age of a society, a collection of individuals, is another. The usual way of expressing age in both cases is chronological, in years since she, he, or it, or they began. But there are age reckonings which are not necessarily chronological, and which need not, or cannot, have anything to do with the calendar. Our four Ages in the life course are conspicuous examples.

TYPES OF AGE AND AGEING: AGELESSNESS

An individual may be thought of as having several ages, though not entirely distinct from each other, and related in slightly confusing ways, because they differ somewhat in character. Apart from his or her age last birthday, given in years and entirely linked to the calendar, an individual may be said to have a biological age, a personal age, a social age or even ages, and a subjective age. A society, on the other hand, like the British nation or nation-state, though it also has a chronological age, or years since its first appearance – an institutional age as we shall call it – cannot have and should not be thought of as having any other of the age

34

characteristics which attach to an individual. But a nation, like any other collection of persons, has an age in a different sense, the age of its constituent population, which we shall call its compositional age. A population is judged old in the compositional sense when there is a relatively large proportion of elderly people in it, or when the general expectation of life is high, or when both are true, as they are for Britain now. We shall see how old the British really are in our next two chapters.

Of the distinguishable ages of an individual, the two first named, *calendar* or *chronological* age and *biological* age, are the most often assumed to be identical. In fact the entire system of age grading in general use – nursery age, youth, middle age, old age and so on – rests on the assumption that years since birth coincide with successive states of the body and of the personality. But it is quite obvious that individuals of the same chronological age differ, sometimes considerably, in bodily development or decline, and in personal development too. It is inaccurate to suppose that there is a 30-year old, 50-year old or 70-year old type common to all individuals. Differences of this kind get more marked as the life course passes, and the elderly are therefore more varied among themselves than any group of their juniors. They make up a very large collection of persons, stretching over a very long range of ages, and they are very miscellaneous.

In view of these facts biologists tend to judge a man or a woman as young or old 'for his age, for her age', that is always age last birthday. This is what we all do in conversation, but from the present point of view, which is to insist as much as possible on the different character of the senses of ageing and to reduce the pre-eminence of the chronological, it would be better if each were kept separate and the chronological sense played down.[1] When they think of their personal ages, for example, people habitually feel themselves to differ from the chronological ages or the biological ages allotted to them, even if they accept these ages for certain purposes. Although they may join willingly with others in the celebration of their birthdays, especially such anniversaries as the twenty-first, there is often anxiety about reaching the beginning of particular years since birth – the fortieth year, for example, or the sixty-fifth. There is in fact a widespread tendency to remain as quiet as possible about calendar age and even to 'fib' about it. The extent of the difference between personal and calendar age is itself thought to be a very personal matter.

The present *personal age* of an individual is that moment in the life course which a man, a woman or a child himself or herself judges to have been reached. It need not be expressed in the calendar way, and could be reckoned, if people so chose, without referring to birthdays by the use of the point judged to have been reached in one or other of the four Ages that we have defined. For readers of this book this would usually be a point within the Second or Third Ages. *Social age*, as distinct from chronological or biological, is the *public age* as attributed by family, friends, acquaintances, employers or officials. All these persons and agencies are likely to express social age in years since birth, which is the invariable rule with officialdom. There are writers on ageing and the Third Age in Britain who resent this imposition of a calendar age on everyone, especially by authority and more particularly by the state, as an unwelcome and unnecessary tyranny.

In a lecture to the Royal Society of Arts in London in December 1990, Michael Young, accepted as the doyen of the social sciences in our country, devastated the custom of labelling all persons with a calendar age for social purposes so as to sort them out and, as he strongly insinuated, to gain initial control over their affairs.

> The State (undoubtedly, the big bugbear here) should have no access to the ages of individuals, and the whole apparatus of selection, promotion, dismissal, retirement, qualification and disqualification based on age last birthday should be brought to an end. The newly arrived society of the huge and growing proportion of persons in later life should become an ageless society in this sense as soon as that can be engineered. The whole monstrous regiment of discrimination and authoritarianism based on calendar age will have to disappear, for children shoved in and out of school as for adults taken into and dropped from the workforce, and for oldies booted out of active and significant life.[2]

Brave words Young's certainly are, and of signal importance at a time when outdated and restricted conventions about age and its labelling potency are in need of radical revisionary attack. But we should perhaps exercise some caution before we go so far as this. It would not advance the cause of enlightenment about our age-transformed society if we insisted on changes which can surely never come about.

Let us return to our consideration of the tendency of social or public age to be identified with calendar age and notice the further complications even here. Those assigning a social age to a person may not really know his or her calendar age, and may be mistaken, even deliberately misinformed. Those close to a person have reservations about mentioning such things. They have a respect for privacy although they may know something about his or her personal age. Nevertheless there is a general curiosity about the calendar ages of other people, which is to be expected in view of the desired secrecy. This may help to explain why journalists insist on publishing everyone's calendar age whenever possible, and along with the points about authority and bureaucracy why the Carnegie Enquiry insisted on giving the Third Age a chronological definition. Let it be repeated here, and with emphasis, that from the point of view of the persons concerned, succession to the Third Age has nothing to do with birthdays. It comes when a person decides that the appropriate stage has been reached, at a point in time when personal and social age simultaneously require the changes.

Because of all these circumstances there can be differences, occasionally wide differences, between personal ages and social or public ages. Variation may even exist between the social age of the same individual, depending on who it is who proclaims the figures. All these reckonings inevitably differ from the *subjective* age of a person, because subjective age can scarcely be reckoned by the calendar or in any other way. It is achronic. There is a succession of events within it but no passage of time. It could be taken to be that which stays constant in order that personal, social and public age can be felt to change.

This is a slightly incoherent picture, but the differences discussed do not seem to cause much difficulty in practice. No uncertainty of this kind was evident, for instance, when we went over the ageing issues facing a person in our last chapter. It is not quite the same with the distinctions which have to be made for the collective age of a society as distinct from individuals, a society such as a firm, a college, a church, a country, or a nation like Britain. The misunderstandings mostly arise under the heading of the country's compositional age, its age as a population, and we shall examine these issues in the next chapter. But confusion is often due to the simple error of mixing up institutional age and compositional age, in spite of the fact that the differences between them are very easily illustrated.

China was founded a very long time ago, and therefore is an old country in that sense, but 'her' population is at present a young one. The state of Florida, if by any freak of fate 'she' became independent of the rest of the United States of America, would be at one and the same time the youngest nation in existence at the moment of 'her' independence and yet 'her' population would probably be the oldest in the world. Compositionally then China is comparatively young and Florida very old, but institutionally it is the other way round.

The words 'her' and 'she' have been given quotation marks as a warning against referring to societies as persons when discussing ageing, its attributes and consequences. It is these which are of importance to us, and in attempting to weigh them for Great Britain we must never, never think of that collectivity as an old lady. Evidently Britain could be declared to be old in both the meanings which have been contrasted. We are aware that we have large numbers of elderly people and so an advanced compositional age, and we are rather proud of the fact that we have a long history as a country, and so a venerable institutional age. But we must recognize that this is only a coincidence, as is shown in the case of China and of Florida. Above all it is not permissible to assimilate the two types of collective age by thinking of Britain as an individual, or as an individual-like entity, for this or any other purpose.

THE INSTITUTIONAL AGE OF COUNTRIES

So strong is national feeling, however, that institutional age does get mixed up with compositional age, especially in support of a claim to superiority. Americans, for example, are likely to insist that theirs is a younger country than those important enough to make the comparison worthwhile, and especially much younger than Britain, the 'old country'. In the early years of American history, American apologists were so convinced of the paint-fresh novelty of their nation that they proclaimed on its coinage that it belonged to a new order of time itself, *Novus ordo saeculorum*.[3] They did so while taking full advantage of the impermissible assimilation of the population with the nation: the compositional age of the American population was then conspicuously weighted in the direction of youth.

One source of these sentiments is presumably to be found in the metaphorical language of parenthood in relation to nations thought of as persons. The daughter nations of the Commonwealth; the mother country, not only Britain for her brood of white former colonies, but Spain for Argentina and a host of Latin American countries; Portugal for Brazil. In the 1960s France for Quebec?[4] All this may make it seem questionable whether we should think of collective age in either of its two distinct meanings as in any way analogous to the age of an individual.

Social traditions may not be transmitted to any great extent by nation-states acting to bring this about, but when transmission occurs, the entities concerned are usually in very close contact. The closest contact of all, of course, is where two political communities are, or have been, united in the same nation-state, or where one is or has been within the empire of the other. Under these circumstances, and especially where joint political life has continued over a long period, people are very likely to move as settlers and founders of family lines, though the extent of influence can be surprisingly great even where the relationship has been of a colonial character over shorter periods. Associations of this kind account for such facts as that American lawyers sometimes have to consult earlier records of the English common law to decide American cases. They are certainly reasons for the use of parental language in referring to relationships between the nations in question.

But neither 'parenthood' nor 'daughterhood' can in fact have anything to do with these circumstances, since we have agreed that nations are not persons, and so cannot procreate each other. Nor do the institutional ages of the collectivities concerned matter much either. Individual members of the population of North America or Australia, even of India, undoubtedly have absorbed English traditions and the English language within the family, from their own, individual parents in fact. Now it is precisely these cultural inheritances which may become important to a society when it calls upon the past for guidance on such questions as the ageing of its population. At this point questions about nationhood and national begin-nings multiply themselves. What about India, once more, with a tiny number of its characteristics drawn from Britain? Or what about Japan or China? All are very old in many directions, but can they be acknowledged as being older than Britain as constituted, sovereign nation-states?

These are historians' questions *par excellence* and we cannot hope to settle them here. In order to decide the age of Britain now, we ought to make ourselves aware of some of the facts about nations, nationalities, sovereignty and legal continuity.

The concept of the nation-state is itself an historical product. It origin-ated in Europe and in France and England particularly perhaps five hundred years ago in the 1400s, or four hundred years ago in the 1500s: historians of ideology and institutions cannot be more certain about such things. The whole set of ideas, and the legal doctrine of national sover-eignty, were not codified and accepted over the European and European-dominated area until the 1700s, and certainly did not become the basis of a world order of sovereign nation-states including all the peoples of the globe until the mid- or late nineteenth century, or even the twentieth. Japan, for example, was not a nation-state in that special, once exclusively European but now global sense, until perhaps the nineteenth century – most Japanese would probably say at the Meiji Restoration in the 1860s, at about the same time that Germany and Italy became nations.

China did not adopt 'nationhood' of this kind until the twentieth century. But China, a Chinese collectivity of a somewhat different kind, was in a position to do many of the things that 'nations' do, such as fight wars, from the beginnings of Chinese history. And so for Japan. As for India, it might now have to be supposed that an Indian collectivity resem-bling the Chinese existed long before the British arrived, or even before the British nation-state was founded. After the British left in 1947, however, it became a sovereign national body like all the others in the world of the 1900s. Is India then a new nation or a very old one? International convention and jurisdiction apart, it becomes increasingly difficult in view of all these circumstances to know what is conveyed by claiming that Britain is older, or younger, than these other nations.

The position of North Americans is relevant here once again. We have seen that the USA was instituted as a nation-state rather late in the period during which nationhood was crystallizing, but that this was nearly a century earlier than was the case for Germany or Italy. When compared with them, or with the scores of collectivities which have attained nationhood in the second half of the twentieth century – and which have incidentally made the whole system look less and less convincing – the United States is a markedly senior country, not a young one at all. There is in fact a rather more refined definition of a 'nation' in contemporary usage, one which incorporates the element of deliberate, revolutionary nation-building against opposition, the opposition of an overlord in possession which had to be defeated and expelled. According to this revolutionist doctrine of the creation of nations the United States could be said to be one of the oldest of the 150-odd sovereign nations of the world whose representatives foregather in New York City at the United Nations. That doctrine, we may notice, leaves Canada, Australia and New Zealand in an interestingly equivocal position, and perhaps India too.[5]

The Americans in this mood are apt, and not unreasonably, to advance the claim that the United States is the oldest of democracies, just as the British will proudly proclaim that theirs is the Mother of Parliaments. We know now that we have patiently to accept the fact that citizens of national societies can wish them or their institutions to be the youngest and the oldest at the same time, if that should minister to their national feelings. Nevertheless age is usually preferred before youth as a boast about nations and institutions; the greater the age, the greater the possibility of influence. Being old, having withstood the buffets of time and misfortune for longest, even possessing venerable objects on the national territory, legitimates.

To this must be added the persistent misbelief, put about by poets but not much weakened by historians, that the 'early ages of man' were simpler, purer, better. 'Early' is the word to ponder here, but the fact itself remains. Age is indeed the great legitimator among the nations, hence the fierce insistence on priority, on having got there first, in international relationships. Commercial undertakings, especially shops, behave in a similar fashion when they display 'Established in 1875', or 1825, or 1675 for that matter, nearly always very dubious claims, but put forward as a recommendation of their priority, their solidity, their trustworthiness. This goes along with a failure to remember what came in between, whether in fact the body making the claim now is in historical reality the same continuing body as the one which did what it is known or said to have done in the distant past.

The real history of the shop which styles itself as a century or a century-and-a-half old would often be unrecognizable to its customers and to those who run it. Changes of location, of premises, of ownership, changes in lines of goods sold, are all concealed behind a continuing name, if indeed the name is genuinely the same as it was in the beginning. With nation-states the tendency to believe what makes a good story is even stronger, and it has palpable consequences, even though the historical inconsistencies are easy to discover. An example is the unchallengeable assumption which seems to be made by the citizens of contemporary Greece that theirs is the nation of Socrates, Sophocles, Pericles and Praxiteles, and the claim of Israel that it is God's chosen people of biblical times. In the United States the search for antiquity to legitimate the new republic led its citizens in the early years to point to rocks of immense geological age on the surface of the ground it covered.

It is understandable in such a situation among the powers of the world, large and small, that every possible effort should be made by the interested parties to stretch national records back as far as possible into the past. Nation-states perpetually exaggerate their ages, however equivocal that expression is. They may have to do so in order to protect what they choose as their national interest. More unfortunate from our point of view is the fact that individuals, seeking reassurance for themselves in the dignity and authority of the countries to which they belong, may feel that they have to accept this political fiction-writing. They should not do so, not if they wish to be clear about institutional age. Patriotism does not demand it.

THE AGE OF THE UNITED KINGDOM AND THE AGE OF BRITISH INSTITUTIONS

Citizens[6] as we are of the United Kingdom of Great Britain and Northern Ireland, we tend to forget that it was England, with Wales precariously appended, which became a nation in the fourteenth or fifteenth century. Scotland did not get included until 1603, or more likely 1707; Ireland not until 1801, to be reduced to Northern Ireland in 1921. Are we to say then that the Britain we are proud of for being so old is a unity which was not finally defined until about seventy years ago? And suppose Northern Ireland should cease to be part of the United Kingdom? Alternatively should we say that it is really English nationality which gives us our magisterial antiquity? If so, what about the Scots and the Welsh? Do they share it? If not, how 'old' are Scotland and Wales? And what difference would it make if these countries, as we may call them, became members of the European Community independent of England?

It would be easy to raise similarly awkward questions about the age of other 'great European nations', and reduce them to a similar futility. Is contemporary Germany a new state because of the recent reunification with its former Eastern areas, for example, and what difference does it make that the change was a restoration? But I may have gone too far in ridiculing the notion of the age of a nation in the institutional sense and so calling into question its consequences for our purposes. Let us conclude that the word 'age' is of uncertain, equivocal meaning when it is applied to the British nation or nation-state. Of itself it has few consequences for our discussion, though we perhaps should not overlook the self-respect which the feeling of antiquity in British society encourages in British citizens late in life or indeed throughout their lives.

The nation-state as a whole is by no means all that has to be taken into account when we ponder the consequences of the age of British national institutions. In the political field the principles we have touched upon can indeed be seen at work. Here our time-honoured, historically legitimated organs of state confer enviable continuity and security. No doubt the authority which attaches to ancientness means that we have gained from the acknowledged antiquity of our Monarchy, our Parliament, our established Church, our Common Law, even our Universities – if only two of them, Oxford and Cambridge. Their conspicuous antiquity has been considerably strengthened by the recent creation of new universities in dozens at a stroke. You have only to ask a Spaniard, preferably a Spaniard of the left, to recognise how valuable the presence and actions of a monarchy can be in a democracy, especially if that monarchy represents an ancient dynasty. The whole array of British political and constitutional institutions is certainly securely established in time, and the word 'Establishment', with the adjective immemorial understood, entirely appropriate as a description. In all such directions being old helps the British, however tricky it may be to define old for these purposes.

But there are patent signs of change afoot in Britain. A recent movement of opinion makes clearer and more formidable a judgement which has been in place in the country for at least a decade. We have been forced to recognise that continuity and legality are not everything in political life and that the perpetuation of the obsolete may be more and more of a draw-back. The symbolic position of the monarchy has had a focusing effect on these blankly anti-establishmentarian sentiments, and the troubles of the Royal Family add to their salience.[7] Moreover, the virtual absence of a really radical attitude and unwillingness to accept the absolutely new seem incompatible with the facts of advanced industrial economic life. When it comes to the organization of production and to particular industries the British early start is cited as an important reason for Britain's continuing decline as a producer of goods and services which are now in demand in world markets. Perhaps we would have been better off in the 1990s and 2000s if we had missed the era of coal, steam and railways altogether, and proceeded directly to oil, electronics, air and motor transport, as many of our successful competitors have done. Oh that James Watt had been a German, one might even say, or George Stephenson a Japanese!

But it must not be overlooked that another influential and expansive body of opinion claims that such statements merely express the all-too-familiar adherence of those who discuss the wealth and power of nations entirely in terms of the gospel of economic growth. It is our values which have been faulty, they believe, as well as our capacity to sustain the 'progress' that these values require.[8]

Now these are very serious issues, perhaps the most important which we have to deal with in respect of our age as a nation, as a society and as a population. We shall return to them several times here, for example when we consider the obsolescence of the educational system. There seems to be very little, however, in the argument which attributes our relative inefficiency as producers to the 'unfavourable' age balance of our population, nothing which we could not remedy by intelligent reform of the content of instruction, and a radical rearrangement of the periods in the life course during which instruction is carried out.

France, we shall see, now with a richer and more resilient economy than Britain for the first time in three or four hundred years or more, has a compositional age which is practically the same, and was older than we were in the earlier phases of French economic growth. Before German reunification, West Germany was compositionally older than both and economically more successful than either. Sweden developed economically when it already had the oldest European population. The population of the Western industrial giant and leader, that is to say the United States, has at the present time an age composition junior to that of Britain and of Europe, in spite of what has happened locally in areas such as Florida. The margin will continue to exist for a couple of generations or more, but it is becoming less pronounced. Indeed the greying of America has given rise to more alarmist comment than the more extreme effects to be seen among the Europeans. This is perhaps natural in a country so very anxious to be young.

Even if it could be demonstrated that the entirely new industrial powers of the present epoch, Japan and its companions in the Pacific, have gained a great deal from their compositional youth, we shall find that this possible source of superiority cannot last for long. Japan is now ageing faster than any other country in the world, and it will be claimed that every population will sooner or later catch up with the Western European populations in compositional age. It is easy then, to dispose of the formal charge that because Britain is old as a nation-state and old as a population, it cannot expect to be as efficient in production and in the provision of services, and so as prosperous, as the other countries to which it was superior until so recently.

Nevertheless, there is no point in passing over the penalties of an early start and the gains which may come from joining the race at a later stage. The fact of having been exceedingly rich, powerful and predominant for such a long period in the past has legitimated much too much for the British in the present. Everything the British did, or believed or established tended to be looked upon for centuries as justified by the record of British achievement, certainly at home and to some extent abroad. This put our attitudes, practices and social instincts above critical examination for far too long, and made them fundamentally resistant to change even after their justification in success had departed. Such a penalty is exacted of all who get to the top and stay there, and the longer the supremacy, the greater the penalty tends to be. One of its effects is to rob the British now of some of the satisfaction from the advances which they certainly make. Because these achievements do not put them back where they had once been they count for less. But the burden of a prolonged period of former success should not, indeed cannot, be construed as an effect of age or ageing, in the society or in the individual. This could only be done if, once again, the institutional age of the British nation-state was assimilated with its compositional age, and by thinking of Britain as a person.

We are in danger of being haunted by a fantasy, widespread and insidious in spite of its unrealistic assumptions and erroneous logic. It depicts a British national community as a senescent, person-like entity, still exhausted by 'her' efforts put forth centuries ago, when 'she' was much younger; composed furthermore of individuals themselves worn out by exertions, military as well as economic, made decades ago when they too were in their youth; a British national community falling further and further behind in the face of competition from newly industrialized nation states, suffused with vigour because of their recent economic promotion and because they largely consist of younger persons.

Since nation-states are not persons or person-like, they do not exhibit either youthful energy or senile lassitude. In the 1990s they cannot possibly be suffering from fatigue because of what happened in the 1770s, the 1850s or the 1900s. National societies are problematic abstractions with problematic histories, constructed for political and ideological purposes, and senior and junior have in fact no meaning for them, in economic competitiveness anyway. The presence of numbers of older and experienced individuals in a population and in its work-force does not in itself have any effect on the vigour and enterprise of their younger contemporaries. It is simply impossible for older Britons to be still exhausted from their exertions in the 1940s. If this could be, why not their German or Japanese contemporaries? The existence of a large community of older dependants, no longer in the workforce, from which many of them have been ejected for reasons of the politics of unemployment, is no greater burden on Britain than it is on our rivals, and in any case its effects on economic output are by no means necessarily depressive.

The waning of energy, adaptability and inventiveness of persons in middle and later life is perpetually exaggerated. Anyone disposed to believe that Britain cannot do what others do because 'she' is old and tired-out is at the mercy of a whole array of misconceptions and misunderstandings. Of these the most serious and debilitating is the unfavourable stereotyping of the individual in later life, the gratuitous error of confusing the Third Age with the Fourth. This dangerous mistake is spread about and occasionally believed in, sometimes for interested reasons, by politicians, by medical men, by administrators, by welfare workers, and even by demographers, as well as by employers. Persuading British people to take seriously the exhortation to be their age may turn out to be a formidable task.

Nevertheless the possibility remains that the transformation which industrial development, that leap into a new order of production and productivity, brings has an arresting finality about it, already evident in cases other than the British. Having made the wrench from traditional arrangements, built the factories and the other plant, acquired the logistics, fashioned the institutions, worked out and adopted the ideology demanded by an industrial order, changing it all over again seems to be a peculiarly formidable task. To be in an industrialized state, however, is a condition of being in perpetual economic change and innovation. Every phase in the process leaves obsolete plant and awkward impedimenta behind, attitudinal as well as material, steam-age opinions as well as the slag heaps and the abandoned mines, the forlorn, corroding factories, the forsaken docks and railway tracks. The longer all this continues, the less appropriate the original adaptation becomes. In Britain it could be suggested that industrialization and the prolonged period of supremacy that succeeded froze the social structure to some extent at the point when self-intensifying change first manifested itself, during the decades on either side of 1800.[9] Only in this remote and incidental sense could the obstacles to our economic progress be said to be due to our age as a country, as the national society which has been longest industrialized.

Historical circumstances such as these are best looked upon in the way recommended by Niccolò Machiavelli once again, this time for political and national disposition. Having reaped the enormous rewards of early industrial supremacy and global imperial power, we must withstand the consequences and pay the price. It is now quite evident, I hope, how little of that price has to do with our present age, or ages, in any of their definitions.

TIME-SCALE OF AGEING IN NATIONAL POPULATIONS

Before we leave the general consideration of the significance to our institutions of our compositional age and proceed to the closer investigations of contemporary demographics, the time horizon has to be widened very much further. When we reflect on the passage of time in relation to the current situation of the older members of our population, the centuries since industrialization first made an appearance begin to look like exceedingly recent history. This is quite apparent, for example, if we consider the familial position of the elderly, and ask ourselves how far it differs today from what it was in the past. By the past we usually mean the long era of traditional English society, before that was disturbed by repetitive, self-perpetuating, technically-based economic change.

An argued reply to this question about the familial position of the elderly in the past belongs to the later discussion of the nature and consequences of the age transformation of our country, which we shall call the secular shift in ageing, where 'secular' means permanent and irreversible.[10] We can state here, however, what is now fairly familiar to historical sociologists but may not yet be known to all students of ageing or to many of the elderly themselves. This is that the family position of the elderly in the traditional past, a subject of interest to Americans, Canadians, Australians, New Zealanders and the many others who look to the British past as the final origin of much of their contemporary social life, was different, but not so very different, from the familial position of the elderly in Britain and in those countries at present. It has been demonstrated that in pre-industrial England the family group was not of the multi-generational character which is conventionally assumed, with a place reserved for ageing parents and relatives. It is simply untrue, therefore, that the elderly have been rejected from the family circle of co-residing children and kin because of economic and social change. They never were there in anything like the numbers which we might suppose.

But the evidence for this pronouncement, though it goes back centuries before the period of first industrialization, to the time of Queen Elizabeth and to the later Middle Ages, is quite insufficient to tell us how long familial arrangements have been like this in England, or whether there was ever a time when all those in the Third and Fourth Ages could be sure of living within a family circle. For all we know the position as we can observe it four or at most five hundred years ago may have been in place among our ancestor populations ever since peasant societies succeeded hunter-gatherer societies, which is what anthropologists commonly suppose did happen in the very distant past. These arrangements could be even older.

This is certainly sententious language, but it is necessary to get the time-scale right. The abrupt upset to the arrangements of societies which has been brought about by the secular shift in ageing in the present century has transformed a pattern which must have existed for far longer than the four hundred years since Queen Elizabeth reigned in England, or than the thousand years and more conventionally reckoned to have passed since the Middle Ages began. We know this from demographic principle as well as from recent advances in our knowledge of demographic history.[11] The advanced age of the British population is therefore absolutely new, on a very long time-scale indeed. This enormous change, however, can scarcely be held responsible for the creation of situations, which, like that of the elderly within the family, were already in many respects much as we know them to be now.

I have talked, as a historical sociologist should, of the intimations from that almost infinitely enduring past experience which might be consulted as we orientate ourselves towards a future in respect of ageing which will be so different from our immemorial past. Where else should men and women go for a precedent, for a scrap of prophetic advice, for a hint that at least something like this has happened before and has been successfully negotiated? The record of the English population makes plain that within the recorded past numbers of young and numbers of old have gone from high to low and low to high, and quite quickly too, though within very restricted limits. Our English ancestors eight or nine generations ago, between the time of Charles II and that of George II, for example, experienced a rise in the proportions of elderly to levels unsurpassed in previous records known to us, and not exceeded until the 1920s. This early-eighteenth-century interlude quickly gave way to a return to the previous position, and we now suspect that over the same generations English people may have witnessed a pronounced decrease and then increase in the numbers of their kin. What happened at this particular period may well have happened before, although no sign has yet been found that any of these changes were noticed at the relevant time. Somewhere in the traditional social structure it would seem, somewhere within the recesses of the manner of living of our forefathers, provision did exist to take account of such vicissitudes in ageing.[12]

Perhaps it will turn out that there is wisdom to be sought and recovered from the past which might give us a glimmer of a notion of what should now be thought and done. But the thinking of our British and European forebears seems to have been singularly banal in the matter of age and ageing, of societies as well as individuals. Solemn pronouncements on the necessity of respect for the old and deference to them in every direction, except perhaps those that really matter, reappear perpetually. The Europeans of the past shared this sentiment with many other cultural areas. From the Greek and Roman classics we have sententious lucubrations in the manner of Cephalus, the Athenian businessman preparing for his exit from the world in the earlier pages of Plato's *Republic*, and Cicero's garrulous and impercipient discourse of old age, *De Senectute*. Subsequent literature is given over to incessant repetition of sentiments of the same character, along with improbable or bogus recipes for the lengthening of life.[13] Magnificent as they could be on the subject of death, not so closely associated for them of course with the later and latest years, our earlier ancestors were tamely conventional on the subject of age.

What has followed in more recent generations is no more realistic or encouraging. Since the time of William Wordsworth at least our English poets seem to have had their gaze unalterably fixed in exactly the wrong direction. What enlightenment for our appointed time and condition could ever come from such famous lines as these?

> Our birth is but a sleep and a forgetting
> The Soul that rises with us, our life's star
> Hath had elsewhere its setting
> And cometh from afar:
> Not in entire forgetfulness,
> And not in utter nakedness
> But trailing clouds of glory do we come

From God who is our home:
Heaven lies about us in our infancy!
Shades of the prison house begin to close
Upon the growing Boy,
Bur he beholds the light, and whence it flows,
He sees it in his joy;
The Youth, who daily further from the east
Must travel, still is Nature's priest,
And by the vision splendid
Is on his way attended;
At length the Man perceives it die away,
And fade into the light of common day.

Time and again we shall find ourselves turning our faces against the temporal set of our literature and our art, which are as obtuse about the ageing of nations as about the ageing of individuals. The cultural strata have been laid down in the wrong direction for our purposes. We shall have to make the artistic universe itself afresh, in respect of ageing anyway.

4 The Age of the Present British Population, with a Glimpse into its Future: Britain Be Your Age! – Second Adjuration

We need two things in order to decide whether the population of our country is really old, a way of measuring its age and standards of comparison. So far we have used proportion of people in their later years as our ageing indicator, but we have referred to expectation of life and this will have to play an equal or perhaps even more important part in our discussion. For standards of comparison we can set British figures as they are alongside those of other countries and, in due course, alongside English figures from the past. No calibration of the composition of societies has so far been agreed, dividing them shall we say into 'very young', 'young', 'middle-aged', 'old' and 'really old'. Nevertheless there would be no difficulty in allocating the contemporary United Kingdom to a place a little way from the top of any such notional scale.

THE OLDEST BRITISH POPULATION EVER KNOWN

Establishing a way of measuring the compositional age of a population, especially for the rather general purposes likely to be in the minds of readers of this book, is not quite as straightforward as might have been thought. Average ages, either the median or the mean, would seem to be the obvious measures. They are sometimes used by demographers and are becoming more important in calculations of the demographic determinants of ageing,[1] especially the median which is the age at which there are exactly the number of older persons as younger persons in a population. But these figures vary on such a small scale and give so little indication as to the number likely to be in the Third Age that they are not very illuminating for our purposes.

Proportions of the population aged 60 or 65 and over are rough guides to relative numbers in the Third Age and there has been a tendency to describe all those who have passed their sixtieth birthday as old, and those past 65 as very old or aged, reserving the ages after 75 for the really superannuated. The close study of the actual relative condition of people at these ages at different periods, however, and of the emergence of the Third Age, have made this terminology obsolete.[2] Moreover, reckonings of this kind give no impression of how long an experience people are likely to have of later life and for this we have to turn to expectation of life.

Expectation of life at birth is a very popular way of referring to age and ageing, of populations and of individuals. It also has its disadvantages and is often used, as I shall try to show, in a mistaken way. All these circumstances and others not mentioned, make it seem best to have a combined criterion of age for populations, including both proportions in later life and longevity. As the most useful preliminary indicator, adequate for the majority of the discussion here, the following dual measure has been adopted. A country is really old when the proportion of its whole population aged 60 and above is at least 20 per cent, and at the same time expectation of life at birth is at least $77\frac{1}{2}$ years for women and $72\frac{1}{2}$ years for men. In the middle of the 1990s the United Kingdom certainly fits, with 20.5 per cent of its people over 60 years old and with women expecting to live 79.4 years, men 73.5. There are only eight other countries which have figures as high as these, or higher, and which have accordingly to be classed as really old along with the United Kingdom.[3]

Expectation of life is much more interesting and significant for individual experience than proportions of the elderly. It is an average which can be calculated for any age after birth, though only for collections of people. In fact of course, it is my own probable prospect of life to come which most concerns me personally, along with that of members of my family, and for these purposes an average is always to some degree unsatisfactory. In thinking about that average we must be careful moreover to avoid the mistake of supposing that at 50, say, when general expectation of life at birth is $73\frac{1}{2}$ for males, there are over 20 years still to go. It is always rather more: for Englishmen today the value is more like 26 years.

Actuaries working for insurance companies can distinguish between 'good lives' and 'bad lives', that is, presumably between lives likely to last as long as or longer than the general expectation and those likely to fall short of it, but no one can tell one particular person for how many more years he or she will in fact continue. Therefore I can have no assurance that I shall in fact have a life corresponding to the expectation of life at birth recognised as the current average in the society in which I find myself. The same applies to the figure for expectation of life at my current age. Nevertheless this natural preoccupation of everyone with his or her allotted time will face us on each page of this book, which is addressed to individuals thinking about themselves as well as about those around them.

A town, village, profession, occupation, even a club or a school can have an average or general probability of years to live for the individuals which that population is defined to include. In this way expectation of life can be regarded as an indicator of longevity for a whole national population, or for any order of persons within it. The average durations of future life at 50, 55, 60, 65 or 70, for example, are of obvious interest to anyone concerned with the Third Age in a particular country. We shall find ourselves concluding that a figure of a slightly different type, the expectation at the age of 25 of living to age 70, is also highly significant in this connection.

In 1989–91 women in the United Kingdom had 21.9 years to live at the age of 60, and men 17.7; at the age of 70 women had 14.3 years and men 11.1. This relatively greater discrepancy between the sexes in later life has probably always existed even in populations like that of India where women have had lower life expectation at birth. The gap between older females and older males grew rapidly in Britain from the 1950s to the 1970s but it fell slightly in the 1980s. Nevertheless, so telling is the greater durability of women that in 1991 there were 1 800 000 more of them aged 65 and over, 5 434 000 as compared with 3 651 000 men.[4] This is a surplus of 39 per cent of women over men, and at ages above 75 it grows to over 90 per cent. Under our own demographic circumstances where, as in all older countries whose populations have been ageing for long periods, expectation of life is beginning to have a considerable effect in increasing the proportion of the old in the population, an effect which is additional to that of the reduction in proportion of their juniors because of the fall in births. The outcome is inevitably sex-differential, leading to progressive feminisation of the older age groups.

MORE PRECISE AND REVEALING EXPERIENTIAL MEASURES OF AGEING

We have already discussed, in a rather general way, the issues raised by comparison between our own low-fertility, low-mortality population today and the high-fertility, high-mortality populations of the developing world, and of the past. But if we are to be as precise as we can about the relative age of our population, we should look at the rather more revealing indicators which would be required for a really accurate comparison.

It turns out that expectation of life at birth is not the best indicator of longevity in deciding how much longer we live now than people lived in the Ancient World, or in Shakespeare's day or in Victorian England, or than they live in contemporary African countries. Expectation of life at ages 1, 5, 10, 15 or even 20 was and is greater in these populations than expectation of life at birth. In Canada in 1831, for example, women could expect to live for 39.8 years at age 0; for 46.5 years at age 1; for 49.5 years at age 5; and for 46.2 years at age 15. If we wanted to compare their mid-nineteenth-century experience with that of English women in the last decade of the twentieth century, when their expectation of life at birth was 78.7 years in 1989–91 and rising, and higher at 0 than at all subsequent birthdays, the figure for the age at which expectation was highest in Canada in 1831, 49.5 years to come at age 5, would evidently be more revealing than expectation of life at 0 in that country at that time. It would considerably reduce the longevity advantage of contemporary women. The same would be true of comparing English persons today with those in contemporary Ghana, shall we say, or Egypt. For these reasons it is more accurate, though even then not entirely satisfactory, to make comparisons of this kind at age 15 rather than at age 0.[5] We cannot go into the numerical grounds for this apparent paradox about expectation of life at birth without making it look even more puzzling to people with no acquaintance with demography. It should be emphasized, however, that for the demographers expectation of life at birth has not been regarded as a measure of experience, that experience of time to come which is evidently of literally vital importance to every member of any population. They have looked at it almost exclusively as a measure of the health and welfare of the people in question, a very important matter of course, but not the really crucial one from the point of view of experience. This to my mind is a telling example of the relative indifference of demographers to the spontaneous interests of the ordinary people around them in the implications of demographic studies.

A similar point about the realistic meaning may be made in respect of figures for proportions of old people. Although the fractions in the whole population of those over 60 or 65 are perfectly straightforward measures, not subject to uncertainties of the kind which attach to expectation of life at birth, they are also less than satisfactory as measures of experience, particularly in relation to the Third Age. In all populations, except again, those of advanced societies in recent decades, so large a proportion of the numbers alive is *young*, anything up to a quarter or a third, or even a half of all persons being under the age of 10, that the ratio of those in later life to the population as a whole is an implicit comparison between the number of the old, which is relatively small, and the number of the young and very young, which is relatively large. To be realistic, realistic to experience once again, what is needed is a measure of the share which those in later life make up of all adults, all mature people. The indicator adopted for this purpose is the proportion of all those over 25 years old who are themselves over 60 or 65 years old rather than the proportion of these elder age groups of the population generally. In 1991 those more realistic figures were 23.7 per cent for those over 65 for the United Kingdom and 31.2 per cent for those over 60, as proportions of all over 25.

The statistics for the United Kingdom relevant to proportions in later life are set out in Table 4.1, along with their projected changes up to 2021. We should not miss the plain message of the figures, that the ratio of our older population both to the whole and as a share of all adults has for the moment ceased to grow, although absolute numbers are slowly rising, and those in the latest age group, over 85, are going up sharply. They are expected to rise in the 1990s by a third for males and a quarter for females. General expansion of proportions at higher ages will start again after the early 2010s and the further prospects may be intimidating as we shall see. But the present respite is of considerable importance for our adaptation to the new era. As we continue the analysis of the transformation, however, and go on to put our country into its European context, we should pause to recognise the intricacies of population measures. The subject of this book cannot be regarded as a wholly simple matter to be grasped from the crude figures bandied about by most commentators, and even by some gerontologists.

But this is as far as we can proceed with the complications which commonly appear when ages of populations are being discussed. We shall usually find ourselves having to overlook them in the present essay, sticking for the most part to the cruder measures we have had to criticize because statistics for more refined measures are unavailable. Of one thing we can be quite confident, however. The statistics we have quoted make the British people in the middle 1990s one of the oldest ever known. It is situated in a continent whose populations must be classed as decidedly older than in the rest of the world, very much older than populations have ever been before, anywhere. To belong as we do, as a country, to this demographic community is to be old indeed. It goes without saying that the present British population is far and away the oldest body of persons which has even inhabited England or the British Isles. And it never will be younger than it is today.

Table 4.1 Figures and projected figures for proportions of the population in the older age groups, by gender, UK, 1990–2021 (percentages)

	Males				Females				Both sexes	
	60+	(60–74)	75+)	85+	60+	(60–74)	75+)	85+	Proportion of the whole population over 60	Proportion of adults (25+) over 60
1991	17.9	(13.0	4.9)	0.8	23.5	(14.6	8.9)	2.3	20.8	31.2
1996	17.9	(12.8	5.1)	0.9	23.0	(13.9	9.1)	2.6	20.5	30.2
2001	18.0	(12.6	5.5)	1.1	22.8	(13.3	9.4)	2.9	20.4	30.1
2006	18.9	(13.2	5.7)	1.2	23.3	(13.8	9.5)	3.1	20.3	31.0
2011	20.7	(14.7	6.0)	1.4	24.8	(15.4	9.5)	3.3	22.8	33.2
2016	21.8	(15.3	6.5)	1.5	25.8	(16.2	9.7)	3.4	23.9	34.3
2021	22.4	(15.9	7.4)	1.8	27.5	(17.0	10.5)	3.5	25.4	36.1

Source: Projections of the Office of Population Censuses and Surveys, based on statistics of 1991.

POPULATION, AGEING AND SOCIAL CHANGE

The situation we are in at the moment as to the age of our population is still only acknowledged, so it seems to me, in a somewhat uncomprehending way by relatively few British people. Not very surprisingly, it might be said, since the facts are unwelcome. They are unpalatable because they are numerical, and easily become technical. They are bewildering because they are so new and their implications so little appreciated, so difficult to explore. They are intimidating because they are irreversible.

We must not exaggerate, however, and we need not be downcast. It is natural that as this situation has unfolded over the last twenty or thirty years, such comment as there has been has taken on what might be called the Wordsworthian theme of regrettable decline; sententious, alarmist, sometimes almost panicky. This has been the case about the ageing of populations ever since the French first recognized, over a century-and-a-half ago, that their population was getting old, older than that of other European nations, a difference which was to be at its most pronounced in the 1930s. The result, some French people supposed, would be national decline, economic, cultural and, worst of all, military decline. The facts of ageing were used to explain the French lag behind Britain in industrial progress and behind Germany in warfare.[6]

Rather ironical, we might declare, in view of the present relative positions of France and Britain in respect of economics touched on in Chapter 3. It has to be said, however, that France was somewhat rejuvenated after the Second World War, when de Gaulle's call for 'douze millions de bébés de plus' was succeeded by a boom in births, though it is highly unlikely that this was simple cause and effect. There was another, even more disturbing, feature of the position of the French during these generations, the possibility of a fall in the whole population, a spectre which still haunts the leaders of that country and those who work at its demography. Both ageing and diminution in numbers as had been said, are usually the outcome of a pronounced and accelerating decline in fertility, rather than of any change in mortality or migration. The fact that increasingly low birthrates, rather than low death rates, have been the operative cause up to very recently of the growth in proportions of the old must perpetually be borne in mind.

During the last decade or so, although they have not dwelt to any great extent on the prospects of a shrinkage in our populations, demographers, sociologists and economists in Britain have written in an unrelievedly discouraging fashion on the menace of our becoming old. Officials have talked woe and potential disaster so as to persuade politicians to recognize that ageing and the support of the old, especially the very old and decrepit, have to be taken extremely seriously. Those concerned with social welfare have intoned in a similarly threatening way, and journalists have been more than usually irresponsible and superficial. They have elaborated their prophecies of doom, without the opportunity or perhaps the training to understand the causes and the issues, and only too aware of the resistance of their readership to numbers and numerical analysis. A sense of proportion is the overriding necessity now, for the citizen in the middle years contemplating growing old, as for everyone at large. Hence the enormous importance of our major theme in this essay, the emergence of a new society with its own collective life and principles, the emergence of the Third Age.

We have already surveyed some of the reasons why we should not think of Britain's present compositional age as a peculiar disability, grounds for self-exculpation, apology or even for self-sympathy. We are in it together with others, all our fellow Europeans in the northern and south-western parts of the Continent, and the figures presented in the next few pages on proportions of the elderly in various countries should make it plain that national ageing differences within these highly-developed areas are of relatively little import. Moreover, advanced industrial nations elsewhere are approaching the European condition at a rapid pace, though with interesting differences. An age composition of the European type is now a recognizable mark of a rich, highly industrial society. At the moment anyway, you cannot have the one without the other.

But although a country, as things now stand, may not be able to be rich without also having an ageing population, it by no means follows that a country with an ageing population will inevitably become rich. There is a strong possibility that poor, undeveloped societies will soon begin to age without being able to afford it. This is certainly no encouraging prospect but it is not a reason to interpret our own more fortunate position as grounds for being pessimistic about the future of the world and about our own position and responsibilities within it. Rather we should look upon what is happening and what will happen as a challenge, as an incentive to action, not in spite of, but because of, our already-so-much-advanced compositional age.

Since it would seem that all the world is finally going to age in the way the populations of the advanced countries have done and are doing, ours is merely one of the first group of populations to get there. Global demography dictates that the populations of the world either have to age or end in that explosion of growth which we have all come to fear. What is done now in Britain and in countries like Britain in appreciating and mastering the situation must be of enormous significance for the future. In this way our subject could be said to have a cosmic interest.

It might be argued, of course, that to be challenged in this way to help to create a policy for a whole world overtaken by the twilight of departed youth is the saddest circumstances of all for us. But this is surely misconceived. No whole set of human conditions can ever be supposed or expected to be markedly better in all directions than any of its predecessors, though there may be improvements and we have justifiably come to expect them. But neither is it sensible to suppose that a new general order can only be worse than what has gone before. In any case, that new general order has clearly come to stay and we are already part and parcel of it. An injunction to Britain to be its age is a demand for us all to get on with it.

AGEING STATISTICS OF CONTEMPORARY EUROPE

The demonstration of our being really old and virtually certain to remain so not only requires that we survey the national statistics of Britain as they have been over the last decade or two, as they are today, as they will be for the next 25 years. It also makes necessary a comparison with the national statistics of such other countries and regions as are appropriate to the purpose. Only in this way will the younger readers of this book get an idea of the facts as they will be as they themselves become elderly.

We begin then, with a set of successive orderings by age proportions of their populations in later life of the more senior nations belonging to the Council of Europe, as they were, are and will be in the course of each decade from the 1960s to the 2020s. Proportions aged 65 and over is the criterion here and the figures have been rounded, since the object is such a general one. Because those for the three later dates are the outcome of projections they may turn out to be slightly inaccurate, but very unlikely to be deceptive.

Table 4.2 demonstrates that for the last thirty years or more the population of the United Kingdom has been at the highest or the second highest rank in respect of the proportion of the population aged over 65 among this group of the very oldest countries. But our country is shown as falling rather than rising in the order and during the second general increase in these figures in Western Europe, which will come during the earlier decades of the twenty-first century, the United Kingdom will stay low on the list. There is not much in it all the same, and will not be. Western Europe seems to continue to grow old as something of a unity, certainly in respect of age composition.[7]

Table 4.2   Proportions of populations aged 65 and over (1960–2020): select countries belonging to the Council of Europe

(Percentages rounded)

1960	*United Kingdom*, Austria, Belgium, France, Sweden	12	United Kingdom at highest level
	Germany	11	
	Switzerland	10	
	Italy, Netherlands	9	
	Greece	8	
1970	Austria, Sweden	14	
	United Kingdom, Belgium, France, Germany, Norway	13	United Kingdom at second highest level
	Denmark	12	
	Italy, Greece, Switzerland, Netherlands	11	
1980	Germany, Sweden	16	
	United Kingdom, Norway, Austria	15	United Kingdom at second highest level
	Belgium, Denmark, France, Switzerland	14	
	Italy, Greece	13	
	Netherlands	11	
1990	Sweden	18	
	United Kingdom, Norway	16	United Kingdom at second highest level
	Austria, Denmark, France, Germany, Italy, Switzerland, Belgium	15	
	Netherlands	14	
	Greece	13	
2000	Sweden, Switzerland, Germany	17	
	United Kingdom, Italy, Belgium	16	United Kingdom at second highest level
	Austria, Denmark, Greece	15	
	France	14	
2010	Switzerland	19	
	Germany, Sweden	18	
	Austria	17	
	Belgium, Denmark, Norway, Greece	16	
	United Kingdom, Netherlands	15	United Kingdom at fifth highest level
	France	14	
2020	Switzerland	21	
	Sweden	20	
	Denmark, Germany, Norway	19	
	Austria, Belgium, Netherlands	18	
	United Kingdom	17	United Kingdom at fifth highest level
	France, Greece	16	

Source: Anton Amman, 'The Changing Age Structure of the Population and Future Policy', Council of Europe, *Population Studies* 18 (1985), Table 4. All countries with higher figures than the United Kingdom in any year are included here, though Italy, which must be in that position in 2010 and 2020, is omitted from the source in those years. Germany is the former West Germany.

THREE SETS OF CIRCUMSTANCES ABOUT THE AGE OF THE BRITISH POPULATION

We still have to make comparisons with other countries on the basis of our second criterion of ageing, expectation of life, in order to complete the details of the answer to the question – *Is the population of our country really old?* These comparisons will concern us in the following two chapters. Having now set out the facts about the conspicuous age of British people at the present time, there are three sets of circumstances on which I think we should reflect. One is to do with the reasons for the conspicuous growth in the proportion of persons in their late and later years. Was it brought about by 'natural' agencies, outside our own control, or does it make sense to suppose that the British and the other elderly national populations brought it on themselves? Another question is the extent of geographical variation in the numbers of elderly. A third is to do with the reasons why it is so unlikely that our population will ever again be much younger than it is and will be during the 1990s.

We shall find that expectation of life is inextricably bound up with all these things although our immediate concern is for the relative weight of the older age groups. It has been indicated several times that rising expectation of life at birth was not the operative cause of the original growth in proportions of those in later life but falling fertility. But falling mortality has of course been the sole cause of lengthening of life and since mortality has been going down during the whole period when our country has been growing older, it is understandable that the error should be made that decreasing death rates have been entirely responsible for population ageing and that this is what always and inevitably happens. Such an error is extremely common with politicians and journalists. But medical doctors and those closely concerned with ageing, even writers of influential studies on the subject, are also liable to make it.[8]

The existence of particular localities where there are large numbers of people living out their later lives, our second set of circumstances, seems to add to the impression that it must be increased longevity which ages a national population. We have already referred to Florida as having a population which is one of the oldest in the world in the compositional sense: 18.3 per cent of the population was over 61 in 1990. This was as high as the proportion of Sweden, the world leader in that year, and almost a fifth higher than the figure for the next of the United States in order, Pennsylvania, at 15.4 per cent. It can be compared with 10.3 per cent in Georgia and 4.1 per cent in Alaska. The excess of older persons in Florida, however, has largely come about because of an influx of people who have chosen to move to that state in order to spend their retirement there. No doubt many of these immigrants do have favourable prospects of survival compared with other Americans, because they are active, often well-heeled people. But there are also Floridans who have migrated there because they are in bad health and so not likely to live long. It is obvious that high expectation of life is not the reason why Florida is old, and we have seen that the US population as a whole is not high compared with ourselves in the proportions of elderly and old people in the population.

Migration upon retirement and becoming old is well established in Britain too, and the south-coast retirement zones have as intense a concentration of elderly people as any in Europe, where every country has similar districts in their warmer, more congenial tracts of town and countryside. In some of the English localities, particularly Sussex, Dorset, and the Isle of Wight,[9] local people and local interests are becoming somewhat restive about this influx. Migration of those early in life can also leave a town, a district, even a city, and especially a decayed city centre, with pronouncedly older populations. In areas of this second kind, however, expectation of life at birth and at all later ages is likely to be relatively low. Movement on retirement happens between developed countries as well as within them, and there are elderly Scandinavians, Germans and Britons in Southern France, Italy, Portugal and Spain. Japan would like to export some of its retired persons to Australia. These movements do not seem likely to be popular in the receiving areas, and the issue of international retirement migration may become of some importance.

If falling mortality and consequent lengthening of life cannot be, must not be, regarded as the necessary and sufficient cause of a large proportion of the population being old, quite how is it that falling fertility has brought all this about? And why has fertility fallen? In order to address these highly significant questions belonging to our third set of circumstances, we should go back a little into the past. As we do so, we must remember that we are concerning ourselves with a record which with variations as to time, place and attitude, must have been similar in other Western nations.[10]

OUR RECENT DEMOGRAPHIC EXPERIENCE

In the late 1870s the birth rate of the English population started to decline, and to decline with that finality and irreversibility which ushered in what is called the demographic transition in our country. At about the same time, mortality began to fall as well, in a similar deliberate, uninterrupted way, and accordingly expectation of life went steadily upwards. The reduction of the British birth and death rates continued for seventy years without a break, though with a perturbation during and after the First World War. By the 1930s and 1940s both fertility and mortality were at a low level, fertility at a very low level.

The baby boom after the Second World War increased the number of births for a while in the 1950s and 1960s. There was also quite a considerable immigration of younger people who had not yet started families or whose families were not yet complete, mainly from the West Indies and Asia, so giving rise to the ethnic communities now an established feature of British national life. But these movements petered out in the 1970s, fertility resumed its fall while mortality, especially infant mortality, was diminishing all the time. The United Kingdom can now be looked upon as a standard example of a low-fertility, low-mortality, low- or no-growth population, properly described, as we have described it, as extremely old. That it was the accelerating fall in fertility consequent upon family limitation, and not the lengthening of life due to decreasing mortality, which was almost entirely responsible for the great growth in the proportions of the elderly, at least up to the last decade or so, is to be explained as follows.

A decrease in the relative numbers of young increases the relative numbers of old, and a reduction of mortality has little or no effect on these proportions. This is because better survival usually benefits the lower age groups more than it does their seniors on average, though concealed in this average is the fact that the very youngest, those in the first year of life, always tend to benefit most from a decrease in the deaths, and this effect can be so pronounced that it actually decreases the proportion, though not of course the numbers, of the population which is in later life. The steadily diminishing birth rate after the 1880s nevertheless was bound in the end to make the relative numbers of the elderly grow large. Still the process took fifty years to become conspicuous in our age structure. Not until the 1920s did the fraction of the population which had attained the age of 60 exceed 10 per cent, a figure which had, we now know, been reached in the early eighteenth century but never surpassed since that time. It is also known that the proportion of this age group in England was smaller throughout the nineteenth century than it had ever been since the mid-sixteenth century. Nevertheless England seems always to have had a markedly higher relative number of older people than the developing or underdeveloped countries of our own day, like Brazil, India or Tunisia.

Expectation of life in England has lengthened since the 1880s from a little over 40 years to over 75, taking both sexes together and reckoning from birth. But if the reduction in mortality leading to greater longevity had been the only effect on the English population over the last hundred years, if fertility had not fallen as well, we should not now have been older in the other sense, that of the higher proportion of elderly. Given constant fertility and so pronounced a rise in the expectation of life at birth, we should have had today a very much larger total population. The proportion of elderly, however, would not be very different from what it was in the 1880s, at between 7 and 8 per cent over the age of 60. This is not much more than a third of what we are likely to have during the next century.

Our prospects for the next twenty or twenty-five years go like this. Should it happen, as seems likely, that zero-growth or gradual shrinking establishes itself as a settled feature of our population, so that we approach a stationary condition, but with a tendency for our numbers to fall after a while, we may expect a fifth to a quarter of our population, or a third of all adults, to be aged 60 or over and these circumstances are those represented in Table 4.1. But even if we are for the moment approaching a quasi-stationary state demographically, this does not seem at all likely to be the permanent position. At the end of the chapter we shall see what might happen in the longer term.

REASONS FOR THE PROBABLE STABILITY IN THE SHORT TERM OF THE PRESENT AGE-COMPOSITION OF THE BRITISH POPULATION

If we ask why this condition is unlikely to alter a great deal in the near future we have to reckon with the following circumstances.

A rejuvenation at the base, through an upsurge of fertility such as occurred to some extent in the 1950s and 1960s, is certainly not impossible. Many of those interested in our population and its prospects believe that everything should be done to encourage such a development and they have a persuasive case. We should certainly stop our tax system and employment practices actively discouraging couples from having children, and we should certainly follow the example of Sweden, which now has the highest birth rate in Western Europe, in providing state support for couples in rearing children. But a rise in fertility could only lead to a substantial decrease in the proportion of the old if it were large enough, and went on for long enough, to give rise at the same time to an appreciable expansion in our total numbers. Perhaps some would welcome an increase of this kind, but all our recent behaviour declarations and resolutions have been against it. And it would certainly contradict the more and more urgent pleas which we have urged on Third World countries to moderate their growth and spare humanity the catastrophe of a global population explosion.

Once set in motion, a really pronounced tendency for fertility to increase above replacement would mean that the population would grow for quite a long time. If the birth rate did go down again to something like present levels, a bulge would travel up through the age structure which would in due course swell the proportion of elderly and old to an even greater extent than before the rise in fertility began, until it finally died out. At that point of course proportions of elderly would be something like what they are now.

Should this happen to our population which has so very many more in the later age groups than it did in the 1950s and 1960s, there would be double dependency – crowds of babies and children, crowds of elders – during the period of heightened fertility. Outward migration would not reduce, but more likely increase, the proportion of the old, because the young and the fertile are always those disposed to leave. Inward migration, on the other hand, could lessen the tendency towards a permanently elderly population, at the cost of sending up our numbers once again. It has to be reckoned moreover that immigration could only come from those countries with a surplus of young persons willing to move overseas to improve their lot and in some cases to escape their persecutors – India and Pakistan, for example, or the West Indies again, or conceivably South America. The newly emancipated Central and Eastern European countries might perhaps be drawn upon for the purpose, and Turkey, the nearest country with a real supply, along with the North African countries. But if immigrants are going to reach a youth-deficient Europe from these sources, it is to wealthier countries like Germany or France, Italy or Scandinavia, rather than to Britain that they seem likely to go. There is a possibility, that we might ourselves supply richer and more advanced countries like Germany or the United States or Japan with some part of our woefully small stock of highly qualified younger people, and so add a mite or two to the growth in the proportions of the older people at home. A university researcher witnessing the depletion of his younger colleagues because of the brain drain can say this with some feeling.

DELIBERATE CONTROL OF FAMILY SIZE

The fall in British fertility, certainly in marital fertility, during the last hundred years has been sudden, as already stated, sudden even as historians reckon time, and almost instantaneous to biologists. As for the voluntary character of this rapid change, all interferences with 'natural' fertility are reckoned to be like this to some extent. No really efficient contraceptive device has been available before our day, and the evidence suggests that the commonest practices in Victorian times and up to the 1950s were withdrawal, abstinence and the increasing use of the sheath and pessaries, along with some deliberate abortion and traces of infanticide. These expedients were surprisingly successful, but decidedly demanding as to willpower. Among well-placed Americans at that time of voluntary reduction in childbearing, coital frequency was about fifty per cent lower than that observed in comparable population groups in the United States in more recent decades. It is not easy to see how representative was the comportment of these élite persons of the rest of the American, or of the British, population at the time, especially among the mass of the people. But they must have behaved in a somewhat similar way.

In our own time of highly effective, almost automatic, chemical contraception, prospective and retrospective, it is hard to imagine how much individual determination went into the steady, virtually uninterrupted decrease in births in England between the 1870s and the 1950s. The contraceptive practices mentioned required deliberate policy, often on the part of the man, and in most instances must have been self-conscious undertakings.[11] In France the same concerted, yet supremely private, campaign went on from a much earlier time, when contraceptive methods may be supposed to have been even more dependent on choice. The difficult decision for our great-grandparents and great-great-grandparents was for how long they could go on taking the precautions which they did to control the size of their families. Today the decision is infinitely easier – if, or when, to have a child by interrupting habitual contraception.

We are now well aware that the purposeful control of numbers of children, inside and outside marriage, in the late nineteenth and early twentieth century was by no means the earliest in demographic history. A voluntary element has been identified at previous periods both in Europe and Japan; in the latter country child groups seem to have been planned by their parents by the use of infanticide and adoption. Such displays of willpower have not been confined to the relatively distant past. It is an extraordinary and somewhat depressing fact that in Central European countries during the period of Soviet domination, and in Russia itself, contraception was effected to a marked degree by abortion. This was so widespread that a standard question put to women attending clinics for gynaecological purposes was, 'How many abortions have you had?' Abortion could be said to be the most voluntary of all birth-control practices. But never in known records has parenthood been deliberately controlled so drastically, with such resolution and for so long as in the Western countries in the late nineteenth and early twentieth centuries. Whatever we may think of the motives of these patient, often frustrated, presumably frequently unsuccessful, but very determined late Victorian and Edwardian couples, we are obliged to believe that they consciously intended to reduce the number of their offspring.

The impression should not be given that up to the time of the decisive change in English procreative behaviour fertility has always been at very high levels, and families of children as large as those which are found in contemporary Africa or Indonesia. We can be confident that in north-west Europe fertility was kept for much of our recorded history at consistently lower levels by late marriage for women and by a relatively large proportion of people never marrying at all. There was certainly a voluntary element in this regulation of the creation of families, even though it may have come about as a result of compliance with general social custom. This form of demographic regulation, which can be thought of as distinctively Western, may well have been a reason why these areas were in a position to keep their populations to some extent above the level of subsistence and finally to escape from what we now define as underdevelopment.[12]

It is probable that a degree of abstinence and withdrawal went along with this marriage regime over the centuries. It seems to me, however, that to prevent conception within marriage on such an unprecedented scale as was done in England in the late nineteenth and early twentieth century at the same time as traditional controls through the regulation of marriage were still in use, at least to some extent, makes the case that the fall in fertility was an essentially willed affair even more persuasive. All signs of traditional population regulation by celibacy, postponed marriage and abstinence seem to have disappeared in the Britain of our day. The present tendency for proportions married to diminish in the younger age groups, accompanied as it is by the rise in procreative unions outside marriage, where procreation is nevertheless kept at the very lowest levels, cannot be thought of in the same way. The classic phase of voluntary contraceptive effort now lies in the past.

WILLING THE AGEING OF THE POPULATION BY ACCIDENT

I have dwelt on the voluntary characteristics of the fall in fertility in England in order to put some questions which seem to me to be of needling importance to our topic. Can it be supposed that all, many, or even any of the people who have acted in such a purposeful way during the century which has elapsed since the 1890s also intended to bring about the ageing of the population of their country? Would it be reasonable to assume of the men and women of the 1990s who decide to have one, two or three children – and this will no doubt be nearly all procreating couples – or even no child at all, that they wish in this way to ensure that there shall continue to be a huge community of the elderly, relative to the rest of our population, a community which they themselves must inevitably join? Can such an outcome really be a part of the deliberate policy of those who applaud zero population growth at home, and who undertake to bring it about in countries which they describe as 'burdened' with a population problem?

We could pursue this rhetorical cross-examination, but with very little prospect of answers in the affirmative. It may be reasonable to suppose that the English persons who began limiting their families a century and more ago, and continued to do so for such a long time, were prepared to risk the *decline* of the population or even, some of them, to help to bring decline about. But it would be unreasonable to hold them in any way responsible for the *ageing* of the population, ageing in the sense of the proportion of elderly, although some of them, probably a very small number, might have known that such ageing could ensue. Even contemporary fathers and mothers, or couples who refrain from so becoming, must surely be for the most part held exempt from any conscious intention of this kind. What has been described is a signal example of the unintended consequences of decisions taken with entirely different purposes in mind, unintended consequences but demographically inevitable nevertheless.

Doctors, welfare innovators and experts and others who have played a part in lengthening life during the past century or so, may have perhaps believed that they were engaged in expanding the proportion of the old in society in relation to the rest. If so, they were in error, not only because the lengthening of life did not have this effect under the then prevailing demographic circumstances, but also because, as is now thought, it was improvement in public health and the rise in the material standards of the mass of the population, rather more than advances in medical or even in state welfare, which improved the expectation of life, at least until the 1930s. What the doctors did by reducing the danger of death was to help ensure that our population was kept from declining and to forward the emergence of the Third Age. Responsibility for our having collectively grown old in the sense of having so large a proportion of persons in later life must be firmly placed on those who deliberately controlled their child-bearing, and thus ensured that the population would grow proportionately old, but without meaning to do any such thing. The story has the quality of tragic drama – watching the actions of myriads of persons who determinedly brought about an entirely unintended outcome unperceived by themselves but now patently obvious to the later observer.

In our own decade in two very different countries the initiation of a similarly tragic theme can be observed, a theme tragic in the same classical, fatalistic sense. The Chinese, by enforcing with such efficiency the most severe policy of birth reduction ever adopted by any country, the policy which in principle permitted only one child to each married couple, set off a process of extremely rapid ageing in their population. If that policy persists, even in the much modified form proclaimed in 1988, China will age at an exceedingly fast pace. The Chinese are well aware of course that an enormous growth in proportions of their elderly is bound to occur if Chinese fertility continues to fall to the levels which have been decided and to stay there for the length of time required to bring population under control. What they may not have reckoned must also happen, what indeed has only very recently been understood by demographers in a principled fashion, is that the numbers of relatives will go down, and particularly the extended households, the horizontal kin links, the cousinhoods, the relationships of uncles with nephews, on which so much of Chinese social life has always depended. The China which will finally emerge from this astonishing demographic experiment will inevitably be profoundly different from the China which decided to undertake it. The change may be even greater than that brought about by the Revolution which created the People's Republic of China in 1948. But it will not occur because it was intended.

This result will not be immediate, it will be marked by an intervening effect. The heavy fall in mortality which accompanies the fall in Chinese fertility ensures that for the near future and some years into the twenty-first century the present very high density of kinship linkages which came into being because of the boom in births which preceded the decision to hold down fertility will be maintained.[13] But the attenuation of kinship will inevitably happen in China, and it will also happen in a society much nearer home, Italy that is to say. Italy is also thought of as highly familial, with large numbers of children to each mother, frequent gatherings of grandparents, parents, grandchildren, uncles and cousins, indeed cousinhood is looked upon as a peculiarly Italian institution. But the demographic facts as they now are put the Italians bottom in the order of European birth rates, which implies that they probably have the lowest fertility in the contemporary world. We have calculated at Cambridge from simulation models that if the current Italian demographic regime is maintained for long enough into the twenty-first century, Italian cousin-hoods will finally shrink to a remnant of what they were in the earlier part of the twentieth. They will be reduced in fact to about a seventh or an eighth of those earlier levels and, although vertical kin links will stretch out over the generations, their numbers will finally go down as well.[14] It has to be further added that the continuance of the extremely low fertility now obtaining in that country will in the meantime have led to a notable fall in numbers, and to a formidable proportion of old people in the popu-lation. How formidable that number could be we shall shortly see.

When this outcome of simulation studies was reported to an audience in Rome in 1992, there was a dramatic impact even though pains were taken to stress its hypothetical character and the fact that the prospect was distant not immediate. It was evident that the Italians present had no inkling that this was what awaited them if they persisted permanently in their extreme behaviour in the control of fertility, although they had antici-pated the possibility of their numbers beginning to decline. Italy has been rather a late-comer to the contemporary European demographic regime. Other countries in the European Union, Britain included, have already undergone a part of the process of kinship attenuation, without recognising the fact. The decline of kinship numbers has in fact been disguised for us by the increasing longevity of those kinsfolk who have been engendered, as is now happening on a much larger scale and during a much shorter interval of time in China. When we come in this book to compare the situ-ation of the English elderly now with their situation in traditional pre-industrial society, we shall have to weigh the importance of the fact that the numbers of their kinsfolk have been very considerably reduced, and that their kin connections are now very different in their relative ages. The great bevies of nephews, nieces, cousins, aunts, uncles, kinswomen and kinsmen, of a more distant kind, which we find in Shakespeare and Jane Austen, no longer exist in our country and those relatives of this kind which we still possess are finally due to be severely attenuated, if not as much as in Italy.[15]

Such kinsfolk as will eventually remain will be vertically connected rather than horizontally, parents, grandparents, great-grandparents when people are younger, children, grandchildren, great-grandchildren when people are older and, for a while in middle life, vertical kin links in both directions. As Patrice Bourdelais rightly insists, this may place those in their sixties right at the centre of familial interaction, and give them a role in kinship which has never before been seen. For the time being, and at least up to the 2020s and the 2030s kinship linkages, horizontal as well as vertical, should be sufficient for the purposes we must have uppermost in our minds in the context of the present essay, that is sufficient for the support of the really dependent elderly. Whether this will be so in the longer term as and when the final implications of our extremely low fertility and mortality work themselves out is much more questionable. Although, for reasons which will become apparent in the next few pages, long-term predictions are seldom discussed in relation to ageing, they are in my view too important to pass over.

LONGER-TERM AGEING PROSPECTS

The major difficulty in considering such issues, it has to be confessed, is the record of the experts themselves since they have been so wide of the mark in the past, certainly in their previous forecasts as to the course of our own population. France is not the only country to have convinced itself that the national population was going to decline and to grow old in the process. In the late 1930s a body of authoritative British statisticians and demographers formed the Population Investigation Committee, one of whose objects was to warn the nation of the impending possibility of an imminent drop in our numbers. In 1936 they issued a pamphlet called *The Future of Our Population*, forecasting a fall beginning in the 1950s and associated with rapid growth in the proportion of those over sixty. By the 1990s our total was to have shrunk to twenty million instead of the fifty eight million now present, and the proportion of those over sixty was to have risen from 12.4 per cent in 1935 to 43.83 per cent: in fact, as we have seen, it turned out to be 20.78 per cent in 1991.[16] But the original projections made sensational news at the time, and the fact that the experts turned out to be wrong shook the confidence of those who had heeded them and has made demographers nervous about committing themselves to projections.

It was the sharp rise in the birth rate in Britain in the 1950s, often called the Baby Boom after its bigger American counterpart, which defeated these forecasts and within a few years the experts were proved mistaken again. With fertility going up and divorce and illegitimacy declining from the high peaks associated with the Second World War and its aftermath, they began talking of a future where the number of births would be high enough to keep the population steady, with stability in the family and ageing levelling out. By the 1970s, however, illegitimacy and divorce had begun to increase at a very rapid rate, fertility had begun to fall catastrophically and there had set in a transformation of procreative activity calculated to bring about a change in the family such as had never before been known or contemplated.

It is understandable, therefore, that projections of this kind should have become unpopular with demographers, who are now disposed to content themselves with statements affecting only a decade or two into the future. They also insist on the arbitrary character even of these brief prognostications. Projection is not much more than informed guesswork, they are apt to insist, simply continuing recent and present tendencies forwards into the fairly near future, though statements over this interval about the elderly are likely to be more reliable than others since the older part of the population is already present to begin with. After twenty or thirty years into the future the degree of possible error becomes so large that the usefulness of the suggested figures can be questioned.

There is a highly expert international body, IIASA, which does venture on longer-span projections all the same.[17] In their recent forecasts for Europe and North America it is stated that unless inward migration to those areas occurs on a considerable scale, and unless particularly fertility recovers there, ageing will persist. The share of the population over sixty in Western Europe will rise from a fifth to a quarter by 2015, and population will start to go down in the 2020s, in North America likewise. These are predictions in which both the population division of the United Nations and the British statistical authorities concur, as can be seen in Table 4.1. After the mid-2020s, however, making the same assumptions, age composition and the size of populations will change drastically in Western Europe, according to the predictions of IIASA. Those over 60 will rise to more than 38 per cent in a decade and the fall in numbers of Western Europeans will become quite rapid. Such forecasts are much in excess of what is expected by our authorities for England and Wales, and it must be remembered that they are presented by IIASA as only one of three possible scenarios.

Between the middle and the end of the twenty-first century, a period for which no British projections have been made, only high immigration and a substantial upsurge in births would keep those over 60 within the previous range in Western Europe, according to IIASA. Continuation of present trends would lead to nearly half (48 per cent) of the population being over 60 by 2100 even if there was a large influx from outside. Without this, those over 60 would come to constitute something approaching 60 per cent of the entire West European population, and numbers would be in full decline. Meanwhile in a separate suggestion, expectations of life at birth are hinted at of an order not often contemplated at least by demographers, conceivably reaching into the nineties or even beyond a hundred years. A society all of whose members could expect to become centenarians might under these highly speculative predictions thus come into being.

The figures for proportions of the population are set out in Table 4.3. It will be noticed that what IIASA names as its two other, alternative, 'scenarios', supposing that birth rates do rise and immigration does occur, yield much more acceptable values. Really high fertility for a decade or two would change everything. But it would inevitably have the bulge and double dependency effects which have been noticed.

The prospect of a quarter or more of the population being in later life in the higher 2020s as the Baby Boom moves into later life, in thirty years' time, that is to say, when our grandchildren have settled into the Second Age, is a somewhat disconcerting one. Still, this is what is expected by our own statistical authorities and we shall ponder its meaning for the Third and Fourth Ages in due course. But even the remote possibility of belonging to a Western Europe where there could be 35 to 40 per cent over 60 years old by 2030, and 50 to 60 per cent by 2100, is something of an entirely different order, especially with just a chance of everyone living for a century. At the second level quoted, those in late and later life would dominate the whole diminishing society, at least numerically; horizontal kinship would practically vanish and vertical kinship become attenuated. This is quite as disturbing as were the prognostications put out in the 1930s for the British population up to the 1990s. Nevertheless, it is my own view that it is right for such extreme possibilities to be made public by the specialists, who should now be confident that the status of their statistics will be understood and alarmism avoided.

The point of greatest significance is that some approach to the most intimidating projections of the IIASA, those in column 1 of Table 4.3 may, at the present time, represent the least unlikely of the possibilities offered. It has to be stressed, however, that this is not the general opinion

Table 4.3   Projected proportions over 60 in the population of Western Europe: Three scenarios (percentages)

	Scenario 1: Low fertility low migration	Scenario 2: Low fertility high migration	Scenario 3: High fertility low migration
1990	19.6 (UK 1991 20.8)		
2030	38.3 (UK 2021 25.8)	36.3	32.1
2100	59.1	48.0	32.8

Source: Figures from IIASA, see text.

among those best qualified to judge. Some of them suppose that European (and British) fertility will come up out of its present abysmal trough and at least ensure that enough children are born to maintain replacement of the population. Such would considerably modify ageing prospects as may be inferred from Table 4.3. Nathan Keyfitz of Harvard, the distinguished demographer who presided over the population programme of IIASA when the projections were made, certainly supposes that this may well happen.[18] In my own view, it would be wise to reserve our judgement as to the possibility of a rise of fertility in Western Europe, in spite of its recent ascent in Sweden, traditionally a low-birth-rate, high-age society, and sometimes viewed as the bellwether of Western demographic behaviour.

However, we can, I believe, be fairly confident that the other nominated cause of excessive ageing, the prevention of immigration, will be maintained for the European West. It is hard to see how influxes of large numbers of people from the areas which have them to offer could be accepted without grave political complications, though illegal immigration might come about on some scale, as it has in the USA. If both the birth rate and immigration do continue to be held down over the coming 100 years, and some version of the extreme results we have run over does make its appearance, then we must remember that we are only being faced with the long-term consequences of our own present policies and actions.

But these consequences have been, and doubtless will be, unintended consequences, exactly like those which we saw were brought about by our Victorian and Edwardian ancestors when they began the purposeful restriction of their progeny and aged their population by accident. Can we be said to be about to witness a further act in that fatalistic drama? Or with a cosmic tragedy standing on its own? There can be no doubt at all that it is a universal drama which may be going to be played out, with issues and outcomes of a kind never before known in the history of the world, the world as a whole and history as all the time for which there have been humans on the earth.

5 The Rectangular Survival Curve and the Secular Shift in Ageing

A curve, as the word is used in ordinary language, can scarcely be rectangular because curves and angles are pictured as opposites. A glance at Figure 5.1, however, should convince the reader that the survival curve, that is the line joining the percentages of a group of persons born in a particular year still alive at successive birthdays, can begin to look as if it could approximate to a right angle. This would happen as more and more people survived to the latest ages. They would all go on until about the age when they ran up against the end of the life-span, or the average age of death of the very old, or whatever concept should be used. The relevance of the discussion in Chapter 2 of how long a human life could last becomes immediately apparent.

THE ABBREVIATION OF THE FOURTH AGE

The message suggested by the diagram for everyone contemplating ageing, her ageing or his, or the ageing of the population generally, is certainly encouraging. A time might arrive when all individuals would come to an end at about the same age, an advanced age on our present expectations. James Fries, the American researcher into the biology of ageing with whom the position has been associated since a study which he published in 1980,[1] maintains that this final point is determined as a characteristic of our species, and is unlikely to be changed by medical intervention. In terms of calendar age the mid-eighties marks the close of the average life-span and the exact figure of eighty-five is often mentioned by him and his associates. As time goes by more people will tend to die a natural death, at ages closer and closer to that critical divide, both above and below it, some of them with few or no symptoms, but affected by mere old age. Final illness – terminal morbidity – will tend to become compressed within that concluding interlude, that is within our Fourth Age. Hence the

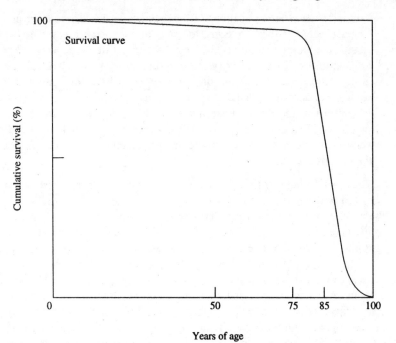

Figure 5.1   The rectangular survival curve
Source: Reproduced from James F. Fries and Lawrence M. Crapo, *Vitality and Aging: Implications of the Rectangular Curve* (San Francisco, 1981).

title of his theory, *The Compression of Morbidity*, though it should be clear that this is accompanied by the compression of mortality as well.

    Survival curves are commonplace in demography and the idea that the human survival curve may tend towards a rectangular shape is well established in that study. It certainly goes back to the Anglo-Jewish statistician Gompertz, who first worked out the mathematics of the human span in the early nineteenth century. But there seems to have been little impact of the notion on those to whom it might matter most, older people themselves, until the publications of Fries and his associates. The title which they issued in 1981, *Vitality and Aging*,, is an informative and persuasive book, in spite of its jaunty, rather dogmatic manner and journalistic style.[2]

    A quotation from this book may help to explain what is at issue. The terms which are used in Chapter 2 above are being explicated so as to make the case.

To understand the implications of the rectangular curve, one must distinguish between the two terms, *life span* and *life expectancy*. The life span is the biological limit to the length of life....Life expectancy refers to the number of years of life expected from birth for an individual or a group. Life expectancy from birth cannot exceed the life span, but it can closely approximate the life span if there is little death at early ages. In contrast to the fixed human life span, life expectancy is increasing rapidly in most countries. Increasing life expectancy is thus on a converging course with the fixed life span represented by the down slope of the rectangular curve.[3]

The position held by these theorists must imply that the numbers of the very old will not go on increasing very much in the future, certainly not the number of very old invalids. Health will be better in any case right up to the approach of death because of medical advances, and arrival at the terminus will remove everyone within a brief period. It must be recognized that the claim as to immobility of the final point, which can only be the end of the average life-span, is crucial to the propositions we are considering. As might be expected, these assertions about length of life and its span being fixed, and as to the number and condition of the very old, have been criticized and we have already been over some of the positions in Chapter 2. The learned controversy that has ensued is not easy for those outside the field of enquiry to follow, though the issues must concern everyone who thinks about the final years.

Those who differ from Fries over these questions insist that the total at the very latest ages will continue to grow, as we have seen them doing in the forecasts for our own country in the 1990s.[4] They counsel against being too optimistic about the prospects of the health of the very old, and against underestimating the difficulty of overcoming not only the degenerative conditions which particularly affect old people, but other diseases as well. AIDS, for example might come to have severe effects on the chances of survival, and so interrupt the tendency of the survival curve towards rectangularity. It seems to be true that most people in our day keep their health and stay active until very late on. But the estimates for expectation of life without disability are rather discouraging especially for the highest ages and there is little to confirm the claim that the period during which they sicken before they finally die is getting shorter. Suggestions have been made, in fact, that the longer the life the longer the final illness.

These suggestions come from a recently instituted set of enquiries into expectation of life in good health, with the capacity to live an active life, as distinct from expectation of life as such, merely going on living without reference to physical and mental condition. Such lines of research, which are going on in several countries, are of evident significance for the topic of the Third Age and its emergence as well as for the possibility of final sickness being short and the survival curve becoming rectangular. We shall have to refer to them when we come to retirement and again in developing the general theory of the Third Age.[5] These studies have an important historical dimension as well. It has been calculated, for example, from the health records of men who had joined the Foresters' Friendly Society in England during 1871–75, that the proportion of working-time lost for sickness was insignificant up to the age of 50, but began rising between then and the age of 60. At that point it went up very sharply indeed until it reached 40 per cent of all working-time between ages 80 and 84 for those still employed, not an inconsiderable proportion at that period. These facts are so impressive that it is worth setting them out in graph form.

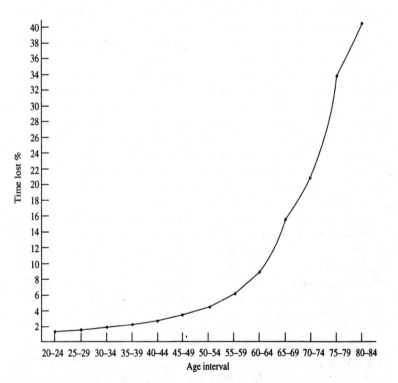

Figure 5.2   Proportion of working time lost through sickness, by age group: members of Foresters' Friendly Society, 1871–75.
Source: James C. Riley, *Sickness, Recovery and Death*, 1989, p. 95.

Who could doubt from this diagram that there was some justification for withdrawal from everyday working life after the age of 65 in that generation? And when faced with evidence from the 1960s to the 1980s of a steady age-related increase in the prevalence of illness and restricted activity throughout working life in four different countries, Japan, the USA, Great Britain and Hungary, who would wish to maintain that sickness is increasingly being compressed into the final years (see Riley, 1992)? The remarkable thing is that during the same time-period and at the same ages when the sickness was growing more prevalent, the death rate was going down rather than up, except in Hungary. The most recent pronouncement about research on these complex issues in the United States blankly concludes 'that it has not indicated a compression of morbidity' (Robine, 1993, p. 15).

If morbidity is not evidently becoming compressed in the way suggested by Fries and his companions, there is likewise a lack of evidence in favour of the assertion that (average) life-span is static at age 85. This is the age, it will be remembered, suggested by Kannisto as the commonest for the death of the long-lived, and by Fries as the average. But Kannisto's published figures and the many further statistics gathered by him show that those over 100 are living longer than they used to, and his statements about natural death have been judged doubtful. Fries' claim that maximum human life-span is exhausted at 115 is scarcely supported by anything yet known to demographers: he seems to suppose that he has caught up with what we have had to describe as a will-o'-the-wisp. Even his colleagues who reject the theory of compression of morbidity, however, show a similar disposition to nominate figures for life-span without accompanying support, and without specifying whether it is average or maximum potential which is intended.

The air of self-assurance and the insouciant manner in which claims and counter-claims are sometimes presented to the general reader on this very serious subject are somewhat disconcerting in the light of the discussion of the human life-span in Chapter 2 above. The interchange seems to lack a sense of responsibility. Roy Walford, for instance, a much-cited biologist of ageing of high standing, estimates of life-span of up to 130 years, and speculates on ways of achieving it, and thus can only be in direct disagreement with Fries. Yet he never alludes to anything written by Fries in his discussion of the subject. His own general book is even more of a journalistic *tour de force*, with autobiographical anecdotes and what can only be called faintly entertaining nonsense mixed in with the results of serious scientific research.[6] Perhaps it is not surprising that the standard of scholarship should be modest in publications of this character. So great appears to be the anxiety of people – some at least, even some very eminent ones – to prolong their lives, and so intractable the evidence, that opportunities abound for facile generalization, and even for quackery.[7]

The effect of all this on the attitudes and expectations of ordinary people, on public opinion and on the journalists must disturb the academic student of ageing as a social phenomenon. It is those who write in the papers and do the broadcasting who are the obvious culprits, but more serious authors join in. There seems to be an established media treatment of the subject which makes an appearance whenever age, ageing, older and oldest people are judged to be newsworthy, along with advances in research. The latest theory about the causes of ageing, and especially about the possibility of lengthening life, is taken up. The more optimistic remarks elicited from experts are duly cited. But one outstanding circumstance is always ignored. This is that prolongation of individual life by heroic and costly intervention, if it became possible, is an entirely different matter from creating a confident expectation that, because of the new 'discoveries', present members of a population can expect to survive for decades longer than they now do, even after the hundredth birthday. It is just such super-survival which people are interested in, and journalists know it.

Great gullibility is shown in these media routines about attained ages, and about areas particularly favourable for long life, but no appreciation of the crucial difference between expectation of life as such and expectation of healthy, active life. It is blandly assumed that an elongated life course would be spent in a state of youth. A recent example of this standard media confection appeared in *The Times* magazine *Weekend* on 6 August 1994 with the title 'Forever Young' and lavish illustration. This at a time when it could not be clearer that the very last thing we need in the era of the Third Age is a prolongation of the cult of youth.

The pity of it is that researchers on ageing themselves, never averse to publicity apparently, and even required by their patrons in the Research Councils to list their media appearances, seem quite willing to play along with the media on these occasions. They never publish criticisms of the rigmarole. In 1991 an author described as a leading authority on ageing, who had chaired a committee of the American Medical Association on the subject, Walter Bortz, published his book with the following title *We Live Too Short and Die Too Long. How to Achieve and Enjoy your Natural Hundred Year Life-Span*. Along with a great deal of good sense about many things, exercise in the Third Age particularly, comes this unrealisable and deceptive promise of a century (it had to be a century) for everyone.[8]

These circumstances make the task of the historical sociologist even more difficult, bent as he must be on discovering what is certainly known

A Fresh Map of Life

on a topic so important to so many people. Nevertheless there is
agreement as to the increasingly rectangular appearance of the survival
curve, and controversy is mostly confined to what goes on at the
bottom right-hand extremity. This is the decisive section of the graph, of
course, since it is here that the fixity of the life-span would show itself.
Fries based his predictions on the fact that Americans have indeed
survived better and better in the twentieth century. They have accordingly tended to die within a shortening stretch of years at the end of
their age range. In Figure 5.3 successive survival curves are set for
females in the United States populations after the year 1890, with a
projected curve for 2050.

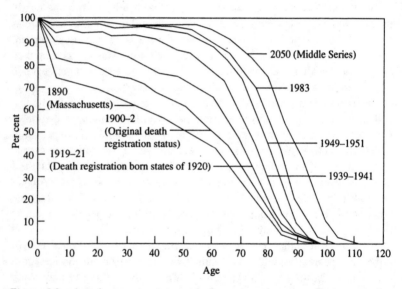

Figure 5.3   American progress towards the rectangular curve: Percentage of a
cohort of white female births surviving to specific ages according to current life
tables for the USA, 1890–2050
Source: Based on Life Tables published by the US Public Health Service,
National Center for Health Statistics and by the Office of the Actuary, Social
Security Administration.
Author's note: This figure is copied from Jacob S. Siegel and Cynthia
M. Taeuber, 'Demographic Perspectives on the Long-lived Society', *Daedalus*,
vol. 115, no. 1 (1986). It is drawn in a fashion which Fries and Crapo (pp. 6–7)
insist is incorrect, because it gives the impression that the life-span is increasing,
as well as expectation of life. For English survival curves over a very much longer
period, see p. 96 below.

The changing shape of these lines of survival is indeed remarkable. Those from earlier in this century and before describe a fairly steady descent in the proportion of survivors after an abrupt drop due to infantile mortality. This descent continues throughout childhood and lasts until about the age of sixty, when the downward slope gets steeper until near the bottom. Since the 1900s the initial drop has been removed and the lines have levelled out for the whole of the first six decades of life, after which an abrupt fall sets in again until close to the bottom. The slope of the final stretch is much more gradual as it approaches the terminus.

The predicted trajectory for 2050, chosen from the alternatives offered by the statisticians, can be taken as approaching the rectangular, though its shape is still a long way from that described by the ideal survival curve in Figure 5.1. Perhaps something not entirely unlike the rectangular survival curve could be on the horizon – or just the other side of it? These established facts must mean that *mortality*, the occurrence of death, is being compressed into the last years of life. Indeed this is what is meant by the claim that those in the Third Age now do nearly all the dying. Not only is this so but a tendency for the direction of the fall of succession curves to point towards the ninth decade of life indicates that something like an average age-limit to the life-span is located in that decade, perhaps even about the age of eighty-five, as Fries suggests with Kannisto concurring. But *mortality*, the occurrence of death, is not the critical issue. It is the compression of *morbidity*, the occurrence of illness and disability, their duration and severity which are under increasingly intense discussion. And the facts we have cited as to expectation of life without disability have demonstrated that the distribution of deaths cannot be taken to represent the distribution of episodes of illness.

THE RECTANGULAR CURVE AND THE CONDUCT OF THE THIRD AGE

The implications of our discussion of the rectangular curve and especially of the compression or morbidity for the major theme of this book should be quite obvious. I have already referred to the apt description of the final Fourth Age which it suggests, especially in the version expounded by Fries and his associates. Many of the statements of Chapter 2 on the prospects of becoming old, as to the extent to which our fears of ageing may be misplaced, will be recognized in the propositions which have been so hastily gone over. Above all, the general tenor of the doctrines being worked out on either side of the debate which has been surveyed is in harmony with one of the principles of the theory of the Third Age.

This precept lays down that the whole course of our experience, and especially the Third Age, must be so conducted by each person, in the continued activity of body and of mind, that the Fourth Age will come as late and be as brief as possible. Evidence is certainly accumulating to support the view that some progress towards this end, both physiological and psychological, is beginning to occur. This evidence is cited on all sides by the geriatricians engaged in the discussion, who maintain that illness and disability are getting less severe in later life, even if they tend to be longer in duration, more so in women than in men. It is not indicated unfortunately that, if final illness comes late, it is likely to be short. But much is made by the experts of being energetic and staying engaged, of systematic exercise and often of a controlled diet, in preventing the conditions giving rise to disabling symptoms and in extending expectation of healthy, active life. On activity and regular physical exertion there seems to be unanimity, as well on the appalling menace of smoking and the dangers of alcoholic excess. Diet is a subject fraught with conflicting opinions and recommendations.[9] Still there would appear to be universal confidence that personal effort can and does postpone decrepitude, and makes older people better company.

We may think it disconcerting that there should be blank disagreement in works of this kind on some topics, even on what seems to be crucial topics. We may find the discussion occasionally dogmatic and offhand, in a way which only medical experts writing for the 'laity' seem able to be. We may be surprised, even astonished, at the present uncertainty as to the fixedness and the potential length of the human life-span. On this depends the very serious matter of the probable duration of the Fourth Age, and hence of the extent and duration of chronic conditions in the last years, conditions which could become such a burden on resources. We may be impatient to know whether anything like an approach to the rectangular survival curve is in fact on the way in Japan, America or anywhere else. We may be taken aback, above all, by the naivety shown by one or two of the medical authors when it comes to the social consequences of the changes which they study and those which they would like to bring about, by the crudity of their concepts of the past and of the future and by the superficiality of their views of social structure. James Fries, for example, should never have talked about the 'rectangular society'.

We must deeply deplore the ignorance and irresponsibility of journalistic comment. But we must also remember the great difficulty of the evidence, arising, for example, from differences between individuals, which grow over the life course and are their widest towards its end. Research in these fields is only beginning, though it seems to be on a scale wholly insufficient to the importance of the problems. Now is the time for bold theorization, so that at present disagreement seems inevitable. It is scarcely just to be hard on medical scientists for the callowness of their comments on sociological matters, since it is for the social scientists themselves to investigate and appreciate the consequences of ageing on the social structure, a task which social scientists can scarcely be said to have begun.

LENGTH AND LENGTHENING OF LIFE AS A UNIVERSAL THEME

In their boldly optimistic presentation of their hypothesis about the rectangular curve, Fries and his collaborator make eloquent use of a popular American humorous poem, or doggerel-poem – 'The Deacon's Masterpiece, or the Wonderful One-hoss Shay'– by Oliver Wendell Holmes, about a horse carriage which supposedly lasted for a whole century, from 1755 to 1855. The conveyance was so marvellously built, with every part exactly as durable as every other, and all fitted together with such flexibility, that it went on and on and on until the very day that the full century was up, when the whole thing shattered to fragments:

>...it went to pieces all at once
>All at once and nothing first
>Just as bubbles do when they burst.
>End of the wonderful one hoss shay
>Logic is logic. That's all I say.

No vivider image could be found to illustrate the account Fries give of death of mere old age, from the exhaustion of organ reserve as he puts it, and which he suggests will eventually become the standard way of going for all those attaining the end of the fixed span of years. Although such circumstances would effectively dispose of one of the more formidable fears of growing old which have been acknowledged here, the fear of spending long years in chronic pain and disability, the whole set of issues surrounding the discussion of the rectangular survival curve raises numbers of further questions, some of them of great antiquity. The appeal to the notion of natural death, for example, has resonances from a long way back in time. Those who maintain with Walford that there is a prospect of the average life-span rising to 100, or even finally to 130 or higher, which last figure would be over half as much again as the present extremely high average level of expectation of life in advanced countries, and surpass the extreme predictions of the statisticians set out in our last chapter, play upon a theme which has persisted from the ancient writers, the theme of prolongation of human existence.

The mythic stories abound in our intellectual and cultural tradition, and regularly reappear in contemporary writings on the topic. Not all of the depictions of prolonged existence are attractive, but the idyllic strain is strong. There is Methuselah, for example, or the Greek legend of Tithonus; Swift's immortal Struldbruggs in *Gulliver's Travels* and, in more recent generations, *The Picture of Dorian Gray* by Oscar Wilde and the Land of Shangri-la, in James Hilton's novel *Lost Horizon*. The artists have painted variations on these literary themes, like Lucas Cranach on the Fountain of Youth. In this splendid picture of about 1546 the fountain stands at the centre of a pool in a garden. On the one side wrinkled, elderly women limp down into the water and on the other side they step out on to the bank rejuvenated, to join a company of eager young men.[10] Unmistakable, it might be said, as a masculine sexual fantasy, and as phallocratic as Machiavelli's metaphor for Fortune. Extending the length of life made up much of the substance of earlier medical and other treatises on ageing, and is clearly still alive in the geriatic and gerontological professions.

The significant point of much of this evidently very appealing literature is that the time gained should be spent not as an old person but as a youth. When Tithonus was endowed by Zeus with unending life, his lover the goddess of the dawn forgot to mention this imperative condition in making her request to the godhead, and the outcome was a tragedy. Tithonus grew ever smaller, weaker, more shade-like, his voice shriller and shriller.[11] More suprising, perhaps, in the outlook of ageing issues in our own day, is the persistent willingness, indeed the eagerness to believe in demographic impossibilities in the contemporary world as confirmation that life can last in particularly favoured geographical situations for a very long time indeed.

We have referred to this credulous disposition, but not yet mentioned any of the people or the places, remote and rather romantic as they tend to be and, like Okinawa, lacking official birth-registration at the relevant times. The mountain villagers – mountains seem to be particularly conspicuous in these accounts – of the Caucasian range in Georgia, when a province of the former Soviet Union, of the Andes in Ecuador, of the Himalayas in Pakistan, are among the simple livers supposedly surviving markedly better in the blessed spots which they inhabit than we do in our polluted, unnatural city environment and with our inorganic nourishment. In sober fact all these accounts are as mythical as Methuselah.[12] The only localities particularly favourable to longevity known to demographers are those chosen by the rich and privileged to live in, and it is these personal attributes which enable them to go on living longer than the rest of us. Some places are healthier than others, of course, and this is why they are chosen for residence by the well-to-do. In England in earlier times remoter settlements on high ground, away from infections and from urban dangers to health could have markedly higher longevity.[13] But there are no known areas where it can be demonstrated that ecological conditions alone keep the old and very old of all social description going on living. It is a different matter with the highly specialized and costly buildings where people may sometimes feel that they are being compelled to stay alive.

Here a spectre glides on to the stage which is entirely of our time and of the rich, industrial countries, namely the elaborate apparatus and practices which our medical men and women supposedly sometimes use in order to stave off the final extinction of life in a body already useless for a life that is worth living. We might conceivably have added the following questions to the list of fears of ageing in Chapter 2. Shall I go on living for too long? Shall I be forced against my will and in defiance of my choice to stay alive?

The issue of euthanasia, that is, the right of an individual to die when he or she decides, or the right of relatives, friends and doctors to end pointless and unbearable existences, are the most sombre of those which come before us when we reflect really seriously on expectation of life and the life-span. Making up our minds about them will be one of the duties listed in our last chapter, when we come finally to assess the responsibilities of the British elderly for themselves and for the future.

AGEING IN THE LONG TERM: THE SECULAR SHIFT IN ENGLAND

We shall reserve to the end of this chapter our judgement on the undoubtedly attractive hypothesis going by the name of the rectangularization of the survival curve. Meanwhile no one could doubt that the upthrust of life expectation which prompted such speculation has been of great social significance. The conspicuous change in the shape of American survival curves since the 1880s portrayed in Figure 5.3 must have been brought about by fundamental developments in American social arrangements, feeding, living standards and health care, as well as by medical advances. The lengthening of life must in its turn have had far-reaching effects on American society and American life, and will have more.

In the British, more particularly the English, case we are in a position to make historical comparisons over a very much longer period. We can show that a transformation as to ageing began with us in the 1890s and came to the pause after the 1980s which is evident for proportions in late life in the figures of Table 5.1. From a plateau, uneven in its surface but fundamentally level, stretching backwards from the 1890s towards the distant, illimitable past, we seem to have climbed almost to the top of an exceedingly steep slope, and to have landed, at least for a while, on a very much higher plateau; perhaps a ledge would be a better description. This abrupt ascent we shall call the *'secular shift in ageing'*, secular being meant to convey the long-term, enduring character of this irreversible change.

Because of the extraordinary and unprecedented penetration backwards in time in English vital statistics recently achieved by E. A. Wrigley and R. S. Schofield and James Oeppen at the Cambridge Group for the History of Population and Social Structure, we can begin to see where we now are by comparing with what we were, at points as distant from the present as 450 years ago.[14]

The two graphs in Figure 5.4 use this hard-won and quite novel evidence, which at the present time has been recovered only for England, to trace out over the whole of that period of nearly 500 years the course of the two ageing statistics with which we have preoccupied, proportions of the elderly in the population – in this case those aged 60 or over – and expectation of life at birth. In the diagram these lines have been projected schematically back into the past and forwards into the future for some five hundred years in each case to suggest the lineaments of two ageing plateaux, the second much higher than the first. Between 1541 and 1800 the liens are to some extent approximate and for the period up to 1500 they represent informed conjectures. After 2000 the graphs attempt to incorporate the projections for the near and distant future which were discussed in Chapter 4. But the upthrust is so pronounced that these uncertainties make little difference to the secular shift itself which occurs during the interlude of the most reliable reconstruction. The astonishing ascent in both graphs during the twentieth century is shown in what can only be its proper perspective in the figure. Such an account of ageing in England and in the United Kingdom, past, present and future, looks fairly reliable in its general outlines, unlikely to be much changed by further historical investigation,[15] but subject for the more distant future to the vagaries of demographic projection with which we have had to become familiar.

Perhaps we should dwell a little further on Figure 5.4 since the observed, projected and schematic demographic changes which are depicted there lie at the heart of the message of this book as to the course of ageing. When compositional ageing resumes in our country in twenty or twenty-five years' time the forecast that there will finally supervene a

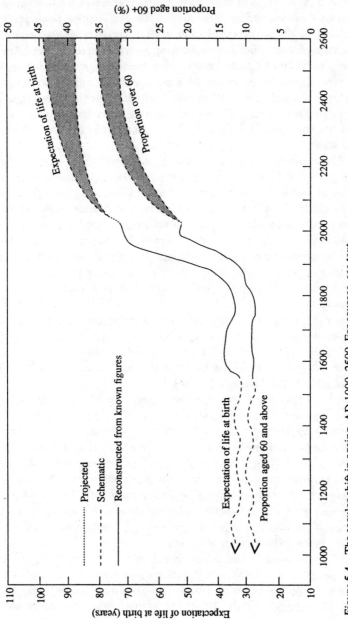

87

Figure 5.4   The secular shift in ageing, AD 1000–2500. For sources, see text.

plateau in ageing is of course a hypothesis. It rests on the commonsense proposition that ageing must come to an end at some point and on the analogy of the lower ageing plateau. But the uncertainties of projection which have been discussed make it necessary to represent the future after the population of England moves from the ledge on which it rests in the 1990s and the 2000s, as shaded areas of possible trajectories for proportions of older people and longevity and not as single trajectories. These possible lines might yet cross the upper or lower bounds of these areas. But we shall talk of a higher plateau in contrast to the lower plateau, all the same.[16]

The message of Figure 5.4 would undoubtedly appear in a figure for any developed country, which, like our own, has competed the demographic transition. In *Necessary Knowledge* evidence is set out which demonstrates this to be so over past periods in France, Sweden and other Scandinavian countries, along with indications of the same pattern beginning to take shape in East Asian countries like Japan and Korea. The trajectories represented in our illustration represent an abrupt, transformative change, entirely unprecedented in the lengthy previous story of ageing in England as we have now got to know it. Indeed when we consider its demographic character and causes we have to conclude that such a mutation cannot ever have happened anywhere or any time before the last hundred years or so and in the history of the developed countries. But everything we know about the abrupt ascent from ageing plateau to ageing plateau points to the probability that all other populations will sooner or later undergo a similar secular shift.

It is no easy matter to suggest the importance of such a transformation in a diagram necessarily gross in scale in relation to the facts. The hypotheseis, it must be insisted, is that the first plateau could be extended backwards indefinitely from 1541 and the second indefinitely forwards from 2051. A change took place, therefore, between the 1890s and the 1980s which was so fundamental that it can indeed be conveyed only in geographical metaphors, using the tens of thousands of years which mark the shortest intervals on the geological time-scale, and transferring the sense of fundamental, physical structure conveyed by the notion of landscape to the architectonics of society.

There are three features of the secular shift which must be recognized if we are to try to appreciate its significance for the theme of this book. One is that its impact fell on a particular generation of Britons, those who are actually experiencing the Third Age in the 1990s. The secular shift has run its course largely within their lifetimes and the resumption of ageing change projected in such variable terms for a quarter of a century hence is best regarded as a separate movement. Another of the features of the shift is its inevitable effect in making accepted and immemorial assumptions about age and ageing obsolete almost overnight. If it is true that we have little idea where we now are in ageing, the secular shift must be held largely responsible. The third of its features is a corollary of the other two, perhaps to some degree a compensation for the second of them. This is the emergence of the Third Age into history as a new social entity, a subject which we shall tackle in our text chapter.

THE SECULAR SHIFT AND CONTEMPORARY EXPERIENCE AND ASSUMPTIONS

In Table 5.1, and Figure 5.5 the secular shift is shown in much finer detail. When the scale is changed in this way, the overall configuration displayed in Figure 5.1 looks much as before. But some circumstances come to light which are of importance to contemporary experience and assumption.

Table 5.1   The secular shift in ageing in England, 1891–2021

Periods and years	Expectation of life at birth			Proportion aged 60 and over			Proportion of adults (25+) over 60
	Women	Men	Both	Women	Men	Both	
Lower plateau	–	–	36.5	–	–	8.0	c. 18.0
1891	45.7	41.9	43.9	7.9	6.8	7.2	15.4
1901	51.6	48.0	49.6	8.1	7.0	7.6	
1911	53.4	49.4	51.3	8.6	7.3	8.1	
1921	59.9	55.9	57.5	10.4	9.0	9.8	
1931	62.4	58.4	60.0	12.5	10.9	11.7	19.7
1941	63.9	59.4	61.4	15.2	12.9	14.1	21.8
1951	71.2	66.2	68.4	17.6	13.9	15.8	24.5
1961	73.4	67.9	70.5	19.4	14.1	16.8	26.8
1971	75.0	68.8	72.1	21.7	15.9	18.9	31.0
1981	76.2	69.8	73.2	23.5	16.9	20.3	31.7
1991	78.7	73.2	75.4	23.5	17.9	20.8	31.2
2001	79.4	74.1	76.3	22.7	18.0	20.4	30.1
2011	79.9	74.7	76.8	24.8	20.7	22.8	33.2
2021	80.2	75.1	77.1	27.4	23.4	25.4	36.1

Source: Census records, *Social Trends*, projections of the Government Actuary's Office.

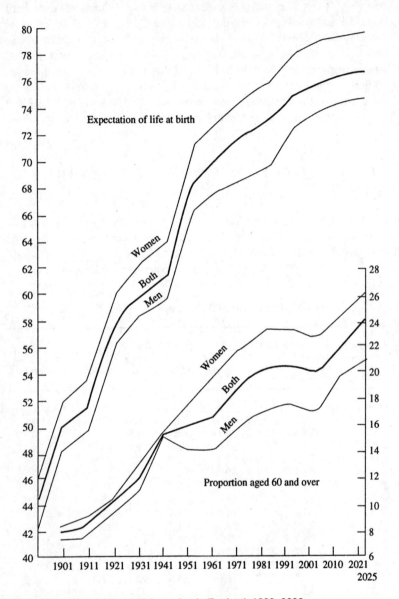

Figure 5.5   The secular shift in ageing in England, 1890–2020
Source: Table 5.1.

Expectation of life rose somewhat sooner and comparatively faster than proportions of the elderly. By the 1920s, when those now in their seventies were being born, expectation of life at birth had already increased over its long-term average on the lower plateau by a half of what was to be its final gain towards the end of the secular shift in ageing in the 1980s. But the percentage of the elderly had only grown by about a fifth, and between the 1920s and the 1970s the pace of gain increased, and the whole process completed itself within the lifetime we have specified.[17] A lifetime, even a lifetime as long as that which corresponds to the life expectancy at birth of the elderly people of today, is a very short period as historians reckon time – in terms of wars, political vicissitudes, technical change and so on. On the biological time-scale, that which might lead to natural selection in response to changed conditions, biological conditions, one lifetime is entirely insignificant. It is evident that in adapting to our new situation in respect of our longer survival we shall get no help whatever from our physiological make-up. This is perhaps too simple-minded a point to maintain, yet remarks are sometimes made which seem to suppose that the physical constitution of British people could have evolved since the 1900s, in ways biologically more fundamental than social change could bring about.

Evolution by natural selection can only be faintly and very distantly influenced by what happens to an animal after the point in life when reproduction ceases to be possible. If some grandparents developed traits which made the production of children by their own children a more efficient process, and thus improved the survival chances of those grandchildren, then there could conceivably be selection in favour of individuals likely to possess those traits when they became grandparents. Some biologists have suggested that the function of grandparents in aiding the rearing of grandchildren is a possible reason why humans survive at all after the cessation of fertility, or why reproduction does not continue until the end of the lifespan. Such an evolutionary process might take a social form, for one can see how a society might encourage efficient grandparenting if it improved child-rearing. but even if any such thing should be going on, its relevance to the other adaptations required to live in the newly-arrived Third Age is difficult for us to conceive. In short, it is hard to see how really long periods of lengthened life, continuing for centuries or millennia on end in the biological or geological fashion, could ever give rise to physiological modifications of the human organism making us better-suited to our new conditions of prolonged life for everyone. All the adaptation that is ever likely to take place because of our altered situation as to age will inevitably be social. It will happen in historical time, though, as we have said, one lifetime counts for little even there.[18]

Little is certainly known about how societies change, in structure, in outlook, in every respect, as they react to a shift of this dimension, and we cannot go very far into discussion of so complex a problem here. We may, however, take note of the fact that those who are elderly in Britain now being brought up and educated in the 1930s and 1940s, at the time when the secular shift was becoming precipitate. They spent their early middle life, in our vocabulary the first part of the Second Age, at the time when the shift was going on at its greatest speed, and when, as we shall see, the likelihood of surviving for a substantial time in the Third Age was becoming a near-certainty, for women anyway. The widening of the gap between male and female in the matter of ageing, expanding noticeably between the 1930s and the 1980s, is a very striking feature of Figure 5.5, especially in respect of proportions in later life.

A WANT OF ROLE MODELS FOR THE CONTEMPORARY ELDERLY

In their later Second Age, the contemporary population of retired people saw the whole process slowing down and now that they are the seniors in society, the acceleration of ageing compositional ageing, has been interrupted, at least for a decade or two. The critical point for the issue of social adaptation is that at no period of their lifetimes did they have what sociologists call a *role model*. The experience, outlook and assumption of those older than themselves, of their grandparents in the 1920s to the 1940s, of their parents in the 1950s and 1960s, were entirely inappropriate as a guide to what things would be like for them in their turn. Both men and women are affected by this lack, but it is particularly evident for women, so much the majority in the Third Age. Childhood memories of their elders taking life easily because they, the few survivors of their coevals, were convinced that they deserved to rest, are of no use in deciding what those at similar calendar ages should be doing in the 1990s and 2000s. Wearing black, looking submissive and regretful, being thankful that no new thing is to be expected of them – these are attitudes which no woman in the Third Age would now wish to adopt, or indeed ever ought, to adopt.

It is often and properly insisted that the cohorts who will succeed the present elderly will have had quite other experiences. They are bound to make a very different thing of the Third Age than the present incumbents of that quite novel social structural position. In so far as these newcomers to later life have a role model, however, it will have to be derived from the outlook and behaviour of those in the Third Age in the remaining years of the current century and the early years of its successor, that is to say the persons whose previous life experience we have been describing. Creative activity is therefore demanded of the present society of those in the Third Age, and of those who are perpetually being added to their ranks. They and only they can elaborate the social patterns which may do something to help their successors. When we come in our last chapter to the responsibilities of older British people now, we shall stress their duty in these directions, their duty to work out a role model on which a different set of attitudes can be based.

In so doing we shall have to bear in mind that those now in the Third Age are in a very different position from younger persons intent on transforming attitudes and changing the structure of society. Even those entering the Third Age cannot have the same sense of life being still in front of them, in spite of the fact that those entering the Third Age in our day have a future approaching a half of the expectation of life of those in their twenties in pre-industrial times.

Nor can today's society of the Third Age be thought of as having a stable membership, since their rate of turnover is so high. The American demographer George Myers tells us, for example, that nearly two-thirds of that part of the population of the United States which was over the age of 65 in 1970 had disappeared by 1980 and been replaced, in fact more than replaced, by members of succeeding cohorts. This rate of change may seem extraordinarily high, so high as to make it impossible to create new models of behaviour for elderly persons and establish them in practice. But as an example of population turnover as such, it is not all that much in excess of what seems to have been normal in pre-industrial English village communities.[19]

When this particular feature of the life of our rural ancestors was discovered, the conclusion was that the structure of village society would have had to be rigid, very difficult to modify if men and women were to be able to make sense of their social world. But a seventeenth-century English village is a very different entity from a whole age group in a huge modern population, especially an open-ended age group such as 'all over the age of 65'. It would perhaps be difficult to show that rigidity necessarily informs the outlook and the relationships of those in later life because they are always arriving and departing, replacing and being replaced. There could, in fact, be a danger of exaggerating the want of continuity and the tendency towards flux among the elderly, for we are told by Myers that in the United States in the 1970s 'the average length of stay within the aged population is roughly 16.7 years'. But the issue of how new social forms could establish themselves so as to take account of the secular shift is far wider than the discontinuities due to turnover or even the absence of appropriate role models. A comparison with what seems to happen among women who become mothers might help us to grasp what the problems are.

Although most young women have their own mothers as role models, more often today than ever before, and although the birth and nurture of babies is all around them, it is a matter of observation that many or most of those likely sooner or later to produce children have little notion of how they will actually behave when challenged with the palpable presence of their own babies. They find it very difficult in fact, and this is surely true of everyone at all stages of their lives in relation to any kind of change which is in store for them, to put themselves in a future position, of being clearly aware of what they will do and how they will do it. This outlook is apparently more pronounced with very young women, although as things now are, most of them can expect to be mothers within twelve or fifteen years after reaching maturity, even if a large proportion of them will still be unmarried when they first give birth.

We have already laid it down that the proper way of looking at your own ageing in our time is to live your life in the perpetual presence of all your future selves. At the age of 25, we shall insist in Chapter 6, it is prudent to think of yourself as you will be at the age of 70, exceedingly difficult as that may appear to be. But the incapacity of girls in their teens to imagine what it will be like in so short a period as a dozen years hence does not mean that when they do come to be mothers they will act as if they do not know where they are or what do to. This is because a great assemblage of social models, norms or practices, tried remedies, supportive institutions and deeply marked attitudes are there to instruct and reassure them.

This is just as well, or else the continuation of any human population might otherwise be in doubt. It could be said in fact that the anticipation of becoming a mother is built into the society, any society, for the girl who will eventually give birth, and if she wishes to be irresponsible she has no need to think about her prospects in that direction. But in the case of women or men faced with thinking appropriately about what things will be like not twelve years hence but four times that amount, forty or fifty years hence, few such built-in social mechanisms yet exist. They have neither models to copy, precedents to take note of, conventions to be guided by nor experience to consult, either personal experience or social experience. Being your age in the last decade of the twentieth century is challenging indeed.

No wonder, then, that we in our own time scarcely know where we are in the matter of ageing, and no wonder the traditional arrangements continue to be maintained in spite of the fact that their reason for existence has already passed away. Like Bottom the Weaver we have been translated, and like him also we are taking an unconscionably long time to put up a hand and feel out the unfamiliar shape which fate has unceremoniously thrust upon our shoulders.

Before we go on to the subject of the emergence of the Third Age into our own century, and recount something about the extraordinary and unfavourable stereotyping of the elderly which seems to have been in place during the same period of years, let us return for a little while to the rectangular survival curve.

SURVIVAL CURVES IN ENGLAND OVER THE LAST 450 YEARS

The survival curves for England over 500 years (set out in Figure 5.6) can be seen to illustrate what has been recounted here about the long-term history of expectation of life and about the secular shift in ageing. Not all the curves now available are shown. Between the 1540s and the 1900s we have presented a line for every half century, and after that, for the twentieth century, a line for each decade. But the same vigorous breasting outwards and upwards, apparently towards the top right-hand corner is evident as in the lines for the USA in Diagram 5.2, shapes which made the final attainment of the rectangular survival curve so tempting an hypothesis. Progress towards that end appears from the long-term English evidence to be the inevitable outcome of the long-term historical process. But a closer look at the lower curves, that is those for earlier dates, shows that these crowded lines are not in date order. The survival curve for 1541–5 is the lowest, the most given to concavity, the least 'rectangular'. But the next in order is not that for 1591–5, its chronological successor in the series, but that for 1741–5, a curve which differs only slightly from that for 1541–5. Survival in the 1590s in fact was better than in 1790s, the 1640s, the 1690s and the 1740s, in that order.

The secular shift is quite evident in the relationship between the lines for the twentieth century, drawn it must be remembered for every decade, not for every half century. It is particularly conspicuous in the gaps between those for 1911 and 1921, and between those for 1941 and 1951, interludes we must remember, of all-out national warfare but also of increase in the distribution of collective welfare. As the 1950s give way to the 1960s, 1970s, 1980s and 1990s the lines grow rapidly closer together.

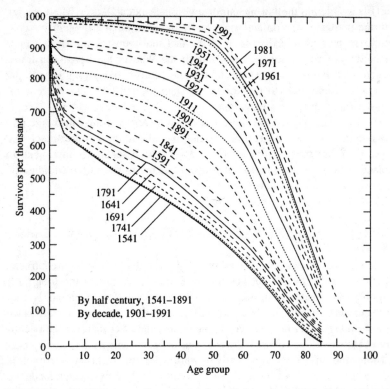

Figure 5.6   Survival curves for cohorts of one thousand newborns, by age group: England, 1541–1981.
Source: Cambridge Group back projection files and English Life tables up to the interim life table for 1989–91. Work of James Oeppen.

This marks the end of the secular shift and the succession of the ledge as we have called it on which we now metaphorically stand. It cannot be very long before successive survival curves begin to jostle and cross each other again, as they will perpetually doing on the lower ageing plateau.

With both the English and the American survival curves in front of us we might venture on a provisional conclusion about the promise or the prophecy of 'rectangularization'. The ideal curve portrayed at the beginning of this chapter in Figure 5.1 differs in two ways from the curves which represent the actual history of mortality in the two countries, one quite conspicuous and one somewhat more elusive. In the representation of the ideal, everything stops at 100 years: virtually no death takes place after that age because compression of mortality has been assumed to range all deaths around the average attainable span of 85. But we now know that survival in the very latest years has not behaved in such a way as to confirm this prediction as it was propounded a dozen years ago. Persistence beyond the group of years when most older people now die has tended to increase attainable age, average or final, and is still entirely open, an ultimate uncertainty.

The implication has to be that the question of the limit to human life, and of the age at which that limit is attained, are the most important objectives of the research now in progress. The ultimate possibility, that the limit to life does not exist, would appear to be out of the question, but it has to be allowed for until such time as these two questions have been given answers. These are the circumstances which seem to be responsible for the second feature of the two sets of survival curves. Their tendency to swell upwards and outwards is not, in reality, directed at the right-hand top corner, but well to the left of it. There are a multitude of conflicting theories as to why the mortality curves behave in this way but many of them, we are told,[20] themselves require the assumption of a compression of morbidity, though not that which has been proposed by James Fries. These competing theories cannot be pursued in an introductory essay like the present one. But it could be said that until the differences between them are resolved it is appropriate that successive survival curves do not appear to be progressing towards the occupation of the upper space still blank in the two figures. The survival curve cannot yet be shown to be tending towards complete rectangularity because its tendency seems not to be finally rectangular at all. The idealised survival curve of Figure 5.1 is something of a distortion.

It would perhaps have been better if the word rectangular had never been used, and certainly better, as has been said, if Fries had never talked in his writings about the 'rectangular society'. It is unfortunate that the hopes and fears about the abbreviation or the prolongation of the Fourth Age, with all that they imply about burdens of support and care, and about our own personal expectations of our own personal futures, should lend themselves so readily to an attractive and dramatic graphical representation. We are left with the realization that it will be up to us to do what we can to ensure that the latest phase of life is as free of illness and discomfort as good health practice can make it. For everyone is agreed that such addictions as nicotine and alcohol, over-eating and inactivity can and do contribute to difficulties in the final years.

We are left too with the confidence that biologists and doctors will continue to prolong our healthy lives by the progress of their researches and their practices and with the hope that dramatic improvements in the degenerative conditions may be brought about. We shall certainly have to be prepared for the consequences of this happening, and that will presumably be a progressive prolongation of life in the Third Age, perhaps finally to an inordinate length. But we are left also with the impression that we have to be rather careful of what is confidently told to us by the experts on these subjects and with wavering uncertainly about our innermost hopes and fears as to the Fourth Age, the social burden of the finally decrepit, and so on.

Survival curves may well make a much closer approach to the right angled form as time passes upon the higher ageing plateau. But there is almost nothing to convince us that the goal will ever be reached. Indeed there may sometimes be shrinkage away from the top right-hand corner of the figure, flaccid depressions in the swell of the survival curves as there must have been in recent decades in Russia. We do not yet know, perhaps we shall never know in our time, whether increased expectation of life at all ages, especially the latest ages, will finally be accompanied by natural death, swift and with little final illness, an outcome which all of us would so much prefer to that which we sometimes observe among those in the Fourth Age at the present time. The rectangular survival curve and the secular shift in ageing have a great deal to tell us about what our attitude to ourselves should be as we strive to be our age in our own generation.

6 The Emergence of the Third Age[1]

The Third Age is not to be defined wholly by the calendar nor are its true limits to be reckoned by birthdays. A point in the personal age of an individual, a point personally chosen, rather than a marker fixed in the calendar of biological, or of social age has to be the occasion of the onset of the Third Age. The Third Age, moreover, is a collective circumstance as well as a personal affair. It can only be experienced by an individual in the company of a nationwide society of those with the disposition, the freedom and the means to act in the appropriate manner. The Third Age, therefore, is an attribute of a population, indeed of a nation, as well as of particular men and women. Populations and nations may nevertheless have some, but not all, of the characteristics which would enable a full community of the Third Age to exist and to flourish within it.

Accordingly the appearance of the Third Age in history must be expected to be developmental, rather than eventful, the setting together of changes in intellectual and cultural, as well as in economic and demographic life, into a general pattern not before seen. In this chapter we have to decide the date – or rather the stretch of chronological time – when these elements first showed themselves, the fresh configuration began to make itself evident and the Third Age to emerge in particular countries, especially in our own country. In spite of their limitations for the purpose, the numerical measures which we shall use to make this judgement will have to be demographic, and to some degree economic. Educational and cultural criteria for Third Age living have to be given in descriptive form. The inadequacies of all these kinds of evidence for the purposes in hand will be sadly apparent and will show themselves again when the general theory of the Third Age is discussed at length in Chapter 10.

Some persons, as we have seen, may and do live in the Third Age from the moment when they attain maturity in the conventional sense, and thus at a point much earlier in their lives than the calendar age at which retirement usually supervenes. Consummate personalities like these, as we have said, can be supposed to experience their Third Age to a greater or lesser extent simultaneously with their Second Age, or, in the case of most athletes, simultaneously with their First Age. These circumstances demon-

strate how ineffective figures, durations and birthdays can be in defining
the Third Age and thus in deciding when it first appears. However, for
most of us, demographic approximations and conventional life-course
transitions are considerably more appropriate, if never entirely satisfactory. Moreover the disposable wealth, both of society and of the individual, is of fundamental importance.

Although we need not, indeed should not, reckon our own Third Age
experience by our birthdays, in practice we have to accept that such experience becomes a general possibility only after the end of the Second Age,
at retirement, which is in fact usually a matter of birthday age. Age at
retirement, then, is of crucial importance to the length of life a person can
hope to spend in the Third Age. Some people can choose when to finish
working, in other words, to leave the Second Age. But for most, certainly
for most men, age of retirement is fixed for practical purposes, fixed by
others – the Government or employers.[2] Women are somewhat differently
placed because the end of responsibility for children, and their departure
from home, marks the close of the Second Age for mothers without jobs.
This juncture is variable in the female life course and need not be connected with leaving work. Since the calendar age of retirement in Britain
is usually inflexible, often for administrative reasons (although employers,
politicians and administrators jiggle around with it to suit their own purposes), length of life after this fixed point in the life course is of crucial
importance to the Third Age. Life after the Second Age has to last long
enough for the whole population of a nation, not simply for the lucky, the
rich, the highly educated and the privileged, to expect to be able to go on
to the Third Age. That the opportunity of living a Third Age should be
open to every single individual in a population who lives long enough is a
crucial circumstance for its emergence.

All of which means that the Third Age can only appear at the time when
expectation of life in the country concerned begins to be high enough to
allow this to happen. Moreover a number of years – perhaps a decade or
two – of a country's history is at issue in the arrival of the Third Age,
rather than a precise date. This is because it takes some time for people to
become aware that they can expect this longer future and start to conduct
their lives with such a future in view. In the meanwhile they are evidently
displaying a particular feature of that lagged condition which we have
alluded to so frequently. They are not properly aware as yet of what has
happened to the age relations of the society to which they belong, and of
its implications for themselves and their comrades. They seem to be
particularly badly informed of the length of time which they and their
contemporaries have still to live.

Further circumstances have to be present for the emergence of the Third Age, apart from the required demographic and economic conditions. Among these are the health, vigour and attitudes which enable people to go on to attain what has been called the 'crown of life' in their latter years, together with appropriate cultural and educational facilities. These conditions will be considered in due course. Here stress should be placed on the fact that people have to be confident quite early in their lifetimes that they will live long enough to experience the Third Age, in order for them to plan for it. We shall have to make an important assumption at this point, the assumption that the Third Age becomes a possibility only when every citizen can be reasonably sure at the onset of the Second Age that there will be a Third Age to come for him or her. By 'reasonably sure', we mean having more than a 50 per cent chance of that happening.

It must already be clear that such circumstances cannot have existed until after the secular shift in ageing had got under way and survival curves had begun to distance themselves from each other as we saw them doing in England during the first part of the twentieth century. We should not be surprised to find, therefore, that the Third Age as we define it only made an appearance in Britain during the 1950s, and that it did not begin to establish itself as a settled feature of the social structure until the 1980s. Most other Western countries have had a similar history in this respect, but the demographic development seems to have come about twenty years earlier for Italy, and in Scandinavia and Australasia some of the requisite demographic conditions are visible even before that. It will be shown that the possibility of the Third Age appearing is already beginning to be present during the 1990s in a select few of the developing countries. It is virtually certain that this demographic situation is here to stay and will finally spread over the world. Once more, the point at issue is whether the economic advantages of the already developed nations will likewise become universal.

EXPECTATION OF LIFE AT BIRTH IN THE TWENTIETH CENTURY IN BRITAIN AND ELSEWHERE

In order to see when enough people begin to live long enough for the Third Age to emerge we have to know some of the facts about expectation of life and its recent history. In Table 6.1 a series of figures for expectation of life at birth[3] are set out for a number of countries so as to place the United Kingdom where it belongs.

A Fresh Map of Life

Table 6.1 Expectation of life at birth in the early 1990s in various countries: in order of values for women (with proportions over 60 for both sexes)

		Women	Men	Proportion of population over 60 Both sexes
80.0+	Switzerland	82.7	75.4	19.7
	Japan	82.2	76.4	17.2
	France	82.0	73.6	19.4
	Spain	81.7	74.9	19.0
	Italy	81.5	74.6	20.8
	Netherlands	81.2	74.3	17.6
	Sweden	80.9	74.9	22.8
	Norway	80.9	73.5	20.9
	Canada	80.8	74.1	16.0
	Austria	80.6	73.7	20.6
	Belgium	80.6	73.6	20.8
	Greece	80.3	75.1	20.5
	Australia	80.2	73.8	15.6
	Finland	80.0	71.4	18.7
77.5–79.9	United Kingdom	79.4	73.5	20.7
	Germany	79.2	72.6	20.6
	Denmark	79.1	72.8	20.4
	USA	79.1	72.2	16.9
	Costa Rica	78.9	74.7	6.7
	Israel	78.9	75.1	12.7
	New Zealand	78.6	72.5	15.5
	Ireland	78.5	72.6	15.5
	Cuba	78.2	73.3	12.2
	Portugal	78.2	71.2	18.5
	Taiwan	77.9	71.5	10.0
	Venezuela	77.8	70.9	6.1
75.0–77.4	Guadalupe	77.3	70.1	10.6
	Singapore	77.2	72.5	8.9
	Poland	77.1	68.7	15.1
	Chile	76.8	69.9	9.3
	Czech Republic	76.8	69.0	16.8
	Mexico	76.4	68.1	5.8
	Panama	76.2	72.0	7.4
	Bulgaria	76.1	69.5	19.2
	Puerto Rico	76.1	68.8	11.6
	Yugoslavia	76.0	70.0	15.1
	Barbados	75.9	70.1	13.4
	Jamaica	75.8	71.6	9.1
	Hungary	75.7	67.6	19.1

Table 6.1   Continued

		Women	Men	Proportion of population over 60 Both sexes
70.0–74.9	Romania	74.9	69.0	16.0
	Argentina	74.3	67.6	13.2
	Soviet Union	74.3	65.0	15.0
	Mauritius	73.9	66.2	8.2
	Tunisia	73.8	70.0	7.4
	Sri Lanka	73.7	68.5	8.0
	Colombia	73.7	68.3	6.2
	Jordan	73.1	69.5	4.0
	South Korea	73.1	66.6	7.7
	Trinidad and Tobago	72.8	67.5	7.6
	Paraguay	72.3	67.3	6.1
	Turkey	72.1	67.5	4.5
	Solomon Islands	72.0	67.2	7.2
	China	71.7	68.3	8.9
	Thailand	71.0	66.2	6.6
	Malaysia	71.0	65.3	5.7
	Syria	70.6	68.3	4.4
< 55	Haiti	55.0	52.3	6.2
	Madagascar	54.5	50.9	5.2
	Tanzania	54.5	49.5	4.4
	Bermuda	54.3	50.3	4.4
	Rwanda	54.2	50.8	4.0
	Cameroon	53.1	49.1	4.9
	Burkina Faso	53.0	51.5	5.3
	Ethiopia	52.9	49.8	4.5
	Bangladesh	52.5	53.5	4.8
	Nepal	50.4	50.8	4.7
	Nigeria	49.8	48.0	4.0
	Central African Republic	48.7	45.4	5.7
	Mozambique	45.6	45.1	4.1
	Afghanistan	42.7	44.2	4.4

Source: US Census Bureau, *Global Aging*, September 1991, wallchart, and for same countries not present there, N. Keyfitz and W. Flieger, 1990, *World Population and Aging*, Chicago.

Getting to the top of the international table of expectation of life is just the sort of game which sovereign nations most like to play. Maintaining or improving their country's rank in the order is an important concern for politicians, administrators and journalists. It also affects doctors and even the general public. Success has been recognized as a sign of good nutrition, safe working conditions, adequate and efficient sanitation and housing, a widespread and comparatively equitable distribution of resources among the population at large, and efficient social services, with medical services prominent among them. A country which falters in this competition is liable to be accused of failure in all these directions, of low morale and even of an oppressive ideology, discouraging to the citizen. It was in this way that evidence of a pause in the rise of expectation of life in the former Soviet Union and other authoritarian socialist countries was regarded in the West before the dissolution of their regimes. Unfortunately, there is as yet little sign of a recovery in this direction in these areas.

The table itself bears out what has been said but is surprising in its placements all the same. Towards the top come the rich nations with high living standards, and the poorer nations come lower, the developing nations lower still, especially those in Africa. In the early 1990s Switzerland was the richest country in the world and had the highest expectation of life at birth. Mozambique was the poorest and comes at the bottom of our longevity list.[4] Nevertheless, the ordering is not identical with the world ordering of national wealth and it is a little disconcerting to see that neither our own country, nor Germany, nor even the USA is in the first division, along with the dozen or so whose life expectation at birth is given as being over 80 years for their women. These large countries are all in the second division, with figures between 77.5 and 77.9 years. That there should now be such a number of nations in that position is a very remarkable fact in itself. Size is a disadvantage in the race, which makes the achievement of Japan with its 120 million people even more impressive, and that of France, too, at about our own size. Numbers of people then do little to explain the modest position of the United Kingdom. In the earlier decades of the century it was consistently at or near the top.

The placements in the competition have become much less clear-cut than we might expect, and judging the order resembles the task faced by a jury of experts at international events such as gymnastics or ice dancing, rather than observing the outcome of a race to get across a finishing line. This is because the values in the table are so close to each other, and because there are other numbers which could be taken into account, such as life expectation with or without disabilities. These would discriminate more accurately especially for our purposes here. In reading the table it has to be remembered that the statistics concerned change rapidly and are published at varying intervals after the observations on which they are based. They are also of course of very varying reliability. It is not possible to present really accurate current values for the populations of interest.[5]

All this means that the ordering itself changes bewilderingly from year to year. Crude as the placements have to be, they are certainly interesting, sometimes surprising, occasionally quite disconcerting.

Our position at the top of the second division of the table, countries with values in the high seventies, puts us, with reunited Germany, somewhat below the other western European countries, not far below Australia, and along with the USA. It is somewhat surprising to see the modest positions occupied by the former USSR and other Eastern European countries, but the position of China is a significant one. The biggest nation on earth, and with an income per head something like an eightieth of that of Switzerland yet with a female life expectation above 70. This is a telling demonstration of the important fact that high expectation of life does not imply a high proportion of the old, especially when a population is growing as fast as China's has been growing.

Expectation of active life, that is life free of disabilities serious enough to interfere with the pursuits necessary for self-realisation, is clearly relevant to the Third Age. A number of the populations of the world have been given estimates for life expectation with varying degrees of disability, from being slightly lame, rather deaf or badly-sighted to being subject to long periods of serious illness and finally being confined to bed, perhaps in an institution. In the United Kingdom expectation of life at birth 'without disability' has been estimated for 1988 at 72.4 years for males and 78.1 years for females, 80.8 per cent and 78.4 per cent respectively of expectation of life altogether.

At birth, then, English boys could expect to spend over 19 per cent of their lifetimes with some sort of physical incapacity and English girls nearly 22 per cent. These are sobering figures, but those for age 65 have to be called shocking. Disability-free life expectation for English men of that age was only $55\frac{1}{2}$ per cent of life expectation altogether, and 50 per cent for English women. This is a complex subject and a great deal depends, as has been said, on the definition of disability and judgement about its degree. The figures for the US, Canada and Germany are not very different, but the outstanding fact is that there is not much indication of improvement in English figures during recent years, and some sign of deterioration.[6]

HISTORICAL AND INTERNATIONAL COMPARISONS IN AGEING: THE PITFALLS OF MODERNIZATION

If historical comparison in longevity is added to geographical we meet something which may strike us as singular. Only the two countries worst placed as to female expectation of life at birth in Table 6.1 – Afghanistan and Mozambique at 45.6 and 42.7 years – have figures as low as those of England when our population was just about to leave the lower plateau and begin the secular shift. At the beginning of the 1880s, after a century of industrialization, expectation of life at birth in our country stood at 47.5 for women and 44.2 for men. The estimated average for both genders combined over the preceding 240 years in our country had been 36.5 years, with a maximum of 41.7 in the 1560s and a minimum of 27.8 in the 1540s. There does not seem to be a country, as distinct from tribal communities or societies, whose record in the 1990s is as bad or worse than this. Indeed it seems probable that no population other than that of Sweden or Norway had an expectation of life at birth as high as that of contemporary Haiti at any time before 1900.[7]

In assessing these comparisons in longevity between developed and developing countries we must not forget what was said earlier about the drawbacks of using expectation of life at birth for the purpose. Moreover, the abnormal demographic condition of most developing areas in our day must be borne in mind when drawing this contrast. These areas are estimated to have an average expectation of life at birth for the sexes combined of 61 years overall, compared with well over 70 in more developed areas. Demography tells us that a population with a life expectation at birth of 61 and which has only 7 to 12 per cent of its people over 60, must be expanding fast. It is impossible that rates of increase now common in the Third World populations can have existed for long periods of past time, when their expectations of life must have been lower and their proportions of elderly probably higher, their populations variable in size from time to time, but not growing at breakneck speed as many of them have done recently. Nevertheless such a two-way comparison, over time and between areas, nations and cultures, has an important bearing on an important issue.

For this multi-dimensional comparison discourages the use of the word modernization in connection with ageing or with the secular shift in ageing. Rising expectation of life has frequently been taken by those who conform to this unfortunate convention to be itself an index of modernization. But England, as has already been stressed, began to industrialize a hundred years before the onset of the secular shift in ageing. In so far as the word has any historical meaning at all, England was already 'modernized' before industrialization ever began in its economy, let alone a precipitate rise in expectation of life.[8] Expectation of life at birth did not rise above its general pre-industrial level there during the whole of the century after industrialization began.

The developing countries today have already been described as beginning to age in the sense of the lengthening of life well before industrialization has been achieved in most of them. If present trends and policies continue, it could be that ageing in the further sense of having large proportions of old will also supervene in these countries, before industrialization and 'modernization' have made much progress. The secular shift for them could well be prior to economic development. This is quite the opposite case from that of England, and very different from that of other already-developed countries, with the somewhat uncertain exception of Japan. If it is true that developing countries now have lower proportions of persons late in life than at earlier points in their history then the structure of their societies is already different in an important respect from what it was in the past.

We shall never be able to be our age in contemporary Britain if we equate our historical experience with that which developing nations are now undergoing. Most emphatically not if we use a term like 'modernization' to cover both their experience and our own.

EXPECTATION OF LIFE AT LATER AGES IN BRITAIN SINCE THE 1890s

The study of ageing has lacked historical depth until so very recently that the creation of a muddle as confusing as that over modernization is not difficult to understand.[9] Let us proceed to the alterations in life expectation which have taken place in our own population since the onset of the secular shift in the 1890s. We shall have to direct our attention to those changes which are significant to the emergence of the Third Age, that is, expectation of life not so much at age 15, as at 40, 50 or 60 and beyond. The details are presented in Table 6.2.

As must be expected since the same demographic changes are at issue, a similar atmosphere of relentless and practically uninterrupted progress suffuses these figures as it did the survival curves considered in Chapter 5. An upward movement shows itself at pretty well every date in the table for every age. But a little differentiation can be descried, which is not without significance for the emergence of the Third Age. Expectation of life at birth went up at all dates in the table, rose fastest in the 1890s and at a considerable pace between 1911 and 1920, the time of the First World War. But it actually went down during the black decades of the 1920s and 1930s, at later ages and for both sexes. It changed course sharply after that, showing its second greatest increase in the following decade, the

1940s, for both sexes again. It is a paradox that the periods of warfare should be marked in this way in spite of the heavy loss of life, and the destruction of assets, social and individual. The reason no doubt was the more equitable distribution of food and other resources which rationing brought with it.

After the 1940s improvement in longevity slowed down a little, as did the growth in the superiority in this particular of women over men. But there has been no further setback for either gender, which is in contrast to the experience of other European countries, especially Eastern European countries. These trends are expected to continue and make the higher plateau, as I have called it, slope upwards for some decades in respect of longevity, perhaps for a long time and perhaps to extraordinary heights.[10] Official British projections suggest an expectation of life at birth of 80.3 years for females and 74.9 years for males in 2001 and 82.6 and 75.4 in 2030. There is, moreover, every reason to expect that the sharp rises in longevity at ages 60, 65, 70 and 80 which have taken place in the last decade or so will continue and probably themselves increase.

Table 6.2   Expectation of life at later ages, UK, 1891–1991

	Females							Males						
	0	50	60	65	70	75	80	0	50	60	65	70	75	80
1891	45.7	19.3	13.0	10.4	8.0	6.1	4.3	41.9	17.5	11.9	9.5	7.3	5.6	3.9
1901	51.6	21.6	14.9	11.9	9.2	7.1	5.4	48.0	19.7	13.4	10.8	8.4	6.4	4.9
1911	53.4	22.4	15.4	12.3	9.5	7.3	5.5	49.4	20.2	13.7	10.9	8.4	6.5	4.9
1921	59.9	24.0	16.4	13.1	10.1	7.6	5.6	55.9	21.6	14.6	11.6	8.9	6.7	5.0
1931	62.4	24.1	16.4	13.0	10.0	7.4	5.4	58.4	21.6	14.4	11.3	8.6	6.4	4.8
1940	63.9	23.9	16.2	12.7	9.7	7.2	5.2	59.4	20.6	13.7	10.8	8.2	6.0	4.4
1951	71.2	26.2	17.9	14.2	10.9	8.0	5.8	66.2	22.2	14.8	11.7	9.0	6.7	4.8
1961	73.8	27.4	19.0	15.1	11.7	8.7	6.3	67.9	22.6	15.0	11.9	9.3	7.0	5.2
1971	75.0	28.3	19.8	16.0	12.5	9.4	6.9	68.8	23.0	15.3	12.1	9.5	7.3	5.5
1981	76.2	29.0	20.6	16.7	13.2	10.0	7.3	69.8	23.1	15.6	12.4	9.5	7.4	5.5
1984	77.4	29.6	21.0	17.2	13.6	10.4	7.6	71.5	24.6	16.6	13.2	10.3	7.8	5.9
1991	78.9	30.6	21.9	17.9	14.3	11.0	8.2	73.2	26.1	17.7	14.8	11.1	8.5	6.4
Index for 1991 (1891 = 100)	172	159	147	172	182	169	191	175	149	149	156	152	152	162

Sources: S. H. Preston, N. Keyfitz and R. Schoen, 1972, *Causes of Death: Life Tables for National Populations*: Government Actuary, *Interim Life Tables*, 1989–91.

From the figures laid out in Table 6.2 readers of this book who are at the mid, and later stages of the life course should be able to understand something of what they need to know in matters of survival. It is not only their own prospects which may interest them, but also those of their parents who are, or might become, dependent on them. The table makes possible, moreover, a comparison with the prospects of our parents and grandparents as to length of life when they were in corresponding positions. The prospects of our children and grandchildren are not, as we have seen, very easy to gauge but it seems wisest to expect steady increase in length of life at these later ages, with all its consequences for the individual and society. Most interesting of all for the persons to whom the present essay is particularly addressed, that is, individuals contemplating their imminent entry into the Third Age, may be their chances of surviving through that period of life as members of pairs of spouses. It is reckoned that nowadays spouses of fifty on both sides have about a 40 per cent chance of spending 25 more years together, though if the man has reached fifty five and the woman fifty the probability falls to about 25 per cent. But the chances on both counts are improving rapidly.[11] We should not, however, allow such concerns as these to draw attention away from the issue of exactly when the demographic preconditions for the emergence of the Third Age as a general attribute of the population first appeared in Britain.

DEMOGRAPHIC INDICATORS FOR THE THIRD AGE

In order to make a clear decision on the time when the Third Age appears and to permit comparison between contemporary populations in this respect, we need demographic indicators for the Third Age. Any such measures will have to be arbitrary, and will have to take account of the circumstances which have been recited. They must capture, that is to say, the prospects of persons at the beginning of the Second Age continuing to live on into the Third Age, and also of experiencing the Third Age over a stretch of years in the company of substantial numbers of other. They must also, I believe, capture the sense of how many *adults* there are in the later range of ages, rather than of how many members of the population as a whole.

We are not dealing here with dependency, which is what most measures of ageing are concerned with, often joining presumably dependent older persons with evidently dependent younger persons to get at the total dependency *burden*, the same slanted language again.[12] With all this in mind, the first measure proposed nominates the age of 25 as the initial point of the Second Age for both sexes, and provides an estimate of the probability that someone at that point in the life course will reach the age of 70, which is taken as situated five, ten or even fifteen years into an individual's Third Age. The second measure suggested requires a proportion of at least a quarter of the national population which is adult to be over the age of 60 for the society of the Third Age to be of adequate proportional size. 'Adult' here is taken to mean being over 25 years of age.

The probability that those who, at the presumed point when the Second Age begins will go on to the Third, can be arrived at by dividing the number of persons surviving to 70 under a particular set of demographic conditions by the number of persons surviving to the age of 25 under these same conditions. In the life table for the United Kingdom based on data for 1989–91, the latest available, 98 750 out of 100 000 women originally born are given as alive at the age of 25 and of these 79 605 are still alive at the age of 70.[13] The value given by dividing the second figure by the first is .806 which means that during those years a woman of 25 had a chance of 806 out of 1000 of surviving until the age of 70. For men the corresponding fraction was 67 571 out of 97 973 or .690. Men, that is, had a probability of a little over two-thirds at the outset of the Second Age of living well into the Third, and women a probability of over three-quarters. In 1991 31.2 per cent of persons over the age of 25 in the United Kingdom were also over the age of 60. In demographic shorthand $\frac{\leq 60}{\geq 25}$ much exceeded .25. Our country, then, is decidedly qualified for the Third Age on these, the demographic, criteria.

We shall call the expression arrived at by dividing male survivors at 70 by those at 25 the Third Age Indicator and refer to it as the 3AI. in demographic, life-table terms, $\frac{l\,170}{l\,125}$ must exceed .5. Since in nearly all contemporary societies, men survive worse than women, it is usually adequate to quote the male 3AI and assume that the female 3AI will be larger. Table 6.3 presents the historical record of Third Age Indicators in England since 1541, at fifty-year intervals up to 1891, the time of the onset of the secular shift, and at ten-year intervals thereafter until 1960. From 1841 proportions aged 60 and above of those aged over 25 are also included (adults over 60). The change in both series which put them above the qualifying levels came in the decade 1951–60. This decade must accordingly be regarded as marking the emergence of the Third Age in England, almost exactly at the mid-point of the twentieth century.

Let us pause for a moment and reflect on what these developments convey for individual and collective experience. A Third Age Indicator of over a half means that a majority of all males, and thus of all females, reaching their twenty-fifth birthday will go on to the seventieth, in other words can and must reckon to live well into the Third Age. In matters like

Table 6.3   Third Age Indicators: England, 1541–2021

	Third Age Indicator Both genders	Adults over 60		Third Age Indicator Women	Men	Adults over 60 Both genders
		%				%
1541	.292	19.19	1891	.372	.301	16.2
1591	.348	18.43	1901	.456	.375	15.4
1641	.325	18.67	1911	.517	.416	15.7
1691	.310	20.53	1921	.582	.492	17.2
1741	.287	17.87	1931	.595	.497	19.7
1791	.338	16.90	1940	.629	.471	21.8
1841	.391	16.30	1951	.695	.532	24.5
1881	.374	16.40	1960	.749	.581	26.8
			1971	.758	.625	30.1
			1980	.776	.634	31.7
			1991	.806	.690	31.2
			2001			28.7
			2011			33.2
			2021			36.1

Source: Calculated from figures in the files of the Cambridge Group for the History of Population and Social Structure. The later figures are for the United Kingdom rather than England and Wales. The Third Age Indicator is measured by $\frac{l70}{l25}$ and adults over 60 by % $\frac{\% \geq 60}{\% \leq 25}$. In earlier printings of this book the measure of the percentage of older persons was those over 65 as a proportion for the whole population.

these an 80 per cent chance, which is what affects English females today, has to be taken as a virtual certainty. For a woman to overlook it, or to behave as if it could be ignored, is surely pretty well impossible, and the chances of seven out of ten which now affect English men in relation to becoming established in the Third Age would also seem to be exceedingly difficult to disregard. Moreover, to live in a society where approaching a third of all adults are over 60 is certainly to be influenced by the fact that a considerable share of the mature population is no longer at work on Second Age employments, no longer producing or even bringing up children, no longer economically productive in the highly restrictive, conventional economistic sense. To be yourself in such a position is to be a member of a large community – if not yet well defined, a community all the same – and all this in spite of the prevalent lack of consciousness of ageing conditions and ageing developments which has so often been stressed in this book. After the 1950s, therefore, personal outlooks on ageing had to begin to change in our country, and those in the Third Age began to occupy so much social space that general social attitudes had to begin to change as well. By the present day such changes are absolutely imperative, but it is still very dubious how far the necessity is recognised.

The 3AI for men for England and Wales for 1989–91 was .690, for Scotland .626 and for Northern Ireland .649. The proportion of adults over 60 was very similar in all areas of the United Kingdom. In this rather rough-and-ready fashion it is possible to pronounce quite firmly that in the 1990s the Third Age in its demographic definition has become a settled feature of British society, varying from region to region somewhat, and varying no doubt much more widely from class to class, occupation to occupation, but highly probable for the whole population. Whether the further non-demographic attributes of a national society necessary for living the Third Age – adequate and fairly distributed incomes for the elderly – are yet present in Britain, with a sufficient share of educational and cultural advantages, is certainly more dubious, especially in view of the present trend in social policy in our country. But it can be said that the possibility of Third Age living has been open to everyone in Britain since the 1950s, and that before the twentieth century this was not so for a majority of the population in any country anywhere in the world.

DISCOUNTING THE POSSIBILITY OF BECOMING OLD, A TRADITIONAL ATTITUDE?

The implications of this last statement are fundamental to our subject, and indeed for the whole study of ageing in late-twentieth-century societies. The proposition could have been put in other ways, approaching the facts about survival and expectation of survival from many different angles. We must recognize that until recently it was not only possible, but in some ways quite sensible, for people over most of the life course to ignore the possibility of living long after leaving active life, and their work. This was particularly so for men. The chance of their surviving into the seventies and eighties were small enough for them to look on old age as unlikely, even as a piece of bad luck, an eventuality to be coped with if it ever should arise.

No doubt people varied, and still vary, in their attitudes towards their survival possibilities – vary by age, gender, nationality, social class, education and other circumstances, especially personal experience. It is difficult to ascertain to what extent a particular person would shrug off the possibility of persisting till late life, but there is evidence that discounting old age was a widespread assumption up to and perhaps into our own time. It may have been a standard feature of the outlook of all but the educated and privileged before the secular shift in ageing began a century ago.

It would have been particularly unlikely to have been questioned among working men during the cloth-cap era of industrial organization, or among the labourers, small farmers or husbandmen, cottagers and paupers, who accounted for the majority of the population in pre-industrial England. For all of these the 3AI had an average of between a quarter and a third from the earliest period we know of until the death of Queen Victoria, fluctuating somewhat from time to time. Chances of one in three or less, it is suggested, can sensibly be disregarded.

'Did the Workers Save for Old Age in Victorian and Edwardian Britain?' is the title of a recent discussion of the topic, which concludes that the working-class made little or no provision for the future out of their meagre resources other than to pay out a few pennies a week for their funerals. A survey of the elderly poor in London made in 1930 shows that at most 10 per cent of those over 65 had incomings of any kind, apart from such wages as they still received, together with their old age pensions and the proceeds of letting rooms in their houses. The total of these extra earnings was tiny, and by no means all of it can have come from savings. A very little may have been money offered to them by their children.[14] If their handling of what funds they did have at their disposal is an indication of their willingness to discount becoming old, they must have done so.

It would not be surprising to find something of this attitude surviving into our own time, one more example of the lag in awareness of what has happened to society concerning ageing. A recent piece of unpublished research shows that those in classes 3, 4 and 5 of the Registrar-General's classification, that is, the majority of the population who are less well-off, received in 1980 only about a pound a week when in retirement from unearned income other than pensions.

It has to be said that for the population as a whole investment income has been of some importance since the 1970s. Eight to 12 per cent of the incomings of those over 60 were from this source in 1971 and 15 to 17 per cent in 1989.[15] But savings on this scale cannot be expected of the poorest and ignoring the possibility of becoming old is more easily done when the people concerned are in no position to do anything effective to provide for a Third Age. They look to collective welfare for support if they should survive after the end of their working lives. We shall see in Chapter 9 that investigations of the history of welfare in our country suggest that they have not looked entirely in vain, even during the infamous era of the workhouse. Those old and past work among the majority of the population in our country and the USA have always been in something of a privileged position in relation to the dispensing of welfare funds, even if all they could ever expect to get was a bare livelihood. The industrious and prudent among them, those who possessed the middle-class virtues which middle-class observers have always singled out for praise, did what they could to provide against the possibility of becoming old. As life proceeded towards that eventuality, all of them may have suffered anxiety about having to go on welfare, or enter the workhouse.

This was a fear with less of a basis in fact than we might expect, for research has shown that the picture of old people being hauled off to the workhouse in Victorian times has been rather overdrawn. They were usually relieved at home.[16] Moreover a counter-current has been detected in attitudes towards becoming old. There was undoubtedly a sense of relief at having reached an age when a claim to public support was recognized as legitimate. A reliable policy of relief for the old must encourage the discounting of the possibility of growing old at all. It would not be surprising if an attitude of letting old age look after itself should have become embedded in the traditional view of the world held by most of the indigent population.

THE EMERGENCE OF THE THIRD AGE; SOCIAL STRUCTURAL ISSUES

The demographic argument for the emergence of the Third Age as a historical novelty in the first half of the twentieth century, and its establishment in the social structure of a number of nations in the last quarter of that century, can be regarded as completed by the figures in Tables 6.3 and 6.4. It will be seen from Table 6.4 that this demographic development has been fairly uniform in the economically advanced areas of the world, and that the United Kingdom passed the level of a male 3AI of .50 in step with the other countries in the West.

We have laid it down, however, that for the Third Age to establish itself demographically in a nation, a Third Age indicator of .5 and above for males is not of itself sufficient. If that were so, a considerable number of countries would now be demographically qualified, since so many have an expectation of life at birth which implies that their males have an indicator of the required value, but they fail to satisfy the second criterion of a quarter of the population over 25 being over the age of 60. As we have shown, the United Kingdom had qualified in both senses the 1950s, but

Table 6.4   Third Age Indicators: Various countries (males)

Sweden	1891–1900	.499	France	1951	.545
New Zealand	1901	.515	United Kingdom	1951	.532
Norway	1910*	.539	Hungary	1960*	.592
Denmark	1921*	.595	West Germany	1960*	.572
Australia	1921	.505	Sri Lanka	1960*	.516
Netherlands	1931*	.587	Japan	1960	.561
Italy	1931	.512	Mexico	1960*	.516
Spain	1941	.525	Colombia	1960*	.512
United States	1950	.541	China	1982*	.601

Source: Calculated from Cambridge Group files and from Preston, Keyfitz and Schoen (see Table 5.2).
* First available record.

Sweden, though it reached a 3AI of virtually .5 in 1900, as we can see from table 6.4, did not qualify on the proportionate count until later, during the 1950s. In fact, no Western nation can be assumed to have had the requisite numbers of older people until the 1930s or 1940s, although fertility was beginning to fall fast in some of them.[17] It is very interesting to see developing countries like Sri Lanka, Mexico, Colombia and even China on this list. None has yet qualified on the proportional criterion, however.

If the criterion of the female 3AI had been at issue, rather than the male, the threshold would have been passed forty or fifty years before. In the United Kingdom the statistic for women had reached .517 by 1911, and .557 in Sweden a decade earlier. The relationship of men to women in this matter is one of a group of rather complex social structural issues about the Third Age which have still to be considered, though this can be done here only in a cursory fashion.

It still seems natural to assume that when someone joins the Second Age and starts working, most of the rest of life will be spent in the labour force, with a short interlude of retirement coming afterwards, if the person survives for long enough. But radical change is coming about in this aspect of the life course. Virtually everybody lives through what are called the working ages and beyond, as we have seen, but they leave the labour force earlier and earlier and live longer and longer after that. Here we take the example of men and consider the balance of work and retirement in their experience.

If all Englishmen actually quitted their jobs at the 'official' British age of retirement of 65, it would mean that their lifetime after work would begin to approach time left to be in work at about the fiftieth birthday. Although the age of leaving the labour force had been falling for some time previously, a little more than two-thirds of men were still on the job during their early sixties in the year 1981. But by 1990 the figure had fallen to a half and is still going down quite rapidly. This means that in the present decade a man who is going to leave the workforce at age 55, shall we say, will reach the point at which work-time to come equals retirement-time by his 33rd birthday. The position is different for women, but the tendency is the same. They will probably soon spend as much of their adult life after work as they do in work, those of them, that is to say, who have jobs throughout the Second Age. Things will no doubt change somewhat for women in Britain after their pension age goes up, but it is certainly possible that the point will be reached in the earlier 2000s when time in work is equal to or even less than time after work for all adults.

This very recent, but rather problematic, extension of the Third Age backwards so to speak, so as to include younger and younger people, is a highly significant development for contemporary experience over the life course. The change, however, less pronounced in Britain than in any other European country except Sweden, which in 1988 had 64 per cent of males still at work in their early sixties. In Germany the figure was half of that, in France it was 25 per cent: in the Netherlands it was as low as 15 per cent, and had come down by no less than four-fifths since 1965. Our country has been in an intermediate position as to the rate of reduction in later-age employment for men, and this fall has not been as much offset by the growth in the rate for women as in most other countries for which comparisons have been made. Nineteen per cent of women were at work in the United Kingdom between ages 60 and 64 in 1988, the second largest group in Europe, but this figure had grown by only a quarter since 1965, the lowest European rate of increase.

The reasons for this general exit from Second Age employment in progress in the West are a subject in themselves. A crucial factor is quite simply a shortage of jobs, for men at least. The growth for women has been largely in part-time employment.[18] There is no reason to expect these tendencies will stay as they are and official retirement ages may well be extensively revised, upwards. But it looks as if the actual point in life when working is given over may stay the same or continue to fall in spite of pension-age changes. The awkward intermediate period – not in work but not retired – may thus get even longer. In France they are beginning to think that this tendency is undermining the division of the life course itself.

The Third Age has come to stay, and covers a considerable and increasing part of everyone's lifetime experience in Western countries. We have already seen that when the children now being born reach their Third Age, that phase of life could last so long and include so many persons that over two-fifths of all adults may be involved in it. All of which drives home the point that it is becoming more and more realistic for every individual to make plans for the Third Age at the outset of the Second.

NATIONAL WEALTH AND THE THIRD AGE

The fact that the majority of those in the Third Age are female, and the further fact that control of economic resources has been and for the most part still is in the hands of males raises the rather difficult question of how an individual can reserve the peak of individual achievement to the period after job and family have ceased to be all-demanding. There is clearly no point in being doctrinaire here. Few, or very few, of the large number of British wives, widows and spinsters as we still quaintly call them who since the 1950s have lived long enough after 25 to satisfy the requirements laid down for the Third Age have been in a position to live a Third Age as it is conceived of in this book. Leisure, independence and education (this is especially so in Britain), have been lacking, as well as money, for both the genders. It could well be said that the principles and ideas of Third Age living are a mockery for the poorer old, who have been and lamentably still are, so large a proportion of those in retirement. The accusation that the idea of the Third Age belongs entirely with the middle classes has inevitably been made. There are political leaders on the left in the United Kingdom who have rejected the name and the notion out of hand.

But in setting out the conditions permitting and accompanying the emergence of the Third Age into a national social structure, we are not required to survey the whole of that structure, in our own country or in any other. Least of all can we be expected to produce a set of expedients which might get rid of class divisions. Nor can we possibly take into account every social circumstance, influence and consequence. The issues of health and fitness, for example, cannot concern us here in spite of the fact that the sick and disabled can scarcely expect to live a fulfilled life in the Third Age. We should certainly be willing to modulate the figures we have used in the discussion of longevity to take life expectation without disability into account, and face the formidable difficulty of allowing for the fact that few forms of disability entirely inhibit Third Age living. This will be done in due course, but at present it doesn't seem possible to go further in such directions.

Nevertheless, there is a set of considerations about the extraordinary development which I have called the emergence of the Third Age, extraordinary because unexpected and unprecedented although ineluctable, considerations which are so important that we shall have to spend a page or two on their discussion. They have to do not only with the resources necessary for an individual to live in the Third Age but also with the wealth required for a whole nation to maintain its retired citizens at a level which would provide these resources for them. The national wealth as a whole must be adequate to finance the necessary incomes, by whatever means (pensions, public and private, investments, savings and so on) and the arrangements for the purpose must be in place and in operation. How all this can best be secured will concern us in Chapter 12.

The proposition is that there now exists a number of countries whose wealth is in fact large enough and widely enough distributed to ensure that those in retirement do benefit to the required degree. Britain is one of those nations, but not at all well placed among them, as will appear when we see our country in relation to its compeers. If we are prepared to set up one more arbitrary standard, this time for the purpose of justifying the financial proposition just put forward, the following is suggested. A gross national product of at least 10 000 US dollars per head of the nation's population at the values prevalent in the early 1990s[19] must be available for the Third Age to be a social reality in those countries demographically qualified. At this level of wealth, it is suggested, it should be possible to provide for fairly comfortable living standards in the Third Age for a critical mass of persons. By this is meant a big enough community of them for the society as a whole to modify its structure in order to accommodate their weight and influence.

For this to work, of course, resources have to be distributed in such a way that those in later life have a share sufficient for Third Age living. The just allocation of wealth between age groups in Britain – indeed in all industrial countries – is one of the most urgent of the issues which face us. There is disturbing evidence that older people are more unequal among themselves in their command of resources than those in other age groups, and even more challenging indications that the rich among the elderly may have become so at the expense of their juniors as well as of their age-mates, among other reasons because of the way in which the welfare state has operated over the last thirty years.[20] In spite of all such considerations the nations listed in Table 6.5 can be suggested as being in a position to support a community of those in the Third Age at the present time. Each now has a 3AI for males well above .5 and a proportion of adults over the age of 60 above a quarter and mostly more like a third.

In the 17 nations in Table 6.5, most of which have more than three times the estimated resources per head general for the population of the world, and some of which have five or six times that amount, the material resources now exist for Third Age living. The range in terms of gross national product per head is very considerable. Switzerland is rated at $27 500 and New Zealand at $10 000. It is a bold assumption that these resources are in reality distributed evenly enough between age groups and classes for the purpose, and that medical, educational and cultural goods are similarly available to their citizens demographically definable as currently in the Third Age. Perhaps therefore even this short list of nations qualifying under all our heads is still too long.

Every one of these countries is in the Western or Northern European area, or is descended from nations in that area, with the single exception of Japan. Over a quarter of them have English as the native language and a considerably higher proportion of their combined populations is British-descended. All of the so-called Anglo-Saxon societies belong within the circle, in fact, but it is notable that, except for Canada, those within the British Commonwealth occupy the lowest positions, and New Zealand might be called marginal.[21] None is in Central or Eastern Europe and the gap is wide. Hungary and what was Yugoslavia had the highest figure in these areas in 1988, at some $2500. A little group of oil-rich countries

Table 6.5   Countries satisfying both the demographic and the wealth criteria for the Third Age and assumed to satisfy those for access to education over the life course, and for cultural development

---

Country (in order of Gross national Product per capita, 1988, minimum $10 000)

---

1. Switzerland	10. France
2. Japan	11. Austria
3. Norway	12. Netherlands
4. USA	13. Belgium
5. Sweden	14. Italy
6. Finland	15. United Kingdom
7. Germany	16. Australia
8. Denmark	17. New Zealand
9. Canada	

Source: World Bank, *World Development Report*, 1990.

qualify as to wealth; Kuwait, Saudi Arabia and so on. None of them, however, satisfies the second of our demographic conditions, a sufficiency of elderly persons in the adult population, a condition which as we have said excludes so many other possible candidates which have the required 3AI, quite apart from the level of their resources.

Nevertheless the suggested omission of nations on grounds of insufficient wealth is obviously unsatisfactory, and poses the most difficult of the questions which have to be left open in this first attempt at a series of knotty problems. Apart from the Central and Eastern European nations which have grown in number so quickly since 1989, there is Russia itself. All of these societies belong with the high civilisation of the Europeans, as do several others omitted in this way, including Greece, Spain, Portugal and Ireland. The conditions laid down here mean that we are able to make no firm judgement on the situation of those of the citizens of these nations who have relinquished the Second Age but have yet to reach the Fourth. The temptation for an Englishman, of course, is to bend the rules for the European names on the list, and include them with their neighbours, leaving the others for later decision. There are advantages, all the same, in the suspension of judgement on particular topics at so early a stage in the appreciation of so novel a set of problems. We should not try to make up our minds too soon.

The same evasive response has at present to be made to an enquiry such as this. Since China and Russia are so large, large enough to have tens of millions, even for the Chinese not far short of two hundred millions, of individuals over sixty years old, might it not be granted that Third Age living is a characteristic of a considerable number of their citizens, especially those in the most favoured social positions, if not a characteristic of those nations as wholes? If an affirmative is given here for the Chinese example, the implication would be that income inequality is indeed so great there that privileged minorities can and do live lives inaccessible to other Chinese people. This would certainly seem now to be possible in spite of its running counter to the official ideology. What applies to China applies to any nation despotically and oligarchically controlled. It could be significant that there are numbers of Chinese Universities of Old Age, since the creation of Universities of the Third Age might be seen as a significant sign of the transformation of the social structure by the emergence of the Third Age. Nevertheless their presence in a nation, even in a nation which did have the required resources, emphatically cannot of itself be a guarantee that Third Age living is a possibility for all the people within it capable of taking advantage of the opportunities. And a Western democrat and egalitarian is disposed to insist that free institutions are an indispensable qualification.

In view of all these exceptions, cautions and uncertainties it could be urged that the Third Age is so imprecise apart from its demography and leaves so many people and populations in an equivocal position that the concept itself is of little practical use. But those who follow this line of criticism have to face the challenge of specifying what other sets of considerations could be used to group more adequately the changes which are going forward. Imprecision and uncertainty are what has to be expected during the time which it will take before the social and cultural landscape settles down after the seismic disturbance caused by the secular shift in ageing.

THE THIRD AGE AND TRADITIONAL ELITES

There are Universities of the Third Age in Poland and in others among the European countries which we have decided to leave in uncertainty for the present in relation to our topic. Indeed institutions of this kind could presumably have existed in any European country at any time, at least during the last four or five hundred years, and no doubt in countries outside Europe too.

This must have been so because all these societies have been marked by cultivated, rich, leisurely élite groups, a proportion of whose members could well have satisfied the first, the survival condition for the Third Age. In England in Shakespeare's day, for example, there might have been some 3500 to 5000 men in the élite whose calendar age was in the mid-twenties and who could expect, whether they had known anything about such things, to live into their seventies. But this amounts to no more at most than one in 700 of the then population of just over four million, making some allowance for a few women who shared the intellectual culture of their husbands and fathers.[22] Numbers and proportions of this kind cannot be considered as showing forth the Third Age as we have been thinking of it. The concept itself was unknown in Shakespeare's lifetime, and the 3AI was well below .5 for men in general, though it had reached a notably high point of .348 in the half decade 1591–5 when *A Midsummer Night's Dream* and the *Sonnets* are thought to have been composed.

The decision to exclude these possible Third Age societies of the past disposes of all other brilliant minorities belonging to historic societies; in eighteenth-century France; in fifteenth-century Italy; in the Athens of the fourth and fifth centuries BC; in the Chinese mandarinate at any of its periods of florescence. Though it does little to help us decide the cases of contemporary Spain, Greece, Poland and the others, qualified on demographic but not so far on economic grounds, such an exercise is useful in other ways. It makes clear that yet a further criterion has to be added in arriving at judgements about the emergence of the Third Age, a criterion of cultural accomplishment, not susceptible to any sort of numerical standard measurement, however arbitrarily decided. What are we to make, for example, of the fact that at least three quarters of elderly people in China today have to be classed as illiterate, or semi-literate, though learning fast?

Such circumstances force us to recognize yet again that the Third Age is quintessentially of the present and of the future, the future in which we may hope that wealth and resources, resources of the intangible cultural kind, as well as the material, will grow everywhere to a sufficient extent, and be fairly enough shared out, to make possible a Third Age for all those whose life situation qualifies them for it. This intensifies the challenge to those in later life who are citizens of countries already fully equipped for the Third Age on the criteria set out. They have to recognize that they may be setting precedents of great importance. Being in the Third Age in the 1990s is a weighty matter as well as a novelty, and, for nearly all of us, a potentially refreshing and enjoyable experience.

7 Hostile and Demeaning Descriptions of the Elderly

There is something of the same hesitation about attaching a name to old people and to the condition of being elderly as there is in talking about death. Circumlocutions are used and absurdly optimistic phrases are introduced to disguise with singular ineffectiveness the unpalatable facts. Such trepidation about direct references is closely allied – the psychologists tell us – with humour. Jokes about death itself are uncommon, and inevitably black, but jokes about dead bodies are quite frequent and acceptable. It is difficult to refer to a corpse, or even a coffin, meeting with an accident without raising a laugh. Unseemly as this conduct may be it is very widespread with deep historical roots, though the dead cannot be injured by it. But the nervous humour which attaches to the old wounds them and degrades the elderly condition. Indeed it harms all of us, since we shall all become old one day.

There are historical reasons why we should have no one neutral and satisfactory term for being old, and why it should have been necessary to adopt anonymous numerical expressions in its place – the Third Age and the Fourth Age. 'Old Age' is entirely tendentious and should disappear as a term except where no other inclusive word will do. But the sad fact may be that the suggested new usages would not last for very long, even it they were universally adopted. For one thing we seem to have no spontaneous disposition to distinguish the varying conditions of people in later life one from another. 'Aged' is used differently for everyone in later life – from the gruesome bent figures pictured on road signs in England giving warning of 'Homes for the Aged Ahead' to the entire population of those in retirement; comprising golfers, cyclists, swimmers, writers, administrators, advisers, artists, the whole inclusive lot. Moreover, terms of age and ageing are perpetually subject to debasement. They are like the notices on buildings such as 'Ladies', 'Gentlemen', and 'Toilet', which have been responsible for degrading expressions of high status and delicacy to the level which was once called smut, and for leading to the use of such objectionable euphemisms as 'Comfort Station' or 'Bucks and Does' on shithouse doors. In Athens the indicator for men is a masculine boot. The Third Age may well not continue in the English-speaking countries as a complimentary or even a neutral description. Tarnishment may come to affect the term. In France, whence the title came, *Le Troisième Age* has already become a derogatory expression, to be avoided as much as possible.[1]

All this may seem natural enough, and understandable in a world where living languages are perpetually in flux, and where everyone, and especially the advertisers, who are the wordsmiths and word manipulators, the word falsifiers of our day, have such a clear interest in exploiting associations, meanings and double meanings. But in the case of age and ageing throughout the twentieth century, something else may have been at issue – animosity. Hostility to the condition of being or becoming old is certainly discernible. Ageism as a specifically social pathology has been identified as a characteristic of late-twentieth-century society in advanced countries along with sexism and racism. Ageism, certainly in Britain, is particularly pronounced and deleterious in matters of employment.

The logic of age is so different from that of sex or race, however, that there are disadvantages in the use of a term to describe prejudice associated with the old as at all closely similar to the prejudice associated with sex or ethnic origin. To dislike the old is hatred of the self, rejection of what you yourself must inevitably become. Eric Midwinter has pointed out that this attitude persists even after late life has arrived. 'Older people', he asserts, 'are as prone to ageism as everyone else' and adds that this might be expected, since 'they are the products, like the rest of use, of an ageing ambience' where 'the public scarcely recognizes that ageism exists' and there is hardly any legal protection against its effects.[2] We have seen how difficult it is to look forward to the Third Age from the First or Second, and it may be that this prevents people from recognizing that in despising the old they are despising not only others but also themselves. The psychology of ageing cannot for this reason be quite the same as that of despising those of different physiognomy and colour.

There are signs that a hardening of attitudes towards the elderly has been reinforced and perpetuated over the last three or four generations by the very developments which intensifying demographic change brought with it, in our country, in the USA and perhaps in other countries too. The final decades of the nineteenth century and the initial decades of the twentieth were years when inflexible retirement was instituted in the lives of officials, and still is maintained in Britain. Compulsory retirement at 65 was introduced into the Civil Service in 1890 and 1898 and 'was encouraged, if generally not mandatory, in some occupational schemes for white collar workers'.[3]

SIR WILLIAM OSLER, AGEISM AND GERONTICIDE AMONG THE DOCTORS

This was an invitation, in a way, to take up the attitude we have associated with the Third Age, but it was evidently not proffered in any realistic or benevolent sense. For it was at the height of this development, in 1905, that Professor William Osler, a Canadian by origin, made his notorious allusion in a lecture to 'the comparative uselessness of people over forty and the entire dispensability of people over sixty'. At 61, he declared, in what he later insisted was nothing more than a playful allusion to a satirical novel by Anthony Trollope, 'a peaceful departure by chloroform might be what was wanted by everyone'.[4] Whatever his intentions, literary or otherwise, the great medical man had got Trollope wrong. Sixty-eight was the birthday before which in the fictional account anyone 'shall have departed'.

Professor Osler, later Sir William Osler, Baronet, was the most eminent physician of his generation in Britain, and perhaps in the United States as well. He expressed these sentiments of final hostility to those in later life in an address which he made on giving up his American appointment to take up the Regius Professorship of Medicine at Oxford. He called his disquisition 'The Fixed Period', a phrase which had in fact been used for the title of a novel published by Anthony Trollope in 1882. In this story everyone reaching the age of 67 was given a year in which to meditate and then extinguished by the injection of drugs. The body was to be burnt, an early piece of advocacy for cremation. All this was to take place in a magnificent institutional building which was the most notable feature of the imaginary island on which Trollope's story was set.[5] When his address was printed for printed for the second time, Osler apologized to old people in the preface to the collection which included it, and protested at being taken seriously on the killing-off of 61-year-olds. But he kept every word of his original spoken script, in spite of the worldwide protests the publication had given rise to, and obstinately repeated his assertion that 'the real work of life is done before the fortieth year', so that it would certainly be best if men were retired as 60. This was a judgement with which even his critics could apparently agree.

Eminent and influential as he was, Osler could not have represented the whole body of medical opinion in his day. Another highly reputed doctor gave a lecture in 1903, *On Longevity and Means for the Prolongation of Life* (Weber, 1919) which went through five editions. He took quite a different line and was free of the demeaning altitudes of the other medical authorities we have quoted. Moreover, Osler has probably been taken too seriously on the annihilation of sexagenarians,[6] and his sentiments and those of Anthony Trollope were certainly extreme even for their day and generation. But sporadic allusions to the desirability, or the necessity of ending the lives of those in their later years because they had become useless or 'in the way' have recurred in Western writings for a very long time. These were usually familial references in medieval or early modern times, black jokes put in the mouths of sons and grandsons about the deliberate homicide of fathers and grandfathers. In 1599 a play was acted which had a different message, 'an excellent comedy' according to the *Dictionary of National Biography* in which Philip Massinger is supposed by some to have had a hand. It concerned the revival by a head of State of an old law by which women were to be done to death at age 60 and men at age 80. This could have been Trollope's source.[7] John Aubrey, the eccentric antiquary, wrote in the 1680s of the 'Holy Mawle' supposed to have hung behind the church door: 'which when the father was seventy the son might fetch to knock his father on the head, as effete, and of no more use'. Aubrey calls this an old Somerset story: a mawle was a heavy hammer.

Nor are these ugly sentiments yet entirely absent from the minds of our contemporary doctors, or even of biologists. In 1981 one of the best-known and most humane of biologists, Sir Peter Medawar, republished a pronouncement originally made in 1946:

> In forty years' time we are to be the victims of at least a numerical tyranny of greybeards.... The problem of doing something about old age becomes slowly but progressively more urgent. Something must be done, if it is not to be said that killing people painlessly at the age of seventy is, after all, a *real* kindness.

In May 1987, just after Medawar's forty-year interval had elapsed, Dr Donald Gould, a prominent medical journalist, evidently writing with an ironic purpose not dissimilar to Osler's, commended the killing-off of all over the age of 75. Though he thought this a bit too strong to be adopted, he published this sentiment in a British journal of scientific popularization with considerable standing, even among scientists. The cartoon which accompanied his *jeu d'esprit* carried the implication that everyone should be despatched at retirement. At 65? 60? 55?

It has already been said that it is inappropriate to regard ageism as interchangeable with sexism or racism. But someone who like myself has passed both his sixty-first, his seventieth and his seventy-fifth birthday can perhaps be forgiven for asking what would happen if anyone so much as ventured to refer in passing to a holocaust of all black people in conversation with such persons as Osler, Medawar or Gould, let alone suggest that they print and publish remarks to this effect. Nevertheless we should not take sentiments such as these to be deliberately or realistically intended. The massacre of the innocent old, it seems to me, occupies a position in the literary, scholarly, medical and scientific outlook somewhat similar to the position of cannibalism. Instances of it may have occurred in the past but it is exceedingly difficult to be certain about time, place and circumstance. I myself vaguely recall reading a record in an English parish register of an old man left outside a house to die, a reference which unfortunately I cannot recover. Which leaves me questioning whether it was seen only in my imagination.

The 'primitive' people discovered and studied by anthropologists may actually carry out geronticide as we may call it, or confess to doing so. But many, perhaps most of the occurrences reported or proposals made, seem, like John Aubrey's story, to be whimsical hyperbole, or guilty fantasies, allied to sensationalism, especially in the medical world. A wish, of which they subsequently may be ashamed, brings about the half-humorous proposal of an Osler or a Gould and may under suitable conditions give rise to reports of geronticide actually taking place. Such instances are seized on by writers like Simone de Beauvoir, using as they do mostly literary evidence.[8] This occurs because such fantasies are very widespread. Every strongly-held principle, even that of the absolute sanctity of human life, is accompanied in imagination by its negation. Instances of such negation, therefore, may perhaps confirm the existence of the principle rather than deny it. But this said, it cannot be without importance for the imposition of stereotypes of unproductive uselessness upon the elderly that Osler made his pronouncement when he did. His apparently authoritative declaration that everyone should be disposed of well before the age of three-score years and ten may have caused a worldwide controversy, but was not out of line with much medical opinion of his time and somewhat before it.

We must not get the impression that doctors were alone responsible for these stigmas, or that attitudes became uniformly and progressively unfavourable. Nevertheless there was a combination of influences present in Britain and other European countries as well as in the United States between the 1880s and the 1920s to encourage the retiring and retired elderly to accept as justifiable these derogatory descriptions of themselves. Such readiness on the part of those labelled to accept the insults written on the labels is a phenomenon familiar to those who study stereotyping.

AGEING AS A DISEASE

Added to this was a waning of interest in the ageing process and a relative neglect of investigation of the particular illness of elderly persons, a neglect which persisted until after the middle of the twentieth century. A strange combination here, the medical profession taking justifiable pride in the lengthening of life, which many of them still seemed to believe was the sole cause of the growth of the proportion of the old in the population, yet a relative indifference to old persons as patients. In France the medical attitudes, especially the failing of interest in research, went along with that deep disquiet about the ageing of the population, in the compositional sense which has already been noticed.[9] What wonder, we may ask, that medical opinion with all its enormous influence in this field on general opinion, and on government, has done so little even now to dispel the confusion and unrealism with which ageing is still surrounded.

The classification of their condition as a disease was undoubtedly damaging to the old. This diagnosis is a whole subject in itself and has been excellently described in a book by Carole Haber.[10] Dissections of the bodies of those dying at advanced ages began to convince nineteenth- and early twentieth-century doctors that the process of ageing itself induced irreversible pathological conditions which made a whole series of illnesses inevitable. All the symptoms shown after what was still called the Great Climacteric ushering in the final phase tended to be regarded as manifestations, at first mild but inevitably to become serious, of that appalling affliction, senile dementia – especially Alzheimer's Disease.

In spite of the signal advances made in the biology of ageing in the present generation, this fateful misdiagnosis continued up until quite recently, if remarks such as the following are correctly held to imply such an error. In April 1987 a very prominent British geriatrician said at a research symposium: 'Translating "senile dementia" into Alzheimer's Disease has undoubtedly produced support for research....If dementia had not been for so many years categorized as normal ageing, the relevant research might have started decades ago.'[11] It may be unfair to describe diagnostic errors as instances of stereotyping, since Alzheimer's disease is notoriously difficult to identify. But it is of great significance to us that the mistake induced in doctors a disposition to look on all or most of the age-related afflictions of their older patients as progressive and irreversible. Their condition and the brevity of their lives to come scarcely warranted research and treatment was problematic. This encouraged the view that the old must be written off as useless. All that they could do was to disengage from their responsibilities and accept the isolation which thus must come about.

It is no wonder that in the 1960s the first distinguishable social, as distinct from physiological, theory of ageing, the disengagement theory, interpreted these medical notions as it did. These physical 'symptoms' confirmed the breakdown in the relationships of older people, which the disengagement theory held to be inevitable, a further contribution to the process of hostile stereotyping. Disengagement theory has now been to a large extent abandoned as anything like a complete or accurate account of the ageing development and now takes its place as part of a much more inclusive set of propositions about the social process of growing old.[12]

The classification of ageing amongst those afflictions which doctors began to name as epidemiologies in the late nineteenth century is still maintained, however. Ageing was, and is, placed alongside malign conditions like tuberculosis, the distribution of which in a population by age, sex, region and so on has to be so carefully determined in order to identify possible causes. The description of ageing as a disease has since been repudiated so doctors protest. The epidemiology of ageing, they insist, refers simply to its distribution as a condition with no implication of its being a disease. But it is hard to see how it makes sense to examine the distribution of ageing with a view to identifying its causes. Ageing is not contagious, and it cannot, as we have seen, be brought about or fended off by geographical position or the physical environment. Epidemiology means illness in every other context and in non-medical usage. If the medical profession wishes to dissociate ageing from disease, this terminology will have to be abandoned. The retention of the 'epidemiology of ageing' as a medical expression must inevitably tend to sanction the demeaning stereotypes.

That the identification of age with disease should have become so common is quite manifest in what Carole Haber's medical writers actually declared, before and during the time when hostile descriptions of old people were so pronounced. One Bernard Van Oven, whose book appeared in London in 1853, had advised that

> it is the duty of all persons who have attained the climacteric [74 years old] to avoid excesses and undue exercise; to watch at all times for the insidious approach to disorders; never to reject any slight ailment, but to regard them as forerunners of more serious derangements; to seek to repair the most trifling irregularities of function and give rest at once to any organ of the body which shows debility or fatigue.

Charles Mercier published a work in 1890 in New York which described the retired middle class man in the following way.

The whole sphere of activities comprised in his business relations is altogether relinquished; the activities necessary for the rearing and maintenance of offspring have been long uncalled for, his daughters being married and his sons providing for themselves. There remains to him only the simple activities requisite for the immediate conservation of life, and after a time even these are imperfectly performed....No longer capable of conserving himself from the ordinary risks of everyday life, he must be carefully watched and tended to prevent some accidental circumstance from exterminating the feeble germ of life that still remains.

Two pieces of advice, we might declare from our own generation, exactly calculated to instil into those in the Third Age what they should never do, under any circumstances, even if not in the best of physical health. Worst of all, by 1904, some doctors had begun to think that it was pointless to treat their old patients at all. Dr J. F. Bishop contributed an article to an American journal in that year saying that 'it was not worthwhile to make any great sacrifice to go in search of health; it will do more harm than good'.[13]

Stigmas and stigmatization only persist if there are enduring reasons for their being acceptable to those who create, adopt or perpetuate them. In this instance the fear and rejection of the ending of life perhaps sufficiently explains the power of the images and their durability. We might go so far as to say that white hair is instinctively rejected as a symbol of death, mocked and denigrated so as to ensure that mortality is kept at a distance. This is particularly evident when white filaments first announce their presence among the black or brown. Going grey, or growing white, is of such interest to everyone at all ages, and to a large section of the cosmetics industry, that it is well worth hearing what a prominent scientific authority has to say about the subject and its limitations as a mark of growing old. Leonard Hayflick writes:

Graying of the hair is probably the most conspicuous sign of ageing but it is by no means universal nor does it occur at the same time in all people. It is caused by the loss of melanin-producing cells and the consequent loss of melanin. Melanin, produced by cells in the hair bulb (the tiny collection of cells in the skin from which the nonliving strand of hair grows), is a pigment that gives color to the hair and skin. Graying usually begins at the temples, then extends upwards to the top of the scalp. Axillary hair graying is common in men and rare in women.

In over fifty measurements of age changes one group of researchers found that graying of scalp hair was the most reliable indicator of the aging process. Yet, it only correlated about 65 per cent with old age; 35 per cent of older people are not gray, or do not become gray, until they are very old.[14]

Considering the question of the greying of hair reminds us again of the necessity of facing our fears of growing old, lest we find ourselves content to take descriptions of the final years or months of decrepitude, the Fourth Age in the theory we have adopted, as covering the permanent condition of all elderly people. It was the same unwillingness to distinguish a Fourth Age from a Third Age for the stereotyping of the elderly which was so telling in the attitude of early-twentieth-century medical writers.

It may be thought that too much is here being made of medical opinion, but it must be remembered how influential in such matters doctors and medical experts always are and ever have been. In all issues to do with later life, governments, legislatures, municipalities, civil servants, administrators of firms, societies and institutions defer to doctors. More important is the fact that old people get their own opinions of themselves, their capacities and their value, to a considerable extent from what they are told in the consulting room or the hospital.

INSURANCE AND STEREOTYPES OF OLD PEOPLE

Of all businessmen, those who are responsible for insurance are most likely to be under medical influence. The beginnings of widespread insurance against invalidity are also to be dated during the years we are reviewing, associated as this was seen to be with becoming old and quitting work.[15] Insurance of this kind rapidly became incorporated into institutions, often national institutions, and into their bureaucracies, along with retirement. Set attitudes and established diagnosis became part of these inflexible structures and etched in the stereotypes. Hence ageing, and its now inevitable concomitant retirement, were indeed regarded as withdrawal into the Fourth Age, not as taking up the Third. This extraordinary and unrealistic assumption is certainly still alive today.

It is not yet known how far the presumption that entering the later phase of the life course inevitably meant bodily decay and uselessness was inherited from the past, a traditional attitude particularly powerful at this juncture. It is clear, however, that by the time working people lost or gave up their jobs in the later nineteenth or early twentieth centuries they were frequently in ill-health and to varying degrees disabled, often no doubt because of long years spent at debilitating tasks under bad conditions.

Such circumstances were entirely consonant with the venerable model of the process of senescence, which supposed that each person began life with a finite store of energy that progressively ran down as years passed. The sum of vital energy could be prematurely exhausted by the bodily insults of a hard life of toil and the privations of poverty. Individuals, especially labouring men, could be convincingly described as old before their time.

Early trade unionists certainly regarded working life as consuming a man's energy and health, leaving him in desperate need of rest and inactivity, since he had been make fit for nothing else. The conviction, not always well-founded, apparently held by younger workers that they themselves had better chances of getting or retaining a job, or of being promoted, if their seniors could be induced to retire must be taken into account in judging the popularity of those views. However this may be, the outcome was the conviction that quitting work meant admitting debility and welcoming restful inactivity along with a degree of self-indulgence the deleterious consequences of which were entirely unsuspected. Women were scarcely in the picture and the possibility that an active life, men and women working at their own dispose on what interested them, for the sake of their well-being and their health, was evidently difficult to imagine at that time. In this sense it could be claimed that the working man genuinely tended to pass directly into the Fourth Age after finishing work, and a large number of the elderly poor certainly were in a physically wretched condition in Britain in 1900. Matters cannot have been improved by the dispensing of free tobacco as a comfort to the dependent old, a practice which can be traced at least as far back as the early 1800s.

There is ample evidence of the poor biological condition of older working people in the literature put out by those who campaigned for old age pensions, and who finally succeeded with the Act of 1908. Such propaganda – and this is unfortunately typical of movements in defence of the old – had the unintended effect of focusing almost exclusively upon their disabilities and helplessness. The healthy and efficient of a similar calendar age, who were likely to be in work and not in want, were overlooked, as was the social value and personal worth of the infirm themselves. In this way the stereotypes were confirmed and perpetuated, just as they are confirmed and perpetuated nowadays by the necessary preoccupation of social administrators, social workers and even social investigators with the dependency, degradation and decrepitude of their subjects. Even such privileges as senior citizens' railway passes 'may serve only to build negative stereotypes, for example that all the elderly are needy'.[16]

The professional and middle-class elderly, those who were so insistently urged by Osler to retire in order to make progress possible in such activities as medicine, scarcely conformed to these descriptions. But if there were reasons in the organization of professional productive and business activities in the market, national and international, for wanting to get them out of the way, and consequently an inclination to reject evidence as to their continuing capacity and possible profitability, they were unlikely to be regarded as counter-examples. It is understandable how it was that the unfavourable stereotypes could have become so ingrained, so difficult to eradicate, even in our own day and even among those responsible for policy.[17]

The continuing existence, even the intensification of the stereotyping of those in later life at the very time of the emergence of the Third Age and its final establishment in the British social structure is an outstanding example of what has been called social opacity.[18] These were the years when the principled study of ageing began its career among scientists, doctors, and finally, sociologists and historical sociologists.[19] During the 1950s and 1960s there was a concerted effort in Britain to correct prevailing assumptions about the capacity of older workers to carry on a job, not simply up to the customary age of retirement but beyond. Unemployment was low and there was a need to retain skilled and experienced workers to maintain production, or even to bring them back from retirement if possible. But the attempt to persuade government, employers and trade unionists to call upon the seniors did not succeed. Immigration of workers from the Caribbean was preferred.

It must not be thought that the study of ageing was at this, or at any time, a central or popular subject for social research, especially in universities. Gerontology remains an unpopular pursuit even now, low in status and underfunded in Britain, a discouraging example of how little social studies relate themselves to social change. It is repeatedly asserted that among doctors specialization in the afflictions of the old carries little prestige and so presumably fails to attract the ablest and most ambitious. Such knowledge as was gained when the older worker was in demand and the study of ageing being to some extent encouraged, made no impact on those responsible for policy, in government or in business. Accordingly, when recession returned in the 1970s traditional attitudes were strong enough to ensure that 'natural wastage', which is the reduction and remodelling of the work force, should be carried out as far as possible by dispensing with older workers. This was seemingly accepted almost without question by government, employers and trade unionists.

Although the attempt at the retention and especially the recall of older workers did not succeed in the 1950s and 1960s, a fact which is itself significant for the outlook which now informs those in the Third Age, the new knowledge acquired at that time made an important contribution to the development of both geriatrics and gerontology. It is on these and more recent researches that the description of older people presented here has been based. It should not be supposed, then, that the continued presence of unfavourable stereotypes interrupted progress of this kind. Nor should it be thought that the economists and other social scientists including the demographers, men such as Maynard Keynes, William Beveridge or David Glass, were consistently gloomy, unrealistic or inclined to be prejudiced in view of the conspicuous ageing of the population, or dismissive of the potentialities of older people. This in spite of their conviction that the British population was due to decline. There was a whole range of views on those topics.

The persistence of stereotypes and their use in marginalizing the retired, and those regarded as due to be retired, if the organization of production so requires it, is not confined to Britain. Xavier Gaullier, the French authority on this development in his own country, portrays the dilemma of the *'preretraités'*, something like the equivalent of our prematurely retired, as being considerably worse than it is with us.[20] Other national societies among the ageing population of Europe can be supposed to display the same social opacity, the same unrealistic, patronizing and demeaning attitudes alongside a growing anxiety about what is beginning to be feared as a series of menacing 'problems'.

But it may well be that Britain has these symptoms in an extreme form. This is indicated in our political life, where those in the Third Age, in their millions of voting, participating citizens, are to all intents and purposes a nullity. The only study ever undertaken on older votes in a British General Election, and that a slender pamphlet, concluded as follows about what happened in the one held in June 1987. By polling day, the topic of age, which had occasionally come up in a superficial, desultory way in the course of the campaign, had virtually disappeared.

When it was mentioned it was seen almost completely as a problem, with the old person as little more than an object of welfare... a striking proof of this was the candidate's standard visit to a sheltered housing complex or a residential care home. This is where the old people live, it seemed to say, in spite of the fact that 96 per cent of older people reside in ordinary housing. The stereotype of elderly people...was depressingly outmoded and restricted. The creation of a life-enhancing constructive and dignified older age...was light years away from this campaign.[21]

WHAT WE STILL CANNOT SEE ABOUT OLDER PEOPLE

Let us list some of the outcomes of the still persisting incapacity to take account of what we could see and ought to see, but cannot see because of the rigidity of our thinking and the obliquity of our vision.

Our present attitude, actions and policies in perpetuating, even intensifying the cult of youth; our persistence with an educational system patently made obsolete by change; the crassness of our continued assumption that productive work is not to be expected from men of the calendar age of 65, 60 or 55, and at even lower ages for women – calendar ages which may be reduced at any point which suits the employment exigency of the moment; the bland assumption that those approaching that point in their lives where conventional retirement could be expected can be regarded as 'natural wastage'; the inordinately exaggerated attention paid to the effect of cold weather on the old, to any crime of violence which happens to be committed against them, to any charitable festivity which tries to cheer them up; the condescension to the 'golden oldies', or whatever we choose to call them, which is as much a sign of our incomprehension as being callous or indifferent.

The effects of the hyping-up by the media of crime against older people are particularly damaging, and virtually isolate great numbers of them within their barricaded homes, especially after dark. Evening meetings have become virtually impossible for those in the Third Age, to the singular detriment of their social lives, and this when 'those aged 16–30 are approximately six times more at risk of crime than those over sixty'.[22]

Politicians, intellectuals, not excluding historians and social scientists; demographers and statisticians; administrators, notably administrators of welfare; doctors and the medical community at large, and most evidently the journalists, all show symptoms of this social opacity and arrested development. They have yet to become properly aware of how far current notions of ageing, theirs as well as those of society at large, perpetuate the notions which were in place between 1880 and 1920. The retention of these stereotypes during the period of the emergence of the Third Age has to be pronounced a failure to perceive that which stereotyped thinking makes seemingly invisible.

The unfavourable images which we have been discussing are not the only reason why the issues on ageing are so difficult to bring into focus for our contemporaries. Nevertheless the perdurance of the stereotypes seems impossible to deny. Rarely enunciated, often unacknowledged, usually repudiated on challenge, they continue to distort our outlook. How long will it be before we in Britain become properly aware of the emergence of the Third Age into the fast-fading twentieth century?

8 The Insufficiency of the Family Group – in the Past and in the Present

On 1 March 1681 John Locke, the philosopher, wrote the following in his journal in his chamber at Christ Church, Oxford:

This day I saw one Alice George, a woman as she said of 108 years old at Alhallontide last [1 November 1680]. She lived in St Giles parish in Oxford and hath lived in and about Oxford since she was a young woman. She was born at Saltwyche [?Salwarp] in Worcestershire, her maiden name was Alice Guise. Her father lived to 83, her mother to 96 and her mother's mother to 111. When she was young she was fair-haired and neither far nor lean, but very slender in the waist, for her size she was to be reckoned rather amongst the tall than short woman. Her condition was but mean, and her maintenance her labour, and she said she was able to have reaped as much in a day as any man, and had as much wages. She was married at 30, and had 15 children, viz. 10 sons and 5 daughters baptized, besides 3 miscarriages. She has 3 sons still alive, her eldest John living the next door to her, 77 years old the 25th of this month. She goes upright though with a staff in one hand, but yet I saw her stoop twice without resting upon anything, taking up once a pot and another time her glove from the ground.

Her hearing is very good and her smelling so quick that as soon as she came near me she said I smelt very sweet, I having a pair of new gloves on that were not strong scented. Her eyes she complains of as failing her, since here last sickness, which was an ague that seized her about 2 years since and held her about a year. And yet she made a shift to thread a needle before us, though she seemed not to see the end of the thread very perfectly. She has as comely a face as ever I saw any old woman and age hath neither made her deformed nor decrepit.

The greatest part of her food now is bread and cheese or bread and butter and ale. Sack [sherry] revives her when she can get it. For flesh she cannot now eat, unless it be roasting pig which she loves. She had, she said, in her youth a good stomach [appetite] and ate what came in her way, oftener wanting victuals than a stomach. Her memory and understanding are perfectly good and quick, and amongst a great deal of discourse we had with her and stories she told she spoke not one idle or impertinent [irrelevant] word. Before this last ague she used to go to church constantly Sundays, Wednesdays and Saturdays. Since that she walks not beyond her little garden.

She has been ever since her being married, sometimes troubled with vapours [either flatulence or depression] and so is still, but never took any physic but once about 40 years since, viz. one pennyworth of jalap [aperient] which the apothecary out of kindness making a large penny-worth wrought more than sufficiently. She said she was 16 in '88 [1588], and went to Worcester to see Queen Elizabeth, but came an hour too late, which agrees with her account of her age.[1]

There are difficulties with this extraordinary account, difficulties which belong with the discussion of the oldest old which has already concerned us. Alice George, if aged 108 in November 1680, would have been born in November 1572, and this would have made her 16 in 1588. I can find no record of Queen Elizabeth going to Worcester in that year, though she did visit the city in 1575 when Alice George was assumedly 3 years old, not 16. To have fifteen successful pregnancies after 30 is exceedingly improbable, if not entirely out of the question, though she may have had one or more sets of twins and thus fewer pregnancies than parturitions. The mother's age looks suspicious and that of her grandmother frankly impossible, in view of what we have learned about length of life. It seems extremely unlikely that Alice George was 108 years old, or even a centenarian: all the other figures she gave may likewise have been exaggerated. Locke did not necessarily credit everything she told him and was perhaps aware of the tendency of the elderly to overstate their ages. This last fact is amply confirmed in parish registers, on tombstones and in the literary and other evidence we have from historical times.

But Locke was a shrewd and sceptical observer, and in spite of his error about Worcester we may accept his description of her appearance, condition and situation as likely to be reliable. This very remarkable excessively old woman as she was in 1681 will serve as our introduction to the life of elderly persons, ordinary English elderly persons, not abject paupers but very poor nevertheless, and to life as it was for them before the secular shift in ageing and before economic development. Standards were so low that Alice George as we see could not always rely on having enough to eat. People similar to her in condition comprised a large proportion of the population, a population seemingly irremovably fixed on the lower ageing plateau. A century was still to elapse before industrialization stirred, and two centuries before the secular shift took place. Alice George and John Locke provide us with a vantage-point, a platform in the past from which we can view a larger temporal landscape than that which surrounded us when we observed the emergence of the Third Age into the twentieth century.

In the remainder of this chapter and the following one we may imagine ourselves overhearing the conversation between the aged widow and the great intellectual. Affable, inquisitive and anxious to know everything he must have been, although perhaps a little distant and reserved and evidently not alone with her since 'we' and 'us' appear in the record. Our first subject is the family group and its perennial insufficiency to provide a place for elderly persons within its framework, in England anyway, and for persons as independent as Alice George. Independence, we shall find, was an unmistakable note in the behaviour of such persons, in the past as in the present. The second of our themes, not quite so evident with Alice George but important to her all the same, will be retirement and the parts played by society, on the one hand and kinsfolk on the other, in supporting elderly people. These we shall consider in Chapter 9. In Chapter 10 we shall come to the General Theory of the Third Age.

OLDER PEOPLE IN THE ENGLISH PAST

John Locke was in his forty-ninth year in March 1681, a natural philosopher, a scientist that is to say, and a medical practitioner as well as a philosopher in our sense of the word, a meticulous recorder and not easily bamboozled.[2] It is interesting to see him enquiring about the longevity of the forebears of Alice George, on the assumption presumably that length of life in an individual was an inherited characteristic, though we now suspect that inheritance explains only about a third of the disposition to survive to a particular age. In Locke's account of this ancient woman we have a document pretty well unique of its kind, if only because he evidently let her speak for herself. Even if she falsified her calendar age for his benefit, and the ages of her relatives, what she testified and he set down is a demonstration that irrespective of the conditions under which a population lives, some individuals are going to survive for a very long time. They will retain their faculties and go on looking hale and handsome, even if most of their contemporaries die much earlier than we do now and tend to lose their looks, their acuteness of vision and of smell sooner than she did, as well as their capacity for entirely independent movement and the ability to look after themselves. We are well aware of the great variation in all these respects which exists in our day within and between the social classes. But it is very interesting to have it confirmed among the labourers – for that is where Alice George must evidently be placed – three hundred years ago and more.

Expectation of life at birth for the cohort born between 1571 and 1575, to which Alice George claimed to belong, has been estimated at 38.2 years, and the chances of living to 100 at between one in 50 000 and one in 100 000.[3] Even if she had exaggerated her calendar age by as much as 15 years and was really in her early nineties, the chances were only about one in two or three hundred. Alice George can in no way be regarded as typical as to appearance, personal condition and capacity. We may look on her as indicating that the enormous variation between individuals in late and latest life existed three centuries ago. Locke's interest in her may not have been particularly objective and we must read even his description of this woman with a little caution. He could have looked on her as an example of the paradox that she had still not exhausted her original store of vital energy, and so have supposed he was investigated a miracle. William Harvey, the discoverer of the circulation of blood, showed no disposition to be critical when he dissected the body of the famous Thomas Parr, 'Old Parr', after his death in 1635 at the alleged age of 152.

However, we should be grateful for such evidence as has survived on individuals whose condition at advanced ages so clearly contradicts the accounts and expectations of the medical writers of the nineteenth and early twentieth centuries cited in our last chapter. Most delineations of advanced age, unfortunately, and most writings on the subject have depicted this condition much more in their terms than in those of Locke's account of his venerable Oxford widow. Seeking guidance from Christian revelation, as their authors were bound to do until recent generations, treatises on ageing often took the form of a commentary on Ecclesiastes 12: 1–6, part of what is called the wisdom literature of the ancient Hebrews.

We still remember some of these verses, even though we now so seldom hear them repeated in church, where, it will be noticed, Alice George attended three times a week:

> And the almond tree shall flourish, and the grasshopper shall be a burden, and desire shall fail, because man goeth to his long home, and the mourners go about the streets. Or ever the silver cord be loosed, or the golden bowl be broken, or the pitcher be broken at the fountain, or the wheel broken at the cistern.

It seems likely that, like their successors in Anthony Trollope's time, those who concerned themselves with old age in traditional England were prepared to accept the Fourth Age as a proper first general description of all those they classed as old. But we shall find when we discuss retirement that they recognised how much people differed as to the point in the life-course when the Fourth Age supervened, if indeed it ever occurred.

The Pourtract of Old Age, a book published in 1666 which has claims to be the first of its kind in the English language,[4] took the form of an analysis of this passage in the Scriptures. Such was the intellectual context, then, in which the conversation must have taken place. From our point of view, however, it is not only the vigour, alertness and comeliness of Alice George, which Locke found so surprising, that is of interest.[5] It is where she lived. She didn't live with her eldest son but apparently on her own next door to him. Although evidence is hard to come by, there are indications that this arrangement was not all that unusual at that time, or before, or after. It may even have been preferred, when favourable circumstances made it possible, as they certainly do on an enormous scale today.

OLDER PEOPLE LIVING WITH THEIR FAMILIES, THEN AND NOW

Nearly all our contemporary married or widowed elderly whose offspring have departed prefer to be on their own whenever they can, in their own homes. But they do everything possible to be within easy reach of their children, in the same town or street, even next door or in a granny flat. 'Intimacy at a distance' is the object, in a phrase happily coined by the prominent Austrian sociologist of ageing, Leopold Rosenmayr. Their children also prefer such an arrangement, to be close enough to go in and out whenever they wish, or whenever it is necessary to help their parents, but not to share the same domestic space. It has to be emphasised that it may cost money to maintain the desired position, independent premises for seniors and intimacy at a distance. Two things presumably follow from this. One is that we should expect such arrangements to be commoner with better-off people, though there is a complication here because even the more modestly placed in that society could have servants, and if they did they ceased strictly speaking to be solitaries. The other inference is that a really poor person who lived alone might have to be classed as a deserted solitary, compulsorily and miserably alone. This was manifestly not the situation of Mrs George.

The discussion of her having behaved in this way, which we tend to think of as typically 'modern', has to be wide in its scope for the following reasons. There is still a very deeply entrenched belief – or rather misbelief – that in the past older people lived universally in families, mostly their own families which they had themselves set up, but if not then in the families of their relatives, usually the families of their married children. Such a supposition is part of the universal tendency to suppose that in Alice George's day all family groups tended to be large in Britain and everywhere else, large multi-generational and kin-enfolding. The task of convincing people otherwise has not been an easy one, nor will it be a simple matter to persuade them of the insufficiency of the family group to contain the elderly, in the past as in the present.[6] Moreover, the demographic transition, and especially the secular shift in ageing, along with economic development, have so transformed the numbers, economic conditions, proportions and duration of life of elderly persons that comparison over time is a complicated matter.

The belief, or misbelief, in the universality of the large, multi-generational household in the past, part of whose purpose was to provide a family position for the superannuated is accompanied by an equally widespread supposition about kinship and its historical development. The strength of kinship ties, it is always assumed, was necessarily very much stronger in the past than it is now, and kinsfolk were a major support, if not usually the only support, of those in later life. In view of their evident importance to the situation of elderly persons, their position in society today and their attitude to themselves, we cannot leave these subjects unexplored. In learning what we need to know for our purposes it is important, I think, that the status of the knowledge we are after should not be exaggerated. Ever since social gerontology first took its place beside physiological and psychological gerontology there has been a tendency for a topic named 'the household position of the elderly' which is usually taken to include kinship support, to dominate the enquiry, especially in respect of comparisons with the position in the past or in different social structures. This preoccupation has tended to turn attention from other important topics in the historical sociology of ageing, and an object of the present essay is to restore them to their rightful position in that study.

Let us start with some results of research on the residential isolation of the elderly in Britain, as it was and as it is with a table presenting a selection of the recovered facts (see Table 8.1).

The figures in Table 8.1 suggest that it was in no way eccentric of Mrs George to live alone as an elderly widow, because over a fifth of all women like her are given as solitaries in the second column which refers

Table 8.1   Elderly persons and their co-residents in Britain since the seventeenth century (persons aged over 65, excluding residents of institutions)

Marital status	Co-residents	*England 1684–1796*		Great Britain 1962		Great Britain 1980–81	
		Males %	Females %	Males %	Females %	Males %	Females %
Married	Spouse only	41	49	67	68	81	87
	Spouse and child	53	42	29	25	19	13
	Spouse and other	7	9	4	7		
	All	100	100	100	100	100	100
	n	76	43	701	510	2736	2062
Non-married	Solitary	20	22	37	45	65	72
	Child	52	55	41	37	15	16
	Others	28	24	22	18	19	11
	All	100	100	100	100	100	100
	n	40	106	303	986	962	3364

Sources: England 1684–1796 – P. Laslett, *Family Life and Illicit Love in Earlier Generations* (1977), pp. 204–5.
Great Britain 1962 – E. Shanas *et al.*, *Old People in Three Industrial Societies* (1968), p. 186.
Great Britain 1980/1 – Richard Wall, 1984, 'Residential Isolation of the Elderly', *Ageing and Society*, 4, 4 (Special Issue), p. 489.
*Persons aged ≥ 65 in the five communities of Chilvers Coton enumerated in 1684, Lichfield (1695), Stoke on Trent (1701), Corfe Castle (1790) and Ardleigh (1796) exclusive of residents of institutions as detailed in Laslett (1977), p. 201.

to her gender and era. What is more, 44 per cent of all married people aged over 65 (41 per cent of men, 49 per cent of women) were experiencing the so-called 'empty-nest' stage, where older couples go on maintaining the household after their children have left, and doing so with or without other co-residents.

If they can be taken as representative, these figures by themselves should be sufficient to dispense with the belief that every old person was a member of a large, extended family in the English past. Some of the individuals who survived until the later ages, a very much smaller number, of course, than survive for so long today, were certainly to be found with persons other than their own children still at home. Those were mostly widowed parents in the households of their married daughters or sons.

Taking your widowed and failing mother, or sometimes father, into your household was a recognized expedient in caring for them and our ancestors did this whenever they could and whenever it became necessary. Their very presence made these households extended. In traditional English society, however, we know that no more than 6 per cent of all households contained three or more generations.

This is not so surprising in itself since old persons were not plentiful and, as we shall see, had their unmarried children living with them until much later in life than they do today. Furthermore some seniors lacked children with whom they could live, because of never having married, or having had no offspring, or because their children had died. Evidence coming to light after Table 8.1 was drawn up has tended to modify to some extent the impression it gives. Nevertheless the demographic facts alone make it clear that there can never have been a time when all elderly English people lived in large, extended households.[7]

There was a particular reason in the demography of families conforming to English and Western marriage and residential rules which made it difficult for the younger generations, especially among the poorer people, to take in their still-living forebears or to offer them much material support. Age at marriage and at child-bearing were such that parents were under the strongest pressure to support their children at just the time when their own parents might perhaps be beginning to fail, to lose their spouses or to approach the dependent Fourth Age. This becomes evident when comparison is made with families in countries like India or China, where marriage was and is much earlier, and children much more likely to have ceased to be dependent during the time of parental need, if indeed that ever arrived. These Chinese children, what is more, were, and are still at home, often married, but contributing to the common resources.

The interpretation of Table 8.1 has to be therefore that given the prevailing demographic regime on the lower ageing plateau and given the family system, not every older person could have lived in a multi-generational household and that it was impossible for the proportion of all multigenerational households to have been high. But the interest of the figures there by no means ends at that point. Its further columns go on to demonstrate how in the early 1980s very much larger numbers of the elderly lived in the empty-nest stage than did so in the past. The proportion has virtually doubled for married couples and increased by two-thirds for the non-married. These circumstances have grown ever more pronounced in recent years: in our day the overwhelming majority of our older persons live with their partners if they have them, or alone.

This tendency is more conspicuous in Europe, especially Western Europe, than elsewhere in the world and particularly so in Britain. A few of these individuals have never been married at all, of course, some of the married have never had children, and a number, a rapidly increasing number, have been divorced. But these are not the really important reasons why so very much of them live on their own. The outstanding feature of older persons now as compared with the past, as we now well know, is the prodigious growth in their numbers and proportions. The number of their juniors has not grown at the same pace but the opportunity for forming multi-generational households has expanded very considerably. The preference for independent living has, however, become very much more pronounced, and the means to do so have risen enormously. What we have to reckon with, in the USA as well as in Britain, is an exceedingly widespread determination of older people to live on their own at just the period when opportunities for living in the households of their children opened up on a large scale. It may be fair to say nevertheless that this change has not exactly contradicted the tendency of traditional family provisions: rather it has taken it to inordinate lengths.

In view of what has been said in Chapter 6 about the decades between the 1950s and the 1980s being those of the fastest transformation in respect of ageing, we must also take good note of the contrast between the facts set out in the two right-hand columns of Table 8.1, for 1962 and 1980–81. In that brief period, as Richard Wall asserted when he published the table, as much alteration took place in the household position of the elderly as took place from traditional times up to the 1960s. Once more it is in our lifetimes, that is in those of our contemporaries in the Third Age in the current decade, that the extreme position which is now occupied as to independence by the English elderly has come about.

Richard Wall, the great authority on these issues, has also shown that, like the emergence of the Third Age, this development is not confined to Britain, but is common to all Western and all developed nations. He strongly insists, however, that the position differs from country to country, even from region to region in our own country. The variation cannot be accounted for simply by the demographic transition, which is now so widespread in the world and of which, as we have seen, population ageing has been a part. The marked increase in resources available to those in retirement is certainly one of the predisposing circumstances, also a universal phenomenon in the developed world and one which we have tried to assess in its bearing on the establishment of the Third Age. Elderly couples can afford to live independently, and so can widows and widowers.[8]

We can sum up in the following way the reasons why so many more elderly people lived with their own families around them in Mrs George's time than in our own, without implying that her position was at all extraordinary, even for a very ancient widowed woman. Many, many more of the past elderly had their own younger children still at home with them, unmarried, not yet launched into the world, though often earning something, dependent to varying degrees. Mothers went on giving birth until far later in life than mothers have done in the twentieth century and especially in recent decades. Even after their sons and daughters had left home, generally to be servants in households elsewhere in the village, or several villages away, they would return from time to time between jobs. In some families girls would leave home earlier than boys, in others the reverse applied: this varied with time, place and occupation. Nevertheless, although children did not usually stay longer with their parents than they do today, elderly widows tended to have daughters still with them, thus maintaining entirely female households.[9] Even after they became heads of their own households, children might send their own offspring back home to stay for a while, either to relieve themselves of the burden of the support of those children, or to help their ageing parents, or both.

Because older people did not live in the empty-nest stage for as long as older parents do now (expectation of life at 50 being under twenty years for women as against over thirty today), the empty-nest state was necessarily shorter in the past. A small number of the grandchildren whom grandparents took in were illegitimate, and a common reason why a few families did come to contain three generations was that parents of unmarried mothers kept daughter and child in the family home. There were other, probably more numerous households, where the generational span was the same, but the intermediate, parental generation was missing, the single mother having sent her baby back to her parents. Here is a vivid contrast with the supposedly isolated single-parent families of our own decade, though instances of just such families can sometimes be found in historical records.[10] In still other cases orphans – mostly orphans of related persons – were also taken in.

Although such emphasis has to be placed on the relative unimportance of extended family living for the historical experience of elderly people in our country, we should be careful not to assume such families to have been entirely absent. At any one time about one English household in ten, on average, had a relative or relatives living in it; that is to say was extended in some way, and one in twenty-five had two family units, a multiple family household. A household with either of these characteristics is called complex and much higher proportions had earlier had, or would later have, such a structure at some point in their existence. Nearly all households with these characteristics would have contained older persons. A good number of those in later life, perhaps a majority, would have lived at some point in their experience in a complex family household, if only for a very brief period.

By no means every one of those complex household arrangements were brought into being for the particular *benefit* of old people, however, and none of these circumstances override the general principle which is so evident in the way of life of the elderly in the English past. That is that they headed their own households for as long as was humanly possible. This meant that they might sometimes end as solitaries. This was the fate of a fifth of the non-married men and over a fifth of the women represented in Table 8.1. We find nevertheless that a proportion of old and older people in the past lived with married children, or with other relatives. What we cannot tell, of course, is how far such co-residence was *chosen* by these elderly people, or how far it was imposed on them by necessitous conditions, or even in the case of the very badly-off, by the dictates of poor-law officers.[11] It is a remarkable fact, moreover, that the numbers of extended families actually rose, and rose quite markedly, during the early period of industrialization in England – between the later eighteenth century and the mid-nineteenth century.

This blank contradiction of the dogma that industrialization invariably reduces the amount of extended family living has been known since the critical study of the subject began in the early 1970s,[12] but the degree to which it affected both English and American households has only recently been appreciated. The change, which has been graphically described by Steven Ruggles in *Prolonged Connections: The Rise of the Extended Family in 19th Century England and America* (1987),[13] gave way after the 1850s to that almost unbroken decline which has led to the practice virtually disappearing by the 1980s.

AGES OF CHILDREN AND AGES OF THEIR PARENTS

As we have already seen, much depends for the size and composition of the families of the elderly on the relationships between the ages of their children and their own ages. In Table 8.2 average ages of children are given, from simulation output, at successive stages in their mothers' later lives, first for the demographic regime of the seventeenth century, second

Table 8.2   Average age of children at points in the later lives of women,
England, seventeenth and twentieth centuries

| Mother's ages | Children's ages (with measures of dispersion) | | Differences |
	Seventeenth century	Twentieth century	
45	11.7 (standard deviation 5.85)	17.8 (s.d. 5.22)	6.1
55	21.0 (6.84)	27.6 (5.91)	6.6
65	30.8 (6.46)	37.6 (5.91)	6.8
75	40.7 (6.46)	47.6 (5.18)	6.9
90	55.0 (6.12)	62.4 (5.96)	7.4

Source: Microsimulation files of the Cambridge Group (J. E. Smith, J. Oeppen):
for a selection of relevant outcomes, see Laslett, and Smith, 1988(c), 'La Parenté
en chiffres', *Annales ESC* (Paris, 1988, 1).

for the demographic regime of the twentieth century, in England in both
cases. It is apparent that at the points in question in the life-course of
women, surviving children are markedly older in the twentieth century
than they were in the seventeenth century.

At the age of 55 under the earlier regime a mother could expect four
years and more to pass before an average child would be likely to marry,
or to set up on her or his own. By the fifty-fifth birthday of a mother in our
day the average son or daughter is already past the usual marriage age. A
contemporary couple can confidently expect to have one or two establishments belonging to their married children. Their predecessors in pre-
industrial times certainly could not count on such a thing.

The use of 'averages' here discloses how vague this indicator is and
the large measures of dispersion (standard deviations) demonstrate that
many of the individuals were a long way from the average in the past.
The numbers of combinations of mothers' ages and children's ages is
enormous and not easy to represent in a table of this kind. The effect,
however, is substantial enough to demonstrate the implications of what
is known from historical demography, that Alice George and her contemporaries bore their children over longer periods of time – hence the
higher standard deviations – and that the average age of those children at
home was younger, because new ones kept arriving for much longer than
today. Late-twentieth-century women generally have one, two or occasionally three children quickly after marriage and no more: these offspring usually leave home 25 or 30 years later. Once more a highly
significant change in the domestic and personal position of older persons

has come about as a consequence, no doubt entirely unforeseen, of demographic development.

In the 1990s, then, many more people get accustomed to living alone with their spouses, if they have them, or as solitaries if they don't, for much longer compared with in the past. But there is an interesting paradox, again arising from changed demographic circumstances. If at the later and latest ages people should wish to live with mature, independent children, or with other relatives, and those children or those relatives should agree, both children and relatives are somewhat more likely to be available today than they were in Alice George's time. This is illustrated in the second of our sets of simulation statistics (Table 8.3).

It appears for the first line of Table 8.3 that when they are in their mid-fifties women today have fewer children alive than women in the late seventeenth century, although this was a historical period when numbers of children born were small. The actual figure was 2.1 children then as against 1.7 now. A fraction of a child seems absurd but is the only way to an exact comparison. Nevertheless in our day fewer women have no living child at all in the mid-fifties, 21 per cent as against 33 per cent 300 years ago. This is true at the two later ages in the table, 65 and 90, but at the higher of the two ages twentieth-century women actually have more surviving children than their ancestors, and a quite markedly lower probability of having no child at all. Indeed in the late and latest years twentieth-century women have as many or more living relatives in all categories and better chances of having at least one adult child to be visited by or to visit, to talk to on the phone and often to help out, especially in matters of home-making, child-minding and so on. Although older parents

Table 8.3 Numbers of kin of women at later ages, late seventeenth and late twentieth centuries, England

At age	Nos of children		Proportion with no child		Nos of descending kin		Nos of lateral kin	
	Late C17	Late C20	Late C17	Late C20	Late C17	Late C20	Late C17	Late C20
55	2.1	1.7	.31	.21	6.2	5.4	4.8	4.8
65	1.9	1.7	.33	.21	7.2	6.6	3.1	4.1
90	1.2	1.5	.41	.24	8.5	10.7	0.6	0.8

Source: Microsimulation files of the Cambridge Group.

today do not usually live with the offspring they have more of them with whom they can interact and also more relatives of their own generation. This last condition will change in due course, as we have seen.

People in later life have a greater probability of children being available now than they did in the past because survival rates are so much better. Markedly fewer children have been born to them, but those that they have had are very much more likely to be alive. Low, static, or often falling, fertility is more than compensated for by very low and continuously falling mortality. These same facts explain why older people have greater numbers of other relatives still living, and why these advantages over their predecessors in the past grow as they proceed from the seventies to the eighties, and from the eighties to the nineties. Here we can see the secular shift in ageing at work all over again. But demography cannot account for the fact that our seniors nowadays so seldom choose to live with their children where that is possible, or even to live with each other. To understand this we have to appreciate how our familial system and familial attitudes differ and have differed from others elsewhere in the world. Let us take a comparative example, an extreme one.

GROWING OLD WITHIN THE PERENNIAL MULTIPLE-FAMILY HOUSEHOLD

We now look to the East, almost as far as it is possible to go within the traditional boundaries of Europe. Dr John Locke and 'Goody' George will appear for a while as a tiny telephoto image in the corner of our picture. ('Goody', in Locke's day, was the word for a little old lady.) What an unlikely couple they make in the picture! What a man for her to be talking to! How extraordinary lucky she is to be able to tell him she had three sons still alive – or any child at all! At her age and in her day the chances of having no offspring surviving were getting on for one in two, and the chances of having three sons alive about three and a half out of 1000.

A hundred miles south-east of Moscow on the Mishino estate of the noble Russian house of Gagarin during the late eighteenth and early nineteenth centuries large-scale, kin-complex, multiple-family households certainly existed and certainly dominated the lives of older people, in fact of the whole population. Between 75 and 90 per cent of all households there were multiple at all times, containing more than one married couple, apart from the head and his wife, and each couple usually had its own offspring. The family group was perennial, that is, it stayed together as head gave way to head, normally though not always by the succession of a married son to his late father. From 55 to 60 per cent of all households had three generations co-residing. Marriage was early for men and women, so that some parents were very young. This meant that between 4 and 12 per cent, depending on the year, actually contained four generations, great-grandparents, parents, grandchildren and great-grandchildren, in the same household.

Four-generational kinship strings are known in America and Europe in the 1990s and are there quite correctly regarded as a novelty, though this will no longer be so in the next century. The members of these strings certainly never live together as family groups in Western countries today nor will they in the future. Rather fewer elderly people were present in this population of Russian serfs than in the England of Locke's generation; between 3 and 5 per cent over the age of 65. But the numbers of the grandchildren of the household head residing in his house were actually larger than the numbers of his children. The average size of these households was between 8 and 9.5 over the years examined, and some reached 25 persons. At Mishino everyone could expect to live until death within a large, complex household like this, sometimes but not necessarily in the same family, in the same small wooden house, nearly always in the same village. During the long, hard central-continental winter, all the members of a household – six, ten or twelve people or more – literally slept on the stove.

When young you had your parents, aunts, uncles and grandparents around you, as well as siblings; in middle life some of these and your own children; in later life grandchildren and great-grandchildren appeared as your own parents and other senior relatives died. Because the head was replaced on his death, the life of the household was continuous over generations, and without this feature the aged would not have been guaranteed a familial circle. Occasionally households divided, or were divided at the behest of Prince Gagarin's agent. But the new units also tended to have, or to grow into, the perennial multiple-household form. The reason for division was often incompatibility: that is, there were quarrels.[14]

Even at Mishino, women usually changed households at marriage, and men, other than those who succeeded to the headship of the household, frequently moved as well. Solitary living could occur, though it affected only one person in 2000 compared with one in 16 in traditional England, and there were some English-type nuclear households. Otherwise arrangements at Mishino can be regarded as coming as close as is humanly possible towards ensuring that no one who grew old would ever find himself or herself outside his or her own family group. It is very instructive, I think, to delineate all the conditions which have to be present if this end is to be secured. Such conditions are certainly very rare, and may have been uncommon even in the Russian peasant past.

Nevertheless the tendency among most people has been, as we have said, to suppose that familial arrangements like this were originally very widespread, or even universal in medieval times and earlier. Allied to this is the thought that older people were much better placed under this system since it ensured a 'natural' family situation for each of them. It has even been suggested that in our own day the vast numbers of older couples living by themselves, and even more the solitary non-married, may feel exiled from the family to which they rightfully belong, and once did belong in a world we have lost.[15] Every elderly mother or father can confirm that the departure of children does leave a sense of loss, an inner sadness which never leaves us. Although it has been shown that in our English past the empty-nest phase was far less common than it is now, every other element in the conventional historical account of the familial position of those in later life is historically false, giving a wrong impression to those who want to be their age in the contemporary world.

The outstanding error, the one most likely to obscure reality, is that the family systems like our own today have their historical origins in systems like the one at Mishino. This cannot have been so if the lifetime of Goody George is taken to belong to a time when everyone like her lived in a family, a perennial multiple family. A persistent search into periods earlier than the one in which she lived, as far back as the Middle Ages in England, has so far failed to find any sign of a familial system which resembled that at Mishino.[16] The familial system which we have inherited from our forefathers of pre-industrial England, along with their treatment of elderly persons is, as far as we know, original to our social tradition and to our social structure.

What is more, it has always been, if not dominant on our continent, then very common there. It is the perennial multiple-family household which has been rare in Europe, confined to these Russian regions, with rather distant approaches to it in the area of the Baltic states, in Finland, in the Balkans and, surprisingly enough, in parts of central and northern Italy. It was as 'natural' for elderly people to have lived in the way Goody George was living in all other parts of Europe, with variations from region to region, as it was for old Russian peasant serfs to have lived as they did.

Perhaps it was even more 'natural' for the English elderly to conduct themselves in the ways we have described. This is because perennial multiple-family household living seems always to have had special predisposing circumstances, economic or even military, and to have been regarded as extraordinary even where it existed.[17] The primary purpose of the perennial multiple household, moreover, certainly does not seem to have been welfare, and this may be the case with other forms of complex household living. Apparently the Chinese family, though it could be of considerable size and complexity, did not always find room for elderly widowers, who have been discovered as solitaries in an eighteenth-century Chinese village where perennial multiple-family households contained most of the population.[18] Nevertheless in China and the rest of Asia the three-generational household has been, and still is, far more frequent than in Europe, and even after these countries undergo the secular shift in ageing they may emerge with living arrangements for the elderly very different from our own. In Japan, the first Asian country to enter the Third Age, 48.9 per cent of those over 65 were living in three-generational households in 1982, although this proportion had fallen from 58.8 per cent in 1967, during the secular shift in that country. Only 13 per cent were solitary. In 1985 65 per cent were reported as living with their kin, 62.8 per cent in the cities and 71.9 per cent in the countryside. A notable contrast here with the situation in our own country.[19]

Here is a further reason why it is inadvisable to think of one modernization process associating together countries as diverse as industrial Britain and industrial Japan as their populations age. Each country or culture seems likely to climb on to the higher ageing plateau with its own traditional familial forms, modified by demography but still in being. Our object here is to persuade those of English and north-western European origin to become aware of what it is that they have inherited from the past, and to recognize what it is that they have never possessed. No one as yet can tell how long the Japanese, Chinese or other peoples with non-Western familial forms in the past will preserve them under changed demographic conditions (see Laslett, 1992(c)). In the European area where Britain is situated it could be said that the traditionally established familial form has survived unaltered throughout the demographic transition and the secular shift in ageing.

Before we break off this abbreviated consideration of the familial position of the elderly before and after the secular shift in our country and take up the very closely related issues of retirement and support, there is one misapprehension which must be guarded against. Living under a set of familial conventions which does not ensure a place in a family group for every older person does not imply that the young and the active did not love their older and less vigorous, often necessitous parents, or that they neglected them. Such records as have come down to us of the attitudes and practices of the younger and the older generations are full of testimony of affection and devotion, of sacrifices made and services given, parent to child and child to parent, even to the ungrateful and the unreciprocating, and this on the part of labourers and paupers as much as of husbandmen, tradesmen, ladies and gentlemen. Such recognition of duty and devotion to parents and older relatives did very frequently take the form of making room for older dependents in the household, where it was wanted and could be afforded. There were, of course, the expected instances of neglect and hostility which served, we must notice, as examples which might strengthen and confirm the attitudes of ordinary, well-disposed people. Those who observe the treatment of old persons located by custom within the families of their offspring in such societies as that of the Chinese or the Japanese find cruelty and neglect as well as charity and support. Intimacy at a distance, if it did indeed describe the reciprocal relationship of younger to older of some at least of our English ancestors, seems to be a genuine resemblance between their social and personal world and our own.

We must take care not to make too much of a particular example of a relationship which we have strong motives to locate in earlier times. But it seems justifiable to claim that the position of old Alice George in respect of her residence and her family was similar to that of so many of our own elderly ladies, advanced in years but proudly maintaining their own establishments and independence. How far, we shall have to try to decide, did her whole situation differ from that which she would have occupied as an antiquated widow embedded in a Russian peasant household? What were the differences in attitudes in people of her kind between Stuart England, Czarist Russia and the society of our own time? What about their welfare – as we conceive welfare – namely, collective support and caring? There is a great deal more to historical comparisons over time than the recording of formal resemblances, far more than we can yet get to grips with.[20]

9 Retirement and Its Social History: Kin and Collectivity in Support of the Old

It is difficult to decide the extent to which retirement is a novelty in our time, a novelty as an established social status, and a novelty in experience, as a personal event. Retirement as we know and practise it is certainly responsible for situations without parallel in the past. 'Husband retired, wife working', if not exactly common, is frequent enough in our generation to be a heading in investigations of what goes on in later life today, and it is genuinely new. A sudden and fundamental reversal of roles between genders, upsetting previous attitudes and assumptions as to relationships between the spouses, this is a telling example of what we now have to regard as an ordinary, even an expected, occurrence if we are to be our age.

This said, retirement has been an accepted institution in Britain for a century or more, although previously it was never so imperative nor so much a universal principle for virtually everyone who reached later life. Moreover, it is difficult to cite any example in the history of European societies where retirement, in some form or other, can be convincingly shown to have been *entirely* absent. The single possible exception has to be sought once again in the perennial multiple-households of the serfs at Mishino in Czarist Russia which were discussed in the last chapter. There an unaltered social environment was maintained even for men until the very end, even when physical disability made it impossible for them to work outside the household.

Living in households such as this has been very rare, as we have seen. Under all other familial systems some discontinuity at this stage in the life course is liable to occur, not only for men but for their wives as well. Everyone knows that having the male, former breadwinner, perpetually around the house instead of out at work may transform domestic life. In Japan, with its lengthy work careers and absentee breadwinners, the spouses of the men who finally come back to live at home all day call them wet leaves. The retirement of women is something which has happened only in recent history. Among our landworking ancestors in the English past, during the time which stretched back from Alice George's day into the Middle Ages, retirement has been supposed by historians to occur at the point in life when the ageing head of the household began to settle his land on his heirs. But by no means all of them had land to dispose of, and little or nothing is known about the retirement of the landless. This does not necessarily imply that withdrawal from work did not occur, even among the humblest. At the Nottinghamshire village of Clayworth in 1688, for example, one household head was described as a 'cast husbandman', a small cultivator who had presumably got past it.

RETIREMENT AND STEM FAMILY LIVING FOR THE ELDERLY OF THE PAST

The position of the serf-peasants on the Mishino estate has been called extreme. But there are and certainly have been other sets of residential arrangements which come closer than our own to providing a familial circle for older and retired people, if not on the scale and with the completeness characteristic of the perennial multiple-family household. Whenever a convention exists which requires one child to remain at home to look after ageing parents, renouncing marriage if necessary, familial company if not a familial circle is ensured for them to the end. This was and is so even in the European West, past and present. Since marriage is and always was exceptionally late for most women in that region, in comparison with what happens and has happened elsewhere in the world, and since many never marry at all, there always have been girls, women, or men too, in the West who choose or feel obliged to remain at home for this purpose. Some of them certainly abandoned careers begun elsewhere in order to return to their parental homes to carry out this duty of affection and of family loyalty.

Nevertheless, it is difficult to determine whether these mature companions of the elderly are found in the parental home because they failed to get spouses. There is nothing on record which might demonstrate convincingly that it is, or has been, a rule, a normative rule, of the Western system for one child to occupy this role. The colonial society of North America is a possible exception, but elsewhere too many examples have come to light of sons and daughters leaving home successively, though not in birth order, until the parents or the widowed parent, lived alone; and here we can zoom back to Alice George.

This could happen, it is clear, even though their married children, or some of them, were present in the parental village. In Denmark, a country whose familial arrangements closely resembled those of England, the records of Hans Anderson's city of Odense have been found to contain phrases like the following in relation to the burial of a pauper during the eighteenth century: 'The children would not pay the funeral costs, as they claimed that they had had no contact with their old father or mother for a long time.'[1] The stem-family form, however, which has been encountered in Central and Southern Europe, especially in the mountainous areas, could perhaps be said to institutionalize the arrangement which keeps one of the offspring, the married heir, within the household, giving support to a retired person or to a married couple of the previous generation. In parts of Germany retirement of this description had a title, *Leibgedinge*, and there seems to have been something approaching a conventional age, 60, at which a landholder would withdraw in favour of his resident, usually married, heir who would succeed and carry on the stem (*stamme*). But there is nothing to show that the displaced farmer ceased work on the land, that he retired in our sense of the word.

This is not the place to go into the question of how widely distributed the stem family was in traditional Europe, or how far it was important enough to be of much significance in ensuring a familial circle for a substantial proportion of the aged. There is certainly little sign of the presence of the stem family in England, and it is my own view that its role in this and other directions has been somewhat exaggerated.[2] There are two features associated with the stem-family form, however, which are of importance for our inheritance from the traditional world in the matter of ageing. One is the evident recognition in stem-family practices of the concept of retirement itself, of withdrawal to live on the proceeds of your parental and working life. The other is the tendency to make out a retirement document specifying the continuing rights of the old owner-manager and the obligations of the new one. Such retirement documents are not confined to areas where stem families have been found as groups of co-residents, and exist in large numbers in many European archives, though they are not all common in England after the Middle ages. It is tempting to look in this direction for the origin of retirement as we now conceive it, retirement which almost invariably stands at the beginning of the Third Age in our day.

There is a great deal to be said against supposing, however, that retirement of this character was a recognized institution of earlier European society, an expected stage of the life course of all individuals. It was confined, for one thing, to the property-owning, specifically land-owning or land-occupying, a minority in England in Alice George's generation and not to be assumed as a clear majority anywhere on our continent at any time. There would be little point in her, or any landless labourer, anticipating retirement or in this sense providing for it specifically, when there was so little to retire upon. Craftsmen or small retailers might have made such arrangements but this does not seem likely and such records have not been found. The drawing up of a retirement agreement does not necessarily point to a regular arrangement. It could be said to indicate that withdrawal into inactivity was not the expected but the unexpected thing. In Chapter 6 a case was made for supposing that people in the historic past, especially poorer people, discounted ever being faced with old age.

The existence of retirement agreements even in small numbers might further imply that those who drew them up were well aware that there were not established rules to provide for older persons if they could no longer carry on. Therefore those who were failing and felt that they would have to give up scarcely trusted their successors to support them without their being tied down by formal instruments. Some of the medieval documents make affecting reading, requiring as they do that the ageing individual be assured of a place by the fire. These agreements often, though not always, give the impression that the Fourth Age was already at hand. Local authority, in the medieval village the manor court, sometimes demanded that an agreement be made as to a person's land and so on, because of that person having ceased to be competent. For every written version of a retirement agreement there may have been hundreds or thousands which were simply spoken undertakings.

The early laws of Iceland, the smallest and one of the oldest independent European polities, are of considerable interest here, although they make no provision for written agreements. In that extremely poor country a failing old person was the legal responsibility of his or her children who were required to support parents in need, if necessary at the cost of selling themselves into bondage to find the money. If that arrangement failed, more distant kin were liable, but only if they were of some substance, and they might fulfil their duty by circulating the dependent old person from house to house. Should that not provide for what was wanted, and these repetitive processes surely indicate that each expedient was often ineffective, then the appeal had to be to the collectively, the *faellig* in the Icelandic case, a civilly responsible band of substantial local people who might also circulate the subject from house to house, though not in this case of households of kin. Recourse to relatives beyond the immediate kin for support is very uncommon in welfare provisions in the past, though there are hints of it in Austrian and Spanish records. No more telling example could be found of the joint interaction of family, kin and collectivity in matters of dependency than the Icelandic laws.[3] The treatment accorded to men over 80, though there must have been extremely few of them in so tiny a population, is particularly interesting. There were discouraged from having offspring and if one did appear, he or she could not inherit.

Retirement and retirement agreements among modest landholders are best looked upon as expedients rather than as settled, customary parts of the social structure.[4] Although allowance must be made for traditional arrangements of this kind in assessing our own retirement notions, late-twentieth-century practice must owe a great deal more to the retirement from politics and active participation in élite life and institutions which privileged persons have always permitted themselves at any calendar age and at all periods.

Ten years after his conversation with Goody George, at the age of 58, John Locke himself 'retired' in this way to a country house in Essex. He paid £1 a week for himself and his manservant, and a shilling (5p) a week for his horse. Retirement was how he repeatedly described his situation, but he spent the 100 warmest days of the year in his London chambers to perform such official duties as he had retained. It was through the communication of retirement in this élite sense to servants of the state, and hence to business undertakings, that the type of retirement which the early-twentieth-century doctors and administrators determined to make compulsory finally spread to the whole population, in all European countries.

Retirement in the past, therefore, seems to have been secured by a miscellany of expedients rather than by a set of recognized usages and institutions. Since the numbers of those who reached the later ages were small, and since relatively few of them can ever have anticipated doing so, this is perhaps what we would expect. Where, as with the perennial multiple-family household, or less effectively with the stem family, arrangements did provide a familial position for the old, this seems to have been incidental to the other functions of those arrangements. The general conclusion to be drawn is that the co-residential family group is very difficult to adapt to all the eventualities of the individual life course, and providing for old age seems to be beyond its capacities; it is successful in this respect only in such unusual situations as that at Mishino. Indeed the crucial condition seems to have been customs which permitted multiple families and not simply extended ones, and multiplicity was virtually absent in the West. Should old age have come upon them, Western individuals in the past would have found themselves in a variety of positions as to their family and kin. One of these, perhaps the one some at least would have preferred, was that of Alice George, intimacy at a distance, or at least at a physical remove.[5]

In 1618 'an old and sicklie woman' living at Hunwick in County Durham finally refused the repeated entreaties of her married daughter 'to come and dwell with her ... for that she had none to look to her'. The old lady apparently insisted on dying alone.[6] There remains one question to be put, therefore. Is it, or has it been desired by older persons to live in familial company, if that company cannot consist of their spouses and still dependent children? Is it even always to their benefit?

The replies given by older people today to questions of this kind are clearly in favour of independent living while they are capable of looking after themselves and we have seen that this preference can be found among people in the past. However, there is a darker side to be considered, for guilty fantasies about disposing of the old are not the only evidence we have of hostility to them in traditional society. There are signs that when older generations were compelled by circumstance, established social practice or compulsion, to live with younger generations, there was sometimes trouble. This is still true in a contemporary society, the People's Republic of China, where the generations usually co-reside, and are expected to do so as a normal thing, and older people declare that they prefer living with their children than on their own. The possibility of neglect and even violence are recognized disadvantages of these arrangements, acknowledged as such by Chinese students of the subject and by Chinese administrators themselves.[7] Living together can be surprisingly unpleasant and unsatisfactory for family members in our own country too. In disposing of the myth that the English elderly in the past always lived and died surrounded by bevies of their relatives, we need not accept the belief that it would always and necessarily have been better for them if these had been the circumstances.

'RETIREMENT' AMONG LABOURERS AND ITS FINANCING

If we bring Alice George and her distinguished interlocutor back into the picture once again we can listen to her telling him how 'her maintenance had been her labour'. As a powerful, active woman she had obviously been very successful at it and proudly boasted that she had earned as much as a man for the same task. At the time of the conversation, however, she was quite evidently no longer living in this way. But even if her son and daughter-in-law next door kept an eye on her and went in whenever help was needed, as children of old people do today on such an impressive scale, we are given no hint that the son supported his mother financially. All that historians have so far found out about this rather difficult subject from before the secular shift in Ageing started a hundred years ago makes it seem rather improbable that much actual money would have passed from elderly son to very aged parent, or from children of any age to their mothers or fathers in later life. Where there was property the direction of assistance was from the old or older to the younger rather than the other way round, which might be expected in a society where young adults were required to set up for themselves, especially at marriage. After 'retirement', such upward transfers as there were can be thought of as being made quite often in the way of repayment of debt. An incidental but very important implication of these facts is that the motive for having children, many more children than we now have, in the traditional English past, cannot have been financial, at least to the extent that is often assumed. This is true over the whole life course of those parents and children but it is especially important that it should have been so in respect of later and latest life.[8]

The great nineteenth-century social enquirer Frédéric le Play and his collaborators did observe some signs of direct financial support by the off-spring generation in various of the countries – not all European – which they studied. So slight, however, were these offerings that they rather confirm than contradict what has been said. The surprise in Le Play's figures is the extent to which the elderly were supported from their own resources. Nevertheless there are records of afflicted parents being kept going by their sons and daughters in the pre-industrial English past. An example of this is Abner Croker, aged 73, who lived in the beautiful village of Corfe Castle in Dorset in 1790, with his wife, also aged 73: they were obviously in the empty-nest stage since the list of the inhabitants of the village where they appear records no co-residing offspring. The following comment is written against their entry, however: 'Abner Croker is blind. He is maintained by his children, etc.'[9]

The last term of this quotation is significant since the other sources to which it refers must have included the Poor Law, which may perhaps have done almost as much as the younger Crokers to keep Abner Croker going. It is a remarkable fact that 80 per cent of all persons over 60 in Corfe Castle in 1790 were being assisted by the Poor Law. It seems to have been a widespread practice to effectively 'pension' the elderly when they were judged past being able to hold a job. In the small country town whose elderly population is best known to us historically, Colyton in Devonshire, the 'pensionable age' was about seventy in the middle of the nineteenth century, during the years just before the secular shift in ageing began.

The word 'pension' was not used, however, and Colyton was quite exceptional, though by no means unique, in that a relief fund for assistance was available from a substantial and well-established local charity as well as from the Poor Law. The papers of this charitable organization have been used by Jean Robin researching at the Cambridge Group to provide the following information about the age and length of 'retirement' among the labouring poor, the first that has ever come to light. The facts set out in Table 9.1 can be inferred from the practice of feoffees, the managers of the trust, of ceasing to give assistance to any person who had received relief from the Poor Law during the past three months. It happens that the feoffees gave a regular dole of one shilling a head to all the poor of Colyton at Christmas. The cessation of such payments, once and for all, to a man aged 70 or thereabouts who has been receiving them for many years and who is known to have remained in the parish for several more, indicates that he went on to permanent parish relief from the Poor Law, and so became ineligible for further help from the feoffees.[10]

This remarkable information illuminates several themes of the social history of retirement, indeed of the emergence of the Third Age and its relation to the Fourth. It confirms that the point at which men withdrew from the regular labour force was variable, spread here over twenty years or more with a marked concentration in the early seventies. That one man should be over 80 before he withdrew as old and infirm is a notable fact and confirms what was cited for Iceland in Chapter 8. Although disability

Table 9.1 Age at, and length of, 'retirement' among labouring men at Colyton, Devonshire, 1851–73

Age at retirement	(a)	(b) *Mean length of retirement in years*	
60–64	5		5.6[1]
65–69	7		4.9
70–74	19		7.6
75–79	4		3.75
80+	1		9.0
Total	36		
Mean age	71.3	Mean length	6.4

[1] If one individual with an exceptionally long retirement on 13 years is excluded, the mean length of retirement in the 60–64 group is 3.75 years.
Source: Communicated by Jean Robin.

must have played a part in the decision to 'retire', or to be allowed to do so – otherwise why the range of 'retiring'ages and the below-average length of retirement of those pensioned in their sixties? – we cannot assume that this disability was usually or often sickness unto death. Expectation of life for these Devonshire paupers of the 1850s to the 1870s must have been in the range of two-thirds of the general national average, which is something of a surprise in itself in persons as poor as these must have been.[11]

Most important of all is the implication that many of these men must have had an interlude after being relieved of regular toil, an interlude when they were at leisure. The question presents itself therefore as to whether this interlude can be taken as representing a Third Age, in embryo at least.

The society of Colyton from the 1850s to the 1870s certainly did not qualify demographically for the Third Age on the criteria laid down in Chapter 6 above. Neither could it be claimed that the country as a whole, or that part of it, was rich enough to provide the other requisites of Third Age living. Although literacy levels were rising fast at this period, the men we are discussing had left school before the reforms which brought that about. They cannot have used much of their free time in reading, or study except for some of them conning the scriptures. Many or most must be supposed to have spent it in idleness, or in the ale-house when they could afford it. There is a well-known Victorian cartoon of an old labouring man sitting on his chair in front of his cottage, declaring 'Sometimes I sits and thinks, and sometimes I just sits.' Some certainly worked at their gardens, where they had them, a typical Second Age activity carried on more exten-sively after chances of regular jobs dried up. Yet others must have devoted themselves to religious exercises, that time-consuming activity character-istic of all traditional societies. Nor must it be forgotten that if a piece of casual work which any one of them could do presented itself, it would have been leapt at.[12]

When all this is said, however, it has to be admitted that this unexpected insight into 'retirement' and its duration before the coming of the secular shift suggests some qualification of the principle that there was no inter-lude between the Second Age and the Fourth, that people went straight from unremitting toil to decrepitude and death. In spite of the relative brevity of periods of illness in the past there is ample evidence that poor people could be invalided over numbers of years, the objects of conspicu-ous charity on the part of the ladies from the Great House and from the professional classes. But by and large the expedients for the care of really dependent old people in Colyton were familial. By the age of 70 more than half of parents with married children were living in the household of one such child, often with extra help from the parish.[13] Infirm persons and widows with young children could likewise be given regular weekly payments for months or years on end. Such remittances can be found in Poor Law and charity accounts could well have been a permanent feature of English poor relief, not only during the period of the New Poor Law from the 1830s to the 1940s, but under the Old Poor Law from the 1600s to the 1830s, and even before. The services of doctors and nurses and the supply of medicines were distributed with even greater regularity.

The age at which the overseers, that is the amateur officials appointed annually under the Poor Law in almost every English parish under the Old Poor Law and the guardians under the New, would decide to pay a 'pension' on grounds of advancing years varied extensively with place, time and circumstances. The criterion never seems to have been age by itself, but a combination of age with chronic disablement, which could come upon a man or a woman at any point but especially after middle life. As at Colyton, only after a pauper had reached the seventies or eighties would most officials admit that numbers of years by themselves justified permanent relief. This is a further indication that retirement in the fixed sense in which we use the expression was not yet accepted, and that genuine old age at that time has to be taken to have meant what we call here the Fourth Age of final decrepitude. They got on well enough without a definition of old age or a set number of birthdays after which it started: so indeed did the Poor Law authorities up to the twentieth century.[14] For all their vagaries, however, local people like this truly knew the people claiming support. They could act with a confidence about the records and characters of their 'cases' which the social worker of our day can only envy, because the average size of communities was so small, with only two or three hundred inhabitants. Poor Law officials could also be braggarts, bullies and petty swindlers and this has made them notorious in fiction.

The 'pensions' which such elderly paupers were paid may look paltry to us, and the medical care of little use. Such persons were perpetually patronized, often treated with contempt and sometimes with cruelty: they can never have felt really secure. But standards of such conduct were very much lower in a pre-industrial society and customary behaviour markedly different. Nevertheless scholarly opinion has become somewhat critical of the view that the twentieth-century welfare state is uniquely different from the Poor Law practices out of which it can now be seen to have developed in Britain. It has been shown that some at least of the traditional horrors of the treatment of the old have rather shaky foundations. It was not the regular practice, for example, for paupers in their last years to be hauled off to the workhouse: in general they were relieved at home unless infirmity made it impossible for them to remain there. If they did reach the workhouse together, elderly married couples were not usually separated as younger couples were, and if they did live apart there it may have been because of illness or even from choice.[15]

Treatment varied from area to area and period to period and Poor Law officials certainly do not all deserve their universally black reputation. Here is an account of a pauper woman's funeral, which took place on Wednesday, 3 September 1800, in the village of Grasmere in Cumbria.

> A fine coolish morning. I ironed til 1/2 past three – now very hot. I then went to a funeral at John Dawson's [presumably the Poor Law Guardian]. About 10 men and 4 women. Bread cheese and ale. They talked sensibly and chearfully about common things. The dead person 56 years of age buried by the parish. The coffin was neatly lettered and painted black and covered with a decent cloth. They set the corpse down at the door and while we stood within the threshold the men with their hats off sang with decent and solemn countenances a verse of a funeral psalm. The corpse was then borne down the hill and they sang till they had got past the Town-end [the end of the village]. I was affected to tears while we stood in the house, the coffin lying before me. There were no near kindred, no children. When we got out of the dark house the sun was shining and the prospect looked so divinely beautiful as I never saw it. It seemed more sacred that I had ever seen it, and yet more allied to human life. The green fields, neighbours of the churchyard, were as green as possible and with the brightness of the sunshine looked quite gay. I thought she was going to a quiet spot and I could not help weeping very much.[16]

This was during the time when the Poor Law was being administered with notable liberality, and it may be that Grasmere was among the generous parishes. It will be noticed that the pauper woman was without relatives; the Poor Law and the village community were carrying out the functions which we usually, and perhaps not quite justifiably, refer exclusively to the family and kin. But subsequently, from the 1860s onwards, the welfare authorities grew much harsher in their policy and attitudes.

Families at that later time were being pressed to support the elderly by themselves, even to take them into their homes to a greater extent than before, and allowances were drastically reduced. There succeeded an interlude of relative generosity after the State pensions began in 1908 to be paid to some – but not all – old people, a change in direction now recognized as typical of the unstable history of social transfers. The pension had the perhaps unexpected effect, in some cases, of causing hard-pressed young parents of families to welcome their own parents into their household for the sake of the support which the five shillings a week paid out to those over 70 might give to the household. But when, after further vicissitudes, the current era of the welfare state began its career, it cannot be any longer supposed that unique, unprecedented generosity to the dependent old became the norm for the first time in history. There is, of course, a great deal of difference between a Poor Law 'pension' and one from the welfare state, in that in our day state pensions are a right, paid to everyone. But David Thomson has claimed that state pensions in Britain, lower in any case, both absolutely and relatively, than in other rich countries, have not improved in relation to prevalent living standards since the 1940s: perhaps the reverse.

Insight into the sources of support for the elderly two or three generations ago as well as of their family and of their work situations is provided by the results of the enquiry already cited into over 28 000 working-class households in London originally carried out between 1929 and 1931. As much as 30 per cent of the 2300 elderly male workers or former workers sampled from this total were living alone after the age of 65 and the proportions grew with age: 23 per cent in the late sixties, 30 per cent in the early seventies, 36 per cent in the late seventies and 44 per cent after 80. The figures were even higher for women: 37 per cent of all of whom were solitaries, and over half of those in their eighties. It is astonishing that the inclination to live alone, often supposed to be peculiar to contemporary life, should have been so widespread sixty years ago, though something under a fifth of all older people were members of complex households. As for earnings, two-fifths of the men and a sixth of the women got at least part of their keep from paid work between the ages of 65 and 74. But three quarters of the income of the sample as a whole came from state benefits, only about a sixth, at most, from 'family'.

The author of this revealing study has some trenchant things to say in fact about family and kin in the support of working-class Londoners in the 1930s. 'The role of the family was minimal, critical no doubt in certain situations, but unable or unwilling to act as principal support mechanism for the elderly.' He concludes modestly enough that his information suggests 'a strictly limited role for the kin in supporting the elderly in the London of the early 1930s, and certainly a role exceeded by the State'. But there are signs 'that kin regarded geographical closeness as valuable, that the family was an important source of informal care of the elderly relatives, and further that that support transcended the frontiers of residence'.[17] Once again, London may have been different in these respects from the rest of the country, but well over a tenth of all English people lived in the area.

When the enormous increase in our absolute resources is duly weighed, it is possible to suggest that today, two generations later or more, we are doing relatively worse rather than better by the individual pensioner than was done in pre-industrial times, and perhaps worse than was done in the 1930s. It is certainly out of the question in the 1990s to return the old to the care of the family group because, as we have seen, the English family group has never been of a character which would enable it to contain and support them all. It is also somewhat unconvincing to accuse ourselves of extravagance in maintaining the old. We are being niggardly rather than free-handed and it could be said that we shall continue to be so while our wealth goes on growing so fast and we fail to expand the share of each poor, dependent elderly person in consonance.

THE ELDERLY AND THEIR KINSFOLK

Transfers to those in the later and latest years of life, therefore, transfers on a considerable scale when considered relatively, are evidently not new in this last decade of the twentieth century. If society in our time is doing no more than its historic duty to those in the Third Age and the Fourth, are the kin of the dependent elderly doing the same, or more? Or less? Kinsfolk here means not simply offspring and those in younger generations, but the kin network as a whole, whatever the distance between relatives.

Perhaps too much time has already been spent on the contrast between family life for older people in the past and in the present. We have still to consider their place in imaginative life, in literature and in doctrine before we conclude the chapter with a demand for invention – the invention of institutions and attitudes which we have not inherited and do not yet possess. The issue about past and present kinship, kinship support and kinship interaction can, however, be disposed of fairly briefly. All that can yet be asserted with confidence is that no convincing evidence of much historical change in kin relations in England has yet been found. This is so anyway in the matter of support, regular reliable support, for such dependent persons as the needy or helpless elderly and old.

This provisional conclusion may seem astonishing, and it certainly contradicts the general presumption cited earlier, the presumption that kinship bonding must have declined in importance over time, and that in the past kinship was a much more important resource to an elderly individual, and a greater control over his or her conduct than is the case today.

If the grounds for this presumption were demanded, the reply might well be that since undeveloped societies are seen to be kinship-dominated in our time, our society must have been so before it was developed and to the same degree: this is the modernization fallacy all over again. The historical evidence so far recovered cannot be said to confirm such an assertion for the English past, and the more plentiful and reliable evidence for the present makes against it. We know for certain that older persons can count on their relatives for companionship and help in the 1990s, especially in emergencies, infirmity or bereavement. Observers are regularly surprised by this loyalty of their kin to the old, though there is nothing to indicate that it is a peculiarity of our own time or social situation. We can infer that our predecessors behaved in a similar way, but we cannot maintain with any confidence that kinship meant more to their elderly persons than it does to ours today.

Comparative studies of this elusive topic, necessarily few because the materials are so sparse and difficult, have concluded that kinship recognition was not particularly well marked in the English past and that kinship connection was generally rather lax. Some outstanding examples of the apparent neglect of the elderly, even by their close kin, in their later years have come to light in the records. Perhaps the most distressing is that of Francis Bacon, the barrel-maker living in Clayworth in Nottinghamshire during the 1670s and 1680s. It was concluded of this man in 1963 that he had moved into the family home with his wife and children at his father's death and taken up the family calling, leaving the widowed mother and sister to live 'in the common houses', that is, in the village establishment for the poor. But we shall never know all the circumstances of such cases, and there are many instances of quite contrary behaviour. Despite the perpetual local movement of persons from village to village which has already been referred to as characteristic of traditional England, close kin cooperation within local communities has been conclusively demonstrated and it has been shown that for all its lack of resident relatives the English household of the past was most decidedly not isolated from the kinfolk of its members.[18]

Nevertheless instability in residence by itself ensured that association with relatives is unlikely ever to have been as important, as close and long-lived as anthropologists have found in African or Asian countries. This must make it likely that kin connections were less reliable for the English elderly in the past than they would otherwise have been. The only investigation which has attempted to compare kinship interaction at two points in time at the same place – that is, the London working-class suburb of Bethnal Green – shows that much faster turnover of population in the 1850s, 1860s and 1870s, and perhaps other influences, seem to have made interaction with kin substantially less important in those decades than it was to be in the 1950s. Ageing mums in mid-twentieth-century Bethnal Green must have had more of the company of their children, grandchildren, siblings and cousins than their predecessors did in the mid-nineteenth century.[19] Turnover of population may have been less in other areas of Europe and elsewhere in the world, and kin cooperation more, perhaps much more, salient in the lives of most people, with important consequences for the old. The parallel with the differences already described between the family group in the West and elsewhere will not have escaped the reader.

We can go no further here into the kin relations of the elderly in the past and in the present, but there is a feature of their interconnections with others, and with the community, which has still to be stressed. In discussing the relative importance of social institutions and the state, the collectively on the one hand and the family on the other, it was evident that the two collaborated in devising and maintaining the necessary expedients for the support of the old. The family here means non-resident kin for the most part, close kin such as children who no longer lived with their now-necessitous parents, but also grandchildren, even cousins. Family in all its senses, is not to be seen as opposed for these purposes, or for any other, to collective social institutions. They always imply each other.[20] At the present time, when the relative roles of family and state in maintaining our older population are so much in debate, it is important that this historical interrelationship should not be lost to view.

Nor must we forget that institutions were invented and maintained in the traditional world particularly designed for the elderly who fell through the net of other expedients. There were the innumerable local charitable funds and institutions like that at Colyton, evidence of whose foundation and existence we can still see recorded in sixteenth-, seventeenth-, eighteenth- or nineteenth-century handwriting on boards fastened to the walls of our ancient parish churches. 'Old and decayed' husbandmen (petty landholders), labourers or craftsmen, 'ancient widows', 'elderly paupers' are frequently named on these fading notices, to be doled out bread or clothing, or pittances in pennies every Christmas, or even every Sunday. Then there were the almshouses or hospitals as they were sometimes called, for the same types of recipient, institutions in which personal and institutional life were mingled. Numbers of these still exist as models, as some see them, for the sheltered housing of our own day, residences for the not-quite independent elderly.

Hard by the cathedral close at Norwich there stands a hospital dating from the thirteenth century which was evidently confirmed in its functions and perhaps refounded as a home for infirm older men by Henry VIII, so often thought of as the great despoiler. It is written on its wall that:

> King Henry the Eight of noble fame
> Bequeathed this city this commodious place
> With land and rent he did endow the same
> To keep decreped age in woeful case.

Here is the Fourth Age of dependency to a T. The hospital maintains its services to the present day, with rows and rows of residential buildings, a hospital for the afflicted old and the ancient church still in use for the spiritual exercises of the whole society and its communal intercourse. This is not the end of the significance of the title of hospital for our subject, since the state workhouses themselves also had the further identity of being refuges for the sick and sites of medical assistance. Jean Robin has found that those few poor older people who did get taken to the workhouses from Colyton in Victorian times were removed there because they had become ill, too ill to look after themselves or to be looked after at home.

The pattern of the charitable foundations could vary in an interesting fashion. In the church of Rothwell in Northamptonshire, for example, there are engravings representing bands of old men, ringing the bells in the tower for services, reading prayers, burying the dead, clad in breeches and gaiters, some with top hats, especially the coffin bearers, others with shovel hats. This was as late as 1918. The twenty-six members of the institution, the Jesus Hospital founded in 1591, got five shillings a week and a dark blue uniform with silver buttons, so a local resident reported. There is the following inscription:

> Christ bless our Governors, prolong their days
> Who placed us here to render Heaven our praise,
> To live contended, private and resigned
> Free from life's toils, and humours of mankind.
> Pleased with wise AGURS mediocrity[21]
> Too low for envy for contempt too high
> What we now have we thankfully possess
> Till we exchange for greater happiness

> Henry Dormer Principal, 1721

Along with these curious and venerable establishments which our ancestors have bequeathed to us, there goes an attitude which we seem to have inherited as well. This is that old persons ought to be, we are inclined to think, indolent, out of the way, and duly grateful for what they receive from us as well as from the past, to be objects of our sympathy and generosity, and perhaps patronized somewhat into the bargain. It is an interesting fact that about the same proportions of elderly persons, about one in twenty, lived in institutions in England during the pre-industrial times as live in them today.

ATTITUDES TO THE ELDERLY IN THE PAST: DOCTRINE, LITERATURE, IMAGINATIVE LIFE

A slightly comic, grotesque but rather ugly and threatening figure faces us as we approach the imaginative life of the past in relation to the elderly population. This is the image of the old woman as a witch. Locke makes no mention of a cat, a 'familiar' that is to say, nor even of a broomstick in his account of Alice George, and the picture he presents is quite unlike that of the half-crazy crones seen today on television and in story books. Nevertheless, the association of old women with witchcraft has to be taken seriously, if only because of the weight of discussion which has gone on about it among psychologists, psychiatrists, sociologists and anthropologists, as well as historians, not to speak of the feminists resenting one more cruel abuse of womankind. Let it be said at once that not all English witches were women, that not all witches were old, and that not all witches were evil: 'white' or benevolent witches bulked larger in the life of our ancestors than those who were black or malign. Literal belief in witches did not survive to the time of the onset of the secular shift in ageing, and enlightening influences in Locke's day had already begun to discredit it.

Women over 50 were two-and-a-half times more likely to be accused of witchcraft than they should have been.[22] But lamentable and conspicuous as they are in the records of certain places at certain times, in early America as well as in Britain and on the Continent, the subject of witches and witchcraft seems to have got out of proportion in the discussions of historians and the rest. There is nothing to suggest in village record books, family letters, and diaries containing the incidental personal information whose survival is so uncertain and on which we have to rely for our knowledge of such things, that solitary, infirm old women were anything but very rarely seen as witches. I have never myself come across a reference in the documents I have consulted on the history of ageing. Witchcraft is a cruel caricature of the life of past elderly persons, engendered by the literary interest which witches aroused in their day and for ever after and regrettably exaggerated in the folk history of the present, history as presented by the media and the advertiser. Particularly dismaying is the prominence of this unpleasant myth in books intended for young children.

The personal status of elderly people when more realistically viewed seems to have been fundamentally ambiguous, both in England and in the English-descended society of the North American colonies, where the subject has been extensively studied. 'God damn me', said a man of 23 in the year 1683 at Scituate, Massachusetts 'if thou were not an old man I would bat thy teeth down thy throat.' He was quarrelling with someone about 65 years old. The American scholar recounting this anecdote goes on to ask, 'Shall we count this as an expression of deference to age? Literally, yes – but in context, no. Certainly it was not the kind of deference presented in the published literature on old age, [for it] seems to imply *contempt* for his adversary's weakness as an old man'.[23]

Quite apart from the commandment 'Honour thy father and thy mother', a great body of advice and injunction contained in books on theology and conduct, in sermons, in poetry, drama and literature of all kinds, enjoined respect, even reverence, for old age, and unvarying obedience to parents at all stages of your life and theirs. Gratitude for their having brought you into the world and for having supported you in the First Age is always earnestly enjoined. But actual conduct seems to have been of a different and decidedly mixed character. Powerful, property-owning parental figures who had grown old were usually deferred to and obeyed: poor, weak, failing, dependent elders were not, especially the women. It made a great deal of difference, particularly among humbler people, whether or not an old man earned money and was head of a household, or whether an old woman was spouse of the head or herself mistress of the household in succession to a departed husband. Lone widows or solitary ancient spinsters were of virtually no social account at all.

The sons and daughters of gentle parents were full of love, duty and obedience in their letters home, and their behaviour on the whole conformed to what was most certainly required of them until the last days of the lives of their fathers and mothers. But even the domineering ministers of the Word of God in the New England colonies complained of losing their influence and command during their years of decline. The poor, who made up most of the relatively small population of the old, were objects of sympathy, and they were relieved in necessity: their handicaps were taken into account, as in the New England story recounted above. Nevertheless, they were shoved aside in economic, social and political life as age overtook them, as much 'marginalised', in a favourite phrase of the moment, as the poor, weak, female, especially the non-white, old of twentieth-century Britain tend to be.

We should not be particularly surprised at the example of a society professing a particular set of values which were only irregularly demonstrated in everyday conduct. But we must acknowledge that respect for old people, duty to them, especially the duty of obedience to parents which, when disregarded, supposedly shortened the life of the disobeyer, is a part of our cultural inheritance, if never as imperative as in many other societies which have been studied. There was another doctrine about becoming old, a doctrine which may have been even more strenuously believed in, but which may also have been frequently defied. This was the prohibition of all overt sexual activity in older persons, as inappropriate, indecent, and against life.

Manifestations of the taboo against manifest sex abound in documents which have survived, but the extent to which the elderly themselves were inhibited by it is not easy to judge. The one absolutely reliable witness is demographic again, the frequency with which an old man marrying a wife still in her reproductive years had a child or children by her. This happened often enough to suggest that the taboo could be ignored, by men anyway and within marriage. The most conspicuous example we have, and fascinating for the survival of vigour in the male, is the baptism of 14 August 1663, of Edward Smith, son of Edward, 'supposed to be about 100 years' (register of St Margaret, King's Lynn, communicated by Mrs Sheila Cooper. We now know how unlikely it is that Edward Smith, the father, was a true centenarian, though he could well have been a very old man). About women's sexual behaviour after menopause we are almost entirely ignorant and may remain so. We should not take the 'literary obsession with lecherous widows [and] their rapid remarriage with younger men', in London anyway, as an accurate indication of what really went on after women ceased to have their 'flowers'.[24] But we have no ground for supposing that they were invariably chaste.

A fact of some significance is revealed by the rarity of remarriage at late ages, especially in women but to some degree in men. Re-creating a conjugal union by taking another age-mate for a spouse as a remedy for solitude in later life was not characteristic of earlier English society. Rich and powerful widowed and older men might take a much younger woman to wife for sexual companionship and to ensure that they were nursed through the Fourth Age. Very occasionally well-heeled older widows might do the same, though for the first reason only of course. Still there were circumstances making against such a decision, since there is solid evidence of widowed women having some standing, an authority which they might not wish to exchange for the duty of wifely deference to a succesor husband. Widows of substantial men succeeded to their command of the household as well as to a part of their property, and the more senior and capable they were the higher their status. They took responsibility, for example, for administering the inheritance and arranging the marriages of their children.[25]

A further limitation which traditional society placed on the freedom of older women has, it is good to say, virtually vanished in recent times. No mention of widow's weeds appears in the description of Alice George. But it is exceedingly likely that she had to wear this distinguishing uniform and to accept it as entirely appropriate, just as she was no doubt required to behave with that meekness and resignation, that compulsory grief and regret for her dead husband, which was commanded of widows at any age, in spite of the considerable respect for the good wife and the position allotted to some widows. Even during the present decade there are some residual signs that inheritance from the past in respect of dress and sexual behaviour still affects older people's attitudes, especially to themselves and especially among women. It is further example of stereotypes being accepted by their victims.

According to English records females were in the majority after the middle years in the past, just as they are in the present, notwithstanding the fact that they were probably worse fed and worse treated in childhood than males.[26] We have said enough, however, to make it clear that what is so far known about their position, outlook and experience in historical times contains scarcely a hint which might help women to decide what to think, to plan and to do now that they are so much more predominant numerically in the new, yet to be everlasting, society of persons in the Third Age. Numbers of women in the Third Age in England in the 1990s are already greater than the whole population of England as it was in Goody George's day. This brief excursion into the life of the elderly and old in an earlier social world, attitudes towards them, and doctrines about them, makes one curt judgement possible. The past has little to teach us, men or women, in fashioning a general theory appropriate to the coming of the Third Age. We are on our own, in time at least.

CODA – A PLEA FOR INNOVATION

This may appear to be an insolent pronouncement, heavily biased in the presentist direction and based on what is still an exceedingly small collection of the relevant knowledge. It passes over the whole body of wisdom about age and its imaginative exploration: not only Aristotle, Aquinas, Kant and the rest of the company of philosophers, but Shakespeare, Tennyson, Matthew Arnold and the rest of the poets, Rembrandt and the other artists of old age.

But no thinker, no writer, no painter, can fashion an image or elaborate a doctrine in respect of a human condition and a state of society which it is impossible for him or her to contemplate. The Third Age of the twenty-first century and beyond could present itself to the persons we have named only as a contrived fantasy, as unreal, and as finally unconvincing, as Plato's *Republic*, More's *Utopia* or the imaginary worlds sketched out by Swift in *Gulliver's Travels* where his awkwardly named death-defiers, the Struldbrugs, are repulsive warnings to seekers after immortality. Universal principles of virtue, prudence, patience and resignation expounded in nearly all of this literature must enlighten and bring solace to those who grow old and very old whatever their circumstances, along with religious doctrine and belief. But they are not practical principles for our conduct in an ageing condition never witnessed before in human history. It is we who are charged with creating principles of this description, for ourselves and our successors.

The world of ageing in the past in which all our predecessors lived out their lives before the secular shift, poets and thinkers along with the rest, was governed by the imperatives of the second age, and wholly dominated by its values. Those still in what we should call the First Age, who made up a much larger proportion of the whole society than they ever will again, were looked upon as a preliminary state, in the ante-room of real life, and their values had not yet come to play anything like as much of a part in the outlook of the population as a whole as they do today. A Third Age could neither be realised nor envisaged, and the Fourth Age as we now know it seems to have been taken as the defining characteristic of the whole of experience between the Second Age and death, even though it did not entirely dominate that experience. Hints of the stigmatization of the older person already present? However this may be, those going through these late and latest years, few in numbers and, except among the great, too often exiguous in resources, could be passed over for most purposes: men and women shut away and sitting quietly in the departure lounge of life.

In spite of being admonished by the Scriptures that the span of life was three score years and ten, and in spite of their disposition to discount their own old age, our ancestors were apparently quite aware of the possibility of living after that decade. This must have been so in early medieval Iceland. They seem even to have been prepared to question being stereotyped as woeful remnants of themselves by the time the Great Climacteric had been passed. The representations of these later stages of life in the very popular charts of the ages of men and women, found all over Europe from an early date, do not always show them in decrepitude even in the seventh, eighth and ninth decade after birth. These wall decorations from the houses of modest Europeans and Americans dated between the fifteenth and twentieth centuries usually present the stages of life in the form of five steps upwards, one for each decade after birth, culminating in a platform for the fifties, and four steps downwards to final extinction.[27]

These representations call into question the common assumption that people looked old in the past much earlier than we do. Nevertheless Second Age values of youthful maturity; of vigour and parenthood; of political and social duty; of work, earning, responsibility, of control of young persons and of providing models for them and of having their seniors going rapidly downhill, at their disposal too; these hold almost complete command of our inheritance from the past in respect of ageing. It would be foolish to give the impression that nothing of this Second Age outlook and none of these activities continue into the Third Age and should not do so. We touch upon these questions when we come in the next chapter to spell out its general theory. But Second Age principles cannot be sufficient for Third Age purposes. They are inadequate, for example, to the creation of the institutions required for Third Age living. The persisting imperial domination of the Second Age and its set of values, extensively modulated as they have now come to be by those of the First Age, youth, athleticism and all the rest, has to be counted a great disadvantage to us now that the Third Age has arrived.

Our situation, as has been said elsewhere, is inescapably, irremediably new. It calls for creation rather than for imitation. What we are challenged to create will form the themes of our discussion of the educational system, especially of the University of the Third Age, and of the present responsibilities of older British people. These responsibilities are certainly very different from those of Alice George, the antique widow of the 1680s, and of John Locke Esq. when he took early and partial retirement of his own choice during the 1690s.

10 The General Theory of the Third Age

Limbo is defined in *The Oxford Dictionary* as the condition of neglect or oblivion, the place for forgotten or unwanted things. For many of the doctors and writers of the time of our grandfathers and great-grandfathers it seems to have been to limbo that elderly people, all those judged past work, or past productive work, had to be consigned. This attitude lingers still. With nearly everyone departing from the work-force at earlier ages during the last decade or two, more and more of the population of our country find themselves being thought of as occupying space in limbo. The general theory of the Third Age addresses itself precisely to these circumstances.

MASS INDOLENCE

If income-producing work, the care of a family and responsibility for others are taken to be what most people find satisfying, then it must follow that relinquishing these activities could signify the end of worthwhile living. It has been customary in recent times to belittle the value of work in personal and social life as a manifestation of the work ethic, apparently undesirable by definition. Nevertheless the immense importance to the individual of obtaining and holding down a job and the enhanced status of the job-holder, which continually grows as the ladder of professional promotion is ascended, demonstrates that the reality is quite otherwise. Not only are personal prosperity and power associated with work, but anything opposite to work is regarded as indolence. A society in which large numbers of persons defined as employable are unemployed, and even larger numbers are defined as unoccupied because over age, has to be called a society marked by mass indolence.

The overriding questions then become the following. Are we really content to have the fresh years of life which have been conferred on all of us spent in doing nothing? Are we not forced to recognize that the constructive and productive use of that time for social and collective purposes, satisfying and satisfactory to the individual, is an imperative challenge?

Do not these circumstances require us to have a theory, a theory of the
Third Age?

In the 1990s the proportions of those who can be described in this way
as indolent in Britain go something like this. Over the last ten years
between 1 750 000 and 3 000 000 of our citizens have had to be described
as unemployed, between 6.5 and 10 per cent of the economically active.
We have no guarantee that the proportion will not rise higher than this
second level, which represents nearly 5 per cent of the whole population,
or 6 per cent of those aged 15 and over. But well over three times the
number of the unemployed, 10 500 000 in 1991, were over the age of
retirement, the sixtieth birthday for women and the sixty-fifth for men.
This is almost exactly 20 per cent of the whole population, or almost
23 per cent of those over 15. We have already seen that many men and
some women now leave their jobs before the official retirement ages, so
that these figures and proportions for those now in retirement must be
regarded as low estimates. Even when allowance is made for further
possible falls in unemployment, and for invalids along with the fragile old
who cannot be expected to be active at all, putting the two totals of
inactive people together leaves between a fifth and a quarter of the population to be classed as in a state of indolence. Taking the higher estimates
and reckoning for adults only, the proportion approaches 30 per cent, not
all that far from a third of all mature British people.

The striking thing about the present situation as to indolence and the
older part of the population is the suddenness of the departure of senior
workers from the workforce, especially men. A fifth of all those qualified
for pensions were in the labour force in 1971, but there are not much more
than a twentieth today and their numbers are getting smaller. The fall has
been the most conspicuous for men and women in the workforce (though
by no means necessarily in employment) aged between 60 and 64. The
proportion officially at work in this age group went down from 80 per cent
in 1973 to 45 per cent in 1992, a drop of well over two-fifths. There were a
third fewer workers or would-be workers aged 65–69 in 1992 than in 1973
(18 per cent and 27 per cent), but the decrease in this group has since
given way to a slight increase, and the level among those 70–74 has been
flat since the early 1980s at about 12 per cent.[1] It seems to be among the
younger senior people them, at the age when changing to the Third from
the Second Age begins to become possible, that leaving work has become
so popular. But there are reasons for this other than the desire to retire.
The supply of jobs becomes difficult, especially for men. And both
employers and government seem determined to get the senior workers off
the labour market. The trade unions are by no means unwilling either.

There is a striking contrast here with the situation as it was when the secular shift in ageing was beginning. In the earlier part of this century, even after the old age pension scheme had been instituted and become reasonably supportive, much higher proportions of those we refer to as pensioners, implying no longer employed for reasons of age, were nevertheless still in work. We have seen that among the poorer people of London in the 1930s two-fifths of men in their late sixties and early seventies went out to work and brought in wages. There are commentators who would now maintain that such men as these, and some women too, have since been stereotyped as unemployable by the late capitalist mentality, ejected from the work-force and barred from re-entry. There can be no doubt at all that successive governments have seized every opportunity to play down unemployment figures, which are so politically embarrassing to a party in power, and substitute figures of those in retirement, which are much less of a liability. We must not overlook the fact that there are people in late life who are self-employed, but these are few, although now perhaps increasing. The treatment of workers as 'natural wastage' when they reach the higher ages is the most obvious and definite sense in which very large numbers of fit and active, potentially highly productive individuals have been *forced* to be indolent in the last few decades.

In the vocabulary which we have been using and which we are about to discuss in detail, these sombre outcomes are the result of literally applying Second Age concepts of status, occupation and the work of the individual to the whole of the life course. But we should be wary of going as far as this in thinking of mass indolence. Neither unemployment nor retirement leaves all the persons affected with absolutely nothing to do apart from keeping themselves going. Most individuals retain nearly all their social and political responsibilities as distinct from their work responsibilities[2] after giving up their jobs, and may even increase them. And retired persons are certainly not in limbo from the private, familial point of view.

The family duties and functions which continue into retirement are rarely those of maintaining familial dependents as a group living together. Retired people often spend much time and money in helping their offspring to establish and maintain their own families elsewhere. They 'work' on many tasks for their now independent children, their kin and their friends, as well as 'working' for themselves. But effort expended in this way does not count as a job for purposes of social recognition, any more than a monthly pension transfer, whatever its size, has the same standing as a monthly salary cheque. The same applies to women: their nurturant home-and family-maintaining work counts for even less when it is directed towards the families of their now officially independent children, except of course in the eyes of those children themselves. It also applies to voluntary offices of other kinds. An unpaid position in a voluntary society, however strenuous the effort required, does not have to be competed for and so is not regarded as a job for the purposes of social standing. Those no longer seeking work, although almost never entirely idle, are not in a recognizable occupation, and much of their time is indeed spend in what are regarded as leisure activities.

The insignificance of the non-earners is accentuated by the fact that, in a market society at the moment industriously re-immersing itself in market values, they are not yet a salesman's specific target. They may be a mass, an enormous mass as we have seen, but they are scarcely a mass market. They do not tend to build, furnish, refurnish or re-equip their own dwellings, however well worn their accoutrements may have become. They do not require family-sized packs of groceries and other household goods; do not buy new motor cars on the scale their juniors do, or have them bought for them and maintained for them by their employers. They most definitely do not insist on that year's model every year, because, and this is the main point about the elderly as consumers, they respond much less readily to fashion, in cars, clothes, furniture, or goods of any other kind. There are striking signs that this may change, both because pensioners are developing a set of market values of their own and because salesmen are beginning to work up a market image for the elderly. A market in housing for the more prosperous among them has certainly come into evidence. However, in the main the goods that the retired are being persuaded to buy on a mass scale are to do with leisure – travel and holidays being particularly prominent. So we have mass indolence, conditioned and enforced by all the means of mass persuasion.[3]

The unemployed cannot afford travel or leisure goods of any kind. They nearly all belong in the Second Age and their indolence, their compulsory inactivity, can only be part of a discussion of the Third Age in one particular. In contemporary capitalist economies the huge number and conspicuous frustrated idleness of the unemployed demonstrate the inadequacy of Second Age values and Second Age institutions to do all that is unthinkingly demanded of them. They simply do not, cannot include all the individual lives which they are reckoned to do.

Jobs being easy to lose and difficult to get towards the end of working life, many a worker goes from his latest spell of unemployment straight into retirement. This is a peculiarly disadvantageous region of limbo in which to find oneself, though it is theoretically open to its inhabitants, especially those in the middle class, to declare themselves as now being in the Third Age. What cannot be accepted is that an unemployed person still in the Second Age, there by choice as well as by personal characteristics, should be treated as if in the Third Age, although he or she wishes to stay in the work-force. In France the numbers of those who proceed from years of joblessness directly into retirement are so large that the adequacy of the concept of retirement itself is being called into question. What is the difference between a man of 57, shall we say, living on unemployment pay and fully aware of the fact that he will never get another job, and a man of 68 who is retired?[4]

The situation of indolence is certainly not new in the late twentieth century. 'Full employment' was reckoned to be achieved with an 8 per cent jobless rate in the classic analysis of Beveridge in the 1940s, and this would leave over two million people out of work in the 1990s. Beveridge was himself an exponent of 'natural wastage' as a way of maintaining full employment. During the late 1930s, looked upon then and since as disastrous from the point of view of idleness and the occasion of the Beveridge Report, 12 to 14 per cent seem to have been in mass indolence as defined here, a seventh or an eighth of the population as compared with the fifth or a quarter we have reckoned for today. Moreover there is ample evidence of under-employment and unemployment in the pre-industrial English economy.

But those out of work in the Second Age are not quite in manifest limbo, not consigned to mass indolence in the same final way as their seniors constituting 'natural wastage', definitely and everlastingly redundant. Most unemployed persons at all times, certainly the younger ones, can expect to find work for the first time, or to do so again, and qualifying themselves for that event is for them a purposeful, a Second Age, activity. To the finally, and usually compulsorily retired, 'industry' in all its now manifold forms, from coal-mining and the manufacture of pottery to computer programming, from horticulture to electronic engineering, has virtually nothing to offer.

There are, as we shall see in the chapter on education, a handful of opportunities for a few highly specialized middle-class retired persons in the Third Age. As for the rest, a man can often get casual work as a handyman or as a jobbing gardener whenever he wishes, and so can some women with equally casual, mostly household work. The very highly skilled person, say in the computer arts, can continue working from home until as late in life as she chooses. But in spite of these exceptions it is certainly a myth that all, or even many, of the retired resent their abrupt ejection from the office or the factory. In fact, the theory of the Third Age assumes that they welcome their freedom, and challenges them to make it a time of self-fulfilment. From the point of view of the world of work, nevertheless, they are in limbo and expected to remain there in case they should take jobs away from those in the Second Age.

The duties of those in the Third Age will be claimed in our next chapter to include such responsibilities as the rescue of cultural institutions, which they and the rest of the population so much need, that is to say the libraries, museums, art galleries, historic houses, cathedrals and other monuments. In arguing this case, hard words may have to be said concerning the monopoly of 'work' by the Second Age.

The general argument in support of the Third Age, moreover, asserts that it is wrong to suppose that the satisfactions which men and women desire for themselves can all be effectively conceived in Second Age terms. The personal achievements which people strive for over the whole of adult life certainly transcend the Second Age, and here we choose to associate those achievements as closely as we can with the Third. Though the Third Age ordinarily comes after the Second in the life course the suggestion has been put forward here that where an individual's 'crown of life' can be attained in the pursuance of Second Age goals and activities, the Third and Second Ages should be supposed to go forward side by side. The fact that mass indolence is now commonly allowed to be the whole description of life after or outside the Second Age, is the most telling sign of all that we have so far failed to be our age. Let us turn to the reasoned consideration of each of the nominated ages so as to give more substance to these propositions.

THE FIRST AGE OF DEPENDENCY, SOCIALIZATION AND EDUCATION

Although I have stated that for our purposes divisions of the life course are not to be defined by calendar age nor are they consistently determined by biology, the First Age is much more subject to these factors than the Second or the Third. Its beginning, birth, is unquestionably biological, and its ending, or series of endings since the age of responsibility is attained at different points for different purposes, are birthdays in most cases.

In Britain, individuals can drive cars after their seventeenth birthday, they can vote in an election after their eighteenth, and they attain conventional 'majority' at twenty-one. Social and personal age are of little import, therefore, to the transition from the First to the Second Age, a transition which is difficult to bring about by choice, in spite of the fact that there is so much variation in the pace at which individuals grow up. Hence the process of biological development as to the size, strength and intellectual capacity required for independent living tends to dominate the experience of the First Age, and along with it that dependence on others, that necessary position of being in training, which is so much its characteristic. We shall reject the powerful and deep-rooted inclination to suppose that because all those in the First Age are under instruction, it follows that education, intellectual development and achievement, are confined to the first Age, inevitably linked to socialization. There are other ways in which traditional accounts of childhood and youth have to be modified in order to accommodate the Third Age and its theory.

It cannot now be maintained that physical maturation signals the end of the First Age, for it has not done so for several generations. If childhood ends with the arrival of sexual maturity, reproductive capacity and full size and strength, then it has to be reckoned as shorter on average by over two years in Britain today than it was, and still is in contemporary traditional societies.[5] Adults may not now be responsible for such large numbers of the young and immature as our forefathers were, but they have to keep full-grown persons for longer and longer in a state of instruction and dependence. Meanwhile, and to some degree as a result of these new circumstances no doubt, the bodily appearance and the physical achievements of these youths, between childhood and full independence, have become more and more significant to everyone of every calendar age.

Exaltation of the prowess of youth at sport of all kinds grows ever more important in our cultural life, and it cannot but affect the self-esteem of those no longer able to compete. The exertions and achievements of the athletes, footballers, horsewomen, boxers, golfers and the rest almost dominate television programmes, which in their turn almost dominate diversion in the contemporary world. To the active of every age, and especially the active in their Third Age, passively watching the telly looks to be the quintessence of indolence, and it is a fact that the older you are, the more time you spend doing just this. But youthfulness is not only salient on TV: it monopolizes the market and the media, obsessively devoted as they now are to youthful looks, shape, size and bearing. Not only is each particular of dress and facial appearance subject to the imperial measures set by those in their teens and early twenties, but every last sign of a decline from those standards with the normal ageing process is singled out for comment and reproach. Anyone doubting the unquestioned dictatorship in these directions of the just-past-adolescent body, or mind for that matter, needs only to leaf over the fashion magazines or watch *The Clothes Show* on television. In all such matters we seem to have deliberately set ourselves every possible obstacle in the way of adjustment to the arrival of the Third Age. There can scarcely be a doubt, however, of the principle which we should now maintain. Standards and values entirely more appropriate to the objective situation as it is for two-thirds of the life of all of us will have to be created for our appearance and our bearing. No theory of the Third Age can accommodate to a position where youthfulness, or its simulation, is the standard for everyone.[6]

The First Age, then, is that of babyhood, childhood, initial instruction and early maturation. It is an age of dependency, dependency which rapidly diminishes towards its close, though at a slower rate in monetary matters. It is one of relative irresponsibility and of little authority over others. The First Age contains the transition from home to school, and often if in Britain not often enough, to subsequent full-time education, and the decisive transition from living in the parental group to independent living, which, usually though not quite necessarily, marks its close. These are the commonplaces of the First Age, but I have already pointed to the paradox of an exceptionally successful athlete getting into a position where the Third Age in certain of its aspects may be lived for a while alongside the First Age.

It has to be admitted that this possibility cannot be said to add to the realism of the Third Age theory: special pleading for an unconvincing hypothesis, some might say. The sight of the slip of a girl just announced to be a Wimbledon finalist, or of the baby-faced Olympic medallist on every television screen in the world, accompanied by sententious voices making sententious claims about 'historic' events fought out by beardless boys, should convince us nevertheless that no straightforward account of the relationship of the climax of personal achievement with the personal life course has much prospect of success.

The life career of the world champion, let it be noted, is required by the theory to work itself out so that the Third Age is divided between an early phase of athletic triumph, and a later phase of much more personal cultivation, usually intellectual and aesthetic, coming after the Second Age. Living out achievements in the imagination fifty years after the event, even in the company of millions of nostalgic television viewers, is no prospect in itself for an admirable Third Age. One should not in retirement spend too much time recalling the achievements of youth. This points in exactly the wrong direction, backwards over previous living.

The calendar age of 25 has been hesitantly suggested as that of the end of the first and the beginning of the Second Age for most people, and at this point it was claimed a man or woman should be able to bring into view all future experience up to and beyond the calender age of 70. This need not be taken to mean, however, that no such steady gaze along the corridor of time to come can be expected from those still in the First Age, or that the life plan cannot begin to be formulated before the Second Age arrives.

Because the young are other-directed, however, because parents and other elders, who know more and see more, who have mastered the arts which bring a living, provide the models for them and mould their behaviour by affection, reward and punishment, the young are in an unfavourable position for making their own decisions for themselves. They can witness the Third Age in others, in grandparents and now more and more in great-grandparents, and in older companions unrelated by kinship. They may form friendships over the generations of a surprising fruitfulness. But the circumstances of the First Age make it very difficult for them to imagine coming to be old themselves. In any case the roles of those who are elderly now, excepting always those who have deliberately adopted Third Age attitudes, are not at all likely to be those which will have to be played out by the young of today when they get to the end of their working lives. Obeying the call to be your age at your twenty-fifth birthday by making this imaginative effort is peculiarly difficult at the present time and is never going to be easy.

Those in the First Age, then, are hampered in the adoption of a life plan properly appropriate to their objective situation, a life plan which would reach its apogee in the Third Age. Nevertheless, the immature can and do acquire experience, habits and techniques which will count towards the fulfilment, the later fulfilment, of life objectives already singled out. Furthermore, their outlook has the important attribute of pointing perpetually forwards, which is one of the conditions which the theory of the Third Age has always to assume. But lack of time, lack of independent control of resources, lack of knowledge, experience and instruction – whoever has recommended teaching the life course to schoolchildren? – all these things inhibit planning and tend to get in the way of achievement in any direction other than the physical. Accordingly, it is very rare indeed for an individual to proceed from the first Age directly to the Third, and live for the rest of life in that condition.

THE SECOND AGE OF MATURITY, INDEPENDENCE, PROCREATION, FAMILIAL AND SOCIAL RESPONSIBILITY

Although this last described condition is not the case of the world-class athletes, it is certainly to be found in the infant prodigies who maintain their early promise, and pre-eminently in the lives of the great artists, who have already been singled out as the pattern livers of life in the mode which our theory recommends. Too literal an interpretation has to be avoided all the same. The general theory of the Third Age might dispose us to assert that the prodigy and the genius can omit the Second Age altogether and sometimes part of the First as well, living their lives after their superiority has declared itself wholly in the triumphs of the Third. Wolfgang Amadeus Mozart composed superlative music and performed under his father's direction as a boy, and whilst he was still dependent on the family of his parents for the purposes of living. The conditions which they maintained for him emancipated him as far as could be from the restraints of the First Age and thus made his achievements possible. But he was still a callow youth and when he gained his independence he had to submit to the demands of earning his keep, of founding his family, of the vagaries of patronage. He had to struggle in fact with all the vicissitudes of pursuing a career characteristic of the Second Age in everyone, obstacles as they often are to the realization of the chosen plan of life. Only in so far as he transcended these limitations can he be claimed to have spent his creative life in the Third Age, or in that condition alongside the First and the Second.

The stories of Mozart and of Chatterton indicate that hardship and obscurity are not by definition absent from the Third Age when it is lived before its usual appearance, though such unwelcome experiences as theirs are uncommon. The achievement which brings about the coupling of two of our ages in this way is first and foremost personal achievement, usually in the end recognized for what it is or was by contemporaries but sometimes by posterity alone. Jane Austen might be an apter illustration. She was born in 1770, five years later than the suicide of Chatterton, 'the marvellous boy', and died unmarried and unnoticed at the age of 41, not recorded as a writer in the family genealogy or even in the inscription on her tomb, yet the author of six of the finest novels in the English language. Working round the house as she had been doing for 25 or 30 years, and sneaking from the kitchen to the parlour/dining room next door to compose her works on those tiny slips of paper, Jane Austen must be supposed to have been living alongside her Second Age of domesticity a Third Age of supreme achievement, comparable as many critics have claimed with the achievement of Shakespeare himself.

But it is somewhat anachronistic to show forth our theory by applying it unqualified to entirely extraordinary persons who lived and died 150 years before the Third Age became a social fact for complete populations. Only very occasionally do we find outstanding individuals looking forward to later life in order to attain what they know to be possible for them. Robert Browning is perhaps the best-known from the poem which he wrote in his early fifties, 'Rabbi Ben Ezra':

> Grow old along with me!
> The best is yet to be,
> The last of life, for which the first was made.
> Our times are in His hand
> Who saith, 'A whole I planned,
> Youth shows but half: trust God: see all: be not afraid!'

Even here, however, we find no hint that the 'crown of life' will come after release from the pressures of the workaday world. For Browning in fact, so our theory would imply, the Third Age was already present directly his superiority had declared itself; he did not need to wait for personal fulfilment. Figures like him and other exceedingly successful individuals are in the same situation in our own day. But for the rest of us it is in a Third Age coming after the Second, not replacing or running parallel to it, that we should seek to find realization of the goals which we set ourselves.

The Second Age is not now what once it seemed to have been, that is to say the whole career after youth and before the final decline. It is being perpetually foreshortened at its beginning through the extension of the period of formation and curtailed at its ending by the lowering of the onset retirement. But it is still the longest of the four Ages, and from the social and the political point of view far and away the most productive and important. These are not the years during which nearly all the work which gives rise to the resources counted as economic resources gets done; they also make up the time when individuals and society reproduce themselves. It seems correct to say that reproduction is of much greater significance to women than to men, and gives the greatest of all satisfactions, being the noblest achievement of their lives. Since the procreation and rearing of children is man's work as well as woman's, and since women are now claiming a larger and larger part in business, in industry and services in the arts, this statement reads a little oddly all the same. There could be no point, however, in belittling the worth of family-forming and of the production and upbringing of children, along with the exploits of what is called business life, the gaining of security, prosperity or of any of the other satisfactions of the Second Age, belittling them because the pinnacle of predominantly personal achievement is to be reserved until the Third.

Nor is it all useful to push what is presented here as a suggestive hypothesis to unconvincing lengths. There are clearly manifold personal attainments and satisfactions for ordinary people in pursuing a career, in starting and running a family, in obtaining and maintaining power over others, all of which come within the course of the Second Age and need have no bearing on a Third. Nevertheless there are features of the Second Age which limit it as an arena for personal achievement, in addition to the fact that its duties and conditions usually balk the individual to a considerable degree, frustrating the attainment of personal ends – frustrating, or, more significantly, postponing them.

FRUSTRATIONS OF THE SECOND AGE

Work may well be justly valued for what it creates both for the individual and for society, but work in the Second Age in our economic order is almost wholly imposed by others than oneself. If it is found satisfying, this is incidental to its purpose, and the work would have to be done even if entirely unsatisfactory to the doer. Moreover, work in the Second Age is inevitably allied with the loss of personal control over time. Your time belongs to the firm directly you enter the workplace, and the whole history of work regulations and of socialist protest shows how thwarting this circumstance can be, especially when there is any reason to believe that the work done in an employer's time is the subject of exploitation of the worker. What your efforts create or help to create is never wholly yours to take a proper pride in, to exhibit or dispose of, and is therefore quite different from what you do in your own time and for your own purposes.

We need not go through the familiar litany of the alienation of the worker from his or her labour, and from what that labour brings into being under contemporary conditions of production, in order to recognize that such alienation may be inseparable from the conditions of the Second Age. The socialist element in Third Age living, where work and its products can be pointed to by workers as their own, wholly their own, may be seen as a recommendation by many. The emphasis here is to be placed rather on the fact that truly personal achievement during the Second Age tends to confine itself to time off. Such are the evenings, the weekends, the holidays, brief periods away from the job and the family which you can use, for example, to win a prize at a show for a flower, fruit or vegetable grown in your own garden and tended in your own time.

In the past, before the Third Age began to be established in the 1950s, most of what we here describe as Third Age living went on during such interludes spent away from earning a living and nurturing a family. Hence there was the tendency for those still in employment to view their retirement as a period when hobbies could be engaged in every day, for as long as you please. But it does not follow from this that Third Age living, now that almost everyone can expect to experience it for a considerable and growing length of time after the Second Age is over, should consist of nothing more than relaxation, the gentle pursuit of hobbies as part of a life of slow-paced indolence.

The circumstances surrounding employment in the Second Age do much to explain the well-nigh universal feeling that when retirement comes what people want to do above all, and what they should be allowed and encouraged to do is to take a long, long rest as a reward for their previous exertions in earning a living. Since the Third Age is a matter of personal choice, this is undoubtedly a permissible attitude, even if it is not true that years of hard work literally leave you in need of rest, and even if spending retirement in this way can scarcely be described as the attainment of the 'crown of life'. Physical sloth indeed is inevitably a liability in older people, a source of bodily and of psychic decline, in its way an invitation to the onset of the Fourth Age. 'If you rest, you rot', might not be too extreme a dictum for those who look upon retirement as a time without exertion of any kind, and as the world now works it is in limbo that you rot.

Not all Second Age activities are those of earning your keep, and by no means all earners have that sense of alienation from their labour which has sometimes been attributed to them. Gaining a living as a professional person is done in your own time to a considerable degree, and the sense of alienation is to that extent less likely. Outstanding achievement in Second Age activities no doubt banishes any feeling of alienation altogether. Moreover, if such success is great enough and goes on long enough the theory lays it down that the Third Age is beginning to be lived alongside the Second Age. The creation and maintenance of a family of children, which may go forward simultaneously with these other activities, is usually supposed to be entirely free of any sense of being used or exploited by others. This is so at least while offspring are in the First Age.

Families are ordinarily set up during the Second Age, and this for mainly biological reasons. But as was the case with childhood occupying the whole of the First Age, it is no longer true that the family group once built necessarily lasts throughout the Second Age of its founders, and decidedly not true that the family will stay together during the Third. In Britain and elsewhere in the West we now live for the first time in history when it can be said that marriage is no longer a lifelong association. Divorce, desertion, adoption of new partners and remarriage have brought about vicissitudes in the careers of families which are wholly of our own day. Moreover, the 'empty-nest' stage is likely to be reached well before the retirement, or retirements, of the couple, in spite of the fact that retirement is getting earlier and earlier. This circumstance, as we have seen, marks a very important difference between later life in the modern world and later life in the pre-industrial past. But familial activity in collaboration with and often in company with now-independent married children and with grandchildren usually continues until the very end. Indeed, since many a young wife and mother spends more and more of her time away from her home in order to earn that second income which is now regarded as a general necessity, the grandparents are entering more and more into the familial life of the generation which succeeds their own, and increasingly resent denial of access to their children's children which divorce and separation may bring with them. In this sense the contemporary family could be said to be decidedly more inter-generational in its scope than the family of our ancestors. It may not be long before great-grandparental collaboration of this kind begin to be quite common.

Such inter-generationalism is ordinarily a source of great satisfaction and happiness. So indeed is the subsequent recall of the interlude, brief in years but large and vivid in the memories both of parents and of children, when the family group did possess its classic form, mothers and fathers perpetually alongside their dependent little ones, and human interaction at its very closest. But there are resemblances all the same between the alienation felt in the Second Age at earning work and the discontent which parents feel at being locked up all day with the children, mothers specially. Otherwise why do married women now flock to the workplace during their childbearing years, the workplace where they are still much worse-placed and worse-paid than men, and even more deprived of personal satisfaction from their work? Why have their husbands so often felt the urge to get out of the house? Why do both wives and husbands so often look forward to a day when their time can be their own? Why is it that the presence of children, though it certainly reduces the likelihood of divorce, is increasingly less likely to prevent it?

There are reasons in the status which we have attributed to those holding down a job, and in the need for two incomes to a household as well as the desire for independence and equality, which help to explain why a married woman takes employment and continues in it as her children arrive. If she is between partners the proceeds from her job are clearly crucial. Also, the company she keeps while at work is of considerable importance to her, an advantage which may be lacking to life in the Third Age. No mother with a child or children at home, however, would be likely to rank the pleasure she gets from employment above that which she gets from her family. Like her husband she earns first and foremost to keep the family going, she works for the extras perhaps rather than the essentials, the expensive school fees, the holidays, the furnishings for the home. But whatever the rewards of family life at home with the children, it is also a mark of success to bring that phase of the life course to a proper end, to see your children well-established as independent persons. Thus satisfaction with the family which you have made such efforts to found and to sustain cannot be permanent. It is not possible, therefore, to regard your family at all exclusively as the acme of your own, your personal achievement, what has been called here the 'crown of life'.

Those in the front office of businesses, doctors and lawyers, writers and professors, independent experts of every kind, are in no position to avoid these limitations on the satisfaction which they get from family life. But their situation as to earning their keep is somewhat different. They do not have to submit to the loss of control of their time to the same extent as the rest of us in the Second Age. Such persons in fact, and this is true to a lesser degree of all professionals, not only dispose of their own time at their places of work, they dispose of everyone else's time as well, especially the time of employees, patients and clients.

There are, in fact, several features of the position of the more fortunate practitioners of the occupations of the Second Age which are of relevance to our general theory. Professional people, for one thing, do for a livelihood what they might wish to do for themselves, for their own satisfaction, even for pleasure. Moreover, because they can dispose of their time to such a great extent, they can develop their interests and plan their satisfactions in ways that others cannot, even large-earning, big-spending, business people. Added to which the professional has a good deal more choice about retirements: there are more options, often opportunities to negotiate. Here the scientists, teachers and particularly literary and artistic persons have the greatest advantages. For them it might be said that the Second Age is generally interfused with the Third Age. The distinctions which we are striving to get clear are of lesser importance.

Still, managing directors have to sit at their over-sized desks, doctors have to attend their surgeries, professors have to lecture and examine, writers have to keep their deadlines, or try to, and broadcasters have to turn up at the studio, at the penalty in every case of a threat to their reputations and earnings. It is only the outstandingly successful who are emancipated to the greatest degree which it is possible to be from the Second Age imperatives, if still subject to its limitations in respect of family life. Prominent among the others who transcend the categories which have been laid down are the wielders of power, particularly the successful politicians.

Not only could it be claimed of them that the 'crown of life' comes in the Second Age, so that the Third Age can either be regarded as irrelevant or as being lived at the same time, but it is also true that the politicians show the fewest social symptoms of the ageing process itself, psychological and even physical. There is a sense in which we all recognized that former President Reagan was always an old man while he was in the seat of power, and that the members of the central committees of the Communist parties which used to run the show in so many socialist countries, and still do in China, were also for the most part old men. But there is another sense in which their age has no bearing on their functions. If they do retire it is not to the Third Age as the rest of us understand it. By and large, however, people as eminent as this escape our theory. Who could say how much our own Lady Thatcher exists in the Second Age, how much in the Third? It has been claimed that for such reasons as these, politicians never experience ageing and old age in the way that their constituents and subjects experience the condition. In this sense, the elderly and old could be said to be entirely absent from the inside of the political system.[7]

THE THIRD AGE OF PERSONAL ACHIEVEMENT, THE FOURTH AGE OF DEPENDENCE AND DECREPITUDE

Transition from the Second Age to the Third Age has already been extensively discussed, as has the character of the Third Age itself. Let it be repeated that the coming of the Third Age from the individual point of view is a personal, not a public occurrence: of itself it has little to do with calendar age, social age or even biological age, and above all it is a matter of choice. All this, so the theory claims, is true in spite of the fact that for most people the Third Age is only possible in retirement, and that the time and conditions of retirement cannot usually be chosen by the person who retires. Such a transition is very much easier in an individual who has used the period of life in the Second Age to work out a plan which will bring final satisfaction in the Third when he or she is free, free to realize personal purposes as completely as possible.

The fifth sense of age which was distinguished when the various meanings of the term were analyzed in Chapter 3 is that of subjective age, where there are events but not duration. It is in this fifth sense that we can live our lives in perpetual awareness of all our future selves, and plan for the Third Age from the very outset of the Second. During the Third Age itself, moreover, subjective age is more important in experience than ever before. It lends a timelessness to that stage of life, in spite of, perhaps to some extent because of, the fact that dying becomes so much more probable. It behoves us, as has been already said, when we are in our sixties, seventies and particularly in the eighties to be prepared to die, as our ancestors schooled themselves to be at all points and in every year of their ages, and yet to continue with our plans for ourselves as if the future were entirely open-ended.

Since life-expectation varies so from individual to individual within the Third Age, looking at the future as open-ended is surely the only appropriate policy for the Third Age, which is has no terminus which can be planned or allowed for. The Fourth Age, or death itself, may supervene when five, ten or fifteen years have passed after the beginning of the Third Age, or may be postponed to twenty, twenty-five or even thirty years later. But to those who die a sudden death, or the natural death which James Fries and Vaïnö Kannisto believe to be a possibility, a Fourth Age does not occur at all. Because the Third Age is the period of completion and arrival it has no necessary temporal structure, for the individual anyway. Ideally he or she should be in a position to savour the experience of the Third Age as an individual for any possible duration of years.

But a community of those who have arrived at their destinations in this way cannot, must not, be without a sense that there is a collective, a social, future which is as much their responsibility as the responsibility of those likely to experience that future for much greater lengths of time. This is particularly so in respect of the responsibility of those in the Third Age at the present time to those who will succeed to the Third Age at a later time. It is highly significant, in my view, that the subject chosen for exploration at the first world symposium of Universities of the Third Age, held in Cambridge in September 1988, was 'Into the Twenty-first Century'. The second, which took place four years later, addressed a very similar theme.

Even more interesting, because it runs up against a traditional dogma about the outlook of older people, and touches on a passionate contemporary interest of younger people, is the recognition that those in the Third Age have a lively sense of the future in relation to such matters as the environment and the preservation for posterity of our cultural inheritance, material as well as intellectual and literary. I have gone as far as to sketch out a suggestion that those in the Third Age should recognise themselves and be recognised by others, as trustees acting in the present on behalf of generations yet to come on matters such as these.[8] This sense in older people of an indefinite social future, one that does not confine itself to their own descendants, immediate or distant, is accompanied as must be expected, by a strong sense of the past, the personal and collective past. Indeed it is my own view that those in the Third Age have a clearer and firmer view of what is or may be still to come precisely because they know what has gone before. They were there to see it happen.

It is a mistake, however, a grave mistake and one which seriously distorts the relationship between the Second Age and the Third, to assume that those in late and latest life are interested exclusively in their own past, and that of the society they belong to. It may be therapeutic to encourage the isolated and depressed old man or woman to undertake recall and rehearsal of what once was, to sing the tunes and recite the events of fifty, sixty or seventy years ago. This seems to be a standard routine in the supportive treatment accorded by the caring and sympathetic to their seniors, especially the casualties amongst them.[9] But those in the Third Age have to live in the present and to think about, provide for the future, although theirs will necessarily be a short personal future on the average. They should not have their gaze fixed on the past, as Wordsworth did, and should not be encouraged to do so. This is one more in the list of duties of older people which we shall leave to consider at the end of the book, but it affects their juniors, those of them who choose to intervene in the lives of older people.

To return from the relation between the Third Age and the Second Age to that between the Third Age and the Fourth, it is important that the process of ageing itself be given stress. Since no once can choose the moment of the onset of final decline, the ageing of a person, especially in the biological and social sense, has a significance for the transition from the Third Age to the Fourth Age greater than either of the previous life-course transitions. An important reason for this is that everyone in the Third Age, especially when he or she is threatened by the Fourth, ought to be aware of when and how to withdraw. To be properly sensitive to the judgement of friends, neighbours, acquaintances, and people at large, expressed, implied, or for reasons of delicacy merely hinted at, is a demanding duty. We have to exert ourselves to recognize precisely when the point has come to resign from this, to cease to do that, to recognize that in this particular respect we have begun to be passengers or encumbrances. This is part of the art of living later life, and it is to be hoped that a body of conventions will be fashioned by those in the Third Age to give guidance to their fellows and successors.

The difficulties of this transition are very well-known, and the greatest of them arises from the circumstances that the Fourth Age may come upon people without their being aware of its arrival, and so affect both their sensibilities and their judgement. Nevertheless, the sharpness of the distinction between the Third and Fourth Ages in this respect should not be exaggerated. There are Third Age occupations and pursuits which can proceed, as every one knows, when physical decline is quite advanced. Becoming unable to leave your house or even your bed does not itself require that a person withdraw from the Third Age, and the process may be very gradual. We have discussed at some length in previous chapters the question of how long the Fourth Age itself is likely to last, and insisted on the obvious point that its onset, and hence its duration, should be put off for as long as possible by appropriate behaviour throughout life and particularly during the Third Age. The biological and medical uncertainties of the length of the Fourth Age, now and in the future, pose perhaps the most serious of all difficulties in the way of accepting the suggested theory of the life course and of the Third Age.

CRITIQUE OF THE GENERAL THEORY OF THE THIRD AGE

An obvious objection to the theory of the Third Age would be that it would not remedy the situation sketched out at the beginning of the chapter. It would not in fact lead to the removal of people in their late and latest years from the limbo to which they find themselves relegated, and so to the lessening of mass indolence. It might be granted that a society of older people engaged at last and to the last in the very activities which each most likes, and has previously planned for, cannot be called either indolent or marginal. But people would not easily be persuaded to live in the presence of all their future selves: not many of them would plan their life courses as theory requires, or at all: they would hardly be willing to accept postponement of personal achievement to the Third Age, or to adopt the suggestion that if such achievement should come earlier, it should be associated with the Third Age in the way which has been set out. In all these respects, it could be urged that the theory is unrealistic.

These objections are not quite true to present facts. Some people have always looked forward to a time of freedom from the trammels of the Second Age in order to do what they have always wanted to do. All of us plan our lives to some extent, and for some, as for the writer himself, the planning process already starts or started at the beginning of the working career. Nevertheless, when questioned, people in their early twenties seem so concerned about the immediate future that they are unwilling to consider their more distant prospects. Up to the present, they, like everyone else, have been able to rely on established custom and outlook to provide for what may, but as they see it, only may happen in thirty or forty years time. They have not grasped the fact that these intimations from an unchanged and supposedly unchangeable set of ageing conditions are no longer of use. The demographic regime which gave rise to them has passed away. The provision of pensions, public and private, is much affected as we shall see by this refusal on the part of young adults to recognise that they will all eventually grow old. At the outset of the Second Age, growing old is both feared and rejected. Those who lead and control them, those whose task it is to inform them, have neither the understanding nor the information to give them guidelines whether they be writers, educators, administrators or politicians.[10]

It is important, however, to distinguish what persons in their position may now say from what, under the different conditions which have now arrived, they may think and do, particularly if they take a better informed and more realistic view of the situation as to ageing. The same applies to the further objection to the theory that it requires a high educational level to appreciate and to act upon. The population at large, so many would claim, and the under-educated British population in particular, are in no position to respond to it. The question of whether the analysis is at all convincing, however, has to be separated from the question of whether it could or would become a part of practice.

It has several times been insisted that the coming of the Third Age, indeed the secular shift in ageing itself, are so recent in what has been called social structural time, that it cannot be expected that many people will yet have accommodated themselves in their objective position as to ageing. There simply has not been enough experience, social or individual, to make a judgement on what is possible in the way of modifying habits, outlooks, expectations in the way which the theory recommends, and this could be pleaded in reply to the criticisms I have made of politicians and opinion-formers. This is as true in respect of those with modest educational backgrounds and in manual occupations as it is of the comfortably placed intellectuals. Moreover, the crucial issue as to the value of the practicality of the theory has still to be considered. What other sets of propositions are there which would meet the case?

It is not a future possibility with which we find ourselves confronted, or a hypothetical case, but a present fact, that the elderly are to such a large extent in limbo. The likelihood of the age structure changing back to a position in which these problems would be less urgent has been duly considered and firmly pronounced against. All the indications at present go the other way. It may be uncertain how much longer people's lives will be in the twenty-first century than at the present time, but no one expects that life will get appreciably shorter or that the proportions of the elderly will go down. Part-time work may become very much more common, especially for women, and this could well have an effect in blurring the distinction between the Third Age and the Second. But it seems improbable that such developments would do more than interrupt for a time the steady growth of the numbers of those in the Third Age. Nor does it seem at all likely that there will ever be a significant demand for older workers to stay in the work-force. If the retirement age is raised, it will be because it is decided that the pension and medical bills can no longer be afforded.

This is not an effective solution; as must be expected, it merely adds to the numbers of older workers without jobs. Not much has so far been said, however, about the alterations in the structure of employment and of production generally which could be put into effect so as to make the theory of the Third Age less appropriate or less necessary. Prolonged retirement at the end of employment could be avoided, for example, by everyone working from 25 to 35, 45 to 55 and 65 to 75, and having time to themselves in the intervening stretches of life. Many variants are clearly possible, though more and shorter periods out would give less space for attaining the realization of the self than continuous retirement. Arrangements of this kind are more usually discussed as a way of sharing out jobs more equitably and helping women to combine their careers with the bearing of children. Alternations between work and non-work over the life course would have the further advantages of enabling people to do their own thing when they were more active physically than many of them are in retirement as we now know it, especially during their later years.

But the impracticability and ineffectiveness of this rather rigid solution to the problem seems impossible to deny. The discontinuities imposed on individuals and on industrial organizations would be very serious indeed, quite apart from the bureaucratic complications. In the vocabulary we have been using, the interludes away from employment would be instalments of the Third Age during the course of the Second, so that the differences between the two sets of expedients is rather less than might be thought. For women, however, the outstanding feature of the activities of the Second Age is the bearing of children, most decidedly not a Third Age activity and not open to being intercalated in later life with the Third Age situation.

Furthermore, having to return once, twice, or perhaps even oftener in a lifetime to Second Age conditions would not be welcomed if what has been set out about the disadvantages they place in the way of the realization of the self has been at all persuasive. The same might be said of working part-time. Very few of the currently retired ever wish to return full-time to the workplace. What has to be accepted on all sides is that the disposition of the life course has now got to be changed. The on/off situation, as it might be called, seems not to be as viable as that implied by the theory of the Third Age. Not the least important reason why this is so must be that the theory of the Third Age makes no requirement as to the fundamental restructuring of the labour market and of much industrial organization as well.

The theory of the Third Age as it has been expounded here no doubt makes numbers of assumptions about individual and social psychology, not to speak of industrial and financial organization, which experts would find questionable. If its abandonment on these grounds led to a different and more effective analysis, then the theory would still have accomplished as much as most first attempts at new problems usually accomplish. Whatever its defects turn out to be, however, it has at least the advantage of adaptability.

There seems to me to be little need to dwell on the limits of that adaptability. I have several times insisted in this chapter that the facticity, as the social theorists would call it, of the Third Age as a social construct, and this must be its technical description for such theorists, rests on two things, one affecting women very much more than men, and the other affecting men rather more than women. The disappearance of the children from the home is the first of them and no social investigator or indeed social theorist denies that this constitutes a watershed in the female life course, nor does any woman with whom I have discussed it. The other is that desire for release from the trammels of having to earn a living under the Second Age conditions as they obtain now, and no doubt always have obtained in some form or other, and always will. The inescapable facts are that both these interludes, paid employment and child-rearing have now come to occupy much shorter relative proportions of a much longer life course.

Although a society is at liberty to ignore or to override these ineluctable circumstances to some extent, the limits are quite narrow and seem likely to remain so whatever happens to length of life or to the physical condition of older persons. This means that it is not a viable response to the demographic and other imperatives which have brought the Third Age into being simply to accommodate them by extending the length of the Second Age by political decree. There is an objective change of life for both sexes at about the time when women cease to have to carry out the duties of bringing up their children and when men reach the end of their work careers. Since men are involved to an increasing extent in the duties I have allotted to women and women in those allotted to men, it is clear that the times of withdrawal for a couple will often differ somewhat. But in general the transition for most couples, the giving over that is of the Second Age and taking up the Third, is likely to occur for both partners within an interlude of months rather than years.

Political life being what it is, and politicians what they are, it seems likely that for a time the pretence will be that nothing has happened in respect of the transition in the life course which cannot be met by fiddling about with retirement ages and pushing all arrangements to points a little later in people's lives.[11] Not so. The phenomena we are considering go so much deeper than this that the proper response to such an attempt to evade their consequences is to refer again to that cultural lag, that false consciousness about ageing which have been diagnosed in contemporary attitudes. Those who accept such superficialities demonstrate the purblindness which accompanies total ignorance of historical sociology. They do not know what we now are, or what they may or must become because they do not know what we have been.

So flexible is the theory of the Third Age nevertheless that some may judge it to be descriptive rather than analytic, with little of the properly theoretical to show. Its claims, however, are not limited to life plans and their strategies: the relationship between society and the individual is also affected by it. Of the two overall theories of individual ageing, that of disengagement and that of activism, the model we are expounding belongs initially with the second. Its emphasis is on planning an doing, up to the very moment of dying or when the Fourth Age makes itself manifest. Leisure as distinct from idleness consists in actively carrying out what is most preferred, and prepared for. Rest is not a value, at least in its more usual connotation. You recuperate, when necessary, by engaging in something less demanding, though that something may be passive reflection while basking on the beach, or while sitting in an armchair, or while doing the washing-up. Withdrawal does not seem to be in question, certainly not withdrawal into indolence, or from your fellows.

The dissociation of the idea of rest, that is doing absolutely nothing, from the concept of retirement will no doubt have its own critics, but these can be left to another occasion. It has to be recognized, however, that the disengagement of persons towards the end of the life course has an indispensable social function, that of permitting replacement and renewal. It was made very clear in Chapter 5 that these essential processes will and must continue, in spite of the claims being made about the prolongation of the life-span, and Methuselah-like illusions about going on indefinitely. For all its activist recommendations, the theory of the Third Age as we have expounded it decidedly includes a doctrine of withdrawal, with-

drawal by choice as far as feasible and desirable from those engagements
with society which are the essence of the Second Age. Of these engagements, the most conspicuous are those made necessary by reproduction,
which is usually completed, as was noted, before the end of the Second
Age itself. Engagements with others in the process of production cease
with retirement, and cannot be renewed for that particular purpose.
Those in the Third Age in fact have withdrawn so as to make way for
their children, and their children's generation: they have withdrawn so as
to open the wealth-creating activities of the Second Age to their
successors.

Although the cessation of reproductive activity is due to physiological
change, in women anyway, this is not a question of fitness, and retirement
from the workplace is not now usually a question of fitness either. Most of
those in the Third Age in our time might make excellent parents and
highly competent workers and executives as well. If absolutely necessary,
some of them could even make satisfactory soldiers, so that the anxiety
which was sometimes expressed in the course of the Cold War over the
ageing of our population on defence grounds scarcely made military sense.
However, the adoption of Third Age attitudes must change the quality of
relationships between oneself and others. In the Third Age it is no longer
compulsory to work to stay alive or to associate with particular individuals
for political or social purposes, or to engage in certain activities to safe-
guard a career. Choice of association goes with choice of pursuits, and
deciding what these pursuits will be is a leading principle of the life course
culminating in the Third Age. Withdrawal into the Third Age is hardly an
appropriate description of a decision to direct your efforts henceforth to
that which interests you most, in active cooperation with others with
similar interests and outlooks.

The Third Age, then, provides both for participation and withdrawal.
The logic of its theory could be extended to show that this is as it should
be. Third Age activities are necessarily voluntary, so that compulsory participation is not in question, and would in any case be rejected out of hand
by those whom it is expected to apply. Nothing in the theory, moreover,
requires that those in the Third Age should isolate themselves from their
juniors, or separate themselves by social class. The diminution of compulsion in social and individual life may yet free those in the years of personal achievement to create forms of social collaboration previously
unknown. In the U3As, the Universities of the Third Age, as we shall see
as we go on to consider the issues of education in our transformed social
structure, we may discover the first of the institutional novelties which
have now become so necessary.

CODA TO THE GENERAL THEORY OF THE THIRD AGE

There are one or two further remarks to be made before we proceed. One is to insist again on the distinction between the Third Age and the Fourth as fundamental to the general theory. It is the interrelation between demographic development and the articulation of the individual life course which has made the position as to ageing fundamentally different in principle in our country and in countries like ours in the present period. Any tendency to run the Third Age and the Fourth together will mask that crucial reality. The Fourth Age, which has been shown to have in the past to have been taken to cover the whole of life after the working career had ended, brings the Third Age into being by apposition, so to speak. The Third Age is the condition of being old, even (in terms of historical comparison) very old, without showing the traditional characteristics, the symptoms, as it might be said, of old age.

Since it has been these symptoms which have given what justification there is to the stigma which has been universally attached to late age, it could follow that under the new arrangement for the life course all the unfavourable stereotypes would attach to the Fourth Age. 'Elevating the Third Age in comparison with the Fourth is treading down even older and more defenceless people' (Young and Schuller, 1991, p. 181). That this could be a consequence of making the distinction is difficult to deny. But do we have to allow ageism in its most prejudiced form to prevent us from recognizing a division which is fundamental to the understanding of ageing as it now proceeds? Is it not the deplorable reality that our disposition to be prejudiced about colour, sex, class, physical impairment and old age seems to be part of a general moral inadequacy? If we are sufficiently wrongheaded to stigmatize ourselves as we shall firmly be, refraining from recognizing a Third Age is unlikely to make the position better.

Associated with these criticisms of the theory of the Third Age, perhaps underlying them in fact, goes an uneasiness with stage-based analysis in general. Tendencies in such analysis to lead to exaggeration of the differences between the phases it sets forth, to exaggerate the homogeneity within them and to dwell excessively on transitions between them, and especially to conjure up an air of predetermined inevitability, in passing from one to the rest, are some of the things which give people pause. It is all too slick, too good to be true, the comment might be.

It should be evident from numbers of remarks made in the course of the present text that I have myself considerable sympathy with these critical positions. The insistence on perceiving the life course as segmentary in its very nature has in my view added considerably to the difficulty in the way of ageing theory and given rise to much vacuity of statement. But the inescapable fact is that people in general do think of their lives in such rigid frameworks and expect any persuasive arguments that they should change their outlook to respect their way of thinking. The theory of the Third Age has to be doctrine as well as a structural analysis. That doctrine, if it is to have any chance of acceptance, has ineluctably to be formulated in terms of stages.

11 The Obsolescence of the Educational System; the University of the Third Age

Teaching, everyone spontaneously believes, is for the young, a task shared between parents, other older relatives and friends, and a group of people who are paid to teach. The teaching process consists, therefore, in older, experienced, authoritative persons providing models for younger, ignorant, powerless persons, that is, children and adolescents. The task requires the moulding of the behaviour of these young people, and drilling knowledge into them. Accordingly those in the Second Age teach those in the First Age. The immediate object is to make those individuals independent, efficient, up-to-date members of the Second Age, and this is what the word education ordinarily means. Its further and wider object is the fashioning of a new generation to succeed the current one, to ensure the continuance of society, its institutions and its culture. Along with the engendering of off-spring, education is part and parcel of social reproduction.

In this established, traditional, rigidly conventional view of the educational system, those in the Third Age have no obvious part to play – active or passive – except as watchful grandparents, at a distance or in an emergency. They do not bring up children, because this is a parental function and they are too old to have offspring themselves. The Third Age is debarred from teaching in the schoolteaching sense because that is a monopoly of the Second Age, of professionals earning their living. Those in later life would anyway have little to contribute since their knowledge is out-of-date and gets more and more so, and is hence of diminishing use to those in the First Age in graduating to the Second. Persons in the Third Age do not learn themselves, both because the capacity is largely lost to them, and because such learning is no longer needed when the Second Age is over. If those past working age are to be admitted at all to a place in the educational process as traditionally conceived it is in refreshing their memory of what was taught to them in the First Age for such use as they can make of it in retirement.

There are two further items in this brief and obviously tendentious vocabulary of established educational concepts – learning in its wider sense, and research. In its initial meaning, learning is what children and adolescents are required to absorb – their lessons – anything from toilet-training to the principles of the calculus, or of even more advanced topics. But learning is also the totality of knowledge available to a society, and is contained in the huge plethora of printed materials which that society accumulates, supplemented in our day by electronic storage. These stored materials are also present in the heads of living persons, and the older a person is the more there is likely to be stored in the memory. So it is probable that many of the learned will in fact be in the Third Age. But in the traditional view nothing of importance is likely to be added to that stock of knowledge during the Third Age itself, and the learning of those in later life is no consequence for the processes of education.

Additions to knowledge are not to any great extent made by teachers, and scarcely at all by their pupils, but by practitioners of the last activity included in the conventional educational inventory – the activity of research. Researchers are unlikely to be elderly because new knowledge in this orthodox conception is made by new people, young, vigorous, irreverent professionals, early in their Second Age. Whoever saw a picture of a bald, wrinkled man stooped over a microscope or gazing at a computer screen? or for that matter a white-haired old woman? Education, then, as it is commonly perceived, is not a system with any scope for the elderly. If professors and researchers continue working when they are old, in the popular image they tend to become comic figures, wizened monomaniacs, slightly funny in the head. Excepting only the senior members of the teaching profession, education is entirely for the young.

EDUCATION AND SOCIALIZATION

Exponents of the theory and practice of contemporary education might well describe the summary set out above as a gross distortion, a parody of what in fact goes on in schools, colleges, universities and other institutions in Britain in the 1990s. The educational needs of people past the age of school, college and university, they would claim, are now fully recognized and have been since adult education began three or four generations ago. But our foremost concern here is with the general assumptions which exist in society, and particularly with the beliefs and opinions of older British people. The majority of them ended their education in their teens and have been sedulously excluded from all but the diminutive adult education section of the official system ever since. Such individuals do seem to think like this: they accept the stereotype of themselves once again as no longer required to learn and as largely incapable of it. Moreover, they make up most of those now in the Third Age in our country, and even of those who will succeed to the Third Age during the rest of this decade and beyond. As must be expected from the ageing of the population, adult education classes now contain increasing numbers of people in later life. But the proportion of all those whom we should classify as being in the Third Age attending such classes at the present time is very small, as is evident from Table 11.1.[1]

What is more, the impression of the British education system given by what has been set out, and of the condition of our country as to teaching, learning and research, is to a deplorable degree justifiable. Britain has one of the smallest proportions of the population over the calendar age of 18 within the educational system among all the advanced, industrial countries although the number has been rising. There is a case for describing the present British elderly as the worst-educated of English-speaking persons. British universities are some of the most exclusive which exist, and are still heavily influenced by the élitist model, enshrined in their two most famous – Oxford and Cambridge. Of considerable significance from our point of view is that even Oxford and Cambridge, for all their cultivation of the former members of their colleges on the Old Boy Network, almost never have them back for further instruction. When these privileged youngsters take their degrees, all is over. It is virtually the same in every other British university or college, who take no intellectual responsibility for graduates after graduation. The association of education with what is

Table 11.1   Third Age participation in study, 1990

Age group	Numbers in the population at those ages	Per cent studying	Numbers studying
50–54	3 100 000	8	248 000
55–59	2 900 000	5	145 000
60–64	2 900 000	5	145 000
65–69	2 800 000	6	168 000
70–74	2 300 000	6	138 000
All 50–74	13 900 000	6.1	844 000

Source: Carnegie Inquiry into the Third Age, Paper 3, 1993. *Learning, Education and Training*, Table 1–4.

called socialization is responsible for the notion of education which has been sketched out, an association apparently indissoluble in the traditional educational model, an association which is responsible for much of its inappropriateness to our needs now that the Third Age is upon us.

Even those who would strongly object to the judgement that the educational system in our country will have nothing to do with the Third Age betray the persisting influence of this association in the vocabulary they feel obliged to use. The section of the educational system to which mature students, older students, or even elderly students are admitted, are coming to be called institutions for 'adult' or 'further' or 'continuing' education. These phrases can only mean the extension of education in the conventional socialization sense, the teaching of youth in 'regular' institutions, that is to say, over some part or even the whole of life yet to come after leaving school, or for a few, after leaving college, or for even fewer, after leaving a British university. Socialization stays at the centre of the model, and these extensions – low in prestige and run on the cheap as they undoubtedly are – remain on the margin of 'real' education.

Our 'higher' education system (the world 'higher' grates a little as you write it), cannot be called an intellectual and cultural resource for the regions in which its institutions are located any more than it is for people at large after the end of their First Age. In this it is very unlike its American counterpart with its network of state universities and established practice of offering graduates instruction in their later years. The French, with all their centralization and bureaucracy, by means of their regional 'academies' spread over the whole country seem to do better in these respects than we do.

For our present purposes, the association of education with socialization consists in the following dogmatic propositions. Firstly, all truly necessary instruction, training, or transfer of knowledge can be and must be carried out in the First Age. Any knowledge which is acquired later on is incidental. Secondly, what happens in the First Age – to children and adolescents acted upon by a contingent of those in the Second Age – is sufficient to last for the rest of the life course. Although we shall have to pronounce both these statements to be false, false in themselves and demonstrated to be so by the arrival of the Third Age, we have to recognize the reasons why they have been and are still widely supposed to be virtually the whole truth about education. This was certainly so during the Before, when there was little to call them into question.

Learning is certainly quicker and easier in the First Age than it is later on, and lessons are retained for much longer, for the rest of life in many cases. In spite of what is urged by progressive educators in favour of learning by doing and by sharing, as against inculcation by authority, it remains true that imitation, reward and punishment are highly effective in the teaching process, and that such methods are at their best when the relationship is between the Second Age and the First. Physical superiority bulks large, and even physical punishment has a residual part to play, though it is the social superiority wielded by the older over the younger which is made most use of in instruction. Standards are insisted upon by those in the Second Age and examinations pitting student against student are established features of the system. They reinforce the authority of teachers and add the fear of other students, so increasing the feeling of intimidation. The impression given by institutions of learning – primary, secondary and tertiary, 'lower, higher and highest' – is that they are to a regrettable extent examination machines, organized into a nationwide examination grid. This tendency seems to be on the increase, and is now being taken to greater competitive lengths by instituting league tables, ranking educational institutions by their examination successes.

Examinations reward the successful and provide incentives for everyone, the teachers and the taught. No matter how dubious, or even fictitious, examination gradings may sometimes be, they make judgements possible on educational progress and on the maintenance of standards. They constitute guidelines for administrators and givers of educational grants. They provide copy for journalists, for whom a teachers' strike interfering with the preparation for examinations or the exams themselves always makes a headline. But as in every competitive system of the kind – and the educational world has many of them reaching right up to the award of Fellowships of the Royal Society and of Nobel prizes – the effect is always to rebuff the many in order to encourage the very few. It is understandable that with their period of education by socialization so far in the past, and with the memory of rejection by their teachers often still lingering, the British elderly of modest means should show so little desire to take up education once again.[2] To them it is going back to school, to the intimidating atmosphere described. It is exceedingly difficult in their condition and situation to see the point of further learning. These circumstances make the whole project of lifelong learning much more difficult.

Educators and educational administrators with the traditional outlook are not alone in their commitment to education by socialization and to its values. Apart from parents whose own competitiveness, as well as their fears and ambitions for the future of their children, conspire with the system of standards, Second Age agencies such as employers and the State appear, at least at first sight, to accept its assumptions without question. Their preoccupation is indeed with the production, as efficiently and rapidly as possible, of candidates fit to take up positions in the Second Age, with the future of industry, the economy and the nation itself in mind. Since the early 1980s the grievance has been that children in schools and students in colleges and universities have been taught badly, that the knowledge, arts and skills essential to success in the Second Age are not being properly imparted. There is also a tendency to deplore the fact that they have been taught the wrong things; too much time is spent on subjects which do not prepare them to be productive employees in industry, in offices and in service occupations. What is the use of an A-level in Latin, is the complaint, or a degree in Philosophy, or a doctorate in History, most of all a qualification of any kind in the so-called Social Sciences, to an electronics engineer, a supermarket administrator or an advertising agent?

However this may be, there can be no doubt on one point. It is a qualification which is imperative from this point of view, a certificate that rote learning has fulfilled its purpose, and a suitable young candidate has been socialized into a particular arena of knowledge or skill. In order to satisfy the labour market, these primary qualifications – elementary mathematics, ability to write intelligible prose, the bare bones of beginner's science and technology – have to be acquired at the stage of first impressions on young minds, so that such indispensable knowledge will have become habitual to those of working age. The first principle as to socialization in education seems therefore to be accepted by employers and officials and they wish to take the most advantage of it. But, as we shall see, these customers of the schools, colleges and universities have less respect for the second principle, that virtually all the knowledge necessary for the life course can and is to be acquired in the First Age.

They are also becoming rather less confident about what the curriculum should be for those socialized into necessary knowledge. It is no longer so obvious that the so-called utilitarian subjects are enough in themselves. A little acquaintance with history may well be quite important to those who will be engaged in the tourist 'industry', one of the fastest-growing of the service and information occupations, though characteristically less expansive in Britain than they are elsewhere. Taken together these already employ a greater number of persons than manufacture in Britain and other high industrial countries, and will do so more and more. When communications and administration are added as quickly-expanding Second Age activities, it becomes clear that what are called the 'Arts' subjects are by no means irrelevant to the training of young persons to earn their livings as individuals and collectively for the living of the nation as a whole.

Since Arts subjects are those of greatest significance to those in the Third Age, here is a spin-off effect which we must not underestimate. But a spin-off it remains. Not one whit of the regular instructional effort we have discussed is deliberately directed towards the needs of persons in the Third Age, that is, the needs of at least a fifth of our present population. Nor is any attention officially paid by the established system to lifelong learning, that attribute which the Carnegie Enquiry recognized as indispensable in every contemporary society with a long-lived population, even though the Enquiry did not espouse the educational theory expounded here.

More significant to us, however, in respect of the increasingly obsolescent model associating education entirely with socialization, is the fact that firms, administrative departments and professions now provide more and more of their own specialized teaching for their recruits or potential recruits. Compulsory courses leading up to professional examinations largely outside the national system have long been common practice. But shorter courses of a more optional kind for those already in employment are being added to them on a large scale. Even Her Majesty's judges now submit themselves to seminars and throughout the business world older executives and employees go on such courses along with younger ones, in order to revise what they should already know, and learn about new methods, products and markets. On these occasions the members of the work-force may find themselves faced with course leaders, specialist teachers or other suitably entitled inculcators – the word teacher is not felt to be quite right and authoritarian instruction impermissible – who have themselves officially retired, who are in the Third Age.

It is interesting that the retraining of personnel at all stages of the work career, including those in the late fifties of their calendar ages, has made an appearance in the service and retail occupations but rather less so in British manufacturing. This last activity, which we still tend to suppose is the only real form of production, is bound to a greater extent by traditions of apprenticeship, which could be called education by socialization in its extremest form. We should be very careful not to allow a survival of this kind to conceal the facts about education and re-education, training and retraining, and retraining again which our transformed situation now faces us with. So far such things are pre-eminently lacking in Britain. This is abundantly evident to the professional historian finding himself being addressed by a tourist guide, the worker on the factory floor, so to speak, in one of the most expansive of our service industries. How woefully inadequate is the knowledge displayed by the guides and conductors at a great country house, even in an art gallery or a museum; how urgent is their need for further instruction on the relevant subjects, not simply a revisionary course but a perpetual updating, a widening and deepening of the stock of knowledge. Only thus can the British spokesman get on terms with the far better-educated tourists they have to address, especially the Japanese. This, as we shall see, is just the opportunity for the enthusiastic member of the Third Age.

The Carnegie Enquiry came to a conclusion of the first importance for the educational prospects of those in the Third Age, and for the general thesis of this book. Training and retraining have to go on throughout life, be available to both sexes and at all ages; with access to everyone, whatever his or her original 'educational level'. In spite of changing attitudes and even some improvement during the later 1980s and since, it is quite unacceptable therefore that roughly nine in ten of older British people receive no training whatever in any given year.[3] We are obviously a very long way from the objective suggested in the first edition of this book in 1989, when it was proposed that retraining should take place at every level, at least until the age of 55.

This was held to be imperative since under the industrial conditions which now, or certainly will obtain, ten years is the longest that a retraining will last[4] and men, in due course women too, retire officially at 65. Some industrialists already realize that older employees valued for their experience will be even more productive when equipped by retraining, and they have no doubt of the capacity of older employees to learn new things. The bosses, if they do bring in retired people for the purpose, implicitly recognize also that those in the Third Age can impart their knowledge as effectively as anyone else: indeed that such persons may have made a particular specialization relevant to their Second Age occupation into a Third Age accomplishment, an avenue of self-fulfilment. Of equal, or even greater, interest to us is the fact that employers have now acknowledged for quite some time that their staff and workers need preparation for retirement. Pre-retirement education is an established activity, if on a woefully limited scale, connected with institutions of adult or continuing education belonging to the official system, but still largely in the hands of business administrators.

INTELLECTUAL DEVELOPMENT OVER THE WHOLE LIFE COURSE

The prospect of trying to retrain and recruit those late in their working life for the improvement of production reveals the insufficiency of the socialization account of education in many ways, therefore. It is certainly an acknowledgement of the capacity of the elderly to learn. It is now known that new skills, new items of information, especially when built upon those already possessed, can be acquired at any age, calendar, biological, social or personal age. Admittedly the time needed to learn gets longer, and the elderly would-be-learner is often exasperated by the inadequacies of his memory, or hers, and sometimes by failure in eyesight or hearing. Clumsiness, inattention to detail, absence of mind, all have to be contended with. But this is what is to be expected, and one more challenge to what we are all so marvellously equipped to do, to compensate for deficiencies as they occur. final mastery of a novelty may be securer in older than in younger learners, and there are business administrators who are well aware that this is so.[5]

In fact, it is not at all certain that the traditional slurs on the elderly as learners are as widely accepted by younger people as they are by elderly people themselves. Those who undertake to arrange or instruct classes of senior students, self-selected as the students tend to be, are regularly impressed by the strong motivation of all of them and by the excellence of some. In the very first attempt made in Britain by elderly people to investigate their own reputation and social position – entirely amateur and unscientific as it was – a good majority of the informants questioned in the Cambridge market-place agreed that elderly people could learn new things.[6] Older learners are nevertheless frequently surprised as well as delighted when they find that they are able to tackle Greek grammar from scratch, computer programming, or organ-playing, so tenacious are their unflattering beliefs about themselves. Every time astonishment is expressed at achievements such as these, every time such phrases as 'It is wonderful that he or she could master such a thing, *at his or her age*' are to be heard, the stereotypes are strengthened.

A further feature of the adult class and the professional course is that competitiveness is scarcely evident, at least in the arts subject. The acquisition of information does not depend on authoritarian inculcation, reward and punishment or a final examination. Such things belong, as we have seen, with the socialization model and, since those in the First Age are assumed to be in need of control, they have to be rewarded and even punished, and thus brought up to examination standard in order to graduate to the Second Age. However, these are not necessary parts of the education process as such, any more than that process is necessarily a relationship between the First and Second Age. To assert that education is inevitably and exclusively a matter of socialization is quite simply wrong.

Our preoccupation here is with the knowledge, skill and confidence which should be acquired through experience, in the First, Second and Third Age, in order to find self-fulfilment in the last-named. In so far as the association of education with socialization retains a hold on the educational world, it is clear that this need will not be met. To this extent the educational system at present in Britain can be judged as obsolescent now that the Third Age is of such importance. The developments we have touched upon indicate that some encouragement and support is beginning to be forthcoming for those concerned with the planning of their lifetimes as a whole, support coming from outlying sectors of the educational system, from those who have begun to study the Third Age and from some employers. But it cannot be shown that preparation for life after the Second Age is an acknowledged object of the whole educational enterprise as a whole, or of any part of it. Pre-retirement courses come too late, and are too much concerned with adjustment to the unexpected to be of much relevance. In fact their institution and character could be claimed to demonstrate how unaccustomed people are to thinking forward from the beginning of the Second Age into the Third, to consider at the calendar age of 25 what things will be like for them when they are 70, as was recommended earlier.

Let us dwell a little longer on the misapprehensions which the close association of education with socialization has given rise to. The concept of education in the discussion should not be confined to the active mood or to the transitive sense. We have talked of inculcation, and teachers may be quite convinced that they literally transfer items of knowledge from themselves to their pupils. But what actually happens for the most part is that through the encouragement, persuasion or cajolement of teachers, pupils learn the facts on their own, even if it is simply by imitation or through such mechanical processes as chanting the multiplication tables as a class. Though such indispensable pieces of intellectual apparatus as multiplication are unlikely to be learned anywhere other than at an official educational establishment, much of what is acquired during socialization is learnt from parents, television, books, and from many other sources, especially from companions. Although this does not include Greek grammar, the calculus or the theory of probability, which are almost entirely the preserve of professionals, it does include a great deal of indispensable knowledge.

Models to copy are undoubtedly essential to the educational process, even more so than books, buildings or the rest of the equipment. The more learned the teacher is and the higher in status, the more profitable such imitation will be. But this does not mean that learning can only take place when the instructor is in the Second Age and the instructed in the First. There is no need for the learner to be younger, or more ignorant in general than the person from whom the learning is derived. There is in fact no final justification for the division between classes of persons into teacher and learner in the educational process.

Education is an interchange between those who know and those who need and wish to know. Because the wish and the need last all life long the interchange is a lifelong matter too. Education during and by means of socialization is no more than one example, one interlude, of the continuing process, and the particular means used during that period – highly disciplined inculcation, competitiveness, examinations and so on – are not necessarily indicated for education at later ages. They are certainly out of place in the Third Age, except under one circumstance. A person may decide that retirement will be used to get a Second Age qualification, a degree in a chosen subject, or the certificates required to become recognized as a qualified professional, perhaps an architect, for example, or an accountant. In such a case it is appropriate that examinations should be taken and passed, along with other younger candidates. Pathetically few of those in the Third Age ever take this step. In 1989 only 739 of those aged over 50 were enrolled at universities for a first degree, and 441 for a higher degree.

EDUCATIONAL NEEDS OF THOSE IN THE THIRD AGE

It is questionable whether a national educational system should be required to admit to its most expensive courses students who will never use their degrees or qualifications, or who can have only a restricted time to do so. Will such a system be able to afford to admit those in later life, even in industrial societies as affluent as they are likely to become in the twenty-first century? Cheaper ways of providing what is required are certainly available since those in the Third Age might be able to educate each other even at a level which would qualify for recognition in Second Age universities. It is also arguable, however, that the creation of future affluence will depend to some degree on the modification of our established educational system to receive back men and women at every stage of their careers after their original 'graduation'.

In Chapter 3 the judgement that Britain was past it because it was an old country with an old population was peremptorily denied. But in order to deploy its working population properly under conditions of ever-accelerating technical change, periodical retraining has become indispensable. We cannot increase, or even maintain, our efficiency in manufacture or in the services with a work-force educated at a time when markets, products and methods were those now pronounced out of date. We shall either have to institute an educational system which can continuously update their information and skills, or accept the fact that as the years go by the members of our work-force will become more and more ineffective, and our economy progressively outpaced by its competitors.

The position is, or soon will be, that the country which can found a system able to keep its work-force up to date by continuous training and retraining will have the long-term advantage. Perhaps it would be better to allow the corporations and professions to organize such special instruction and updating procedures for themselves, independently of the educational system of schools, colleges and universities which we all pay for and which will have to be maintained, and ought in any case to be enormously extended. It will have to be maintained because, as we have seen, education at the socialization stage is and always will be crucial in preparing people to proceed to the Second Age. This applies to the knowledge and skills which are required by individuals preparing for the Third Age too. Because these Third Age requirements of the official educational system are so continuous, that system will have to become party, the important supply-side party, to the educational interchange, however far the official education system is encouraged to leave industrial, commercial and professional updating to other agencies. The determined expansion of our only means of equipping ourselves intellectually and technically for the realities of economic and social life, in a world where we lag so much behind already needs neither explication nor defence.

For those preparing for self-realization in the Third Age, the established educational system is indispensable, even though they are so much more self-contained as learners than adolescent students. It is to the classrooms, lecture rooms, libraries, art collections, even the grounds and sporting facilities which these institutions maintain that Third Age learners most need access. Their situation, in fact the situation of every one of us if we are properly to be our age, demands that the educational system, and particularly what is called the higher educational system, recognize immediately the lifelong partnership described.

Although it has been insisted that access is in question, access to teaching premises and learning premises for everyone at all times, technical change has begun to ensure that this will not necessarily imply throngs of persons of every age crowding the available spaces. One of the conspicuous features of recent decades has been the development of open learning, where the teaching resource is accessible from a distance at the convenience of the pupil, not of the instructor. Without moving from where they live people now can, and increasingly will, learn for their own purposes at their own pace and their chosen times, subjects of their own choice, combined or mixed in a pattern selected by themselves. Indeed, within the 'regular' university system itself, courses are already being taught entirely by video recording, and this develops a pattern which might lead in time to a system of perpetually available, broadcast instructional programmes, international as well as national, a veritable 'university of the air'. The immemorial association of education, learning and research with a particular site, a set of buildings and a named place may in due course be accompanied, even to some extent replaced, by a service universally available to all persons at all times. Should these things come about (perhaps I ought to say *when* these things come about), the abstract and problematic ideal of universal lifelong learning begins to look more like a practical, perhaps an imminent, reality.[7]

But even developments as radical as these, especially at their inception, would raise questions of resources, institutional identity and change, staff allocation and training, and a host of others. However much technical advance might ease the problems of mass teaching, universal lifelong learning would place immense strains on laboratories, galleries, museums and so on. There are all the makings of a political crux, arising at a time when the dominant political mood is to reduce the scale and expanse of educational activity. It is not my view, as will become apparent, that the resources required by the educational process as a whole will have to be increased anything like proportionately with the growth in the elderly population and the lengthening of life. In providing support in the form of public and private pensions for so many millions of people well able to instruct themselves and their age-mates, and well able to service institutions of all kinds, libraries, museums, monuments, educational and cultural establishments, we are in a sense already paying most of the bill. But there may have to be a struggle to deploy dormant resources where they are needed, and this may pit the Second Age against the Third.

The maintenance of a continuing relationship by educational institutions with their alumni (former students) as the Americans call them, and a right of access for those alumni, even for periodical interludes of residence, needs to be introduced into Britain forthwith. So also should the American institution named 'Elder Hostel', which provides for older people to visit universities for short periods to learn from the internal staff. 'Regular' (socialization stage) students would not lose: where those in the Third Age have been given such access it has been judged that both sides benefit.[8] It has to be noted that these are costly expedients, quite unable to take advantage of the economies which are secured by the last institution we shall consider in this chapter, the University or Universities of the Third Age, British model.

Let us consider for a moment what people will now do in their retirement of a cultural character. They will watch appropriate television programmes and listen to appropriate radio broadcasts; they will embark on consistent, often directed, courses of reading; they will cultivate their skills as sculptors, carvers, painters, designers, potters, weavers, embroiderers, cabinet-makers, metalworkers and players of musical instruments – the list is indefinite. They will visit castles, cathedrals, houses, churches, monuments of every kind. They will look at pictures, statues, buildings, landscapes, the whole of the contents of museums and galleries; and they will inevitably travel abroad in pursuit of these things and so as to experience other cultures. To do all these things and others which I have not mentioned, they will need knowledge, on the one hand – some of it surprisingly specialized, for instance, linguistic knowledge – and they will need access, on the other hand. The libraries, museums, churches and so on will have to be open, as far as possible, all day and every day. At the moment they are decidedly not.

It may be only a small minority of the retired who yet travel with these expectations, but those who do may face disappointment and frustration. When they are open, that is when they can afford the wages of a staff in the Second Age, sites of all the types mentioned above are thronged with tourists, a high proportion of them being retired. But too often these tourists are listening to droning voices describing either details which they, the visitors, cannot understand, or recounting only trivialities because the speakers realize that their audiences do not know enough to appreciate what they have come to see. The tourist guides turn in desperation to the enormous cost of the artifacts they are discussing, the time taken to make them, the fact – how significant this is in our machine-minded, machine-dominated age! – that these fascinating objects were all handmade. A pathetic admission of futility this, and an evasion of the following patent truth. To experience what a museum or church, house, garden, or even a 'cultural' television programme has to offer you have to have background, to have experienced the interchange with those who know for which I have been pleading.

Leisure without background and training is undeniably indolence. A Third Age, lacking these and deprived of any standing connection with institutions which can provide them, must turn out to be indolence indefinite, limbo in fact, the limbo which in the preceding chapter was indicated as that which the Third Age was intended to replace. Should a regression to limbo supervene in this fashion it would be a historical betrayal on the grand scale. For it would be a mockery of the centuries of effort made in the past by men and women who had no leisure of the kind that we can experience, who could expect no Third Age, but strove so to advance the material level of their societies as to ensure that for us, their successors, it would be otherwise.

But even this miscarriage of human intentions is not as crass as the fact that we now have people with time enough, and an increasing proportion of them with information enough to appreciate our cultural inheritance, while the institutions which alone can make their inheritance available are scarcely accessible for the purpose. Because of the accepted definition of what is work and what is not, because of the relationship which has been established between the Third Age and the Second, we have convinced ourselves that we cannot afford to keep cultural institutions open to the public for long enough to be of use.

In my own locality for example, one of the richest cultural sites as well as seats of learning in the country, the Fitzwilliam Museum, an assemblage of paintings and other objects of art of world importance, is at present open only in the mornings for the viewing of paintings and in the afternoons for the viewing of its other collections.[9] Both cannot be seen at the same time: on Sunday mornings and for the whole of Monday there is no access at all to the public. The Cambridge University Library, a huge accumulation of literary and cultural capital amassed over five hundred years and more, is closed from Saturday midday until Monday morning, and for the later part of every evening of the year except for a few weeks in the early summer. These are particularly the times when those preparing themselves for the Third Age might wish to make their visits. A truly realistic policy would keep the place open to readers day and night every day, all year, as the library at St Petersburg is reputed once to have been open. The situation is similar, if not so serious, in the richest country of all, with the New York Public Library and the Library of Congress. In the Netherlands, as every frustrated visitor has discovered, absolutely everything is shut on Mondays, and after five o'clock on opening days. So also after three o'clock throughout the week in Italy.

There are many reasons, of course, including technical reasons why we are increasingly unable to give access for enough people to our cultural capital in the West just as they are beginning to need it most. The grounds usually given for justifying the current limitations are shortage of staff. However, there is no shortage of persons in the Third Age and even a minute proportion of them would suffice to keep our cultural capital in working use, whatever those in the Second Age may say and do. Those in the Third Age will have to see to it that the galleries stay open, that the libraries are ready for use, that the ancient churches and other monuments are properly guarded and available for viewing. They must do it

themselves: *we must do it ourselves*, and we can do it for love. We are
pensioned-off.

EDUCATION AS A VALUE IN ITSELF

The analysis of education from the point of view of the Third Age has
taken us from the desks in primary school, to the television studios producing cultural programmes to the galleries and museums, and on to the
remote village church which has preserved its medieval paintings on its
walls. All this in addition to distance teaching and national open universities. We might have paused at the teaching hospital, where rote learning
and repetitive examinations are at their zenith so as to protect us all
against the ignorant doctor, and we might have looked in at the research
laboratory as well, where the new knowledge which teachers will use and
the factories will exploit first makes its appearance. For education is a
wide-ranging concatenation of activities, not to be grasped in the discussion of learning methods and the learning situation. What is more, education is a value in itself. All knowledge acquired and skills perfected are
sources of satisfaction, without reference to their usefulness or to anything
else. So also are reflection upon what is known, meditation in all its manifestations. Taken together these things offer intellectual health to those in
the Third Age in a way parallel to physical exercise, promoting physical
health. They can provide a sense of identity and just the kind of self-
esteem which vocational and parental roles provide for those in the
Second Age.

It is in this respect that research is crucial to the lifelong educational
interchange which is necessitated by the arrival of the Third Age. If learning new things is an end in itself for every individual, extending knowledge is even more so. But fundamental discoveries about the physical, the
physiological and the psychic world are only possible under the rigid
disciplines which scientific research imposes.

Similar regimentation is usually necessary for the attainment of new literary and social knowledge, though there are not wanting voices which
proclaim that mathematics and physics do not provide the only or even the
appropriate models for advance in those directions. However – and this
is where we reach the point of importance to those in the Third Age –
researchers, especially researchers in the social subjects but other
researchers as well, may need collaborators outside the library, the labora-
tory or the computer room. Moreover, the activity unsatisfactorily named
research in the humanities, the discovery of previously unknown 'facts'

and the schooling of yourself in fresh methods of appreciation of literature, the arts and history, is an essentially social, often a group activity. Such objects are not satisfactorily pursued by the solitary individual working alone. Finally it can be said that all new knowledge, all discovery, however arrived at, adds something worthwhile to experience – personal and collective.

These considerations enable us to see how it is that education in this, its widest connotation, is the Third Age pursuit *par excellence* and that such education cannot be pursued in an entirely solitary fashion. Reading in a literature, mastering a language, unravelling a point in logic or philosophy, understanding the objectives set for themselves by poets, dramatists, painters, novelists or architects and the works they have created, these things extend your appreciation and your mastery of your world, your objective and subjective world alike. So also does critical reflection on the life situation, your own and that of others, along with the critical aware-ness, the *Ideologiekritik*, which is so much the preoccupation of the philosophers of our day, social philosophers or philosophers *tout court*. All these are fulfilling activities, and adding to other people's knowledge, knowledge in all these senses, is the most fulfilling of all. We shall shortly touch upon such participation in 'regular' research as can be organized for those in the Third Age.

The confinement of the team 'researcher' to the white-coated labora-tory worker early in the Second Age is as much a distortion of reality as any other part of the account of education as socialization with which we began. It is inconsistent in any case with the general notion of the Ages which has been expounded. A successful researcher, indeed anyone capable of being a full-time research worker, may have to be classed as belonging to the Third Age as well as to the Second Age because they are engaged for a living on that which they would want to do in any case and which they are good at carrying out. Nevertheless, and especially during the last few years, professional researchers are less and less permitted to set the agenda for their own research, and political values, even party political priorities, do much to determine what kind of work shall be done. Things like this make the relationship of adding to knowledge with self-realization over the life course rather less straightforward. There is, more-over, a tendency for those in the Second Age to assume that persons in their position should control every aspect of educational activity, even those set up for themselves by those who have retired.

Even in the classes run by University Departments of Continuing Education (originally named Extramural Boards), the Workers Educational Association, local authorities and so on, which now receive older learners on an ever-increasing scale, these learners do not choose their curriculum, their instructors, or the way they shall be taught. And these learners certainly do not instruct each other. Until very recently there was no institution belonging to those in the Third Age which could do such things, and the only one which yet exists is the University of the Third Age.

It is when the University of the Third Age begins to be described that the persistence of features of what I have called the socialization model of education is most plainly apparent. Intellectual activity, and especially organized instruction not using established standards and not regularly checked by properly organized examinations, are not easily accepted by the educationalists of the Second Age, even if no degrees of qualifications are offered. They are looked at askance by those engaged either as teachers or as learners, and no one can be both at the same time in that highly professional activity: it would be deeply disapproved of by educational administrators.

The implications of this last remark are serious enough. In our own country there is a strong surviving tradition of independence in education, however hard the government of the day may strive to override it. It is a tradition unfortunately so deeply implicated with élitism and class exclusiveness that it is well-nigh impossible to separate the two. But British university teachers are not, or are not yet, acknowledged employees of the Ministry of Education as they are in France, for example, with even their notepaper bearing the Ministry's name. In Britain, therefore, and in Australia and New Zealand, Universities of the Third Age can proceed as they wish under any name they choose, provided they do not pretend to award qualifications.

THE UNIVERSITY OR UNIVERSITIES OF THE THIRD AGE (U3A)

In the University of the Third Age (U3A) which began its career in Britain on a July evening in 1981, every member is expected to learn, and, if he or she is in a position to do so, to teach as well. Otherwise, the members are expected to offer services, organizational and such like. They learn, and help each other to learn, in small groups, mostly small enough to fit into a room in the private house of a member.[10] There is therefore no division between teacher and taught: there are no staff and no students, only members. Since members join voluntarily, and pay to join, and since it is the members who take the classes and organize every other activity of the University, the exchange of money is of very little importance. Those who have neither salaries nor administration to pay for can be financially independent of the established educational system, however, important it is that that system should give access to its premises and teaching occasions. Members of a U3A can choose their own subjects, their own teachers, their own methods of learning. Should it be thought that this must mean that nothing significant will be taught or learned, let it be borne in mind who it is who are in the Third Age: professors, schoolmasters, lecturers, researchers, experts of every kind retire. This huge pool of talent is otherwise unused. Our experience has been that a number of these people, especially of the successful ones, are quite willing, often enthusiastic to teach during their retirement. Their enthusiasm is quite decidedly met by enthusiasm in their classes. Everyone who comes into contact with them is impressed by the eagerness for knowledge of members of the U3A.

Among those members are sometime accountants and income-tax collectors, administrators and executives, which means that a U3A can be excellently administered. Qualifications are not required from those who join, not even the qualification of having passed a particular birthday, though there has been a little controversy over this important point. It could be said, however, that those not prepared to support the university's activities, not willing to take part in a learning exchange, should think hard before taking on membership. Qualifications not being in question on joining, and qualifications not being what joiners want of the U3A, qualifications are not offered, indeed cannot be officially offered even if they are demanded. There are, therefore, no examinations, and the University is not in the business of choosing one of its members in preference to others, or of encouraging competition between them. Anyone whose plan for the Third Age does require qualifications is expected to try to gain access to a 'regular' university, particularly the Open University, to obtain them.[11] Since such a person should have made this plan during the course of earning life, it is to be expected that the money will have been saved to pay the fees.

Nevertheless emulation is not itself discouraged in the U3A. If a class did decide to recognize the achievement of particular students in any way, the University would no doubt leave that to the class. But it will not as a body award distinctions of this kind. Such actions are most likely in language classes, or in classes where a considerable degree of disciplined effort is required. It is also in classes of this type that instruction from outside is most likely to be sought, and paid for, at a level within the ability of the association to meet from its own resources. Although smaller classes, meeting in the homes of members, had been envisaged as the major activities of the U3A, larger gatherings of seminar size have increasingly been set up. Truly public occasions have also been a feature of the life of U3A in Britain as in other countries. Public lectures given by a sympathetic outsider are likely to attract quite a proportion of the membership. Though not originally contemplated as an institutional feature, these occasions make it possible for a substantial muster of members to discuss the policy of their University among themselves at frequent intervals, opportunities which their keen commitment to their institution, their own institution, makes very welcome.

In the specification first though up for U3A in Britain, everyone was expected to have a research interest of his or her own. There was, moreover, to be a collective research undertaking in the form of a committee of the University. This committee was to organize and carry out projects which might lead to published results of the usual academic character, and aid individual and other smaller-scale research projects. These plans and particulars will be found in a document reproduced as an appendix to this chapter and we need to go no further with description. The Aims and Objects set out there were composed in a deliberately idealist way, with only a superficial acquaintance with the Universités du Troisième Age in France to help the planners. Since the name and idea were new in this country, since the appeal had to be to the imagination, and since it was a time of discouragement, even disillusionment with educational expansion and change, only idealism would do.

It was fully expected that the paper project would become increasingly irrelevant and might soon be lost sight of if a genuine movement got under way and real working institutions came into being. In the event, the project succeeded against the social grain of the 1980s. As is stated in the preface of the second version of *Aims and Objects* (1984), it is surprising to the author of the document how many of the original provisions, especially the principles, have survived the intervening years, which have seen the creation of so many U3As in various cities, towns and some rural areas, in our country. Nevertheless, as is usually the case with schemes drawn up ahead of practice, some of the suggested principles have been found impractical, or even an interference with progress, and have accordingly remained inoperative. As the U3A has developed, some of the founding notions have been judged too academic in both the meanings of that word. They have been extensively abbreviated, simplified and written out in plainer language. This has happened both at the centre, where deliberately revisionist exercises have been carried out, and in individual local U3As, as at Warwick.[12]

The general conviction is that the novel institution, or congeries of institutions, should develop as experience requires and as situations unfold. There is value, however, in retaining the original, then largely abstract, exercise, if only to make it possible to register what evolution has occurred and is occurring, to see how much survives and is likely to survive further. Every living movement needs its scripture, even though that scripture is widely regarded as unsuited, unintended for literal observance.

No British U3A is a part of an official, state-founded, established university with its professional teachers and administrators. A local U3A is set up at the instigation of a particular individual or group, which can seek the help of the national organization, the Third Age Trust, for guidance. When it is judged that a U3A has got big enough, another is formed. There are three in the Oxford area, for example. It is a considerable advantage of the British model that U3As can come into being in any locality where people willing and able to support it are living.

Classes in our U3A are not being taught as a matter of duty by Second Age professionals, professionals do not choose the subjects and the methods. All are entirely self-governed in a democratic fashion, and all are engaged in a range of activities other than teaching and learning classes. There are visits within the country and outside of it; painting, pottery, sculpture and handicrafts are offered; so also are dramatics – as producers, actors or members of theatre audiences, especially in London; there are reading parties, dancing classes, discussion circles and debating societies; there are sports, in fact, in these respects it is just like a 'normal' university. All our U3As make efforts to raise the status of elderly people in their areas and in the country as a whole, especially, of course, in educational matters. All also recognize that the U3A, is not, cannot be, and never was intended to be, the whole response to the challenge to education posed by the emergence of the Third Age.

In describing and recommending the British model abroad, especially in Europe, I have ventured to define its membership as the vanguard of the new society of the Third Age. Its remit is the intellectual mobilization of this new society, to raise its awareness, to give it a policy, to speak in these matters for all the millions of that society, which is so often spoken for by others, younger, Second Age others. What has to be combated is the tendency for those in the Second Age not only to suppose that they can speak for those in the Third, but that the Third Age cannot be supposed to be able to speak for itself, think for itself, indeed control itself. At the extreme there seems to be an assumption that the Third Age is at the disposal of the Second. These are the grounds which seem to me to justify an address delivered in several European countries in 1993 and 1994 with the title 'The liberation of the Third Age comes before solidarity between the generations'. In finding its position and function in the twenty-first century world the U3A has more to do than learn, teach, research, reflect and meditate, central as these things are to its being.

OBSOLESCENCE, ITS AVOIDANCE AND TRANSCENDENCE

'*Ce n'est qu'un début*' was the commonest of the slogans used in Paris by the embattled students of 1968. Like their evanescent intellectual communes, to which it has a family resemblance, the U3A is only a beginning, though it has already shown itself to be very much more durable, if not as controversial. There has been controversy, however, controversy which has helped the movement to get started by giving it an issue, and which has surrounded the word 'University' in the title.

University is undoubtedly a class-infused term in Britain and is unlikely to be adopted by any society whose membership is predominantly working-class. This underlines the fact that other, different, not yet worked-out expedients will have to be found to meet the case of that great majority of people in or approaching the Third Age to whom anything as academic as a university seems irrelevant, if not to some degree obnoxious.[13]

All this exemplifies what was meant when it was insisted earlier that today is a time for innovation by the elderly themselves, in ways not yet all that easy to descry. A dispute over the title 'University' may scarcely seem worthwhile, for word are only words. Nevertheless if the historical view is taken, university, *universitas*, had originally no specific intellectual connotation: it simply meant an association for a named purpose. But there is no need to go as far as J. H. Newman's phrase 'the idea of a university', to recognise the fact that there is a general tendency to suppose that there is such a thing as a named purpose, indeed a set model of a university in the minds of most people who use the word.[14] It is a model which everybody uneasily feels is scarcely borne out by the practice of the universities we have, but if an attempt is made to judge the U3A by ideal doctrines and abstract principles, U3A, British model, does rather well.

Knowledge, so the ideal of a university would have it, must always be pursued for itself alone and never for what can be made out of it. Success in that pursuit becomes evident from changes in the state of mind and personality of the pursuer, not from achievements in competitive examinations. The role of the university is to elevate its students culturally, intellectually, socially and to add to their knowledge and to knowledge generally, rather than to place its graduates in employment. It should be no part of its functions to maintain institutions designed to judge between its members, certainly not to do so on behalf of outside agencies such as employers and the state. In this vision of the university, education is indeed an end in itself. Now these are the objects and intentions which members of the U3A in Britain in the 1990s are enthusiastic for. Those belonging to our local society in Cambridge may perhaps be forgiven if they refer in a humorous way to that *other* University in their town, the one whose members have long ago lost sight of the original and proper objects of their world-famous intellectual institution.

The U3A does engage in teaching, learning and research, the three objects for which, for example, Trinity College, Cambridge is required by law to use its ample funds. Moreover, the U3A does this in ways which are in direct opposition to those demonstrated by the association of education with socialization. If it is attachment to socialization which threatens existent British universities and indeed the whole of our education system with obsolescence now that age relationships have been transformed, then the very different principles of the U3A are of considerable importance to our intellectual, cultural, perhaps even our economic future.

These principles are consonant with the developments of our time in other ways as well even if they are a long way from the emphasis on productivity and utilitarian training so prominent in the present official attitude to institutions of learning. The U3A does in its way demonstrate the principle to which we referred at the conclusion of our chapter on the general theory of the Third Age: it is a social form without compulsion. It does provide for its members an instrument which gives definition to their status in society, a historically novel status it has to be admitted, a status which differentiates them from their juniors, yet allows for the closest of collaboration and interaction with them. The very title which has been adopted for their peculiar institution, 'The University of the Third Age', underlines the fact that its members have left the Second Age and made way for their successors there. Nevertheless, those juniors are simply themselves as they were a few years previously, and dynamic continuity over the life course has been a recurrent theme of the present book. Although the U3A takes due account in this way of the segmentation of the life course, its whole ethos is directed towards the realization of individual aspiration, the culmination or 'crown' of individual plans of life, which the general theory of the Third Age requires.

Phrases like these may seem to lack reality, inevitably perhaps when the situation is so much without precedent that there is no indication as to its proper delineation and its possible development. Before we go on in the final chapter to the responsibilities of the present elderly in Britain, one of which will certainly be the consolidation and elaboration of the principles of practice of the U3A, we may take one or two concrete instances of what could be achieved.

When the research activity of the U3A was first mentioned, an illustration was promised. At the Cambridge Group for the History of Population and Social Structure the largest body of data about the demographic history of a country which exists anywhere in the world has been assembled since 1966 by the efforts of volunteers associated with the professional researchers at the Group. It was from this body of data that it finally became possible to work out the trajectories which showed forth the secular shift in ageing. A national organization like the U3A could extend such activities in every direction. A remarkably similar enterprise but much bigger has been set going by a geneticist for the study of ladybirds, the Cambridge Ladybird Survey, whose number of recorders of sightings of that insect has exceeded 5000.[15]

The third example is of a different character, and does not lie so evidently within the field of research. At the Royal College of Art in London there is a project called Design Age. Its object is to reshape the common objects of daily life – from toothpaste containers and plastic wrappings round food, from light switches to men's and women's pullovers and ballroom gowns; from the notices on pictures in Art Galleries to the doors, sitting angles and other aspects of motor cars – to redesign them all so as to make them suited to the Third Age. This has indicated a natural alliance for the U3A and it is good to say that in the winter of 1944/5 a marriage was being arranged. Not before time, it could be said, because the motto of Design Age is 'Live in the presence of your future selves'.

These projects are not in themselves either radical or impractically idealistic, and what has been said in this chapter does not advocate anything which would be properly called a revolution in education. Revolution is a tired word in any case, and proposals for the recasting of the whole of society by instituting a radically new educational programme or organization have repeatedly demonstrated their inefficacy ever since the time Plato wrote out his utopian *Republic* for the ancient Athenians. Idealism may be in order, for nothing new and worthwhile ever got into the daily life of any society without it. But the members of the British U3A are most decidedly not utopians. Piecemeal rearrangement for entirely original and previously unheard of purposes is what we are all at.

APPENDIX
THE UNIVERSITY OF THE THIRD AGE IN CAMBRIDGE:
OBJECTS, PRINCIPLES AND INSTITUTIONAL FORM

Objects

First, to educate British society at large in the facts of its present constitution and of its permanent situation in respect of ageing. One of the first of the 'old' societies, we find ourselves in a position which is bound to be shared by all developed countries, and finally the whole of the world's population.

Second, to make those in their later years in Britain aware of their intellectual, cultural and aesthetic potentialities, and of their value to themselves and to their society. To assail the dogma of intellectual decline with age.

Third, to provide from amongst the retired the resources for the development and intensification of their intellectual, cultural and aesthetic lives. In this way to help them to make effective and satisfying use of their freedom from work at the office, shop or factory. To devise methods of doing this which can be afforded in Britain.

Fourth, to create an institution for those purposes where there is no distinction between the class of those people who teach and the class of those who learn, where as much as possible of the activity is voluntary, freely offered by the members of the university to other members and to other people.

Fifth, so to organize this institution that learning is pursued, skills are acquired, interests are developed, for themselves alone with no reference to qualifications, awards or personal advancement.

Sixth, to mobilize members of the University of the Third Age so as to help the very large numbers of elderly persons in Britain standing in need of educational stimulation but who have no wish to engage in university studies.

Seventh, to undertake research on the process of ageing in society, and especially on the position of the elderly in Britain and the means of its improvement.

Eighth, to encourage the establishment of similar institutions in every part of the country where conditions are suitable and to collaborate with them.

Principles

1. The university shall consist of a body of persons who undertake to learn and help others to learn. Those who teach shall also learn and those who learn shall also teach.
2. Joining the university shall be a question of personal choice. No qualifications shall be required and no judgements made by the university between applicants.
3. Everyone joining the university shall pay for its upkeep and for instruction received. These payments shall be the sustaining revenue of the institution apart from gifts by foundations and other patrons. No support from the funds of local or central government shall be expected or sought.
4. No salary, fee or financial reward shall be paid to any member of the university for teaching other members, counselling them, or helping them in any way.
5. All members of the university shall be expected to offer voluntary service to it and to its activities in relation to society at large, especially to the elderly.
6. Members shall be prepared to help to organize assistance in the way of voluntary manpower for educational, cultural and other institutions which may be able to use such manpower, and which under present conditions are prevented from fulfilling their functions as they would like. Examples are art galleries, museums and libraries.
7. The undertaking of all members to teach as well as to learn may be fulfilled in the following ways other than instruction:
    Counselling other members;
    Taking the university's offerings into the homes of the housebound, the bed-ridden, those in retirement institutions or in hospitals;
    Helping the effort to provide intellectual stimulus for the mass of the elderly in Britain;
    Taking part in any other offer of manpower made by the university to educational or cultural institutions which stand in need of it.
8. The University of the Third Age shall not itself engage in the activity of judging between its members. There shall be no examination system; neither degrees, diplomas nor certificates shall be awarded. Nevertheless, classes within the university engaged in any particular intellectual or other exercise may decide on ways of recording an individual's success in the exercise in question.
9. The curriculum of the university shall be as wide as resources permit, ranging from mathematics and the natural sciences, by way

of philosophy, literature and history, to music and to aesthetic, practical and physical training. Nevertheless, the preference of members will be the only criterion of what is done, and it is recognized that humane subjects are likely to predominate.

10.   The standards of the university shall be those set by its individual classes, and ways shall be devised to permit each member to find his or her own level. There shall be no attempt to set a university-wide standard, or an assimilation with university standards elsewhere.

11.   Studies related to the specific situation of the elderly – social, psychological, physiological – shall be included as a matter of course. They will be given no particular prominence in teaching, but high priority in research.

12.   In pursuance of the aesthetic, art historical and topographical interests known to be popular with the type of student likely to be members of the university, special arrangements shall be sought with national bodies such as the Arts Council, the National Trust, English Heritage, the Nature Conservancy and the Forestry Commission, so as to obtain the facilities required to develop instruction and research in these fields. Regional institutions like the Folk Museum in Cambridge and the Museum of East Anglian Life at Stowmarket will be of particular importance. Voluntary assistance where appropriate (see above Principle 6) shall be offered in return.

13.   Strong emphasis will be laid on research in all the university's activities. Every member will be encouraged to join in the widespread accumulation of scattered data required for advancement in knowledge of certain kinds (for example archaeology, natural history, the history of population and social structure, the history of climate and geological events). Every member will be expected where possible to have a research project of his or her own, and to write up its results. Engaging in research, however, shall not necessarily count as fulfilling the obligation to teach.

14.   Insistence on learning as an end in itself shall go along with an emphasis on the value of making things and on acquiring and improving skills of all kinds. The curriculum shall therefore include, if there is a demand, and if facilities can be found, such subjects as computer programming, accountancy, business and managerial studies, spoken languages and handicrafts in textiles, metal work, wood work, bookbinding, printing and so on. Painting, sculpture and music shall be given high priority.

15. Special importance shall be attached to physical training and suitable supporting activities, and negotiations entered into for these purposes with local institutions disposing of the facilities.

16. The closest possible collaboration shall be maintained with the Extramural Board of the University of Cambridge, with the WEA Eastern District and with all providers of adult educational programmes in the area. Ways shall be sought to take advantage of all such teaching and research facilities as may be available in any local institution, especially the University of Cambridge, and to negotiate for the services of any individual willing to assist the University of the Third Age though not himself wishing to become a member.

17. The form taken by each individual pursuit within the University of the Third Age shall be decided on each occasion by members collaborating for the purpose. Though the conventionally taught 'class' will often be the form adopted, every encouragement will be given to seminars, with many participants; acting; visits to sites of scientific, archaeological or historical interest; to museums, art collections, houses and so on.

18. Although the University of the Third Age in Cambridge will be the first of its kind in Britain, it is reasonable to expect that others will soon be founded in our country. Every effort shall be made to encourage interchange with these institutions at home and abroad, to exchange teaching with them, to collaborate on research with them, to unite with them in the furtherance of the intellectual interests of the elderly, especially in Britain.

19. Apart from the voluntary research undertakings of its members on every suitable subject, the university shall seek to collaborate with professional research activity on the process of ageing, especially ageing as a social phenomenon.

20. ....

PETER LASLETT,
16 September 1981

12 The Burden of the Elderly and Paying for Your Own Third Age

This essay began with the burden of the elderly which is a persistent refrain throughout its text. The phrase and the sentiment have had a very important part to play in lowering the self-esteem of those in later life, convincing them that there is nothing that they can now do which will be of significance to other people, and inhibiting them from taking up the Third Age as the time of their self-fulfilment. The sense of being no longer wanted, of getting in the way, of taking up resources which are grudged to you and of which others have greater need lowers self-confidence and harms the personality. It might end by turning every one of us into a Mrs Gummidge.[1]

In its most injurious form, damaging to the thesis of this book and hence in my view harmful to the condition of older people, this reproach to their very existence might assert that our society cannot afford to continue to support them, certainly not at our present standards and at theirs. The vision of a Third Age as the time of personal self-fulfilment and the crown of life accordingly vanishes. The reality to be reckoned with would go like this. All that we can justly be expected to spare for those past productive work is a subsistence strictly regulated by our available resources and evened out over their ever-growing numbers and the ever-lengthening duration of their lives. Not only must we adjust their incomes in this way to our present and expected means, we must see to it that their share of our medical assets is kept within reasonable bounds. This will have to be done even if it means acting in accordance with the following satirical sentiment expressed by Arthur Hugh Clough,

Thou shalt not kill. But needst not strive
Officiously to keep alive.[2]

Perhaps it is unfortunate to have introduced in this somewhat flippant fashion the extremely serious and difficult topic of rationing health services by age. Even in the United States where the medical costs of the elderly are highest and the outcry against these costs and the 'greediness' of older persons is at its strongest, such a sentiment would be regarded as inhumane.[3] But the inordinate expense of medical services to the old and especially to the very old is a considerable element in the notion of the burden of the elderly. They drain away the time of doctors and nurses. They fill up the hospital beds. They settle and stay in costly nursing homes, taking to themselves in these ways hard-earned and grudgingly transferred resources which would better be spent on needy babies, children and stricken younger people who have productive lives still to lead. The increasing disproportion between what we spend on the old and what we spend on the young makes evident how burdensome the elderly are now and how disquieting it is that their deadweight upon us will inevitably grow. Hence the more menacing to our economic welfare, indeed to our welfare in every direction, the ageing estimates come to be, the more probable a final crisis of old age. Averting that crisis must mean tighter rationing of the transfers we make to the elderly, and stricter controls on the way in which these resources are used.

Working through the phrase 'the burden of the elderly' in this way and taking up some of the suggestions it makes, gives us some further insight into the situation as it might be if the concept of the Third Age had never made an appearance, and the traditional outlook on late life had never been questioned. Such a persistence of older attitudes from before the secular shift no doubt helps to explain something of the disposition to count the elderly as a burden and nothing more. We begin our discussion of these issues and of the recommendations suggested by the second phrase at the heading of this chapter, 'paying for your own Third Age', by turning our attention to the manner in which the plaintive resentment against the elderly is expressed in the preceding paragraphs. 'We', who support, are there blankly opposed to 'They', who receive and are supported. 'We' at the same time seem to be talking for the whole society.

Now this is unmistakably the language of the Second Age talking of and to the Third and the Fourth, combining them into the traditional, now obsolete, category of 'old age'.[4] The clear assumption is that the total resources of the society are at the entire disposal of the Second Age which can and should treat the Third and Fourth in an instrumental fashion. The injunction 'live in the presence of all your future selves', looking, that is to say, on those in later life as standing for what we ourselves must inevitably become, is completely disregarded. The 'we' and 'they' account of the relationship of younger and older, moreover, fails to reckon with the fact that when succession takes place, when 'we' become 'they', further successors will appear. We may use these obvious but somewhat compli-

cated circumstances to put forward three principles for the proper understanding of the generational relationships implied by the transfer of means
to support the old. The principles belong to the recently established study
of generational equity, one which we cannot conscientiously ignore in the
present essay.

JUSTICE BETWEEN AGE GROUPS AND GENERATIONS

The reader may find the exposition of this topic, and of the three principles *Vocab.*
which we shall consider, somewhat confusing. This is due I believe for the
most part to the restricted range of the available vocabulary. Some words
and expresssions have to have several distinct significations, a sign of the
undeveloped state of the area of enquiry. Moreover the concepts themselves are rather complicated and elusive, as is the required manner of
thinking about them, thinking over time, or processional thinking, as it
will be called, the type of thinking implied in the very phrase 'live in the
presence of all your future selves'. Those with no more than a general
interest in ageing may choose to pass the following discussion by.

The question of justice between people and collections of people differing in birth date is, however, of evident importance to the full concept of
the Third Age and to the articulation of all the four Ages, so as to make up
the completed theory of the life course being developed in this book. It is
moreover a question which conscientiously concerns many people now in
the Third Age, who can be forgiven if they do not find the issues easy to
understand. One of the objects of writing out the following summary is to
try to provide an exacter phraseology, clearer and more definite concepts
and a more logical and systematic analysis of relationships over time and
the justice which they intimate than has been usual in the discussion of
these issues. Many commentators seem to be content with sketchy descriptions and vague suggestions, invoking some undefined 'social contract' rather than specifying who it is who owes what, and to whom, and
for why.[5]

Let us turn to our three principles, the first of which states that relations
between age groups and generations cannot be understood in the way that
the 'we/they' construction attempts to understand them. In the demographers' language which had to be used in earlier chapters the cross-sectional
view is insufficient for the analysis of cohort phenomena. The appropriate
metaphorical terminology is rather to be drawn from the image of a procession of mortal humans wending its way over the years, the decades and the
centuries. In such a procession, relationships between members of the

cortège are strictly limited in particular ways, the most evident being that they can only interact with their neighbours, that is their contemporaries. Even then it is very rare for an individual to share his or her whole life-span with another individual: longer or shorter lengths stick out at either end.

Although members of the temporal procession can affect their contemporaries so defined, and affect their successors as well, they cannot affect their predecessors, even if those predecessors have in the past been contemporary with them and even though these predecessors have decidedly affected them. Under these and all the circumstances to be described, the primary subjects for analysis and judgement are cohorts or sets of cohorts. Cohorts consist of collections of persons all born at the same time (year, or group of years, month(s) or even day(s)) and members of them can interact with each other. Provided that they share at least a part of the same time-space, that is are contemporary in the sense just described, whole cohorts can also interact with each other. The four Ages, it will be remembered from Chapter 1 above, consist in bracketed groups of such cohorts as their members pass through the four stages recognised in our definition of the life course.

'Generation' can also be defined as cohorts have been defined. More usually, however, the word generation conveys the image of all those alive at any one time of whatever age, as contrasted with those alive at another time; and this is quite a distinct concept. Generations so described are often divided into age groups. It follows from these definitions that processional justice maintained as a trust between cohorts during the highly variable periods over which these cohorts can interact with each other is the appropriate criterion for judging relationships between young and old, retired and not yet retired. Traditional, static justice, as it might be called, between age sets of persons as they exist at any one time, and almost always loosely called 'generations', is simply insufficient.

The second basic principle of relationships and of justice over time goes like this. Members of senior, earlier-born cohorts, can count on the support of members of junior, later-born cohorts, not so much because they, the seniors, have supported these juniors earlier on, as because they, the seniors once again, have in the past supported their own seniors and predecessors many or most of whom have disappeared. Analysis over time discloses the existence of a perpetual understanding that predecessors are to be supported by successors because those predecessors have in their turn supported their own predecessors.

We must notice that this second principle of processional relationships and processional justice goes beyond that which obtains between earlier and later cohorts sharing, or rather partially sharing, the same time-space. It also applies to longer periods, to whole generations, and to questions other than support, including questions of the environment. We owe to our generational successors, shall we say successors whom we ourselves will never see, unabated and unspoilt, the totality of the environment handed down to us by our own generational predecessors of the eighteenth and nineteenth centuries, generational predecessors whom likewise we have never seen. This larger, longer understanding over time is contract-like rather than trust-like and has been given the title intergenerational tricontract. Its relationship with the inter-cohort trust need not concern us here.

It is to be observed, however, that it is through the instrumentality of the inter-cohort trust rather than through any generational or age-group contract that the spontaneous support extended by parents to children and children to parents is made operative as a generalized social practice. Such parental and parent-like relationships are not appropriately described as contractual, if only because they normally consist in ties of affection. But they do partake of trust. Fathers and mothers do *trust* their children to help them when in need and when the children are able. They themselves can reciprocally be *trusted* to do all that occasion demands for their children at all times. It is likewise with younger and older citizens, though here personal affection is largely transcended.

The third principle of processional justice is a further extension of the concept of trust. The members of the entities we have described are required to trust one another, so to behave that as far as possible each gives and receives sufficient for every member of every cohort to go through his or her life course at an equivalent level of satisfaction and welfare.

I have myself suggested (Laslett, 1992b) that it would be advantageous in securing these principles of justice if a regularly instituted inter-cohort trust were to be presumed to be in being. This perpetually existing trust – the word 'contract' being reserved, as has been suggested, to the larger understanding between whole generations – would include the state or government as a regulative party. It would exist, the supposition being in fact that it does already exist, to ensure that each cohort when that cohort's turn to pay into the inter-cohort trust comes round – that is, when passing through the Second Age – will give the means needed for their subsistence to dependent older and younger members of the society, belonging of course to other cohorts, those passing through the First, Third and Fourth Ages. The further understanding is that this transferred support shall ensure maintenance at roughly the levels to which persons of the Second Age were accustomed during their own First Age, and to which members of the Third and Fourth Ages were accustomed during their own Second Age.

Allowance has to be made of course for changes in the standard of living during the periods of transition, for the special nurturance and educational needs of those in the First Age, and especially for the physical dependence and costly medical care coming in the Fourth Age. The adjustive and regulatory function of the state or government acting as part of the trust is particularly evident here. In short, in relation to the recipient elderly, because of the maintenance of the inter-cohort trust, those passing through the Third and Fourth Ages can rely with implicit confidence on those in the Second Age maintaining them, just as they, those in the Third and Fourth Ages, supported their now vanished predecessors earlier on.

The motivation, as distinct from a sense of obligation, of those in the Second Age for sustaining the inter-cohort trust, and the donative arrangement with their seniors which that trust requires, should now be quite apparent. Within an average interval of some fifteen or twenty years, they themselves will be going through the later ages. As things now are, they can expect at birth to spend about two-thirds as much time in the Third Age as they spend in the Second Age, obeying during that Second Age its imperatives in the way of work, saving and supporting others, but also preparing for their own Third Age when they will in turn be supported and live their own lives for themselves, and further preparing for the possibility of a dependent Fourth Age.[6] 'Supported' here, it will be suggested, should consist as far as possible in living on their own savings, that is, on the savings they made for themselves while they were in the Second Age, directed and assisted by the state in the way that will be described.

SELFISH GENERATIONS AND THE THIRD AGE TODAY

Having picked our way through the intricate pattern of inter-relationships, obligations and transfers over time, lifetimes and periods of time, we have to reckon up their implications for our chosen theme. Perhaps the most important is this, that the behaviour of members of a particular cohort, age group or generation can be more or less generous, excessively free-handed or positively selfish in its treatment of its successors. In this way a generation may desolate the environment and violate the intergenerational tricontract, and a cohort or set of cohorts may breach the inter-cohort trust or even conduct itself as if such a trust did not exist.

In his remarkable essay entitled *Selfish Generations?*, David Thomson sets out to demonstrate that one particular set of cohorts, whose members were born during the 1920s, 1930s and 1940s in his own country of New Zealand, have in fact behaved in an exploitative fashion in relation to their successors. They continue to do so, he believes, through the operation for the most part of transfers between cohorts embodied in the welfare state, though in other ways as well. It was to be expected that such suggestions, that a particular set of cohorts has simply not played fair in respect of inter-cohort trust, should be highly controversial, and heated discussion continues.[7]

Thomson maintains that his analysis applies to all the Western societies which he has investigated, though to Great Britain to the least extent. In spite of his challenging title, he does not suppose that his selfish generations have deliberately distorted the operation of the welfare state in their own favour. Indeed conscious policy on the part of interested groups of individuals themselves, or even of government, is difficult to discern in such a complex arena as the flow and counterflow of welfare funds and taxation inputs. This is shown by the singular unwillingness of affected younger people even in New Zealand to voice their resentment at what in Thomson's view is going forward at their expense. The inequitable operation of the inter-cohort trust, he believes, is rather the consequence of the way in which the welfare state was established and has been maintained since the 1940s than of any premeditated policy.[8] Nevertheless, the reaction to his suggestions as they might apply to Britain was swift and began even before *Selfish Generations?* appeared in Wellington. Two considerations came from the welfare state programme then in operation at the London School of Economics, both setting out to vindicate the British welfare state from Thomson's charges on particular counts.[9]

The conclusion arrived at in the second paper by John Hills, after an extremely detailed numerical analysis of all 18 of the five-year cohorts born between 1901 and 1990 in respect of education, health and social security, is that the British welfare state has been remarkably even-handed in its treatment of different generations, at least in these respects. But he adds that those born between 1900 and 1920 have done somewhat better than their successors out of the welfare transfers. Moreover the defence of the British record of inter-cohort equity has been deployed over a much narrower front than Thomson's original offensive.

The anxiety of those who reject the thesis of inequity in the treatment of successive cohorts seems to be informed by their fears that it is the welfare state itself which is being attacked, that the principle of transfers from the earning young to the needy old, the healthy, the active and the prosperous to the sick, the workless and deprived is in danger of rejection. This seems to be entirely unjustified as an inference from Thomson's writings, whatever may be the case of supporters in the USA of the organization called AGE, Americans for Generational Equity, with their loose talk of greedy geezers and their querying why it is that 'we should pamper these whingeing pensioners'.[10]

In fact transfers of the type which we associate with the welfare state have always been a fundamental of political association, in the West anyway, as has already been stressed, however pronounced the change-ability of welfare policy has been. Whatever is thought of David Thomson's critical propositions, no one should seriously suppose that they are irrelevant, no more than a diversion, that is to say, from the really dangerous onslaught on welfare provision coming from the individualistic marketeers. The tendency to think of welfare states in the plural, which affects Thomson himself as well as others, adds to the impression that governments of Western societies are at liberty to institute inter-cohort support systems or to go without them. This cannot be the case in spite of the rapid succession of one set of such provisions to another, differing as to size, origin and destination of transfers.

There can be no doubt than that Thomson has been right to raise the questions which he has done. The comparisons he makes between the treatment meted out to his Earlies (those born in New Zealand in and around the 1920s) and his Lates (those born in the 1950s) in the matter of inter-cohort welfare transfers convince me that there has been substantial inequity in New Zealand. His further comparisons show that there has been almost as much inequity in other advanced countries, even though this inequity may have been least marked in the British case. Accordingly we have to reckon with a possibility that is of prime significance to the general thesis of this book. David Thomson's Earlies, now in their seventies in New Zealand and Britain, have to be identified with those individuals belonging to the cohorts which are experiencing the Third Age in the 1990s. Even if the much narrower counter-analysis of John Hills is accepted, older members of the Third Age in Britain, those between their 75th and 90th birthdays at the present time (mid-1990s) have gained appreciably more than their successors from the welfare flows Thomson analyses. This comparative advantage, John Hills insists, is a long way from making them a generation which in Thomson's phrase 'make contributions which cover only a fraction of their benefits'.[11] But it exists nevertheless. It is we ourselves, therefore, Britons at present in the Third Age, who have to face the possibility that we may have breached the inter-cohort trust, wittingly or unwittingly. This would mean that we help to make up a selfish generation.

When we come to consider the duties of those now in the Third Age, it will be laid down that one of them is to do all that can be done to cease behaving towards our successors and juniors in this fashion if we have done so. On Thomson's own showing there is now very little we could undertake in the way of restitution. But considerable amends might be made in the way of persuading government to modify arrangements so as to prevent generational inequities of the kind he describes from ever occurring again. In the rather laboured language we have had to use, citizens in the Third Age should act within the inter-cohort trust so as to restore inter-cohort justice by requiring government to correct the present and prospective distribution of welfare flows. This may turn out to be a very difficult task, and the securing of complete and continuing equity in the interchange between cohorts too much to hope for. But the effort must be made.

A further outcome of Thomson's critical enquiry, and one which is recognized as persuasive by those who differ from him, indeed by all observers of contemporary social structure in relation to age and the distribution of income, is that the differences between the rich and the poor among older persons have widened and are widening in Britain. In Thomson's view, and this seems to have been accepted without demur, the welfare state has been ineffective in redistributing resources between classes, which was its primary object, but has certainly succeeded in redistributing them between age groups even if in a manner which he and others find inegalitarian.

It was stated during the course of the discussion of the emergence of the Third Age that condition of life could mean very little to a British working-class pensioner on income support, even less to his widow or to an unmarried older person with marginal means. If then it could be claimed to be part of the duty of those in the Third Age to become aware of the possibility that they may be, or have been, exploiters of their juniors, it is even more the case that they should recognise the widening of the divide between those well- and those ill-provided-for in later life. They are challenged as citizens to do everything possible to remedy the position. This divide and this challenge have existed for young and for old, for predecessor and successor in the temporal procession, for as long as we have knowledge. It is somewhat disconcerting to have to contemplate the possibility that the emergence of the Third Age has made things worse.

The reader will undoubtedly have recognised that the unsettled controversy over the record of transfers between older and younger persons during the last half-century is pre-eminently a political one. The rejection of collectivism and the adoption of what has to be called Thatcherite social practices in many countries as well as our own, show through the scaling down or abandonment of much in the way of social policy which once underwrote the younger worker, his family of children, their educational prospects, their employment prospects and the provision of housing. In this way the emergence and perpetuation of the Third Age has, as must be expected of such a movement, got caught up in the politics, political opinions and ideologies of our own day. The same is true, we shall find, of the recommendations we shall make about paying for retirement, accepting the analysis of those who rely on capital accumulation, saving, that is to say, voluntary and enforced, on the part of the individual to play a major part. Socialist critics might say that the effect could be to ensure that in respect of retirement all of us would become possessive individualists, in an entirely capitalist world.

THE HISTORY OF DEPENDENCY AND OUR PRESENT SITUATION

We shall certainly have to reconcile such a live-as-far-as-possible-on-your-savings policy with the trust obligations which have been laid down. But we have yet to complete our consideration of the charge that transfers to the Third and Fourth Ages constitute a burden on contemporary society which is uniquely depressive in its weight and to do so in historical terms. We shall try to compare our own position with that in the past, and especially with things as they were in the immemorial past which came before the secular shift, that past whose now anachronistic attitudes to age and ageing and to persons in late life are still in the way of an objective recognition of where we are and where we are going.

We have to acknowledge that we are not, in the 1990s, in precisely the same position as our predecessors in the past have been in respect of the support given by the young to the old. This is so in the first place because living in the presence of your future selves is a very different proposition now, when all of us must confidently expect to last into that future, than it was when, as we have seen, most people could not expect to proceed from the Second Age to the Third, when in fact it might often have made sense to write off the prospect of ever becoming old. In the second place, which is in fact the same set of circumstances looked at from a different point of view, the relative expense of supporting those in late life was much smaller then, when the elderly were few, than now when the elderly are so many and growing. Ungenerous and hurtful as is the phrase 'the burden of the elderly' it has at least this historical justification. Never before has the cost been greater, the cost to the creators of wealth of supporting those past creating wealth, or judged to be so and accordingly retired.

This last fact can easily be demonstrated using the English historical statistics from which inferences about ageing were made in earlier chapters, though the comparison with present-day statistics is not quite as straightforward. In the middle of the sixteenth century there were about 6.75 people at the working ages, (here between ages 15 and 59), for every person of 60 or over. The figure seems to have risen gradually until the secular shift in ageing set in at the end of the nineteenth century. It was about 7.2 working persons to every older person at the end of the sixteenth century, 6.5 at the end of the seventeenth century, 7.6 at the end of the eighteenth century and 8.06 in the early 1870s. Nowadays there are well under half that number of persons in the working ages for every person in the pensionable ages (over 65 for men and over 60 for women): 3.3 persons in 1990 and in 2000, estimated to fall quite strikingly after 2020.[12]

However, this is decidedly not the whole historical story of the total 'burden of dependency'. In addition to the 10.4 million men and women of pensionable age, it is estimated that those of working age in 2000 will have to support 12.4 million persons not yet in the work-force, those in the First Age in our own vocabulary. Taking the First, Third and Fourth Ages together as being dependent, the Second Age at a strength of some 34.7 million in 2000 will make transfers to 28 million persons dependent on them, a total as large as 80.7 per cent, a good four-fifths of their own numbers. Expressed like this the total looks formidable indeed. It begins to seem more understandable that growth and prospective growth in such things as medical expenses which have never previously bulked large, should make the 'burden of the elderly' so resented.

But consulting the historical record makes this look differently again. Remembering their slightly different numerical basis, the estimated percentage for total dependency, the numbers of those in the First and Third and Fourth Ages as a proportion of those in the Second Age were 75.3 per cent in the middle of the sixteenth century, 72.4 per cent at the end of that century, 68.0 per cent at the end of the seventeenth century, 80.1 per cent at the end of the eighteenth and 77.1 per cent on the eve of the secular shift in ageing. However disposed those currently in the Second Age may be to feel aggrieved about their commitment, their apparently open-ended commitment to the support of their elders, they do not yet seem to be much worse off numerically, that is comparing their own count of persons to the total count of their dependants, than former generations of producers responsible for their non-producing juniors and seniors. The longer-term prospect may be very different of course, as can be inferred from the last section of Chapter 4 above.[13]

The matter cannot rest even here because supporting younger dependants, particularly your own children, is not at all the same thing as supporting older dependants, even your own parents. It is generally reckoned that the cost of maintaining older individuals is greater than that of maintaining younger ones, and the rising cost of medical care ensures that the disproportion will grow. It is then the Fourth Age, not so much the Third, which is expensive, and becomes more so as time passes.

There is a further comment which has to be made about the assumptions implicit in the language and terms of the discussion so far. They have been wholly economistic, confined to productive, marketable values transferable from individual to individual, cohort to cohort, age group to age group. The unmarketed, perhaps mostly unmarketable, services which older and younger persons perform for themselves and for society as a whole, including the Second Age, have been ignored. The support offered by the Third Age, particularly in postponing or preventing those in the Third Age from falling into the Fourth, is certainly considerable, and is certainly growing. As for inter-age support-flows originating in the Third Age, they are already a significant element in the care and support of the Fourth Age and in the upbringing of the children of the Second Age. Those in the Third Age, who act in this second way are accepting some of the responsibility for the cohorts of their grandchildren and no doubt will do so increasingly. Though the First Age is the primary object of such activities, those in the Second Age certainly benefit from them since they lessen the opportunity costs of child-rearing. This service to successors goes back a very long way and has been observed for several centuries. It is highly conspicuous today.

It can be supposed that econometrists could calculate these values in their persistent and ingenious way, and come up with an amended, market-terms balance sheet for the transactions between producing cohorts and dependent, non-producing cohorts, thus producing a meticulously revised estimate of the burden of dependency at the present time and its prospects for the future. But it must be questioned whether they can ever hope to allow for the incommensurables. John Locke declared, and all parents will confirm, that an individual is profoundly gratified by the very existence of her children or his, simply seeing them is a considerable pleasure and there is always present the knowledge that without those children and the cohorts to which they belong there would be no posterity. How are these values to be treated? And above all how can account be taken of the reciprocal fact that if it were not for procreative actions, the loving care, the innumerable sacrifices of those predecessors represented at any one time by members of the Third and Fourth Age the Second Age, the producers, the transferrers could not have existed at all?

It is true that economists, especially those who expound contemporary classical economics, do maintain that there are useable methods to allow for such variables and to settle the awkward questions which they raise. Developed in relation to environmental decisions Contingency Valuation Methods (CVM) rely on Willingness To Pay (WTP) or Willingness To Accept (WTA). In WTP an affected person is asked how much money he or she would be prepared to pay, for example, not to have a view obscured by new building, an inhabitant of a house in Tokyo, shall we say, for a prospect of Mount Fuji. WTA asks the further question as to how much money would he or she accept as compensation for never again being able to see Mount Fuji from the house. These terms and the tenor of the decision of CVM by economists have only to be set out in relation to generational issues in order to demonstrate how unsatisfactory they are. Certainly courts of law try to estimate in money terms such things as the loss to a parent coming from the death of a son or daughter. But everyone agrees that such damages fall short of the psychic, the existential tragedy of never being able to see your own child again, they constitute symbolic, not substantive compensation. And when it comes to questions about your own existence CVM simply makes no sense. How can the question 'How much would you accept in dollars as compensation for never having been born at all?' possibly be given an intelligible answer?

We can go no further into the critique of economistic discourse when directed to issues of justice between the Second Age, the Third Age or the fourth Age, indeed the First Age, from its original purpose of settling dilemmas to do with environment.[14] It has already been hinted how even environmental questions can in fact be translated into issues of justice between generations, between removed generations for the most part rather than between cohorts sharing the same time period.

Considerations like these coming from very recent theorization about justice over time, nevertheless belong to the immemorial discussion of age, age group and generational relationships which is encountered in all the world's cultural traditions. Their brief rehearsal here is surely enough finally to establish that the concept of a 'burden of the elderly', belongs to a disputable conceptual framework. The time horizon is wrong, the theory is inadequate, the values are undetermined and finally undeterminable in market terms, and hence the calculations are without the capacity to convince. It could still be true, however, that there is at present and in prospect for the future an objective excess of dependency of the older on the younger, of the combined Third and Fourth Ages on the Second. This is the possibility to which David Thomson draws attention in expounding his theory of *Selfish Generations?*

PAYING FOR YOUR OWN THIRD AGE

I have elected to take the long-term view of ageing changes in this essay and it would certainly be surprising if a radical and irreversible long-term change such as that brought about by the secular shift could take place without a serious disturbance of the traditional, perennial support relationships in place when that shift began. The tendency has been, as with everything else to do with the growth in proportions of older people and their very much longer lives, to assume that the time-honoured arrangements which have been inherited from the lower plateau would continue to suffice, with an appropriate modification in scale. We have surveyed the character of those support arrangements in Chapter 9 above and concluded that the intergenerational tricontract and the inter-cohort trust were fulfilled not by a single expedient but by a combination of them. Family and collectivity interacted with each other in a variety of ways such as were demanded by particular situations to provide for the dependent older individual. It was done by what might be called *bricolage*, by a varying mixture of expedients, one element of which, a small element and presumably confined for the most part to the minority of substantial property-holders, consisted in the savings deliberately set aside in earlier life by the now-dependent elderly individual. This seems to be true of Europeans anyway, though people of the much richer society of the USA seem to have saved for old age at every level above the lowest (among the blacks, for example) and from an early period in their history (see Haber and Gratton, 1994).

'Saving up for a rainy day', 'putting this or that aside for my old age' (not necessarily money) have always been parts of the proverbial attitude towards the inevitability of ageing, in spite of the much lower probability in former times of ever experiencing old age. Nevertheless, even after the enormous growth in the general wealth of the society which made possible the social insurance programmes which have come to characterise the welfare state, and which have frequently imposed a degree of compulsory hoarding for the purpose, the element of personal saving has usually been small. We have seen, for example, that the London poor of the 1930s saved, not for their old age, but for their funerals. It is important to notice that having to save for your own late life might seem to run somewhat counter to the principle that everyone has a right to support from successors in virtue of what he or she had done for predecessors. It could also be said to be inconsistent with a very much more widespread belief in and practice of adult children supporting their failing parents out of affection and on the grounds that those parents engendered them and supported them while they were children. These principles and practices have been brought within the purview of the inter-cohort trust. Nevertheless in proposing that the proper response to the outcry against the 'burden of the elderly' and to the mounting difficulties encountered at the present time by pension funds in our country and in every other is the establishment of a means whereby everyone can pay for his or her Third Age, we are recommending quite radical reform.

There is in fact a more substantial reason why the traditional arrangements in operation before the secular shift in ageing are less acceptable today, and so contribute to the resentment of the burden of the elderly. We do not know with any precision what the material standards of those in late life were, during the Before, and how they compared with those of their juniors. Where there was property, landed or otherwise, the older can be expected to have been better off than the younger. But the poverty which came with age is a prominent theme of the references to late life in past time and lists of paupers contain a high proportion of the old and the oldest, especially widows. No doubt their incomes were at the margin in the lowest social ranks, not far above minimal subsistence. Still we have seen that their expectation of life was not necessarily all that much lower than that of their age-mates in the more substantial classes, and we can be reasonably confident that they could at least count on being kept going; the inter-cohort trust worked for them to this extent, in the European West at any rate.

But guaranteeing this prospect for every one of the old, was, as has been shown, far less of a drain on the resources of the working population in relative numerical terms than it would be at today's standard and with today's expanding numbers. It is true that the working population was at the same time maintaining a proportionately enormous number of children so that total dependency was larger on the head-count criteron than it is today.[15] But this was so much an accepted part of social life and universal expectation that it never seems to have been questioned. In effect by offering this degree of certainty to its superannuated members, traditional English society transmitted to modern English society a set of expectations which appears to many of our contemporaries in the late twentieth century to be wholly out of proportion, given present numbers. They misunderstand the situation but it is not difficult to see why they think as they do.

The case will be that the emergence of the Third Age demands that personal savings should come to play a very much more substantial part in the support and care of the old and the oldest than it has ever done before. The new division of the life course into the four Ages which have been defined requires that everyone should, as far as possible, plan and provide for his or her own means of subsistence after the Second Age is over, just as Third Age intellectual activities have to be planned, promoted and provided for over the whole course of the previous earning career. The phrase 'paying for your own Third Age' should not, however, stand alone. Coupled with it should be the injunction 'and doing so in such a way as to even out incomings and outgoings over your whole life course from the beginning of the Second Age to the end of the Fourth, or to death'. The two last phrases cover the question of expenditure on health over the life course. Provision and plans should be made in anticipation of medical costs escalating towards the end. Here the imperative to live in the presence of all your future selves is given its financial content.

We have already seen that the difficulty of carrying through this apparently simple piece of practical advice is enormous. Along with the new and appropriate attitudes to age and ageing which the end of the secular shift demands, it requires wrenching yourself away from a whole set of dispositions inherited from the immemorial past and previously unquestioned. It has seen that the simple act of putting yourself in the place of a 70-year-old when you are 25 goes beyond the imagination of most people, the unaware and uninstructed particularly. This fact is illustrated by the discovery that people between the calendar ages of 16 and 24 have so little idea of what late life is like that a fifth of them are prepared to say that someone under the age of 45 is already old.[16] And where is yet to be found a body of doctrine or institutional arrangements to teach young people what it will be like to go through the life course and get older? To convince them that this process will inevitably happen to each and every one of them, almost as certainly as that they will finally die? Death and old age are instinctively rejected by those that do not suppose that they have to face up to either of them, not yet anyway, and we have emphasized that the link between the two last has never been tighter.

Foregoing present gratification in favour of future security and comfort, deliberately lowering the standard of living of yourself, your spouse and your children in favour of a future which is likely to be almost exclusively your own and your spouse's, these are exceedingly difficult prospects to contemplate. They would quite certainly be neglected by many people, probably most people, if left to their own devices, which is why the voluntary tone of the phrase 'paying for your own Third Age' will have to be stiffened by a modicum of compulsion, political compulsion, and one of the reasons why the proposed arrangements will have to be complicated, not simple after all.

However, the plethora of literature about pensions in our country is beginning to suggest that this do-nothing-radical policy about pensioning, about paying for the expensive Third Age and meeting the escalating costs of the Fourth, may no longer be open to us at least in the long term. A fresh pension regime will presumably have to be instituted under all circumstances and, in my view, it is essential that it contain provisions to ensure that as far as possible those who will from then on be able to expect to proceed to the Third Age will be required to pay for their subsistence during that Third Age, and to do so as far as possible from the proceeds of a capital fund accumulated annually by being required by law to put aside the requisite sums from their earnings during the Second Age.[17] This is not only just, in as far as the prospective difficulties of the pension system are coming about largely as a consequence of the appearance of the Third Age, but also because paying for your own Third Age is indicated by the character of the Third Age itself.

EVERYONE SAVES AND OWNS HIS OWN PENSION OR HERS

There is no call to go over the difficulties facing the current agglomeration of pension arrangements in Britain. It is sufficient to rehearse the desirable pension scheme criteria set out by Jane Falkingham and Paul Johnson[18] in order to demonstrate their failings.

A pension scheme, they pronounce, should in the first place be adequate, providing under all circumstances and economic vicissitudes including prolonged inflation, an income which is a reasonable replacement of what was being earned in the Second Age. It should cover all the to-be-retired and the retired irrespective of sex, marital status or employment history. The pension itself, and all contributions made by the pensioner-to-be and any others including the state towards its funding, should belong to the pensioner-to-be, and so be portable from job to job, independent of the wage level in the final year of employment and securely safeguarded against the manipulation of employers. It should possess what they call distributional transparency, that is, in their own words, 'contributors should know how much they are paying into a pension scheme and what they can expect from their contributions. This means that the intra-personal and inter-personal elements of any pension scheme should be clearly identifiable and separately financed.' It should be stable, 'isolated as far as possible from short run fluctuations in capital markets'and from political interference, this last applying particularly to pensions paid out of current taxation. These then are the essential conditions laid down by Falkingham and Johnson for their unified pension scheme, the major element of which is the pension fund each individual will be required to build up by personal contributions assisted by public money in ways we shall now attempt to describe.

In the above account 'intra-personal' means savings in the straightforward sense, money put aside at an earlier stage of a person's lifetime to be drawn out at a later stage, and represented here by the contributions made to his or her Pension Retirement Fund (PRF). 'Inter-personal' means money to be transferred for welfare reasons from one person to another and plays the following part in the scheme. Annual savings for retirement should build up a capital sum sufficient at the end of the Second Age to ensure to pensioners an inflow of a third of their average income when they were in employment. Estimates are also given for a replacement income for a half rather than a third. Any individual falling short in savings will receive 'top-ups' from general taxation to make them up, and this constitutes an element of inter-personal assistance, distinctly financed, it will be seen, from the individual contributions. Provision is also made for special capital levies on all personal PRFs at times of capital boom and they suggest that the proceeds should be used towards top-ups required in the latest years of employment, which they anticipate would leave large numbers below the required level in ther PRFs. Income in retirement would not be the same for all persons, but it would represent the same proportion of Second Age income. Full transparency would be guaranteed by every individual receiving periodic statements setting out exactly where he was or she was in relation to his or her pension fund. Arrangements would be provided for joint, spouse and spouse, contributions. Using the phraseology suggested earlier, we can regard the complete set of proposals as intended to direct the inter-cohort trust to be managed by government in the specified manner in respect of the pensioning of individuals.

The outstanding feature of the scheme is that all transfers from present to future in a person's lifetime and from person to person irrespective of cohort or age, could be said to be personally possessed capital sums. During the Second Age, and perhaps beginning in the First, an individual might well receive top-ups in the earlier years and if a substantial income begins to be earned subsequently pay back the value of those top-ups, thereafter being a net contributor, and helping as a taxpayer provide the the top-ups due to the less fortunate. The authors use the example of a poor student who turns into a well-heeled professional, and present a table (Table 1 on page 25) of payments in and out between ages 21 and 27. Income rises from 0 to £22 000 over these years, with top-ups received in the first two years totalling £2700 and repayment of this total by the end-year, when the value of the individual's retirement capital would be £12 150, the nucleus of the final fund for investment which might provide for the pensioner interest equal to half of the average earned annually in the Second Age.

We shall have taken as read the other provisions of this highly original and ingenious set of proposals intended to satisfy the ideal conditions which have been described. The reader cannot fail to notice the vivid contrast with the experience he or she has had with pension arrangements as they are in Britain today. One of the features of the proposal which has to be noted is how the enormous costs of getting the scheme going are to be met. Their estimate is £300 billion at the lowest (page 47), equivalent to over half the Gross National Product of the country. But this is no more than two-thirds of the capital already present in pension funds in this country, so huge are the sums involved in financing retirement. Since the national pension system may have to be reformulated anyway, which is bound to require expenditure of this order, Falkingham and Johnson judge their estimates to be acceptable. They go to some trouble, however, in recommending the means of covering these formidable costs.

Here then is a seemingly practicable scheme for paying for your own Third Age and one which makes every adult a pension-owner. In the same way as at present people do their best to secure a retirement income extra to the annual dole, which, in this country at least, is barely sufficient for life at the lowest standard, so the PRF scheme would exist alongside corporate pensions and other income producing capital accumulation made independently. It can be shown that this is not a method of 'privatising' pensions because of the inter-personal payments from taxation which have been described. It is also possible to show that these arrangements would in no way contradict the general principles laid down earlier in this chapter about successors perpetually supporting predecessors. The use of taxation funds to provide the requisite top-ups in order to ensure that everyone at the end of the Second Age has the necessary capital sum is a straight-forward example of successors at large undertaking the support of their predecessors at large. And they are doing so, our theory would add, because they can rely on their successors doing the same thing for them.

If any version of such a set of arrangements should come into being, and it seems certain that a difficult and perhaps lengthy transitional period would have to intervene, this would undoubtedly have economic, social and even political consequences beyond the attainment of a recast system of pensions. From our point of view the most important of these would be the institution of a mechanism of support for those no longer in work peculiarly suited to the theory, aims and ideals of the Third Age. We have to be aware, however, that it would indeed make of every retired person a capitalist or rentier, and that this might well intensify that class inequality among those in late life already commented upon. It is one of David Thomson's grounds of complaint against members of his unwittingly 'selfish generation'that they, now the seniors in society, are the capital-owners tending to use that position of financial power even though unconsciously and unintentionally against the interests of capital-deficient younger persons. It is true that the Falkingham–Johnson scheme would make every pensioner a capital-owner from the beginning of his or her earning career, but it enshrines the principle that the older a person gets, the richer in capital, with all the status, security and social weight which capital ownership brings with it.

It is evident that the intelligence, the skill and above all the integrity of those involved in the inter-cohort trust would be immensely important in such a situation. So also would the accuracy and extent of the information at the trust's disposal and the prudence of its practices. A great deal would also depend on the financial market which would handle the gigantic investment funds. We can be fairly confident that the City of London would rise to the occasion, in spite of the fact that recent events are hardly reassuring and that the record of British private pension agencies leaves a lot to be desired. In developing countries the financial markets are in no position to take on pension business on the required scale, which is a reason why, at the present time, the savings pillar, as it is called by the World Bank experts, could not be as important as it might be in Britain. This is unfortunate because of that invaluable feature of these arrangements which more or less guarantees that governments could not divert the savings of pensioners-to-be to other purposes, now happening on such a large scale in the non-industrial and industrialising areas.[19] Decreeing the dispossession of every citizen of all or any part of his pension fund is surely beyond the capacity of even the most dictatorial regime.

More significant in the eyes of highly authoritative economists and equally famous philosophers of generational justice, would be the predominating element of savings in such a pension plan. 'We should save more in our own economic interest', declares the very eminent economist James

M. Buchanan in the title of his contribution to the collection *Justice across Generations*, and he roundly declares that a dollar saved is a dollar earned.[20] The 'just savings principle' informs the entire discussion of the claims of the future generations on the present one by John Rawls, acknowledged as the leading contemporary philosopher of justice.[21] Financing retirement in the way recommended in this chapter should make it possible once again to maintain and extend the necessary substructures, invest in the contemporary productive processes, build the hospitals, schools and other capital goods which David Thomson claims have been progressively neglected in recent decades, much to the detriment of those who use them most, that is, younger persons in the Second Age and their families.[22]

It is not for an outsider to economic argument to pronounce on just how beneficial a radical increase in personal savings would be to our future prosperity, conceived of in conventional terms. But it would seem apparent that paying for your own Third Age would add to our assets as a society in many directions. It would certainly considerably enhance the notion of the Third Age itself, if only by removing the dependence on direct doles of public money as an essential source of income during that phase of life. However difficult, costly and time-consuming its introduction would be, it is much to be hoped that some version of the pension arrangements favoured by Falkingham and Johnson, and favoured also to a considerable extent by the Policy Research Report of the World Bank will come to replace the current British pension regime. This is surely an expedient to avert the old-age crisis, to quote the somewhat old-fashioned title of that publication.

DO THE THIRD AND FOURTH AGES DESERVE THE SUPPORT OF THE SECOND AGE?

In setting out in this chapter to dispose of the impression that older people, unproductive in the economistic sense, can be regarded as a burden on society, and in suggesting a juster, more efficient and appropriate way of securing their livelihood, no mention has been made of what they deserve to get, their deserts. This is in sharp contrast to the declarations and appeals of the British pensioners' organizations, which are perpetually appealing for more generous pensions, further allowances, and for greater consideration and respect as well. They frequently do this on the grounds that they, the retired, have done signal service to the whole community during their long years of hard work and played the principal British role in the dramatic and tragic events of the twentieth century. Even John Hills, when he discovered that those born in the early 1900s have been the most conspicuous gainers from the flow of welfare funds for education, health and social security, concludes by saying, 'Given that they lived through the Depression of the 1930s and were the generation who had to fight the Second World War, it might be thought churlish to begrudge them this gain: after all, intergenerational equity is not just about the Welfare State.'[23]

Gallant as this sentiment may be thought to be and widespread as is the belief among older people that they are entitled to the respect of younger people and do not get enough of it,[24] desert does not seem to me to provide much in the way of justification for the claims of the Third and Fourth Ages at any one time to the share which they enjoy of the wealth being created largely by the Second Age at that time. We receive this income, and I write as one currently in the Third Age myself, who served for four years in the wartime British Navy as a right under the inter-cohort trust and on the strict understanding that producers of that value, that is to say those who are in the Second Age, will themselves be in our position in due course, receiving their support from their own successors. Indeed it has been insisted that the people who work to create the wealth so transferred should best regard it as being paid to themselves as they will be when they leave the Second Age. The question of whether those who receive that support have deserved it, or deserve more of it than they are getting, simply does not arise as an issue between age groups sharing the same time-space. It has to be dealt with by the inter-cohort trust which deals in the whole life-span of cohorts.[25]

It will be seen how much more convincing these considerations would be if everyone in the Third and Fourth Ages were paying for themselves from their earlier savings in the way which has been set out. Under these circumstances, the tendency of older people, and their younger champions and spokesmen, to proclaim that 'the old' deserve more than they might get might be lessened. That tendency presumably ultimately derives from the widespread conviction, a traditional Second Age conviction for the whole discourse is shot through with Second Age attitudes and values, the conviction that to be older is to be worse-off, finally to be pitied and so compensated simply because of advanced age. Such an outlook is entirely inconsistent with the concept of the Third Age as it has been worked out here and commits the solecism of taking the Fourth Age for the Third.

It may seem paradoxical, that 'the old' and those who elect to speak for them proclaim that these older persons deserve more than they get at the very time when there is so much complaint about the burden of the elderly. This clash in currents of opinion could be explained as a dialogue, the party for 'the old' using the argument of desert against the party of the age-denunciatory young. The attempt here has been to demonstrate that both attitudes are mistaken in their ideas of what constitutes processional justice, justice between age groups and generations.

No cause is furthered by adopting faulty arguments and that of the autonomy of the Third Age has certainly been damaged by the emphasis on how deserving older persons are, and by a further set of appeals, to the necessity of restoring and reinforcing what is called solidarity between the generations. This rather unhappy phrase rests, so it seems to me, on a somewhat questionable reading of history, inaccurate observation of the relationships between young and old at the present time, an instrumental attitude on the part of the Second Age to the Third, and a refusal to allow those from the Third Age to make their own choices, work out their own policy, and negotiate with their juniors from a position of independence. Nothing was added to the effectiveness of the European Year of Older People in 1993 by subjoining this phrase to the title.

The historical analysis contained in our earlier chapters does not indicate that there was a time, a world we have lost, in which there was greater interaction between generations (in whatever sense of that multivocal word) more understanding and interdependence, warmer sympathy, larger preparedness to offer necessary support, whether in the form of house room or otherwise, than is the case today. Since there has been a marked reduction in coresidence between older and younger people, especially in recent decades when opportunities for co-residence have increased so much, the continuous interaction which living together implies has certainly got less, much less than might have been the case. But on the whole the strength of bonding between old and young, like bonds of family and kinship generally, have been remarkably constant over time and on the whole independent of the great increase in living alone which sometimes, and questionably, is called the residential isolation of the elderly. Whether these attitudes and practices can survive the familial alterations of our own day, the transformation of procreative practices, the multiplication of divorce and the attenuation of kinship numbers, is the crucial issue for our increasingly long-lived society, as has been insisted several times in this book.[26]

No amount of insistence on generational solidarity as it is claimed to have existed before these changes took place seems likely to have much effect under these circumstances. Would those who plead for greater generational solidarity advocate the overriding of decisions by parents to live apart from their married children? Setting ourselves a somewhat peripheral objective might hold back the full recognition of what is really new in the matter of ageing, that is to say, the emergence of the Third Age as an entirely responsible body capable of making their own decisions, working out their own policies, collaborating of their own free choice in maintaining a social fabric in response to and in the face of demographic and economic vicissitude.

This was the reason for my personal decision to adopt as the theme of the first Dutch National Lecture on Gerontology the claim that the independence of the Third Age comes before solidarity between the generations.[27] It might perhaps have been expected that the move among those in the Third Age, initially in Britain, but subsequently in Australia and elsewhere, to organize their own universities, the U3As, in collaboration with sympathizers in the Second Age to begin with, but subsequently wholly on their own, should meet with criticism and even opposition from Second Age professionals engaged in the instruction of adults outside the University and intent on conducting their activities as community education. On the continent of Europe and especially in Germany and France, in which last-named country the first Universities of the Third Age were brought into being, these institutions are still for the most part controlled, organized and taught by Second Age professionals. Some of them, so impressed are they by the necessity of reinforcing generational solidarity and by the personal rewards of being taught alongside students at the regular (ie. socialization) stage of study, have changed the names of the Universities of the Third Age to Universités de tous les Ages (Universities for All Ages).[28]

These are not urgent issues however, and their importance should not be exaggerated. So new is the recognition of the vital necessity of intellectual and cultural instruction and activity in late life, that any contribution ot that end coming from any source has to be warmly welcomed. But it seems that many years of experience of the Third Age will have to elapse before those in that phase of life enter into their entire intellectual independence, and here the word 'their'had to be considered as that of persons now in the Second Age who will have proceeded to the Third Age by the time the change comes about.

A proposal about these Second Age/Third Age relationships, institutional or personal, seems to be in order here. As the future unfolds, the activities of the charitable institutions founded before the Third Age arrived to succour those at the end of their lives should be directed in accordance with the original impetus, and confine themselves to assistance to those in the Fourth Age, whose situation largely corresponds to that of 'old age' before the middle of the twentieth century. In that important, indispensable task they must be able to count on the collaboration as partners of those in the Third Age, in relation to whom Second Age activists, as they might be called, should renounce entirely any role of spokesmanship. Let us in the Third Age speak for ourselves. As for those whose Second Age commitment is to community education, it is surely evident from what was said in Chapter 11 that their function is the preparation of everyone in the Second Age for succession to the Third Age. Whilst those in the Third Age must rely on them for much needed resources they should allow us in the Third Age to get on with our own education and cultural self-realisation.

The consideration of the complaint that the elderly are a burden and of the case of paying for your own Third Age has led us to cover a great deal of the ground already surveyed in earlier chapters. This should cause no surprise since our subject is so fraught with intertwined relationships that its exploration can scarcely be progressive. Rather it is the successive viewing in depth of the whole phenomenon from different points of view. But the one thing the whole discourse makes obvious is that those in the Third Age have duties as well as privileges. Although it is a time of release and fulfilment, the Third Age is also one of responsible citizenship and continued activity in certain familial matters. It is to the duties of those in the Third Age that we turn in our final chapter.

13 The Responsibilities of Older British People

Growing older does not absolve a person from responsibility, certainly not responsibility for the social future. It could be claimed, indeed, that many more duties of older people go forward in time than is the case in those who are younger. This follows from the fact that they owe less to their own individual futures – now comparatively short – and more to the future of others, all others.[1] It is those who have lived longest who have done the most to bring about the situation which is experienced at any one time. In shouldering their responsibilities for that current situation, older people will do all they can to ensure the future is as good as it can be. In this the elders of any society can be said to be *trustees* for the future.

NB

The facts and circumstances, demographic and otherwise, with which we have been concerned in this book make this clear. It is shown in Chapter 4 that the actions of parents and grandparents of people now in later life were responsible for bringing about the great proportionate increase in older age groups. But it has been the more recent and the present elderly who have ensured that the ageing of the population should continue. They have done so primarily by continuing the policy of producing fewer children, but also by fostering the practices and institutions which enable everyone to go on living longer.

Those who have recently retired from careers in medicine, social services and administration have made the greatest contribution to the rise in expectation of life, and thus have helped to bring the Third Age into being. Since the responsibility of the dead cannot enter into the question, we can regard the results we have described as in good part due to the actions of still-living people. It is surely proper that those living people should accept their share of responsibility and their continuing duties to the social future, doing what it is open to them to do.

This may in fact be very little, but we all have responsibilities which we find difficult or impossible to fulfil. Those relinquishing positions in which their achievements have been considerable certainly merit the satisfaction which they get from the advances which they have helped to make. It seems hardly right that they should leave all the consequences to their successors. In the course of this book, moreover, stress has been placed time and time again on the things which the elderly can do now, and should do if they possibly can, because no one else can do them.

As we outline the opportunities for taking action, for recognizing the shape of change and modifying attitudes, the boundaries of the possible must never be lost sight of. The present British elderly may not be peculiarly victimized by the facts of historical development. This is a claim which every generation, every group within a generation, is tempted to make for itself and must resist. But the older people of our time and in our country, or most of them at least, have been singularly badly prepared for the challenge which they find facing them as they take up their position in the new social formation of the Third Age. They have neither the position nor the power, the educational advantages, the money or the means to do what they might wish. What is more, as we have seen, many of them have neither the health, nor the strength, while the intentions of all of them are restricted by the time which they can now expect to have left to them. But when all is said and done their opportunities are remarkable, and it is right to exhort them to take proper account of them.

Let us look once again at the character of those responsibilities and dwell for a while on one or two illustrative examples. First and foremost it must be said that those in the Third Age who have by definition learnt to be their age, that is they have recognized what it means to belong to the oldest English population which has ever existed, and in this case to be an older member of that population, must do their best to see that other Britons come to their senses too about ageing. It is a responsibility clearly shared with all other citizens, but rests particularly on them. Their further obligation, however, is entirely personal. It is to fulfil themselves as far as personal circumstances and history permit, to use their Third Age in fact in the ways which have been suggested here.

Finding self-fulfilment implies making the judgements which are necessary to sustain independence, to create a proper relationship with others, especially in the interchange with younger members of society. This interchange has a particular importance in view of what was said about the lack of role models for late-twentieth-century elderly and to-be-elderly individuals. The example set by those in the Third Age in present society must inevitably be of significance to their successors, must serve as hints of what they might do or avoid doing when they themselves become members of that society. Those now in the Third Age have an obligation to recognize that the persons perpetually joining them in that status from the Second Age have been differently and better educated, more comfortably placed financially, with quite other past experiences. There should accordingly be no question of a forced relationship. Familiarity at a distance, which we have taken as the preferred relationship of the elderly with their families, might serve to cover this relationship as well. Being sensitive about when to withdraw from situations where remaining in them would interfere unjustifiably with the purposes of younger people, is also of the first importance. If it is true that those in the Second Age have to respect the autonomy of those in the Third, it is also true that those in the Third Age have to give a free hand to those in the Second. This may be particularly important when the control of capital and resources is in question.

The elderly should not isolate themselves nevertheless, and it may be the duty of younger persons to help to ensure that this does not happen. But it should be made clear that it is the right of those in later life to make their own terms on which this interchange shall take place, and that their privacy should be protected as they see fit. An eloquent, if minor, example of this for some members of the U3A concerns swimming. Older women, and older men as well, whose bodies no longer conform to the ideals of youthful vigour and beauty, meretricious as some may think these ideals have become, surely have a right to enter the pool with their age-mates and with no one else. An even more conspicuous example of their duties which are also their rights can be illustrated from the questions which may or must arise about the ending of life, questions of far greater significance to those in the Third and Fourth Ages than to any of their juniors.

Difficult and debatable as these questions are, subject to differing religious and ethical beliefs, they are inescapable by older people. In my own view it is the duty of the elderly to work out and maintain a code of theory and practice in these matters, in consultation with younger persons and with the professionals who may have to carry out the necessary actions. But the final responsibility should be reserved to themselves. It is inequitable, a breach of the principles of justice between age groups, to leave the issues entirely to those in the Second Age and especially to medical staff, as seems to be the present situation. The creation of such a code is the duty of such institutions as the University of the Third Age. A major clause in such a code would have to be the requirement that everyone in the Third Age who has not done so already should make a Living Will giving directions as to what should be done if a point is reached when she or he would not wish life to be further prolonged. It is imperative that this not be postponed to the Fourth Age. It is also desirable that citizens in the Third Age should press for legislation in these areas.

The next set of responsibilities which arise for older British people is to provide as far as it is open to them for justice between age groups and generations, above all in matters of support and welfare reaching them through the Welfare State. The lineaments of the present situation and the arguments for and against the supposition that those at present going through the Third Age have tended to exploit their successors have been set out in Chapter 12 above, sufficiently I hope to require no repetition here. What may need most emphasis is that the issues and circumstances as to the distribution of wealth over time affect the political responsibilities of those now and to be members of the Third Age, both because they are responsible citizens and because they have been the only witnesses of the developments in question. They are, therefore, in the preferred temporal position to make the proper judgements. Their interest, moreover, is in the establishment of a set of relationships between cohorts and generations in a permanently age-altered society which does secure continuing justice over time, to advise the administrators of the inter-cohort trust in their enormously demanding task. It is in ways like those in late life they can fulfil their forward-reaching social responsibilities, and secure for the whole of society something which may approach an equitable relationship with the future.

Actions, plans and purposes like these demand a self-awareness so far conspicuously lacking among the British elderly, and the development of a policy on the matters which affect them because of their particular position. This means that they must make a considered use of their political allegiances and of their political potential. That political potential, as all the commentators have agreed, has yet to manifest itself in action in this country. It was evident in the description of the electoral insignificance of the elderly that they possess neither institutions nor instruments which might mobilize and express their power. Apart from associations concerned almost entirely with the issue of pensions, and social and recreational clubs, such as the still-youthful Association of Retired Persons, seemingly very unlikely to become anything resembling the AARP, the U3As in Britain seem to be alone as organizations founded by those in the Third Age, for their own purposes and under their own control. Political representation of the elderly here is largely undertaken by what I have called Second Age Institutions like Age Concern, whose tendency to adopt an attitude of spokesmanship towards the Third Age has already been sufficiently discussed. There are those in the Third Age in this country, well-represented in the U3As who deliberately resist any discussion of issues of ageing in political terms.[2] They seem to fear being used as instruments by existent interests and parties.

But if democracy in our country is to function as it should, it is necessary that this political potential make itself manifest in choices, policies and movements, even if a Third Age party or faction may not itself be recommended. This is the obvious responsibility of those in Britain now in later life, and it is only in this way that they can do what can be done to bring to an end that cultural lag as to age and ageing, to which repeated reference has been made. It could be said that the ageing of the population has divided the political nation by bringing into being a huge body of the politically inert. It is surely up to the society of those in the Third Age to ensure that this rent in the political fabric is knit up, in so far as this can be done from the side on which they are placed. That change in this direction is occurring elsewhere in Europe and is leaving Britain behind is shown by what has happened in the Netherlands. There no less than three political parties came into being in the interest of older people at the General Election of 1994.

In all these directions older people have a special responsibility to their more immediate juniors, those who can reasonably expect to join them in the Third Age over the next decade or two. It has several times been insisted that it is for the present elderly to prepare a place and set precedents for them, precedents, many of them, for further innovation. To illustrate what has to be done, we may move from major social issues and return to the obligation of the contemporary elderly to act as cultural trustees, and pay a little attention to craftsmanship.

One of the outstanding features of cultural interest in the material objects which have been inherited from the past lies in the expenditure of time which each of those objects represents. Indeed, as has been remarked, in attempting to explain its significance to the tourist, guides frequently spell out the number of work hours, work weeks or work years which were needed to create a particular object. Now it is a fact of the greatest significance that such expenditure of highly-skilled workmanship for such purposes has vanished for ever. The work-time available to professional craftsmen in the Second Age, who could earn their livings, maintain their families, pursue their careers in fashioning objects of the quality we must have in mind when we speak of British culture, is quite simply no longer available.

The very circumstances which make us richer than our predecessors, healthier, longer-lived and more comfortable, are also the circumstances which ensure that the time of those who earn their livings in the Second Age is immensely more valuable and therefore proportionately scarcer than it was in the past. Today it is only during the Third Age that people have world enough and time to conduct themselves as traditional craftsmen used to do. The retired, of course, have the hours, days, weeks, and months to spend at a task because they do not have to earn a living wage for what they do.

It may well, therefore, become the long-term duty of those in the Third Age to assume responsibility for the maintenance of the tradition of crafts-manship in our country and its role in our cultural life. Craft activities are already widespread at centres for the deprived elderly and in institutions for the very old, and in the judgement of those who arrange such things these have a rehabilitatory effect as well as providing satisfaction to their subjects. In these instances, however, it is not clear how far objects of laboured hand-manufacture are being produced for their value in them-selves or how far their production is being used to occupy those with too much time on their hands. And neither rehabilitation nor the filling-up of vacant time was in the minds of the craftsmen and craftswomen of the past. To them it was a vocation, a vocation for life, and it had to yield a living too. Moreover, an aptitude, long experience, extensive practice in the craft concerned, an apprenticeship with a master or a mistress, all these were, and may still be, essential for the fashioning of craft objects exquis-ite enough to enrich our cultural tradition. The professional craftsmen of the past did it for a living as well as for love. We shall have to learn to do it for love alone.

The example of craftsmanship provides an opportunity to estimate the proper relationship of those in the Third Age with the unemployed, those other members of the community of the indolent by compulsion which has been described as typical of late-twentieth-century industrial society. Could not their interests and energies also be recruited in an effort to pre-serve and intensify the craft tradition in our culture? To the extent that they resemble the dependent old, the unemployed may have a need for therapy through the exercise of craftsmanship. As far as any of them have chosen this as the source of their self-fulfilment in the Third Age, more-over, in so far as this would be an alleviation of the burden of their indo-lence, those out of work most certainly should be encouraged to take up arts and crafts.

But we have seen that society can, or will, no longer afford to provide a living wage for a full-time occupation of this kind, and it is in training for a full-time occupation that the unemployed should be engaged. Even though the membership of the University of the Third Age must be open to them as to everyone else, instruction in view of a full-time job is no proper function of that voluntary, intellectual and cultural society. The instruction and rehabilitation of those in the Second Age who are out of work is a Second Age rather than a Third Age responsibility.

It can be seen then that not all the activities of the Third Age is fulfilling a trust for the maintenance of the cultural life of our country would be as strenuous as those which were mentioned earlier as guarding the monuments, keeping the libraries and museums in full-time operation, the practice of weaving or of wood-carving. Not all indolence is idleness. Having time to read poetry, or to write it; to look at pictures, or to paint them; to go to concerts, or to play an instrument; to do these things at leisure – at an unhurried pace – is the essence of self-cultivation and of social cultivation too. The tendency to remove from schools and universities subjects for which a leisurely pace is required, subjects whose justification is almost entirely cultural – music, the classics, the fine arts, the rarer languages, and so on – is particularly pronounced in Britain at present. This grudging attitude to the humanities has been characteristic of what we have called education at or through socialization for much of the present century and previously. It is a circumstance, as has been shown, which puts us in an increasingly unfavourable position in relation to the expanding tourist 'industry'. It is certainly inconsistent with the emergence of the Third Age, and with the proper use of time in the Third Age for those who come to participate in it.

If they were given the opportunity to acquire the elements of these arts of cultivation while they were at school and university, above all if they had the opportunity to maintain repetitive contact with those institutions and the professionals who teach in them, those in the Third Age could come to be exponents, advancers, indeed practitioners of the humanities. Leisure is traditionally associated with the aristocrats and the wealthy, and it has to be recognized that they have been the patrons and guardians of our culture to a considerable degree, at least in the matter of the fine arts. They continue to regard themselves as trustees of these activities, a point which is demonstrated with irresistible force to the visitor of the great houses of the British countryside. It should also be recognized that their way of living is now anachronistic, as well as being in full decline: their functions of this character are entirely inadequate for these purposes.

But time, or leisure rather, and a means to use it, have ceased to be the monopoly of an élite made up of hundreds, thousands, or at most in tens of thousands of persons. It is becoming a commodity possessed by millions of our citizens, our elderly citizens, those in the Third Age. Some way, therefore, must be discovered to entrust them with our cultural future, and by the same means to relieve them of the burden of their present indolence.

We may press the comparison of the cultural function of the Third Age today and tomorrow with those of the aristocracies of the past with a citation from what was said when it was suspected that the Third Age might form a National Trust for the future on the analogy of that remarkable institution, the British National Trust itself.

After citing Edmund Burke's famous phrases about partnership over time, partnership in the temporal procession, a partnership not only between those who are living, but those who are dead, and those who are to be born, the address continued

What is patently evident is that the duties of all of us require a partnership reminiscent of the partnership which Edmund Burke is so eloquent about and involving, as he assumes, the collective institutions of the State. (Here he might be thought to have had in mind what I have called the intercohort trust and the generational tricontract.)

It is a partnership between individuals of all ages and all professions requiring from everyone a vigilance even more constant than John Stuart Mill required for the retention of our liberty. Never to use too much water, too much heat, too many materials; never to pollute anything anywhere; never to discard anything which will not disappear instantly and of itself; never to join in an activity which will tend to depopulate the earth of any of its species, defoliate the landscape, upset the global atmosphere, desolate our habitat and so the habitat of all our successors. The list is infinite and goes far, far beyond the genteel structures and their comforting contents protected by the British National Trust, along with the entire body of objects which rest on the shelves of the museums of the world.

Universal as these duties are, however, essential as it is that experts and administrators in the Second Age should take much of the action and decide the policy, it is for members of the Third Age, as I have tried to show to see themselves as the nominated trustees for those who are to come. It is for them to prompt, inform and support the administrators, curators, keepers and librarians of the National Trust, the museums and so forth. I would go so far as to say that these officials, professional and amateur, insofar as they have persons to whom they should feel a responsibility, should turn to those in the Third Age. It follows therefore that every sensitive, informed, conscientious member of the Third Age should do everything possible to be aware and informed of the needs of posterity, of the rights of posterity, of the things which posterity would most wish to inherit from us and of the things which menace those rights, of the habits and outlook which have to be transformed if posterity is to be given its due. (If it be asked on what principle we are compelled to fulfil this debt to our successors in the world, the answer can be summarised with the terms used in Chapter 12 above.) We are obliged to hand over to them what we have inherited from the past in the condition in which that inheritance was received. We do for those who follow us what has been done for us by those who preceded us.

The address ends by asserting,

> It has been the aristocracies, which until recently have had the means, the leisure, the cultivation and the taste to act as trustees of the cultural and national societies and for such entities as the society of Europe at large. You have only to contemplate the elderly eighteenth-century aristocrat supervising the planting of a great avenue before his splendid house, knowing that he himself would never live to see the trees grow as tall as his own shrunken height,[3] to recognise that these past patrons of the arts must have been conscious that they were representing the future. Though the structures and the objects which this social order created still survive, at least in part, the age of aristocratic patronage has virtually passed away. It is the leisured members of the Third Age who should recognise that it is for them to take over where the dukes, the earls, baronets and plain esquires have had to relinquish their responsibilities. They will have to recognise moreover that leisured life of this kind means work, very hard work.

An even more determined idealism about the Third Age might see it as performing all that the cultured, the intellectual, the accomplished and the creative of any social group or class have ever undertaken in historical time. A twenty-first century utopia begins to come into our being. But we must content ourselves here with a beginning which is infinitely more modest in its scope.

Such a beginning can be descried in the growing numbers of voluntary associations which are growing up around institutions of learning and of culture – the Friends of the Royal Academy, or the Tate Gallery, for example, or of the British Library and the Bodleian, most of whom must be in the Third Age. But the scope must assuredly be widened, the catchment enlarged. A better model might be the membership of the National Trust. Their numbers have been expanding at an astonishing rate. There were a million-and-a-half in 1988 and over a quarter of a million joined during that year. The rate of expansion has slowed somewhat in the 1990s, but there are now over two million members. Perhaps a third or more of these interested people, alert as they can be supposed to be to the questions about the cultivation of our culture and its transmission from the past to the present and to the future, are estimated to be in later life.

Simply belonging to the National Trust, however, may imply very little in the way of service to that institution. Regular attendance to carry out work is undertaken only by a very small proportion of the membership. Perhaps the most important of all the duties of the present elderly, however, is to recognize that persistent, recurring, daily attendance, with periods to themselves, will increasingly be expected of them in Third Age institutions as Third Age living takes its hold. Grateful as they are for such voluntary help as they at present receive from the retired in keeping their exhibits on view, directors of art galleries consistently complain that unpaid service of this kind is unreliable.

Even the U3As have found that keeping office hours, answering the telephone, making copies of the documents, and all the other routine duties of administering their own organizations are better carried out by paid assistants than they are by members honouring their duties by giving freely of their time. It is one of the accepted privileges of retirement that your time is your own to stay at home when you feel like it, to visit relatives and friends on any day you choose, to be with your children and their families whenever that is desirable or necessary and at short notice. Reconciling these hard-won privileges with the duties of the Third Age may turn out to be difficult. But it will have to be done. This is an especially urgent matter if, as has been hinted in the course of the text, the familial changes now afoot and to come in British and Western society require that the Third Age collaborate deliberately and publicly with the Second Age in the raising of their grandchildren, and in the care and nurture of the large numbers of children in the future who may have no parental attachment. This is a theme which we shall have to relinquish at this point. It goes too far and requires too much in the way of decision about the uncertainties of the future shape of high industrial society to be adequately treated in an introductory text like the present. But I hope to return to it on a future occasion.

If this present book reads as an injunction to hard-pressed working men and women when they come to retirement to take up pursuits for which they have neither the inclination nor the preparation, it will have missed the mark. If it fails to convey the message that nearly all the attitudes and institutions appropriate to an era of transformed age relationships have yet to come into being, it will have been misunderstood. If it is interpreted as maintaining that the Third Age can only be satisfactorily lived by those sufficiently instructed to join in what for want of a better expression must be called university-level studies, it will have been fundamentally misjudged. The fact that it is not at all clear as yet how best those not intellectually motivated can fulfil themselves in the Third Age has been called the greatest of all the challenges which the emergence of that new phase of life has brought in its train. Meeting that challenge is decidedly a duty of older British people, along with their companions elsewhere in an ageing world. To those who might interject that the institution of something like the U3As can hardly be expected to make much progress in answering that challenge, I can only respond – what then? What other starting point? In what other direction should we be expected to go?

A twentieth-century industrial society does not solve its problems of social distribution, its problems of class and income inequality, and inequality in eduction and cultural enrichment, by becoming old. But these things may come to be seen in an entirely new light as the social structure changes in an elderly direction. So it might be for the woman in middle life whose feelings, fears and expectations about her age have been behind the text which stands completed. The facts may turn out to be numerical, numerical to a wearisome degree. Their arrangement may be complex and tedious to unfold. But to know their lineaments, even in a preliminary way, reveals the shape and contours of a landscape so far never seen before, in

> The light that never was, on sea or land,
> The consecration, and the poet's dream.

Notes

PREFACE

1. In the United States as well as here, in spite of all the efforts of the great lady of ageing studies at the National Institute of Aging in Washington, Matilda White Riley. Witness her latest publication, *Age and Structural Lag*, ed. Matilda White Riley, Robert L. Kahn, and Anne Foner which appeared in May 1995.
2. In that country a committee of the House of Representatives published a report in April 1992 which adopted the life course divisions laid down in this book and reproduced extensive extracts from it. The party of government, the Australian Labor Party and especially its Chairman Barry Jones seem to have adopted its revision of policy towards older people. See Chapter 12 below.
3. See Bibliography, Laslett 1994(b) and the discussion in Chapter 12 below.
4. It is present in the American republication of the book (Harvard, 1991) but not in the Italian version (*Una Nuova Mappa della Vita*, Universal Paperbacks II Mulino, Bologna, 1991, translated with an introduction by Pier Paolo Viazzo) nor in the German version (*Das Dritte Alter*, Juventa, Weinhem and Munich, 1995, translated with an introduction by Axel Flügel). Neither of these versions includes Chapter 11 on education, and in both the text has been rearranged to suit the countries concerned. They are therefore slightly different books from the original, which is appropriate enough for the following reason. Each contains in addition to, or in place of, the statistics drawn from Britain, statistics applicable to the two countries concerned. In this way it is hoped to make the work genuinely European, or at least of the European Union, since other translations, including the one now in progress in Spain, will have their own national statistics on ageing.
5. See Laslett 1991(a) ('The duties of the Third Age: should they form a National Trust for the future?') and compare what is said in Chapter 12 with its references, especially to Laslett 1992(a) ('Processional justice').
6. *Generations Review, Journal of the British Society of Gerontology* 5:2, June 1995, p. 10.

1   A NEW DIVISION OF THE LIFE COURSE

1. See Chapter 7 below, with its references, especially Hazan, 1994.
2. For a scholarly survey of these terms and divisions in medieval and early modern times, see Burrow, 1986 (*The Ages of Man*). I know of no inclusive discussion of later usages and practices. The most important consideration

of the topic is Bernice Neugarten, 'Age Groups in American Society and the Rise of the Young Old', 1974. I am grateful to her for discussing the concept of the 'young old', which is not quite identical with the Third Age.

3.   See Laslett, 1994(a), *The Third Age, the Fourth Age and the Future* a review of the Carnegie Enquiry into the Third Age. The four numbered Ages were first suggested in Laslett (1987b), and the division of the life-course sketched out.

4.   Most recently the one implied by the phrase 'the third quarter of life', for all over 50, suggested by Alan Pifer, not unattractive but unfortunate in that it seems to leave us 25 years to die. See Pifer and Bronte, 1986; and my review of that book (Laslett, 1986). Both the system adopted here and that of Alan Pifer (who was a number of the Advisory Committee of the Carnegie Enquiry) finally derive from the study of the life-course in relation to the developmental cycle of the family group, from its formation at marriage, its expansion as children arrive, its diminution as they depart for work or for marriage, and so on. When the empty-nest stage is discussed in Chapter 7 below, for example, extensive use is made of this development typology. But it is not well suited to comparative study, and its complication makes exposition difficult. In 1987 the terms First, Second and Third Age were used in the study of the ageing population published by the Office of Population Censuses and Surveys (Jean Thompson, 1987, 'The Ageing of the Population: Contemporary Trends and Issues'). But no Fourth Age was named and the First ended on the sixteenth birthday. In the Carnegie usage the Third Age is strictly a period of years lived, from the fiftieth anniversary of birth, irrespective of whether the individual has retired, to the eve of the seventy-fifth. It is thus implied, and there are allusions in the Research Papers which bear this out, that all life lived after the seventy-fifth birthday is lived in the Fourth Age, an unacceptable proposition to those in later life who have reflected on the issue, and certainly unacceptable to me.

5.   See Chapter 12 below with its references, especially Thomson, 1991 and Laslett, 1992(a) and (b).

6.   See Chapter 12 below and Laslett, 1991(a), 'The Duties of the Third Age. Should they Form a National Trust for the Future?'.

2   HOW LONG CAN ANYONE GO ON LIVING?

1.   Thatcher and Kannisto, 1993, ('The plausibility of certain reported cases of extreme longevity'). For Mr Thatcher's original opinion see Thatcher, 1992 ('Mortality at the highest ages'). I am grateful to Roger Thatcher for many discussions of these topics and for his further papers about them, especially a draft of December 1994 ('How much do we know about maximum length of life?'). It is evident that Norris McWhirter, editor of the *Guinness Book of Records*, still accepts Izumi's record. See *The Times Weekend Supplement*, 14 Oct. 1995. But the Japanese experts now suppose that his age at death must have been well below 120.

2.   The French take great pains with recordings of latest life and French demographers have a project for monitoring the condition of every French cente-

narian. There is an institute in Paris devoted to this project, the Fondation IPSEN: see Allard, 1993 (*A la recherche du secret des centenaires*).

3. See the celebratory volume issued in 1994 for Jeanne Calment's 120th birthday, and Allard, Michel, 1993. In discussion with those in France who have worked on the record of her life and her genealogy it has become evident how difficult it must have been to apply to her case the name-matching principles which have been worked out by historical demographers to whom name-matching is an important issue. The tremendous publicity surrounding her age, however, and indeed the age of all those who attract attention because of exceptional survival makes it seem tactless even to mention such details for fear of giving offence.

4. Mr Thatcher is a member of the Cambridge consortium, along with Dr Väinö Kannisto, formerly adviser on population statistics to the United Nations. This gives the project the character of a set of persons themselves in the Third Age working voluntarily in their own locations on issues of great significance to all their age mates and so putting into practice one of the original principles of the University of the Third Age (see Chapter 11 below). The third member is Professor James Vaupel, Director of the Odense Research Unit, the only one of us not in the Third Age. At Cambridge we also interest ourselves in individual instances of very long life. The testimony of her family has enabled us to investigate the case of Mrs Charlotte Hughes, who died aged 115 in March 1993, the oldest English person whom we can confidently pronounce as ever having lived. The *Guinness Book* gives Daisy Adams, born 1880 as the oldest English woman now alive and Edgar Sharpe, born 1886, as the oldest man. The oldest man in the waved (and the oldest ever to have lived) known to the consortium is Christian Mortensen, a Danish immigrant in California, recently discovered to have been born on 16 August 1892 and so to have reached 113 years. Information from John Wilmoth, University of California, Berkeley.

5. These principles, derived from the application of the Gompertz law, are best described in a further unpublished paper of the length of life project, (Zhao Zhongwei, 1994, 'Record longevity in Chinese history; the evidence of the Wang genealogy'). They do not imply that no 98-year-old could ever be found in a small population with a low expectation of life. It is rather that they would appear so rarely that hundreds and hundreds of years would have to go by with the whole population under perpetual observation to be confident that an instance would be observed. Zhao's case is that the population of China has been so large for so long that some cases must have been forthcoming although life expectation was modest for most of the record.

6. At the world conference on ageing in Budapest in July 1993, several such sessions were organized, and in the case of the Brazilian session, for example, seemingly incredible claims were put forward.

7. See Väinö Kannisto, 1988, 'On the Survival of Centenarians and the Span of Life', his book of 1994 already cited, and Thatcher, 1987 and 1992 ('Trends in Numbers and Mortality at High Ages in England and Wales)'.

8. Kannisto, op.cit., 1988. The collection of data there used formed the core of the Kannisto/Thatcher database. In a further unpublished paper of 1993,

written with Roger Thatcher, Kannisto produced estimates for *living* centenarians in a current population of some 430 million in 1990; there were
18 600 in total alive aged 100 and over. In 1990 there were 3942
alive in England and Wales (see Chapter 5 below, note 4).

9. The original article is to be found in *Journal of the American Medical
    Association*, 28 May 1982, vol. 247, no. 20, Robert R. Kohn, 'Cause of
    Death in Very Old People'. Kohn states that 'no acceptable cause of death
    other than ageing could be found in at least thirty per cent of autopsies
    carried out on persons dying over the age of 85'. He proposes that 'the
    ageing syndrome should be viewed as a universal, progressive and
    ultimately fatal disease'.

10. Fries, James F. and L. M. Crapo, 1981 (*Vitality and Aging*); see Chapter 5
    below.

11. Compare a review by Michael R. Rose of *Human Longevity* by David
    W. E. Smith in *Ageing and Society* 14, 1994. The statement quoted in the
    text was made by Rose in a letter to the Review Editor of the Journal. The
    extraordinarily contemptuous attitude in the published review towards
    Smith's book and all preceding theoretical positions should be noted, and is
    observable in Rose's own book of 1991 (*Evolutionary Biology of Aging*).

12. See Molleson, 1988 (*Skeletal Age and Palaeo-Demography*). 'Commonest
    age of adult death' is one of the definitions of life-span listed by Thatcher,
    1994 as being used for comparing species.

13. For justice between age groups see Chapter 12 below and its references,
    especially Laslett and Fishkin, 1992 and Daniels, 1988 (*Am I My Parents'
    Keeper? An Essay on Justice Between the Young and the Old*). On p. 91 of
    this last book Daniels refers to the discussion of the life-span in relation to
    ethics, Veatch, R. M. (ed.), 1979 (*Life Span: Values and Life Extending
    Technologies*), which I have been unable to consult.

14. See Chapter 12 below, where it is suggested that terms like 'afford' and
    'burden' reveal a misunderstanding of the pattern of relationships and duties.

15. Such as *finem respice*, 'have an eye to the end', for the family of Laslett.

16. Katzmann, Robert, 1988 (*Alzheimer's Disease as an Age Dependent
    Disorder*). In Carnegie Research Paper no. 9, 1992, the prevalence of all
    forms of dementia is given at 5.6 per cent from 75 to 79, 10.5 per cent 80 to
    84, 20.8 per cent 85 to 89, and 38.6 per cent 90 to 95 (p. 66, quoting
    A. F. Jorm, 1990). Hayflick, however, gives a rate of 47 per cent in those
    over 85, presumably Americans (1994, p. 164).

17. See Nicholas Coni, 1985 ('Alive and Well: Geriatic Medicine in the UK
    in 1984'), figures somewhat revised from more recent evidence. Britain
    has markedly low proportions of old people in institutions; about a half of
    those in Denmark, for example, or a fifth of those in the Netherlands.

18. See H. B. (Tony) Gibson 1992(a), *The Emotional and Sexual Lives of
    Older People*. The figures cited are given in Table 2.1 on page 36, and
    were derived from a study by B. D. Starr and M. B. Weiner. Over 40 per
    cent of the women said that sexual experience was better in later life. In
    his second book, published in 1992 (*Love, Sex and Power in Later Life*)
    Tony Gibson provides a list (p. 17) of myths about sexuality in later life
    consonant with the list we are commenting upon here. The whole of this
    small book is illuminating and useful, and in Chapter 8 he considers an

issue of extreme importance, though one which is rarely discussed: the extent of a change in sexual orientation among the partnerless woman in later life for whom the chances of a male partner are becoming almost impossibly small.

19. See yet a further short and readable work by Tony Gibson, the first specifically addressed to this salient problem for those in the Third Age, apt in its title and in that of its publisher, *On the Tip of Your Tongue: Your Memory in Later Life* (Third Age Press, 1995).

20. Carnegie Research Paper 9, 1992, pp. VII–IX, excerpts.

21. In Chapter 12 below, it is insisted that those at present in the Third Age in Britain should be deeply concerned about the increasingly poverty, absolute and relative, of their age-mates with the lower and lowest incomes.

22. See Laslett, 1991 (*Duties of the Third Age*), and Chapter 13 below.

3   THE AGE OF BRITAIN AS A COUNTRY

1. There are average bodily states, of course, corresponding to particular chronological ages or stages in the physical life course but variability due to diet, living conditions, heredity and so on are enormous. This is a subject of study in itself, called auxology. See for example the authoritative work of J. M. Tanner, *A History of the Study of Human Growth*, 1981. Psychologists of ageing distinguish psychological from biological age, here considered as one, and add functional age which I find difficult to distinguish from psychological (see e.g. Birren and Schaie, 1977, pp. 4–5). They also consider someone whose performances are markedly different from the mean for his or her chronological age as old or young 'for his age'.

2. Quoted from Laslett, 1991, 'The Ageless Society', a review of Michael Young and Tom Schuller 1991 (*Life After Work. The Arrival of the Ageless Society*).

3.. Still to be seen on the silver dollar. David Lowenthal, 1985, is a mine of interesting information on such subjects.

4. In the *Petit Larousse Illustré*, a book to be found in most French households, the flag of Quebec is included with other flags of the sovereign nations of the earth.

5. For the notion of revolution as crucial to the contemporary sense of nationhood, which might perhaps be held to disqualify Britain altogether because in the view there presented there never was an English or a British national revolution, see P. Laslett, 1983, Chapter 8 – 'Social Change and Revolution in the Traditional World'. Dutch nationalists might dispute the claim that the American was the first national revolution against an overlord, insisting on their national origins in the fight against Spanish rule in the sixteenth and seventeenth centuries. It seems likely on the other hand that fresh 'revolutions' of this kind will soon take place in Australia and perhaps other *ci-devant* British colonies in abolishing the monarchical institution shared with the 'mother country'. These decorous legal and constitutional processes stand in striking contrast to the earlier violent disruptions and the whole revolutionist tradition is running down, even in the successor polities of the former USSR.

6. Or rather 'subjects as we are' of the crown which technically rules over us. Contemporary republicans stress this point; Britons do not own themselves, they are owned by the queen as her subjects.

7. See, for example, the forceful republican and a reformist book by Stephen Haseler, *The End of the House of Windsor and the Birth of a British Republic* (1993).

8. Of the large number of titles on this topic, by environmentalists especially, *Sleepers Wake* by Barry Jones is particularly illuminating.

9. For the view that the *ancien régime* was not subverted in England by the new industrial order until as late as the 1820s, see J. C. D. Clark, 1985 (*English Society 1688–1832*). And for a formidable argument demonstrating that Britain's success was not entirely due to industrial innovation, but to supremacy in pre-industrial, especially agricultural techniques, combined with the new manufactures, see Wrigley, 1988 (*Continuity, Chance and Change: The Character of the Industrial Revolution in England*). In Wrigley's authoritative view the British lead in the new economic order disappeared much more quickly than is usually thought.

10. For the past position of the elderly in the English family, see Chapter 8 below and its references. As for the antiquity of the nuclear family itself, a prominent archaeologist of the Middle East has documented its existence at an epoch called in the title of his book 'the dawn of history', at and before 2000 BC. See Postgate, 1992 (*Early Mesopotamia: Society and Economy at the Dawn of History*), esp. p. 93.

11. See Laslett, 1995a (henceforth this reference will be named as *Necessary Knowledge*). One of the important reasons why older people did not form multigenerational households with their married children was lack of opportunity owing to demographic conditions: see Chapter 8 below.

12. See *Necessary Knowledge* pp. 20–1. For changes in numbers of kin because of demographic fluctuation, see Laslett and Smith, 1988.

13. See Laslett, 1987(a). And on the Greek and Roman philosophers, Finley, 1984.

4   THE AGE OF THE PRESENT BRITISH POPULATION

1. See Preston, Himes and Eggars, 1989 ('Demographic Conditions Responsible for Population Ageing'). This study stresses the very important fact that in most populations now classed as old, ageing in the very recent past has been due to falling mortality more than to the still falling fertility, which has accounted for practically all the ageing taking place earlier in time in those populations, and still does for populations which are compositionally young. It is not the actual level of either which ages a population further so much as an increase over an established trend.

2. It is now being suggested that it is pointless to seek for any age last birthday after which persons are to be classed as old: see the discussion in Chapter 10 below.

3. The countries are Sweden, Norway and Denmark; Belgium, Germany and Austria; Italy and Greece. See Table 4.2 and 6.1 for an international comparison. The US National Institute of Aging ranks the United Kingdom as the fifth oldest country in the world.

4. *Social Trends*, numbers 18 (1988) to 22 (1992), (Government Statistical Service). All unreferenced figures for the United Kingdom come from this publication.

5. These somewhat confusing points, which form a real barrier to the recognition of age in the study of the population at large, are set out and explained in *Necessary Knowledge*. See pages 30–3 for the Canadian example.

6. See *Necessary Knowledge*, pp. 38–41, and Myers, 1985 ('Aging and Worldwide Population Change'), pp. 173 onwards. Bourdelais, 1993, gives full details of the rise of disquiet in France over ageing and of the natalist reaction which this brought about. He goes as far as to imply that the very notion of ageing (*vieillissement*) came into being in this way.

7. See Amman, cited for Table 4.2 Spain has the single medium large population (39 million in 1991) which might be described as clearly younger on this score than the large European ones. But he shows that Spain is catching up.

8. See, for example, Phillipson, 1983 (*Capitalism and the Social Construction of Old Age*), as corrected by R. M. Smith, 1984 ('The Structural Dependence of the Elderly as a Recent Development: Some Sceptical Historical Thoughts'). It is perhaps to be expected that historians should be unaware of this misconception, even historians of the family; see e.g. Hanawalt, 1986 (*The Ties that Bound: Peasant Families in Medieval England*), p. 231.

9. Carnegie Enquiry Research Paper 5, 1992, Tony Warnes (ed.), Homes and Travel, p. 17. By the late 1980s, however, a change had occurred, 'a clear trend for the most popular retirement-age destination to shift from the traditional south coast counties towards the periphery of the densely settled urban industrial area of southern England'. Nevertheless the highest proportions of the elderly in the population in 1989 were to be found in the areas named in the text, with the addition of Norfolk, and Mid and West Wales.

10. What follows is a much modified version of part of Peter Laslett, 'The Centrality of Demographic Experience', The Galton Lecture, 1979, printed in D. F. Roberts and R. Chester (eds), *Changing Patterns of Conception and Fertility* (1981). The history being discussed is that of England and Wales rather than that of the British Isles.

11. How demanding in self-control these practices must have been can be judged from the frequency with which young people fail to use condoms at the present time, in spite of all the warnings about the danger of AIDS.

12. See Laslett, 1988(a) ('The European Family and Early Industrialization').

13. See Zhao Zhongwei, 1994(b), ('Demographic conditions and multi-generation households in Chinese history').

14. See Laslett, Ocppen, and Smith, 1993(b), ('La Parentela Estesa Verticalmente Dell'Italia Del XXI Secolo').

15. We have in contemplation at the Ageing Unit at the Cambridge Group a project which would work out the kin linkages of our population in the next century, given not only the projected rates of fertility and mortality, but also the very high rates of divorce and birth outside marriage which seem likely

then to prevail, and which were not allowed for in the Italian simulation which was a rough-and-ready affair. We hope to do this comparatively with the position as it will be in the population in the United States, where divorce rates are even higher and where results of this kind are already becoming available(see Wachter, 1995).

16. The pamphlet was written collaboratively by C. P. Blacker, a distinguished physician, and D. V. Glass, who became the best known British demographer. The Committee went on to found *Population Studies*, the major demographic journal in this country. The very similar developments in France which began earlier but were in full vigour at the same time, are interestingly described in Bourdelais, 1993. I know of no important connection between the two movements, however.

17. The International Institute of Applied Systems Analysis at Laxenberg, Austria. The publications of this body cited here are its newsletter *Popnet*, 23, Summer 1993, Lutz Wolfgang, Christopher Prinz and Jeannette Langgassner, 'World population projections and possible ecological feedbacks', and Wolfgang Lutz (ed.), 1991, *Future Demographic Trends in Europe and North America: What can we assume today?*

18. I am grateful to Nathan Keyfitz for helping in interpreting these materials: see his IIASA Working Paper, 1989, 'Measuring in Advance the Accuracy of Population Forecasts'.

5 THE RECTANGULAR SURVIVAL CURVE AND THE SECULAR SHIFT IN AGEING

1. See James F. Fries, 1980, ('Aging, Natural Death and the Compression of Morbidity') and at greater length in James F. Fries and Lawrence M. Crapo, 1981 (*Vitality and Aging: Implications of the Rectangular Curve*). He develops his notions and replies to his many critics in Fries, 1984 ('The Compression of Morbidity: Miscellaneous Comments about a Theme') and Fries, 1989, ('The Compression of Morbidity: Near or Far?').

2. See Alex Comfort, 1978 (*The Biology of Senescence*, 3rd edn), for comment on writings of this kind by gerontologists, though Comfort himself cannot be said to be always judicious and undogmatic in his general publications. The first edition of this book of Comfort's in 1956 seems to have contained the earliest extensive discussion of the rectangularization of the survival curve in the terms later used by Fries.

3. Fries and Crapo, op. cit., p. xii. B. Bytheway (*Ageing and Society*, vol. 2, no. 3 (1982) p. 389), is highly critical of their statistical argument.

4. See Table 4.1 for those over 85. As for the oldest of all, the rigorously corrected counts of centenarians in England and Wales show them increasing from 300 in 1951 to 570 in 1961, to 1237 in 1971, 2288 in 1981 and 3942 in 1990 (Thatcher, 1992, 'Trends in Numbers and Mortality at the Highest Age in England and Wales'). Compare Chapter 2 above.

5. Interesting from the point of view of the compression of morbidity is Robine, J-M. 1993, ('Trends in Disability: Life Expectancy'). The evidence on the Foresters' Friendly Society is set out in James C. Riley, 1989 (*Sickness, Recovery and Death,*, Chapter 3 on Sickness Risk), and for the

four countries in James C. Riley, 1990 ('The Risk of Being Sick: Morbidity Trends in Four Countries').

6. Roy I. Walford, 1983 (*Maximum Life Span*). This book is recommended to be taken in earnest by medical reviewers; see *Journal of Gerontology* (1983), p. 634.

7. For the absurdities surrounding the life-prolonging drug 'Gerovital', for example, in relation to such persons as Charles de Gaulle and Somerset Maugham, see Walford, 1983 and Hayflick, 1994, p. 276.

8. However the way-out possibility that 100-year expectation of life at birth by 2100 hinted at in the final pages of Chapter 4 above could come about, would surely never be described as 'natural'.

9. Expert judgments as to the effects of regular exercise on longevity nevertheless tend to play down the extreme claims of some enthusiasts, who have tended to make particular forms of exercise into a cult. As for the claims about diet it is difficult for an outsider to judge of their validity. Some of them appear to be improbable and even irresponsible; the food fad does not seem to be far beneath the surface. The implied recommendations of severe under-nutrition (two fast days a week), for example, or the ingestion of chemicals associated with longevity in laboratory animals (Walford, Chapters 5 and 7) do not inspire much confidence. The best guide to the facts and the clearest recommendations come from Carnegie Research Paper 9, 1993, already cited.

10. Picture at Berlin, somewhat luridly described by Walford, 1983, p. 133.

11. See Tennyson's poem *Tithonus* in which, 'this grey shadow, once a man' laments his 'cruel immortality', envying 'happy men who have the power to die'. In one version of the myth he was finally locked up in the bedroom of his mistress where he turned into a cricket (*cicada*). Hayflick, 1994, has an excellent discussion of these literary and artistic contexts.

12. The most recent discussion in English of the Georgian evidence is by the Russian immigrant scholar Z. A. Medvedev, 1986 ('Age Structure of the Soviet Population of the Caucasus: Facts and Myths'). This tells an extraordinary story of exaggerated claims, unsubstantiated by evidence, over-registration of the numbers of centenarians in the Soviet Census, official obstinacy about correcting the figures and admitting earlier errors, and even the encouragement of local people to turn alleged longevity into a tourist attraction. In judging the Soviet record, we should bear in mind that the former Registrar-General, in his study of our centenarians, shows that the British Census also exaggerated their number (Thatcher, 1981).

13. Hartland, in Devonshire, was an example. See *Necessary Knowledge* for further discussion and for the surprising indications coming to light at Cambridge that in the past the élite groups did not necessarily live longer than the population generally, at least until the eighteenth century and after infancy and childhood.

14. E. A. Wrigley and R. S. Schofield, 1989 (1981), *The Population History of England 1841–1871*. The statistics used for Diagram 5.4 come from their Table A31, pages 528–9. The same authors have in preparation a new volume of the same kind, based not on 'back projection' (for this term see their text of 1989) but on family reconstitution. It is not expected that its statistics will require very much change to the account of ageing given here.

15. The rise in expectation of life is frequently supposed to have started earlier in the nineteenth century over much of Europe: see for example J. P. Vandenbroucke, 1985, ('Survival from the 1400s to the Present'), and its references. Though this may be true of the élite, including the British peerage, especially at the latest ages, it is not true of the population of England and Wales as a whole. Expectation of life at birth did not exceed the highest figure in the Wrigley and Schofield estimates (41.68 years for both sexes in the half decade around 1581) until 1881 (males 44.26, females 47.49) and there was a sharp fall for both genders in the half-decade around 1891. At the later ages no definite move upwards is evident until 1901 or later. In Britain, anyway, the secular shift in expectation of life cannot be placed before the final decade of the nineteenth century. For more comparisons with results for the population histories of other countries, see *Necessary Knowledge*. where the Demographic Transition is discussed in relation to the secular shift in ageing. This transition from high to low fertility, high to low mortality, has occurred in all developed countries, and is now being experienced by most developing ones. The transition lies behind the shift, but the relationship is not quite straightforward.

16. See *Necessary Knowledge* for a fuller exposition. Several authorities suppose that proportions of older people will became stable, and that perhaps fairly soon, at levels not much higher than at present, in spite of the possibilities sketched out in Chapter 4 above. As for longevity, its possible levelling-out rests to a considerable extent on the outcome of the remarkable rise in the survival of the old and very old which has been discussed, and on the (pretty safe) supposition that no genetic change for a higher or continuously increasing human life-span is occurring or will occur.

17. The final gains, by 1991, were a doubling in expectation of life at birth, and multiplying of proportions over 60 by two-and-a-half (two-and-a-quarter in proportions of adults over 60). These statistics are somewhat played down in *Necessary Knowledge*, p. 5.

18. For these considerations, which are significant to any study of ageing in the longer term, but which might take us a long way from the theme of the present work, see Laslett, 1988 ('Social Structural Time'). Social structural time, in which adjustment to the secular shift would have to take place, is there described as the slowest order of social time, though of course it is nothing like as slow as biological or geological time.

19. See Laslett, 1977 (*Family Life and Illicit Love in Earlier Generations*), Chapter 2 – 60 per cent turnover in population within twelve years 1675–88 in a rural village (40 per cent less births and deaths). Turnover in the US population over 65 is reckoned in George C. Myers, 1985 ('Aging and Worldwide Population Change'), in Binstock and Shanas, eds, 1985.

20. See Robine *et al.*, 1993, p. 5

6   THE EMERGENCE OF THE THIRD AGE

1. An earlier version of this chapter was published in *Ageing and Society*, vol. 6, no. 2 (1987).

2. The possibility that jobs will become intermittent over the life course rather than occupying a continuous stretch of time complicates the issue but does not

affect the principle. In some of the definitions of the Third Age now becoming current, retirement is ignored and age bands only are used. This seems to me to void the subject of most of its meaning and to misunderstand the composition of the age groups in question, especially that of the 50s. See the Preface above and Laslett, 1994 ('The Third Age, the Fourth Age and the Future').

3. For the limitations of this statistic in making comparisons between long- and short-lived populations, see Chapter 4 above. It did not prove possible to find figures for expectation of life at 15 for more than a few of the countries.

4. Gross domestic product per head in 1990, Mozambique estimated at $100, Switzerland at $27 500, China at $340 (*World Development Report*, 1990, published by the World Bank).

5. This version of Table 6.1 is very different from that originally published in 1989 using data from the later 1970s and earlier 1980s. For example, the USA (eighteenth in Table 6.1) was then seventh in order of female life expectation at birth, above France, Norway, Spain, Australia and Canada: the United Kingdom (14) was thirteenth.

6. See Robine and others, 1993, Tables 3 and 4, pp. 32–3. Estimates for disability-free life expectancy at birth in the United Kingdom since the year 1976 are 58.2 for males (1981 59.5; 1982 58.7; 1988 58.5); for females 61.7 (60.6; 61.5; 61.2).

7. Expectation of life at birth for Sweden 1816–40, 39.5 years for men, 43.6 years for women (Sundbärg, 1970. (*Bevölkerungsstatistik Schwedens, 1750–1900*), pp. 52–3). The figures Sundbärg prints (p. 156) for the 11 most favoured European countries before 1900 show only Sweden and Norway with an expectation of life at birth of over 50 for men, and that in the 1890s.

8. See Wrigley, 1972 ('The Process of Modernization and the Industrial Revolution in England'), and Wrigley, 1988. Compare Laslett, 1976(a) for the difference between England and other European countries in the relationships between the secular shift in ageing and industrial change, and on the ageing of the population of developing countries, *Necessary Knowledge*, especially Zhongwei Zhao's treatment of some East Asian countries (pp. 55–61).

9. For further discussion of the disadvantages of the term and concept modernization in relation to ageing, see the fuller version of this chapter in *Ageing and Society*, with Laslett, 1987(c) and also 1992(c) ('The family in the industrial West and the industrializing East'). Compare also the doctoral dissertation of Carmen Avalos del Pino on ageing and modernization in a Catalonian town in progress at the Cambridge Group for the History of Population and Social Structure.

10. See the discussion in Chapter 4 above.

11. See *Carnegie Research Paper*, 5, pp. 4–6, Table 1.2. It is the lower longevity of men of course which accounts for the surprising extent of the drop and for the much greater probability of the woman being widowed. Britain, however, is not making progress of this sort as fast as other advanced countries and shows little sign of catching up (ibid., pp. 19ff.).

12. The concept of burden in relation to age is cleverly explored by Anthony Warnes: see Warnes, 1993, and compare Chapter 12 below.

13. Figures supplied by the Government Actuary's Department which calls the resultant life table 'Interim' in character, to be replaced by a more accurate one in due course. The life table is the major instrument used by

demographers for the analysis of mortality, with columns for probabilities of dying at every age, for numbers of survivors, for expectations of life, etc. It is described in every text on the subject, and particularly well in R. Pressat, 1972, (*Demographic Analysis*), Chapter 6.

14.   See Paul Johnson, 1985 (*Saving and Spending: the Working-class Economy in Britain, 1870–1939*) and Chris Gordon, 1988, 'Familial Support for the Elderly in the Past: the Case of London's Working Class in the Early 1930s'. The estimate for 1980 in the next paragraph is taken from a contribution by Christina Victor and Maria Evandrou to the meeting of the British Sociological Association's annual conference at Loughborough in September 1986. Compare Carnegie Paper 2, Table 3.5 (£2 a week from investment for those in income deciles 1 and 2 in 1979). These circumstances were evidently very different in the USA, a much richer society, and the emergence of the Third Age must have taken a different form there. See Haber and Gratton, 1994.

15.   Carnegie Research Paper 2, 1993, Table 1.1. This excludes those over 75 years old, and so may overestimate slightly the value for the Third Age as a whole, an example of the distortion created by the definition used in the Carnegie Enquiry.

16.   See David Thomson's Cambridge PhD dissertation, 1980, 'Provision for the elderly in England, 1830–1908'. The older view is still being expounded, however; see Jennifer McLarran 1993, 'Saved by the hand that is not stretched out: the aged poor in Hubert von Herkomer's "Eventide": a scene in the Westminster Union'. It has to be said that in London elderly paupers were more often taken to the workhouse than they were elsewhere in England.

17.   France had qualified by 1946 on the proportionate count and was quite probably the first to do so. The issue could be settled, of course, by reference to the records of the countries concerned, a task which remains to be done. But it seems quite unlikely that the conclusions would be otherwise than in the text.

18.   The figures cited here are given in Carnegie Research Paper No. 1, *Employment*: see Table 3 for comparison with other countries. The US is included in the survey and has employment levels much the same as in Britain for men at the relevant ages, though markedly higher for women, and with an even lower rate of recent increase. Details are given in Haber and Gratton, 1994.

19.   Figures for GNP are notoriously volatile and uncertain. The task of ranking them as has to be done here is hazardous, and the table should be treated accordingly.

20.   See Chapter 12 below. In what follows it is not intended to imply that wealth is anything like equitably distributed among elderly people (or among all people) in the United Kingdom or in any of the countries named.

21   Iceland, population 200 000, GNP $13 500, has been omitted as too small, as has Luxembourg ($16 000, population 400 000). In a population of this order the retired seem likely to be too caught up with their fellows to live in a separately identified Third Age society.

22.   See Margaret Ezell, 1987 (*The Patriarch's Wife*.)

7   HOSTILE AND DEMEANING DESCRIPTIONS OF THE
     ELDERLY

1.   On these points see Laslett, 1993 ('What is Old Age? Variation Over Time
     and Between Cultures') and 1994(b) ('The Third Age and the disappearance
     of 'Old Age''). It is there insisted that the discontinuance of the use of 'Old
     Age' as an expression should not be absolute, nor become subject to PC.

2.   See E. Midwinter, Carnegie Research Paper 8, 1992, *Citizenship from
     Ageing to Participation.* This paper is an admirable commentary on the
     themes of the present chapter.

3.   Pat Thane, 1994 'Ageing and the Economy, Historical Issues', discussion
     paper, 194.

4.   William Osler, 'The Fixed Period', published in 1904 in *Aequaenamitas,
     with Other Addresses,* reprint of 3rd edn (1939), p. 382. Osler's attitude in
     this and in his other writings on ageing could be said to be the polar
     opposite of that which gave rise to the concept of the Third Age.

5.   Anthony Trollope, 1882, *The Fixed Period*, reprinted 1993 (World's
     Classics paperback, an edition with an informative introduction and notes
     by David Skilton).

6.   By W. Graebner, for example, in *A History of Retirement: the Meaning and
     Function of an American Institution, 1885–1978*, 1980. The issue is dis-
     cussed with due solemnity by G. J. Gruman in 'Cultural Origins of Present
     Day Ageism', 1980. Weber treats Osler with offhand coolness, simply
     saying. (1919, p. 4) that he would not discuss the mental changes Osler
     mentioned. This is an example of the equivocal character of literary
     evidence in historical enquiry.

7.   Play published in 1656 and read by Trollope in 1876; see Skilton's
     'Introduction' to *The Fixed Period*, attributing the play to Massinger alone,
     and referring the reader to a source which gives an account of the plot which
     is entirely different from his own. The age difference at their execution of
     women and men should not be missed. For the Holy Mawle, John Aubrey,
     '*Three Prose Works,* ed. John Buchanan Brown, 1972, p. 154: for Medawar,
     The Uniqueness of the Individual, 2 edns, 1981, and for Gould, 'Death by
     Decree', *New Scientist*, no. 1560, 1987.

8.   Simone de Beauvoir, 1977 (*Old Age*, translation of *La Vieillesse* (1970).
     The word used above for the killing of old persons, geronticide, does not
     appear in the Oxford English Dictionary, which seems to contain no
     expression for the practice.

9.   See Bourdelais, 1993, Chapter 10.

10. 1983, (*Beyond Sixty-five*).

11. Professor J. Grimley Evans of Oxford reported on p. 47 of CIBA
     Foundation Symposium Report, 134, 1988. The whole lengthy discussion of
     a paper by Evans recorded there is of interest to the topic. That the condi-
     tion, or some of the conditions, known as dementia, including some now
     classified as belonging to Alzheimer's disease, are in fact continuous with
     ageing itself at its latest stage, is still supposed by many experts.

12. See for example, Hochschild, 1975 ('Disengagement Theory, a Critique and a Proposal').
13. Haber, op. cit., pp. 71, 79 and 80. The exclusive concern for the middle-class male, the professional man, on the part of these physicians should not be missed. There is an exquisite contrast between their views, assumptions and advice and that of the Carnegie Research Paper 9, *Health*, 1992, of which Grimley Evans is the first-named author.
14. Hayflick, 1994, p. 176. All that he has to say in the chapter of his book where this passage appears, about height, weight, wrinkles, hearing, taste, smell, sight, sleep and so on, is of great interest to everyone contemplating her ageing or his.
15. See Christoph Conrad, 1985, 'La "Senilité", Problème Social: Causes de Decés, d'Invalidité et de la Pauvreté (Exemples allemands du XVIIIe au XXe Siècle)'.
16. Norman Daniels, 1988.
17. Graebner, 1980, p. 98 and others diagnose retirement as characteristic of a phase in the later development of capitalism, reinforced by a determination to increase national competitiveness, including military competitiveness. Retirement has several uses for employers, of course, especially as a control of the labour force. The social construction of old age for interested reasons is being analyzed for the contemporary world by Alan Walker, Chris Phillipson, Carroll Estes, Anne-Marie Guillemard and others; see a number of studies published in *Ageing and Society*, and a strongly argued collection of essays by Chris Phillipson and Alan Walker, 1986 (*Ageing and Social Policy: A Critical Approach*).
18. For this concept see Laslett, 1985 ('Gregory King, Robert Malthus and the Origins of English Social Realism').
19. This effort of investigation was largely due to the Nuffield Foundation and to the remarkable series of research undertakings by Frederick le Gros Clark.
20. Xavier Gaullier (*La Deuxième Carrière, Ages, Emplois, Retraités*). He claims that France has more such people, and a greater problem with those in their fifties, or even the late forties, than any other country.
21. Eric Midwinter and Susan Tester, 1987 (*Polls Apart? Older Voters and the 1987 General Election*).
22. See Midwinter, 1992, Carnegie Research Paper 8.

8   THE INSUFFICIENCY OF THE FAMILY GROUP

1. Quoted from Laslett, 1983 (*The World We Have Lost*, Third Edition), pp. 124–5.
2. On John Locke, see Laslett, 1995(b) (1960) ('Locke the Man and Locke the Writer'). His only slightly critical attitude to Alice George and her age was normal in his time and for a century and a half afterwards. Francis Bacon, in spite of his reputation as institutor of the scientific attitude, could record without comment impossible stories about great age (centenarians performing Morris dances). See below for William Harvey.

3.   Cohort life expectation (both genders) from Wrigley and Schofield, 1989. Chances of reaching 90 or 100, from Coale and Demeny, 1983 (*Regional Model Life Tables*, 2nd edn) model North, females, extrapolated between levels 8 and 9.

4.   By John Smith, second edition; copy in the possession of the author: no example of a first edition seems to be known.

5.   See p. 175 and note 27 of Chapter 9 below for the appearance of elderly people in the past.

6.   For references to the works which have shown this assumption to be inaccurate (works written after the appearance of the first critique in 1965) see Laslett, 1972 (*Household and Family in Past Time*) and Laslett, 1983 (*The World We Have Lost*, Third Edition). Strictly speaking, it is the household rather than the 'family' (a word of multiple and often ambiguous meaning) which is at issue, though our British ancestors themselves often used the word family to signify household and vice versa.

7.   The statements in this paragraph rest on a considerable literature, which is cited in the *Special Issue on History and Ageing* in Peter Laslett (guest ed.), *Ageing and Society*, vol. 4, no. 4 (1984) (hereinafter cited as *Special Issue*) where Table 8.1 first appeared. Since 1984 the study of kin availability by the use of demographic microsimulation (see p. 69 and note 4.13 above) has modified the view that the residental choices of older people were as much a matter of choice as had been supposed. Ruggles, 1994, undertakes to prove that in the USA from 1880 onwards a very high proportion of old people who were in a position under the prevalent demographic regime to live in multi-generational households did so. It is not yet clear whether this was the case in traditional England, but the indications are against it.

8.   See Richard Wall, 1989 ('The Living Arrangements of the Elderly in Contemporary Europe in the 1980s'), and 1995 ('Elderly persons and members of their households from pre-industrial times to the present') 81–106 in Kertzer and Laslett.

9.   See Richard Wall, 1987 ('Leaving Home and the Process of Household Formation in England').

10. For illegitimates and the household position of bastard-bearers, see Laslett, 1980(b), in Laslett *et al.*, (eds), *Bastardy and its Comparative History*.

11. Although it was in general true that the poorer the family, the less likely it was to be extended, there is evidence that true paupers – those in receipt of poor relief of whom elderly people were so considerable a part – were more often extended than those immediately above them in the social scale. See T. R. Sokoll, 1993 (*Household and Family among the Poor*), especially pp. 167–71. We do not know how far living in the households of married children was made a condition of receipt of poor relief by a necessitous elderly parent. But instances of this have certainly been found.

12. See the now famous remark by Michael Anderson on p. 223 in P. Laslett and R. Wall (eds), *Household and Family in Past Time* (Cambridge, 1972): 'The urban industrial revolution, then, seems, contrary to all expectations

ten years ago, to have been associated with a considerable increase in the co-residence of parents and married children.'

13. Ruggles's text becomes very involved and rather obscure in its account of reasons for the change. Nevertheless he makes an interesting case, which he has since extended (see note 7). It may be that too strong an insistence has been laid on the claim that in earlier times English people on the lower ageing plateau invariably preferred independent nuclear families.

14. See the quite remarkable work of Peter Czap, especially his essay of 1983 ('A Large Family, the Peasant's Greatest Wealth: Serf households in Mishino, Russia, 1814–1858'), and his article of 1982. 'The Perennial Multiple-family Household, Mishino, Russia, 1782–1858'. For four- even five-generational kinship strings in the contemporary USA and Europe, see G. O. Hagestad, 1986 ('The Family: Women and grandparents as Kin-keepers').

15. For the 'world we have lost' syndrome, see Laslett, 1983 (1965) (*The World We Have Lost*) and Laslett, 1976. I now think that exaggerated emphasis was placed on the feeling among our contemporaries of alienation from the family arising from these circumstances.

16. For these facts see the contributions to the *Special Issue*, particularly that of R. M. Smith and Smith's own contributions to the volume edited by him, *Land, Kinship and the Life Cycle* with its references. Compare also Barbara Hanawalt, 1986, *The Ties that Bound: Peasant Families in Medieval England*, Chapter IV, 'Stages of Life'.

17. The notorious Zadruga of the Balkans, for example, is often attributed to the conditions of the frontier with the Turks; the Italian *mezzadria* is usually associated with share-cropping. For these points, see the contributions in R. Wall *et al.*, (eds), 1984, *Family Forms in Historic Europe* and especially Laslett's final chapter, providing for four suggested sets of household tendencies in Europe, all of which have implications for the household position of the elderly. John Hajnal regards the Western system as one of the 'two household formation systems' extant in the world: see Chapter 2 of *Family Forms*.

18. Hajnal has also reckoned, in an unpublished paper, that in the 1980s old people lived alone as to 1.8 per cent in rural China, 2.4 per cent in Korea, 7.1 per cent in Malaysia, 2.0 per cent in the Philippines, 2.0 per cent in Fiji and some 8 per cent in India. The familial systems of none of these Asian societies seems to have been able to provide a domestic niche for each and every old person. In none of them, however, does the proportion of couples in the empty-nest stage attain an eighth.

19. *Annual Report on the National Life 1983*, Economic Planning Agency, Tokyo, table p. 224, and a paper by Makoto Atoh of the Japanese Ministry of Health, presented to a seminar of the International Union for the Scientific Study of Population, Tokyo, December 1988. In this source only 9.2 per cent are given as 'single'. For welfare and the complex household, see Laslett, 1988(a) ('Family, Kinship and Collectivity as Systems of Support in Pre-industrial Europe: A Consideration of '''The Nuclear Hardship Hypothesis'''),. In China in 1982, 17.2 per cent of all households (not simply those of the elderly) had three or more generations, as against 12.8 per cent in Japan, and under 6 per cent in traditional England. On multigenerality in China, see Zhongwei Zhao, 1994(b).

20. For the strict limitation on evidence about household composition and demography as a guide to the situation of older people in the past, see Laslett 1984(b), p. 384. An adequate study 'would have to proceed from the demographic realities now so conveniently available, to the innumerable other features of social relations, attitudes, habits, customs, rules (whether deliberately or instinctively obeyed), religious observances and so on, which are relevant to ageing'.

9   RETIREMENT AND ITS SOCIAL HISTORY

1. See H. Chr. Johansen, 1987 'Growing Old in an Urban Environment'.
2. See Laslett, 1978 ('The Stem Family Hypothesis and its Privileged Position'). In Ruggles, 1994 (The Transformation of American Family Structure') discussed in Chapter 8 it is insisted that in the nineteenth century the stem-family form did predominate, or come to predominate, in America, and that it did so because a married child (not specified as to son or daughter) remained at home with a spouse, not because elderly parents entered the households of married children. It is just possible that this might have occurred in a population consisting of small farming landowners, but that of the US seems to have been much less like this than the theory requires and to lack the other characteristics of the stem-family tradition. In English family arrangements none of these characteristics was apparent in any but an insignificant minority of households at any period known to us.
3. Compare Laslett, 1988 ('Family, Kinship and Collectivity'). The information on Iceland was communicated by Frederik Pedersen, on attachment to the Cambridge Group from Denmark. He states that something like these Icelandic regulations, the earliest to have survived, underlie the practice of all the Scandinavian countries. Gisli Gunnlaugusson, 1993 shows that living arrangements of older Icelanders in the nineteenth century and later were recognizably descended from the early medieval ones, and illuminates all the retirement arrangements discussed here.
4. See David Gaunt, 1983 ('The Property and Kin Relationships of Retired Farmers in Northern and Central Europe') and Thomas Held, 1982 ('Rural Retirement Arrangements in Seventeenth Century Austria') For medieval England, see especially Elaine Clarke, 1982 ('Some Aspects of Social Security in Medieval England'). A market could grow up in such agreements, so that complete strangers could be found supporting a retired person. Substantial people had other expedients, like retiring to monastic foundations: see M. Mitterauer and R. Sieder, 1980. Such persons can be seen in the corrodians, retired people who were resident in the hospitals in England and elsewhere in the later Middle Ages, and who made gifts to the endowment of these institutions. See Peregrine Horden, 1988.
5. For a fuller discussion of retirement and its relationship with the Third and Fourth Ages, see Laslett, 1993(a). It is argued in this paper that the undifferentiated concept of old age is now obsolete in societies where a Third and Fourth Age can be distinguished.

6.   Christine Issa, PhD dissertation, Faculty of History, University of St Andrews, 1986, p. 251: this is called an isolated instance. Margaret Spufford, 1974, has shown from the evidence of wills that customs as to the residence of widows varied from manor to manor. In most the willmaker expected their widowed wives to reside with a married son or daughter; in others they lived as solitaries, or with unrelated persons, or in an almshouse.

7.   See the contribution of Zhang Chun Yuan to *Changing Population and Family Structure in China* (Beijing 1989), the published papers of an international conference arranged by Chinese and English researchers in Beijing in October 1987. The extent of the disharmony is difficult to gauge and should not be exaggerated. For friction in English families see Gordon, 1988. A possible, and tragic, indication that co-residence with relatives is not necessarily an advantage to the older person comes from Japan. There, as in China, levels of co-residence are very much higher than with us, but suicide among the elderly is commoner than anywhere else and commoner than at young ages. No clear causal connection has been demonstrated to my knowledge, however.

8.   For a reasoned argument that children did not necessarily possess much in the way of economic value to their parents in the European societies of the past, see Cleland and Wilson, 1987.

9.   Laslett, 1977, p. 180. Le Play's results are analysed by R. Wall, 1983(b), pp. 28–32.

10. Of the three major classes of those recorded as entitled to relief from the Poor Law, those with many children, the sick and the old, the old were the best defined and the most regularly supported, see Laslett, 1985. The collaboration between the Colyton charity and the Poor Law officials is an outstanding example of how transfers to the needy took place under the English *ancien régime*.

11. Male expectation of life at birth of about 46 estimated for the whole country in the 1860s implies a male expectation of life at 70 of about nine years: at 75, seven years (Princeton life tables, Coale and Demeny level 15, North, Males). The favourable rural character of the settlement has to be borne in mind in judging the comparative figures, but what has been said about the surprising tendency for older poor people to survive almost as well as their betters must be borne in mind.

12. On the topic of how later life was spent before the Third Age emerged, see Laslett, 1993. Proletarians had never been employed full-time all the year round in pre-industrial English society. Much of the winter must have been spent in the way indicated above, and under-employment was widespread.

13. Apart from Jean Robin's work in progress see her articles of 1984 ('The Role of Offspring in the Care of the Elderly') and 1990, 'The relief of poverty in nineteenth century Colyton'. See also R. M. Smith 1984(a) and 1984(b).

14. For this intricate subject see Janet Roebuck, 1979 ('When Does Old Age Begin?'), and Laslett, 1993 ('What is "Old Age"?'). In using the term Fourth Age in contexts such as these it is important to bear in mind that it is not always in late life that it may supervene. Before the secular shift, and occasionally in our own time, it might arrive at any calender age.

15. London was the exception here and the large bands of poor old women in the London workhouses may have done much to establish the somewhat misleading image of the Poor Law treatment of the old. See note 16 to Chapter 6 above.

16. Dorothy Wordsworth in Mary Moorman (ed.), *Journals*, 2nd edn (Oxford, 1987), p. 38. Dorothy was herself buried in Grasmere churchyard in 1855: it lies on the lakeside, well below the village and the house where she was standing.

17. See Gordon, 1988.

18. See Laslett and Smith, 1988, 'La parenté en Chiffres'('Kinship in Numbers'), which reviews this literature and presents a series of kin counts. The relevant titles include the classic monograph of Alan MacFarlane, *The Family Life of Ralph Josselin* (Cambridge, 1970), Keith Wrightson in *Land, Kinship and the Life Cycle* (Cambridge, 1984 ed. R. M. Smith) and M. Chayter, 'Household and Kinship', *History Workshop*, 10 (1980), together with studies by R. M. Smith (medieval kin bonds) and David Cressy (kinship and emigration). The Bacons, the coopers of Clayworth, are discussed in Laslett, 1977, Chapter 2. The suggestion made in Laslett, 1988(b) ('Kinship and collectivity ... ') that inter-household kin-links might even have been stronger in communities marked by nuclear family living, has been tested on Italian evidence and found non-proven.

19. See M. A. Clarke ('Household and Family in Bethnal Green, 1851–71): P. Willmott, 1987. ('Kinship in Urban Communities, Past and Present'). Willmott reviews the development in kinship relations over time in Bethnal Green and elsewhere, and adopts the conclusion presented here, that no consistent difference can as yet be demonstrated.

20. See Laslett, 1979 ('Family and Collectivity') and 1988(d), 'Family Kinship and Collectivity'as well as R. M. Smith, 1984 and the same in a recent masterly survey of the evidence on that hypothesis and of family and collectivity generally in relation to the support of the dependent (R. M. Smith, 1995).

21. See Proverbs 30:8. 'Mediocrity' was the condition between poverty and riches which Agur asked God to vouchsafe him.

22. See Edward Bever, 1982, 'Old Age and Witchcraft in Early Modern Europe'. The classic English discussion, especially of the benevolent witch, is Keith Thomas, *Religion and the Decline of Magic* (1971).

23. John Demos, 1979 ('Old Age in Early New England'). For our own country little has yet been done, and the best discussion remains another book by Keith Thomas, 1977 (*Age and Authority in Early Modern England*).

24. This was an expression for menstruation. See Vivien Brodsky, 1986 ('Widows in Late Elizabethan London') p. 126. Widowhood was not confined to the later ages: an eighth of all women under the age of 45 were widows, as against a fiftieth today; inferred from J. E. Smith, 1984, Table 2, p. 433.

25. See M. Ezell, 1987.

26. See Chapter IV above and, for treatment of girls, see Wall, 1981, ('Women Alone in English Society').

27. See a volume entitled *Die Lebenstreppe: Bilder der Menschlicher Lebensalter*, being an amply illustrated catalogue of an exhibition mounted

in various places in the Rhineland in 1983 and 1984. There have been other such exhibitions, including one in Amsterdam in 1993.

10   THE GENERAL THEORY OF THE THIRD AGE

1.   See Carnegie Paper 1, Employment, p. 5.
2.   Where they are allowed to do so. Those over 60 are barred from jury service in Britain, and there are numerous other disqualifications. See the list printed on pp. 18–19 of Carnegie Paper 8, *Citizenship: from Ageism to Participation*.
3.   This is evident at meetings such as that staged by *The Economist* in May 1987, on 'The Ageing Population: The New Growth Market'.
4.   See Anne-Marie Guillemard, 1989 ('The International Trend towards Withdrawal from the Work-Force'); and 1990 ('Les nouvelles frontières entre travail et retraite en France').
5.   Menarche in women came between 14 and 16 in pre-industrial European society, as against between $12\frac{1}{2}$ and 13 today with considerable variation in both cases. The reduction in menarcheal age was closely associated in time with industrialization, and among middle-class girls (university students) seems to have been static since the 1960s. See Laslett 1977, Chapter 6, and Dann and Roberts, 1993, ('Menarcheal age in University of Warwick young women'). These changes, which have occurred in males as well, along with the prolongation of the years of education as conventionally conceived, comes second only to the emergence of the Third Age in its importance among the modifications of the life course over the last hundred years or so, and its social effects have been manifest in the 'revolt of youth' since the 1960s.
6.   In Britain the institution most strongly committed against the perpetuation of First Age imperatives in the design of clothes, furniture, utensils and other articles of use seems to be the Royal College of Art, where the Design Age programme directed by Roger Coleman has committed itself to development of decidedly more various and suitable shapes and structures. In December 1994 an alliance was struck up between Design Age and the British Universities of the Third Age.
7.   See Jean Lambert and others, *The Image of the Elderly on TV*, a research publication of the University of the Third Age in Cambridge, 1984.
8.   See Laslett 1991(a) ('The duties of the Third Age: Should they form a National Trust for the future?'). Although there is a little evidence to show that an interest in the future is more characteristic of older than of younger people, too little is yet known to be confident of the facts about personal age and time to come.
9.   There is now a Reminiscence Centre in London making a long series of claims about how reminiscence extends 'knowledge and understanding of issues affecting populations and the lives of individual older people'. This

strikes me as a conspicuous example of the attitude of Second Age people to their elders, all their elders.

10. But compare Barry Jones, member of the Australian House of Representatives, and National President, Australian Labor Party, and his book *Sleepers Wake! Technology and the Future at Work* (1993 (1982)). Compare also the references in Laslett, 1994(b) (Review of the Carnegie Enquiry).

11. See Laslett, 1994(a) on the Carnegie Enquiry. The Lords debate on that enquiry which took place on 15 December 1993 (Hansard vol. 550, no. 16) showed plentiful signs of the evasive complacency described above. This debate can be contrasted with the contents of the document published in April 1992 by the Committee of the Australian House of Representatives for Long-Term Strategies and entitled *Expectations of Life: Increasing the Options for the Twenty-First Century*. I am indebted in some of the following discussion to Paul Ramcharan of the Centre for Social Policy Research, University of Wales, Bangor.

11 THE OBSOLESCENCE OF THE EDUCATIONAL SYSTEM; THE UNIVERSITY OF THE THIRD AGE

1. Because the Carnegie Enquiry omitted all persons over 74 years old, these numbers are incomplete for the Third Age as defined in this book. They seem also to be optimistic for the age groups included. Estimations made ten years earlier gave a proportion studying of half or less. The Labour Force Survey reckoned in 1990 that 68 per cent of men now aged 50–64 had left school at age 15 or under, and 63 per cent of women. A further 23 per cent and 29 per cent had left by 18.

2. Carnegie Paper 3 reports that 'members of social classes A and B' are over twice as likely to participate in study 'than those from classes D and E' (page 13). Women are more likely to do so than men.

3. Paper 6, *Employment*, p. 67; Paper 3 *Education*, pp. 25–37. The figures given are rather difficult to follow and the actual situation hardly clear, though the evidence presented implies that the statement in the first edition of this book could have been somewhat misleading.

4. First edition, p. 187, in the chapter dropped from the present edition.

5. See, for example, Pratt and Wood, 1984, ('Cognition and Elderly People'), and many other studies, British and American. The persistence of the capacity to learn in later life could now be said to be quite securely established, together with the extent and manner in which learning differs from that which is characteristic of younger persons, for the most part, but by no means entirely, in its lesser efficiency. The Open University regards older students as among its best and has demonstrated their superior achievements. See Clennell *et al.*, 1984 (*Older Students in the Open University*).

6. This was in March 1982, during the initial demonstration of the feasibility of the model of the University of the Third Age which came to be adopted in Britain.

7. This prospect was sketched out by Michael Young, Lord Young of Dartington, in a remarkable speech made in Churchill College, Cambridge on 15 April 1994 on the occasion of the 25th anniversary of the British Open University, which was the first of the numbers of national institutes of the kind which now exist in the world and which quite evidently might presage a development of the kind described above. Young himself pronounced against a worldwide sustaining broadcast programme and recommended to the International Extension College, and the English National Extension College, a rather different future policy, though he insisted on the prospective severance of learning from particular sites. The two institutions named, whose specialism is open learning, grew out of the movement in the 1960s, largely based on Cambridge where Young and I were collaborating on means of opening up learning to the wider public. We also worked hard at using electronic techniques to link traditional universities together, and on the kind of wholly recorded courses of instruction now just beginning to appear. 'The University of the Air' was the name which we, as pioneers of this movement, gave to what finally came into being as the Open University. A version of Young's speech was published in the journal *Open Learning* in February 1995.

8. See, for example, O. Cibulski and S. Bergman, 'Mutuality of Learning Between Old and Young. A Case Study in Israel', *Ageing and Society*, vol. 1, no. 2 (1981). Elder Hostel has begun to develop many of the characteristics described below as features of the British University of the Third Age. But it continues to base itself on existent, Second Age, universities.

9. In 1995 it was announced that this limitation on opening hours was to be relaxed.

10. It should be stressed that the phrase University of the Third Age is used here in a collective sense. There are now in fact, in the autumn of 1995, over 300 societies affiliated with the central body (*The Third Age Trust*) and, sad as it is to report, a small group of U3As which are not so affiliated, including the society which was first started in Britain, Cambridge U3A. At present the number is growing rapidly. The movement has spread in its English form to other English-speaking countries, and flourishes in Australia and New Zealand. The original Universités du Troisième Age in France, Italy and Spain, which made their appearance during the 1970s are organized on somewhat different lines, in effect being part of existent universities, which do the teaching, and much less under the control of the members. The present membership of U3A in Britain, 50 000 or more, is probably already larger than the numbers involved in Universities of the Third Age in any other country.

11. The Open University, and the other open learning institutions in Britain (see note 7 above), as the earliest established, are well advanced in the techniques and of high standing. In our interchanges with those responsible for Third Age education on the Continent we have found that the combination

of the U3As with these organizations in our country provides a highly effective service to Third Age learners, securing access to professional teaching and other resources which amply compensates for the want of an organized relation between U3As and Second Age universities.

12. A short page of straightforward statements constitute the 'Guiding Principles' of the Warwick District U3A, with no reference to the original series reprinted here. I am grateful to Roy Harris, the chairman, for discussion of these issues, and to Jean Thompson and Audrey Clouet for information about the activities of the central body and national annual general meetings in relation to U3A principles.

13. See a report composed in 1979 by Peter Laslett published in a shortened form as 'The Education of the Elderly in Britain' in Midwinter, (1984), (*Mutual Aid Universities*). The University of the Third Age was only one of the new departures suggested there, as affecting the most part the middle class among the elderly. Much of the discussion in that essay was of distance-teaching methods (see above), especially radio and television, but correspondence as well. The U3A itself is not yet in a position to exploit these techniques but one of the Carnegie recommendations is that distance teaching should be put into the hands of those teaching the Third Age.

14. See Peter Laslett, 1967 ('The University in High Industrial Society'). In this essay it is questioned whether institutions should be thought to embody ideas. Newman's principles are analysed, and the regrettably élitist use subsequently made of them is severely criticized.

15. See Michael Majerus, *Ladybirds*, 1994 (*New Naturalist* series no. 81) p. 15.

12 THE BURDEN OF THE ELDERLY AND PAYING FOR YOUR OWN THIRD AGE

1. The lone, lorn widow in Dickens's *David Copperfield*. As to the persistent refrain on the elderly as a burden, see Warnes, 1993 (Being Old, Old People and the Burden of Burdens'), and Walker 1990 ('The economic 'burden' of ageing and the prospect of intergenerational conflict').

2. The echo in Clough's jingle of disposing of the useless old discussed in Chapter 7 above should not be missed. I owe this reference to Professor J. Mirrlees.

3. In recent years, especially in the USA and particularly since the publication in 1987 of *Setting Limits, Medical Goals in an Aging Society*, by Daniel Callahan, the increase in the cost of medical care with age has become a subject of widespread discussion and controversy. All the issues to do with the right to euthanasia, the living will and so on are being debated, but especially the financial facts which reveal that a very high proportion of all medical costs over the life course are incurred during the final years. Gillion, 1991 ('Ageing populations: spreading the costs') reckons for 1985 that health costs per capita (weighted) were almost twice as high in the USA

as in Sweden, the next in order of the countries compared ($1056 as against $559) and the relative pension costs also the highest, though not much in excess of those in France.

4. On the obsolescence of the term 'old age' see Laslett, 1993(a) ('What is Old Age?'), and Laslett, 1994(b) ('The Third Age and the Disappearance of Old Age').

5. This part of the text is a summary and development of Laslett, 1992(b) ('Is there a generational contract?' in Laslett and Fishkin (eds), *Justice between Age Groups and Generations*). In many ways the clearest exposition is to be found in the World Bank report of 1994 *Averting the Old Age Crisis*, simultaneously appearing as a pamphlet summary. Two further titles have to be taken into consideration, both published by organizations of, or acting on behalf of, old people. L. M. Cohen (ed.), 1992, *Justice across Generations* (American Association of Retired Persons) and David Hobman, (ed.), 1994, *Uniting Generations* (Age Concern England). The inexact arguers about the *contract* (not often even specifying 'generational contract') include several of those involved in the current controversy over the theories of David Thomson discussed below, especially Alan Walker.

6. The position summarized above is close to that of Norman Daniels as set out in his contribution to Cohen (ed.), 1992, under the heading 'The prudential life span account of justice across generations', recounting the thesis of his book *Am I My Parents'Keeper? An Essay on Justice between Young and Old* (1988). His account of cohorts and generations is different, and not in my view entirely satisfactory, and he does not avoid Second Age attitudes and vocabulary, talking as if that Age were the whole society. Daniels himself admits that environmental justice is left out of account.

7. See David Thomson, 1991, book published in New Zealand and using evidence derived from that country, and in course of publication in Britain, using additionally British and other national files as evidence. Several earlier statements of his thesis had appeared before the book itself came out.

8. For the numerous attacks on his argument, see the references in the English republication of *Selfish Generations?*, Chapter 8. Two particularly critical considerations have been made, by Alan Walker and Eric Midwinter, who have dismissed Thomson's arguments as getting in the way of enquiry. Walker's latest published démarche is in Hobman (ed.), 1994.

9. See Paul Johnson and Jane Falkingham, 1988 (*Intergenerational Transfers and Public Expenditure on the Elderly in Modern Britain*), and John Hills, 1992 (*'Does Britain have a 'Welfare Generation'? An empirical analysis of intergenerational equity'*).

10. David Lovibond, *David Telegraph*, 15 January 1989, quoted by Malcolm Johnson in Hobman (ed.), 1994, p. 28. Lovibond was commenting on a visit to Britain by a representative of AGE.

11. Thomson's response to these conclusions, a response which carries considerable conviction, is to be found in Chapter 8 of the new version of *Selfish Generations?*.

12. The historical figures have been calculated from Wrigley and Schofield, 1989, Table A3.1, and the contemporary figures from the Carnegie Enquiry paper 2, *Income, Pensions, Earnings and Savings in the Third Age*, Table 6.3. The two sets of statistics are not quite comparable, as will be seen, and

those for the older section will have to be corrected for the coming equalisation of the retirement age for men and women.

13. These crude estimates of dependants per person of working age roughly correspond to the weighted figures worked out in Gillion, 1991, ('Ageing populations: Spreading the cost') for France, Germany, Japan, the Netherlands, Sweden and the USA for 1987 and for 2040. This is in spite of the fact that no account is taken here of such factors as wholly dependent non-earning women, unemployment and possible migration. If it is permissible to argue from his estimates to the British case, our country is located among those with lower numbers of dependants to workers and will be so in 2030 and 2040.

14. An illuminating discussion of Contingency Valuation Methods (CVM) is contained in a special number of the journal *Environmental Values*, entitled *Values and Preferences in Environmental Economics* (vol. 3, no. 4, Winter 1994): see particularly the article by Jack L. Knetsch, 'Environmental valuation: some problems of wrong questions and misleading answers' (pp. 351–68). The volume edited by Laslett and Fishkin, 1992, has some analysis of the kind applied to age groups and generations, especially in relation to the outspoken contribution of Richard A. Epstein ('Justice across generations'), a devotee of market values and market solutions to dilemmas of decision.

15. See above. There are uncertainties here which call for investigation. It is not yet known how much children, even very young children, brought in during the pre-industrial era in the West, and whether it made up as substantial a part of their costs as Das Gupta has reckoned for contemporary low-subsistence societies, especially in sub-Saharan Africa (Das Gupta, 1995). See also Haber and Gratton for familial contributions in nineteenth-century America. The earliest numerical evidence from Britain which dates from 1790s (see David Davies, 1795, *The Case of Labourers in Husbandry*) suggests that after the age of about ten a child might contribute more than a trifling amount. It seems clear that poor societies must have paid relatively more out of their slender resource than would be required today just to keep an individual alive, with in the West, especially in England, a little surplus above that level per head of the population supported

16. *The Gas Report*, 1991, Table 3.

17. I am here following the analysis of Dr Paul Johnson of the London School of Economics and his associate Jane Falkingham, as well as that of his namesake, Paul Johnson of the Institute for Fiscal Studies, and his associates, in their Research Paper no. 2 for the Carnegie Enquiry. I adopt Paul Johnson's recommended solution as set out in Jane Falkingham and Paul Johnson, *A Unified Funded Pension Scheme (UFPS) for Britain*, Discussion Paper WSP/96, April 1993, of the Welfare State Programme of the London Schoool of Economics.

18. The criteria are listed on pages 13 and 14 of the UFPS study. To the conditions laid down there may be added those specified in the *World Bank Report*, such as tax evasion, particularly widespread in developing areas but not unknown in developed countries.

19. For these points see the *World Bank Report*. Since under the scheme corporate pensions, such as those whose capital assets were so criminously

appropriated by Robert Maxwell, would not be the sole and seldom the most important pension pillar for the individual, abuses of that kind could scarcely occur.

20.   Cohen (ed.), 1994, pp. 269–82. It has to be said that David Friedman, of roughly equal standing, begs to disagree; pp. 287–90.

21.   John Rawls, 1972, *A Theory of Justice*, where this principle is introduced under Section 44, 'The problem of justice between generations'. Rawls' notion of generation differs from that expounded here.

22.   David Thomson in several contexts, for example his 'Generations, justice and future collective action' Chapter *X* of Laslett and Fishkin (eds), 1992.

23.   Hills, 1992, p. 38. He does not use the word 'desert', but Daniels does, three times (Cohen, ed., 1994, p. 210). Unfortunately, he spells it as 'dessert', an afterdish, appropriate only in an Alice in Wonderland mode.

24.   In 1991 59 per cent of the older people interviewed for the Gas Report agreed that they did not get enough respect from younger people, and over a quarter of the sample felt strongly about it (Appendix, Table 17).

25.   Compare Daniels' account of what he calls 'the prudential life span account of justice across generations' in Cohen (ed.), 1994, and in Daniels, 1988. In the allocation of means between cohorts, the inter-cohort trust might decide to make symbolic extra payments to particular groups, which could justify statements like that of John Hills. Symbols scarcely affect rights however: compare Laslett, in Laslett and Fishkin, 1992, p. 41.

26.   A cautious claim that in the USA the attenuation of kinship due to low fertility, and the dilution of kinship bonding brought about by extremely high divorce levels and extra-marital births, will not have catastrophic effects on the kinship support of the elderly, is made in Wachter, 1995. This is a preliminary report on the simulation work going on at the University of California, Berkeley, forecasting the future US kinship network, in the way that we hope to do in Cambridge for the United Kingdom.

27.   Laslett, 1993(c), *The Third Age, A Fresh Map of Life*.

28.   See Laslett, 1994(b), address to the meeting of the International Union of Universities of the Third Age at Jyvaskala, Finland, in course of publication.

13   THE RESPONSIBILITIES OF OLDER BRITISH PEOPLE

1.   For duties 'going forward in time', see Laslett, 1977 ('The Conversation Between the Generations') and 1992(b). For the sense of the future in older people and trusteeship for the future, see Laslett, 1991(a) ('The Duties of the Third Age').

2.   See Eric Midwinter and Susan Tester, 1987, and Carnegie Paper 8, on the resistance of the British elderly to political mobilization.

3.   Leonard Hayflick tells us that 'On average the lifetime loss in standing height in women was almost two inches and in men one and a quarter inches' (Hayflick, 1995), p. 187.

Bibliography

Ageing and Society, 1984, Special Issue on *History and Ageing* no. 4, 4.

Allard, Michel, 1993, *À la recherche du secret des centenaires*, Paris, La Cherche Midi.

Amman, Anton, 1985, 'The Changing Age Structure of the Population and Future Policy', Council of Europe, *Population Studies*, 18.

Annual Report on the National Life, 1983, Economic Planning Agency, Tokyo.

Anderson, Michael, 1972, 'Household Structure and the Industrial Revolution', 215–35 in Laslett and Wall, eds.

Atoh, Makato, 1988, 'Changes in the Family in Various Countries and in Japan', paper to the Seminar of the International Union for the Scientific Study of Population, Tokyo, November.

Aubrey, John, 1972 [c. 1688], *Remaines of Gentilisme and Judaisme*, in *Three Prose Works*, ed. John Buchanan Brown, Fontwell, Sussex, Centaur Press.

Australian House of Representatives, Committee for Long Term Strategies, 1992, *Expectation of Life: Increasing the Options for the Twentyfirst Century*.

Baechler, Jean, J. A. Hall and M. Mann (eds), 1988, *Europe and the Rise of Capitalism*, Oxford, Blackwell.

Beauvoir, Simone de, 1977 (1970), *Old Age* (translation, *La Vieillesse*), London, Penguin.

Bever, Edward, 1982, 'Old Age and Witchcraft in Early Modern Europe', in Peter Stearns, ed.

Binstock, Robert H. and E. Shanas (eds), 1985 (1976), *Handbook of Aging and the Social Sciences*, New York, Van Nostrand.

Birren, James and J. M. Schaie (eds), 1977, *Handbook of the Psychology of Aging*, New York, Van Nostrand.

Bittles, A. H. and K. J. Collins (eds), 1986, *The Biology of Human Ageing*, Cambridge.

Blacker, C. P. and D.V. Glass, 1938 (First Edition 1936), *The Future of our Population*, London, The Population Investigation Committee.

Bonfield, Lloyd, R. M. Smith and K. Wrightson (eds), 1985, *The World We Have Gained*, Oxford, Blackwell.

Bortz, Walter M., 1991, *We Live Too Short and Die Too Long*, New York, Bantam Books.

Bourdelais, Patrice, 1993, L' Age de la Vieillesse [*The Age of Old Age*], Paris, Odile Jacob.

Brodsky, Vivien, 1986, 'Widows in Elizabethan London', in Bonfield, L. and others, *The World We Have Gained*, Oxford, Blackwell.

Buchanan, James N., 1993, 'We Should Save More in Our Own Interest', chapter 16 in Cohen, ed.

Burrow, J. A., 1986, *The Ages of Man*, Oxford.

Bytheway, B., 1982, contribution to Review Symposium of Fries and Crapo, 1981, *Ageing and Society*, 2, 3, 381–92.

Callaghan, Daniel, 1987, *Setting Limits: Medical Goals in an Aging Society*, New York, Simon and Schuster.

Carnegie Enquiry, 1993, The Carnegie Enquiry into the Third Age, *Final Report, Life, Work and Livelihood in the Third Age*, Bailey Management Services, 127 Sandgate Road, Folkestone, Kent CT20 2BL.

Research Papers, 1992

1. Trinder, Chris, G. Hulme and U. McCarthy, *Employment: The Role of Work in the Third Age.*
2. Johnson, Paul, A. Dilnot, R. Disney and E. Whitehouse, *Income: Pensions, Earnings and Savings in the Third Age.*
3. Schuller, Tom and A. M. Bostyn, *Learning: Education, Training and Information in the Third Age.*
4. Midwinter, Eric, *Leisure: New Opportunities in the Third Age.*
5. Warnes, Tony (ed.), *Homes and Travel: Local Life in the Third Age.*
6. Askham, Janet, E. Grundy and A. Tinker, *Caring: The Importance of Third Age Carers.*
7. Smith, Justin Davis, *Volunteering: Widening Horizons in the Third Age.*
8. Midwinter, Eric, *Citizenship: From Ageism to Participation.*
9. Evans, J. Grimley, M. Goldacre, M. Hodkinson, S. Lamb and M. Savory, *Health: Abilities and Well-Being in the Third Age.*
10. Mangan, Ita, *Irish Perspectives*, Proceedings of the Ireland Seminar.

CIBA Foundation Symposium Report, 134, 1988.

Cibulski, Ora and S. Bergman, 1981, 'Mutuality of Learning between Old and Young: A Case Study in Israel', *Ageing and Society*, 1, 2, 247–62.

Clark, J. C. D., 1985, *English Society, 1688–1832*, Cambridge.

Clark, Elaine, 1982, 'Some Aspects of Social Security in Medieval England', *Journal of Family History*, 7, 4, 107–20.

Clarke, Martin A., 1986, 'Household and Family in Bethnal Green, 1851–71: The Effect of Social and Economic Change', PhD dissertation, University of Cambridge.

Cleland, John and C. Wilson, 1987, 'Demand Theories of the Fertility Transition: An Iconoclastic View', *Population Studies*, 41, 5–30.

Clennell, Stephanie *et al.*, 1984, 'Older Students at the Open University', Milton Keynes, The Open University.

Coale, Ansley J. and P. Demeny, with B. Vaughan, *Regional Model Life Tables and Stable Populations*, Second Edition, New York, Academic Press.

Cohen, Lee M. (ed.), 1992, *Justice across Generations: What does it mean?* The Public Policy Institute for The American Association of Retired Persons, Washington, DC.

Comfort, Alex, 1979, *The Biology of Senescence*, Third Edition, New York, Elsevier.

Coni, Nicholas, W. Davison and S. Webster, 1986 (1984) *Ageing: the Facts*, Oxford.

Coni, Nicholas, 1985, Alive and well: Geriatric Medicine in the UK in 1984, *Health Policy* 5.

Conrad, Christoph, 1985, 'La "Senilité" comme Problème Social: Causes de Décès, d'Invalidité et de Pauvreté (exemples allemands du XVIIIe au XXe Siècle)', *Annales de Démographie Historique*.

Czap, Peter, 1982, 'The Perennial Multiple-family Household: Serf Households in Mishino, Russia, 1752–1858', *The Journal of Family History*, 7, 1, 5–26.

____, 1983, 'A Large Family, the Peasant's Greatest Wealth', 105–52, in Wall, Robin and Laslett, eds.

Daniels, Norman, 1988, *Am I my Parents' Keeper? An Essay on Justice between Young and Old*, Oxford, New York.

____, 1993, 'The Prudential Life-span Account of Justice across Generations', pp. 243–7 of Cohen, ed.

Dann, T. C. and D. F. Roberts, (1993) 'Menarcheal Age in University of Warwick Young Women', *Journal of Biosocial Science*, 25, 4.

Das Gupta, Partha, 1995, *Scientific American*, Feb., 272, No. 2, 26–31.

Davies David, 1795, *The Case of Labourers in Husbandry*, G. and J. Robinson, London.

Demos, John, 1979, 'Old Age in Early New England', in D. van Tassel (ed.), *Aging, Death and the Completion of Being*, University of Pennsylvania Press, 115–64.

Environmental Values, 1994, 3, 4, issue on *Values and Preferences in Environmental Economics*.

Epstein, Richard, 1992, 'Justice across Generations', in Laslett and Fishkin, eds.

Evans, J. Grimley, 1988, remarks in CIBA Foundation Symposium Report.

Evans, J. Grimley and others, 1992, *Health*, Carnegie Enquiry Paper 9.

Ezell, Margaret E. M., 1987, The *Patriarch's Wife*, Chapel Hill, University of North Carolina Press.

Falkingham, Jane and P. Johnson, 1993, *A Unified Pensions Scheme (UFPS) for Britain*, Discussion Paper WSP/96 of the Welfare State Programme of the London School of Economics.

Finley, Moses, 1984, 'The Elderly in Classical Antiquity', *Ageing and Society, 4.4 (Special Issue on History)*.

Fries, James F., 1980, 'Aging, Natural Death and the Compression of Morbidity', *New England Journal of Medicine*, 303, 130–135.

____,1984, 'The Compression of Morbidity: Miscellaneous Comments about a Theme', *Gerontologist*, 24, 354–9.

____,1989, 'The Compression of Morbidity: Near or Far?' *The Milbank Quarterly*, 67, 2, 208–32.

Fries, James F. and L. M. Crapo, 1981, *Vitality and Aging: Implications of the Rectangular Curve*, San Francisco, Freeman.

Gas Report, The, 1991. The Gas Report on Attitudes to Ageing, London Burson-Marsteller, for British Gas.

Gaullier, Xavier, 1988, *La Deuxième Carrière, Ages, Emplois, Retraités*, Paris, Seuil.

Gaunt, David, 1983, 'The Property and Kin Relationships of Retired Farmers in Northern and Central Europe', Chapter 8 in Wall *et al.*, eds.

Gibson, H. B., 1992(a), *The Emotional and Sexual Lives of Older People, A Manual for Professionals*, Chapman and Hall, London.

____, [H. B.] Tony, 1992(b), *Love, Sex and Power in Later Life: a Libertarian Perspective*, Freedom Press, London.

____ (1995) *On the Tip of Your Tongue: Your Memory in Later Life* (Third Age Press, London).

Gillion, Colm, 1991, 'Aging Populations: Spreading the Costs', *Journal of European Social Policy*, 1, 2, 107–28.

Gordon, Chris, 1988, 'Familial Support for the Elderly in the Past: the Case of London's Working Class in the Early 1930s', *Ageing and Society*, 8, 3.

Gould, Donald, 1987, 'Death by Decree', *New Scientist*, no. 1560.

Government Actuary, *Interim Life Tables 1989–91*.

Government Statistical Service: see *Social Trends*.

Graebner, William, 1980, *A History of Retirement: the Meaning and Function of an American Institution, 1885–1978*, New Haven and London, Yale.

Gruman, G. J., 1980, 'Cultural Origins of Present Day Ageism', in G. T. Spicker *et al.* (eds), *Aging and the Elderly*, Atlantic Heights, NJ.

Guillemard, Anne-Marie, 1989, 'The International Trend towards Withdrawal from the Work-Force', in Johnson, Conrad and Thomson, eds.

——,1990, 'Les Nouvelles Frontières entre Travail et Retraite en France', *La Revue de IRESCO*, 2, Paris.

Guinness Book of Records, 1994, London, Guinness Publishing.

Gunnlaugsson, Gísli, 1993, 'Living Arrangements of the Elderly in a Changing Society: the Case of Iceland, 1880–1930', *Continuity and Change*, 8, 1, 103–25.

Haber, Carole, 1983, *Beyond Sixty-Five*, Cambridge.

Haber, Carole and Gratton, Brian, 1994, *Old Age and the Search for Security in American Social History*, Bloomington, Indiana University Press.

Hagestad, G. O., 1986, 'The Family: Women and Grandparents as Kinkeepers', in Pifer and Bronte, eds.

Hajnal, John, 1984, 'Two Kinds of Household Formation System', in Wall, Robin and Laslett, eds, 65–104.

Hanawalt, Barbara, 1986, *The Ties that Bound: Peasant Families in Medieval England*, New York.

Haseler, Stephen, 1993, *The End of the House of Windsor and the Birth of a British Republic*, London, I. B. Tauris.

Hayflick, Leonard, 1994, *How and Why We Age*, New York, Ballantine Books.

Hazan, Haim, 1994, *Old Age: Constructions and Deconstructions*, Cambridge.

Held, Thomas, 1982, 'Rural Retirement Arrangements in 17th to 19th Century Austria', *Journal of Family History*, 7, 3, 227–34.

Hills, John, 1992, *Does Britain have a 'Welfare Generation'? An Empirical Analysis of Intergenerational Equity*. Discussion Paper WSP/76, Welfare State Programme, London School of Economics.

Hobman, David (ed.), 1994, *Uniting Generations: Studies in Conflict and Co-operation*, ACE books, Age Concern, England.

Hochschild, A., 1975 'Disengagement Theory: a Critique and a Proposal', *American Sociological Review*, 40.

Horden, Peregrine, 1988, 'A Discipline of Relevance: The Historiography of the Later Medieval Hospital', *Journal of the Social History of Medicine*, 1, 3.

Issa, Christine, 1986, PhD Dissertation, University of St Andrews.

Johansen, H. Chr. 1987, 'Growing Old in an Urban Environment', *Continuity and Change*, 2, 2.

Johnson, Malcolm, 1994, 'Generational Relations under Review', Chapter 1 in Hobman, ed.

Johnson, Paul, 1985, *Saving and Spending: the Working-class Economy in Britain, 1870–1939*, Oxford.

Johnson, Paul, and J. Falkingham, 1988, *Intergenerational Transfers and Public Expenditure on the Elderly in Modern Britain*, Discussion Paper 254, Centre for Economic Policy Research, London School of Economics.

Johnson, Paul, C. Conrad and D. Thomson, eds, 1989, *Workers versus Pensioners: Intergenerational Justice in an Ageing World*, Manchester, Manchester University Press.

Jones, Barry, 1993 (1982), *Sleepers, Wake!*, Melbourne, Oxford.

Jorm, A. F., 1990, *The Epidemiology of Alzheimer's Disease*, London, Chapman and Hall.

Kannisto, Väinö, 1988, 'On the Survival of Centenarians and the Span of Life', *Population Studies*, 42, 3, 389–406.

____, 1994, *Development of Oldest Old Mortality, Evidence for 28 Developed Countries*, Odense, Denmark, Odense University Press.

Katzmann, Robert, 1988, *Alzheimer's Disease as an Age Dependent Disorder*, in CIBA Foundation Report 134.

Kertzer, David I. and P. Laslett (eds), 1995, *Aging in the Past: Demography, Society and Old Age*, Los Angeles, California University Press.

Keyfitz, Nathan, 1989, 'Measuring in Advance the Accuracy of Population Forecasts', IASA Working Paper.

Keyfitz, Nathan and W. Flieger, 1990, *World Population and Aging*, Chicago, Chicago University Press.

Knetsch, Jack L., 1994, 'Environmental Valuation: Some Problems of Wrong Questions and Misleading Answers', *Environmental Values*, 3, 4, 351–68.

Kohn, Robert R., 1983, 'Cause of Death in Very Old People', *Journal of the American Medical Association*, 28 May 1982, Vol. 247, no. 20.

Lambert, Jean and others, 1984, *The Image of the Elderly on TV*, University of the Third Age in Cambridge.

Laslett, Peter, 1967, 'The University in High Industrial Society', Chapter 8 in Bernard Crick (ed.), *Essays in Reform, 1967*, Oxford.

____, 1972, ed. with the assistance of R. W. Wall, *Household and Family in Past Time, Cambridge*.

____, 1976(a), 'Societal Development and Aging', 87–116 in Binstock and Shanas, eds.

____, 1976(b) 'The Wrong Way through the Telescope: A Note on Literary Evidence in Sociology and Historical Sociology', *British Journal of Sociology*, 26, 319–42 Shanas, eds.

____, 1977, 'The Conversation between the Generations', Chapter 11 in Peter Laslett and James Fishkin, eds, *Philosophy, Politics and Society*, Fifth Series, Yale.

____, 1977, *Family Life and Illicit Love in Earlier Generations*, Cambridge.

____, 1978, 'The Stem Family Hypothesis and its Privileged Position', Chapter 6 in Wachter, Hammel and Laslett, eds.

____, 1979, 'Family and Collectivity', *Sociology and Social Research*, 63, 3, 432–53.

____, 1980(a) 'Introduction: Comparing Illegitimacy over Time and between Cultures', 1–64 in Laslett, Oosterveen and Smith, eds.

____, 1980(b) with Karla Oosterveen and R. M. Smith (eds), *Bastardy and its Comparative History*, London, Arnold.

____, 1981, 'The Centrality of Demographic Experience', pp. 23–40 in Roberts and Chester, eds.

____, 1983 (1965), *The World We Have Lost*, Third Edition, London, Routledge; New York, Macmillan.

_____, 1984(a), 'Family and Household as Work Group and Kin Group: Areas of Traditional Europe compared', Chapter 17 in Wall, Robin and Laslett, eds.

_____, 1984(b) 'The Significance of the Past in the Study of Ageing', written as guest editor, *Ageing and Society, Special Issue on History and Ageing*, pp. 369–79.

_____, 1984(c) (1979), 'The Education of the Elderly in Britain', Chapter 2 in E. Midwinter, ed.

_____, 1985, 'Gregory King, Robert Malthus and the Origins of Scientific Realism', *Population Studies*, 39, 351–62.

_____, 1986, Review of Pifer and Bronte, 1986, *Ageing and Society*, 6, 3, 412–14.

_____, 1987(a), Contribution to symposium on Burrow, 1986, *Ageing and Society*, 7, 103–5.

_____, 1987(b), 'The Emergence of the Third Age', *Ageing and Society*, 7, 133–60.

_____, 1987(c) 'The Character of Family History and the Conditions for its Proper Pursuit', *Journal of Family History*, 12, 263–84.

_____, 1988(a), 'The European Family and Early Industrialization', Chapter 14 in Baechler Hall and Mann.

_____, 1988(b), 'Social Structural Time', Chapter 2 of Young, Michael and T. Schuller, (eds), *The Rhythms of Society*, London, Routledge.

_____, 1988(c), with James E. Smith, 'La parenté en chiffres' (Kinship in figures), *Annales, Economies, Sociétés, Civilisations*, 1988, No. 1.

_____, 1988(d), 'Family, Kinship and Collectivity as Systems of Support in Pre-Industrial Europe: a Consideration of the Nuclear Hardship Hypothesis', *Continuity and Change*, 3, 2, 153–75.

_____, 1991(a), 'The Duties of the Third Age: Should they form a National Trust for the Future?' *R.S.A. Journal*, No. 5748, 386–92.

_____, 1991(b), 'The Ageless Society', *R.S.A. Journal*, No. 5751.

_____, 1992(a), Introduction (with James S. Fishkin) entitled 'Processional Justice', Peter Laslett and James S. Fishkin (eds), *Justice Between Age Groups and Generations*, New Haven and London, Yale University Press.

_____, 1992(b), 'Is there a Generational Contract?' Chapter 1 of Laslett and Fishkin, eds.

_____, 1992(c), 'The Family in the Industrial West and the Industrializing East'. Paper to a meeting on Family Formation and Dissolution, Taipei, May: forthcoming.

_____, 1993(a), 'What is Old Age? Variation over time and between Cultures'. Paper to the meeting of the International Union for the Scientific Study of Population, Sendai, Japan, forthcoming.

_____, 1993(b), with J. Oeppen, J. E. Smith, 'La parentela Estesa Verticalmente Dell'Italia Del XXI Secolo', *Polis* (Bologna) VII, 4, 121–39.

_____, 1993(c), 'The Third Age: A Fresh Map of Life', First Dutch National Gerontology Lectures, Bunnik (Netherlands), LSOB/NIG.

_____, 1994(a), 'The Third Age, the Fourth Age and the Future, a review of the Carnegie Report', *Ageing and Society*, 14, 436–47.

_____, 1994(b), 'The Third Age and the Disappearance of "Old Age".' Paper read to the meeting of the International Association of Universities of the Third Age (IUATA), Jyvaskala, Finland, forthcoming.

_____, 1995(a), *Necessary Knowledge*: 'Age and Ageing in the Societies of the Past', Introduction to Kertzer and Laslett, eds.

____, 1995(b) (1960), Locke the Man and Locke the Writer, Section 1 of Laslett's edition of John Locke, *Two Treatises of Government*, 8th printing of Students' Edition, Cambridge.

Lebenstreppe, Die, 1983 (described in text at note 27 to Chapter IX).

Lee, Ronald B., 1994, 'The Formal Demography of Aging: Transfers and the Economic Life Cycle', Chapter 2 in National Research Council, *Demography of Aging*.

Lowenthal, David, 1985, *The Past is a Foreign Country*, New York, Oxford.

Lutz, Wolfgang (ed.), 1991, *Future Demographic Trends in Europe and North America: What can we assume today?* Laxenberg, IASA.

Lutz, Wolfgang, C. Prinz and J. Langgassner, 1993, 'World Population Projections and Possible Ecological Feedbacks', *Popnet* 23.

Macfarlane, Alan, 1970, *The Family Life of Ralph Josselin*, Cambridge.

Majerus, Michael, 1994, *Ladybirds, New Naturalist* Series 81, London, Harper Collins.

McLarren, Jennifer, 1993, 'Saved by the hand that is not stretched out: the aged poor in Hubert von Herkomer's "Eventide": a scene in the Westminster Union', *The Gerontologist*, 33, 6.

Medawar, Peter, 1981 (1946), *The Uniqueness of the Individual*, Second Edition, New York.

Medvedev, Z. A., 1986, 'Age Structure of the Soviet Population of the Caucasus', in Bittles and Collins, eds.

Midwinter, Eric (ed.), 1984, *Mutual Aid Universities*, London, Croom Helm.

Midwinter, Eric and S. Tester, 1987, *Polls Apart? Older Voters and the 1987 General Election*, London, Centre for Policy on Ageing.

Mitterauer, Michael and Reinhold Sieder, 1986, *The European Family*, Oxford, Blackwell.

Molleson, T. I. 1988, 'Skeletal Age and Palaeo-Demography', CIBA Foundation Report, 134.

Myers, George C., 1985, 'Aging and Worldwide Population Change', in Binstock and Shanas, 173–98.

National Research Council, 1994, Demography of Aging, ed. Linda S. Martin and S. H. Preston, National Academy Press, Washington, DC.

Necessary Knowledge, see Laslett, 1995.

Neugarten, Bernice, 1974, 'Age Groups in American Society and the Rise of the Young Old', *Annals of the American Academy of Political and Social Science*, 415, 187–98.

Osler, William, 1939 (1904), 'The Fixed Period' in *Aequaenamitas, with other addresses*, Third Edition.

Phillipson, Chris, 1983, *Capitalism and the Social Construction of Old Age*, London, Macmillan.

Phillipson, Chris and Alan Walker, 1986, *Ageing and Social Policy: A Critical Approach*, London, Gower.

Pifer, Alan and L. Bronte (eds), 1986, *Our Aging Society: Paradox and Promise*, Norton, New York.

Postgate, Nicholas, 1992, *Early Mesopotamia: Society and Economy at the Dawn of History*, Cambridge.

Pratt, J. D. and L. E. Wood, 1984, 'Cognition and Elderly People', *Ageing and Society*, 4, 3, 249–72.

Preston, Samuel H., Keyfitz, N. and Schoen, 1972, *Causes of Death: Life Tables for National Populations*.

Preston, Samuel H., C. Himes and M. Eggers, 1989, 'Demographic Conditions Responsible for Population Aging', *Demography* 26. 4.

Pressat, Roland, 1972, *Demographic Analysis: Methods, Results, Applications*, London; Arnold; Chicago, Aldine Atherton.

Rawls, John, 1972, *A Theory of Justice*, Oxford.

Riley, James C., 1989, *Sickness, Recovery and Death*, London, Macmillan.

____, 1992, 'The Risk of Being Sick: Morbidity Trends in Four Countries', *Population and Development Review*, 16, 403–12.

Roberts, D. F. and R. Chester, 1981, *Changing Patterns of Conception and Fertility*, London, St. Martin's Press.

Robin, Jean, 1984, 'The Role of Offspring in the Care of the Elderly', in the Special Issue of *Ageing and Society*.

____, 1990, 'The Relief of Poverty in Nineteenth Century Colyton, *Rural History*, 1, 2.

Robine, Jean-Marie, 1993, 'Trends in Disability Free Life Expectancy', Paper at the IUSSP and WHO meeting on Health and Mortality among Elderly Populations, Sendai, Japan, April.

Roebuck, Janet, 1979, 'When Does Old Age Begin?' *Journal of Social History*, 12, 13, 416–29.

Rose, Michael R., 1991, *Evolutionary Biology of Aging*, Oxford, New York.

____, 1994, Review of David W. Smith, 1993, *Ageing and Society*, 14, 641–2.

Ruggles, Steven, 1987, *Prolonged Connections: the Rise of the Extended Family in 19th Century England and America*, Madison, University of Wisconsin Press.

____, 1994, 'The Transformation of American Family Structure', *American Historical Review*, 99(1), 105–28.

Shanas, Ethel, P. Townsend, D. Wedderburn, H. Friis, P. Milhøj and J. Stehouwer, 1968, *Old People in Three Industrial Societies*, New York, Atherton.

Siegel, Jacob S. and C. M. Taeuber, 1986, 'Demographic Perspective for a Long-Lived Society', *Daedalus*, 115. 1.

Smith, David W. E., 1993, *Human Longevity*, New York, Oxford.

Smith, James E., 1984, 'Widowhood and Ageing in Traditional English Society', in the Special Issue of *Ageing and Society*.

Smith, John, 1666, *The Pourtract of Old Age*, London.

Smith, Richard M., 1984(a) 'The Structured Dependence of the Elderly as a Recent Phenomenon', *Ageing and Society*, Special Issue, 4, 4, 409–28.

____, 1984(b) (ed.) *Land, Kinship and the Life-Cycle*, Cambridge.

____, 1995(c), 'Welfare, Social Institutions and Demographic Regimes: The Case of Early Modern England', Contribution to the Conference on Population and Security, Centre for History and Economics, Kings College, Cambridge, Feb.

Social Trends, 1988–1992, nos. 19–21, Central Statistical Office, London, HM Stationery Office.

Sokoll, Thomas, 1993, *Household and Family among the Poor*, Bochum, Arbeitskreis England Forschung 18.

Spufford, Margaret, 1974, *Contrasting Communities*, Cambridge.

Stearns, Peter (ed.), 1982, *Old Age in Pre-Industrial Society*, New York, Holmes and Meier.

Sundbärg, Gustav, 1970, *Bevölkerungstatistik Schwedens* 1750–1900, Stockholm.

Tanner, James M., 1981, *A History of the Study of Human Growth*, Cambridge.

Thane, Pat, 1984 'Ageing and the Economy, Historical Issues', Centre for Economic Policy Research, Discussion Paper 194.

Thatcher, A. Roger, 1981, 'Centenarians', *Population Trends*, 25.

____, 1987, 'Mortality at the Highest Ages', *Journal of the Institute of Actuaries*, 116, Part 2, no. 457.

____, 1992, 'Trends in Numbers and Mortality at the Highest Ages in England and Wales', *Population Studies*.

____, 1994 (Dec.), 'How much do we know about Maximum Length of Life?' unpublished draft.

Thatcher, A. R. and V. Kannisto, 1993, 'The plausibility of Certain Reported Cases of Extreme Longevity', unpublished draft.

Thomas, Keith, 1971, *Religion and the Decline of Magic*, London, Weidenfeld & Nicolson.

____, 1977, 'Age and Authority in Early Modern England', *Proceedings of the British Academy*, 205–48.

Thompson, Jean, 1987, 'The Ageing of the Population: Contemporary Trends and Issues', *Social Trends*, 50.

Thomson, David, 1980, 'Provision for the Elderly in England', PhD Dissertation, University of Cambridge.

____, 1991, *Selfish Generations? The Ageing of New Zealand's Welfare State*, Wellington, NZ, Bridget W. Williams Books.

____, 1992, 'Generations, Justice and the Future of Collective Action', pp. 206–25 in Laslett and Fishkin, eds.

Trollope, Anthony, 1993 (1882), *The Fixed Period*, ed. David Skilton, World's Classics, Oxford.

US Census Bureau, 1991, *Global Aging*, Department of Commerce, Washington, DC.

Vandenbroucke, J. P., 1985, 'Survival from the 1400s to the present', *American Journal of Epidemiology*, 122, 6.

Van Tassel, D. (ed.), 1979, *Aging, Death and the Completion of Being*, Philadelphia, University of Pennsylvania Press.

Veatch, R. M. (ed.), 1979, *Life Span: Values and Life Extending Technologies*, New York.

Wachter, Kenneth W., E. A. Hammel and P. Laslett, 1978, *Statistical Studies in Historical Social Structure*, London, Academic Press.

____, 1995, '2030 Seniors: Kin and Step Kin', unpublished preliminary draft, Department of Demography, University of California, Berkeley.

Walford, Roy I., 1983, *Maximum Life Span*, New York.

Walker, Alan, 1990, 'The Economic Burden of Ageing and the Prospect of Intergenerational Conflict', *Ageing and Society*, 10, 4.

____, 1994, 'Whither the Social Contract. Intergenerational Solidarity in Income and Employment', Chapter 2 in Hobman, ed.

Wall, Richard, 1981, Women Alone in English Society', *Annales de Demographie Historique*.

____, 1984, 'Residential Isolation of the Elderly', *Ageing and Society*, Special Issue, 483–503.

____, 1983(a), Introduction to Wall, Robin and Laslett, eds.

Wall, Richard, 1987, 'Leaving Home and the Process of Household Formation in Pre-Industrial England', *Continuity and Change*, 2, 1, 77–101.

____, 1989, 'The Living Arrangements of the Elderly in Contemporary Europe in the 1980s in Bill Bytheway and others', Chapter 8 in *Becoming and Being Old*, Sage.

____, 1995, 'Elderly Persons and Members of their Households from Pre-Industrial Times to the Present', 81–106 in Kertzer and Laslett, eds.

Wall, Richard, J. Robin and P. Laslett (eds), 1983(b), *Family Forms in Historic Europe*, Cambridge.

Warnes, Anthony M., 1993, 'Being Old: Old People and the Burden of Burdens', *Ageing and Society*, 13, 3, 297–338.

Weber, Hermann, 1919 (1903), *On Longevity and the Means for the Prolongation of Life*, fifth edn, London, Macmillan.

Willmott, Peter, 1987, 'Kinship in Urban Communities', Dyos Lecture, Leicester University.

Wordsworth, Dorothy, ed. Mary Moorman, 1987, *Journals*, Oxford.

World Bank, 1990, *World Development Report*, New York, Oxford.

____, 1994, *Averting the Old Age Crisis* (a World Bank Policy Research Report, also issued in summary form), New York, Oxford.

Wrigley, E. A., 1972, 'The Process of Modernization and the Industrial Revolution in England', *Journal of Interdisciplinary History*, iii, 225–59.

____, 1988, *Continuity, Chance and Change. The Character of the Industrial Revolution in England,* Oxford, Blackwell.

Wrigley, E. A. and R. S. Schofield, 1989 (1981), *The Population History of England, 1541–1871*, Cambridge.

Young, Michael, 1995, 'The Prospects for Open Learning', *Open Learning*, February.

Young, Michael, and T. Schuller, 1991, *Life after Work: The Arrival of the Ageless Society*, London, Harper Collins.

Zeng Yi, Zhang Chun Yuan and P. Laslett, (eds), 1989, *Changing Population and Family Structure in China: a Comparative Approach*, Beijing.

Zhang Chun Yuan, 1990, 'Family Size and Structure and their Trends in China', Chapter 6 of Zeng Yi, Zhang Chun Yuan and P. Laslett.

Zhao, Zhongwei, 1994(a), 'Record Longevity in Chinese History. The evidence of the Wang Genealogy', unpublished draft.

____, 1994(b), 'Demographic Conditions and Multi-Generation Households in Chinese History, Results from Genealogical Research and Microsimulation', *Population Studies*, 48, 2, 413–26.

Index